Corporal Punishment of Children in Theoretical Perspective

EDITED BY MICHAEL DONNELLY
AND MURRAY A. STRAUS

Corporal Punishment of Children in Theoretical Perspective

Yale University Press
New Haven &
London

Chapter 15 is reprinted by permission from *Transaction* and chapter 16 is reprinted by permission of Cambridge University Press.

Set in Postscript Sabon type by Keystone Typesetting, Inc.
Printed in the United States of America.

Library of Congress Cataloging-in-Publication Data
Corporal punishment of children in theoretical perspective / edited by Michael Donnelly and Murray A. Straus.
p. cm.
Includes bibliographical references and index.
ISBN 0-300-08547-8 (alk. paper)
1. Corporal punishment. 2. Discipline of children. I. Donnelly, Michael, 1949– II. Straus, Murray A. (Murray Arnold), 1926–
HQ770.4.C66 2005
649'.64–dc22

2004030552

A catalogue record for this book is available from the British Library.

The paper in this book meets the guidelines for permanence and durability of the Committee on Production Guidelines for Book Longevity of the Council on Library Resources.

10 9 8 7 6 5 4 3 2 1

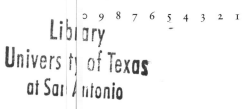

Contents

III. Psychological Theories

IV. Sociological Theories

Acknowledgments

The editors wish to thank colleagues past and present at the Family Research Laboratory of the University of New Hampshire. Doreen Cole and Radim Hladick provided detailed editorial assistance. Erin K. Carter and Lawrence Kenney helped to shepherd the manuscript through its various stages at Yale University Press.

PART I

Current State of Theory

Theoretical Approaches to Corporal Punishment

MURRAY A. STRAUS AND

MICHAEL DONNELLY

Corporal punishment, as we use the term in this book, is:

the use of physical force with the intention of causing a child to experience pain, but not injury, for the purpose of correcting or controlling the child's behavior.

The phrase "pain, but not injury" helps to distinguish corporal punishment from physical abuse: our subject is socially acceptable and legal corporal punishment. The phrase "with the intention of causing a child to experience pain" distinguishes corporal punishment from acts that have other purposes but may also cause pain, such as putting an antiseptic on a cut. It also makes explicit the fact that causing pain is intentional, not incidental. This point may seem obvious, but it is salutary to emphasize, since our culture leads people to focus on why the child was hit, rather than on the fact that hitting hurts.

When one applies this definition to specific acts in order to identify corporal punishment, many questions arise. The most frequent forms of corporal punishment are spanking, slapping, grabbing, or shoving a child "roughly" (with more force than is needed to move the child). But should hitting a child with an object such as a hairbrush, belt, or paddle be included? Traditional cultural norms permit that. Such norms were upheld as recently as a 1992 decision of the New Hampshire Supreme Court. On the other hand, hitting with an object poses a significant risk of causing an injury which may require medical treatment and from that point of view might be considered physical abuse rather than corporal punishment. In fact, public opinion seems to be moving in that direction. A 1978 survey in Texas, for instance, found that only a third of the adult population regarded hitting a child with a belt or wooden paddle as "physical abuse." When the study was repeated in 1991, however, almost half regarded these acts as physical abuse (Teske and Thurman 1992: table 12); close to a majority now regard hitting with an object as abuse rather than corporal punishment.

Ordinary language is also ambiguous. In many poor and minority communities "beating" is a generic term for any corporal punishment. To some, "spanking" means slapping a child on the buttocks (traditionally, the bare buttocks). For middle-class Americans, it tends to be a generic term for slapping or hitting any part of the child. Probably the most frequent form of corporal punishment is slapping a child's hand for touching something.

Whatever the ambiguities in how we think and talk about corporal punishment, the overwhelming majority of adult Americans approve of it. Many regard corporal punishment positively as a customary and necessary technique of child rearing, and almost everyone believes that it may be necessary at least as a punishment of last resort. Close to 100 percent of parents use corporal punishment on toddlers. Just over half of all American children are still being hit by their parents in adolescence, and for about a quarter hitting continues until they physically leave the family home (Straus 1991, 1994).

The legitimacy of corporal punishment, moreover, is firmly reflected in and backed by law. The state laws of Texas and New Hampshire, to cite two examples, provide clear illustration of the legal status of corporal punishment. In the Texas Penal Code the section entitled "General Justification" of violence declares: "The use of force, but not deadly force, against a child younger than 18 years is justified: 1. if the actor is the child's parent or step-parent or is acting in loco parentis to the child; and 2. when and to the degree the actor reasonably believes that force is necessary to discipline the child or to safeguard or promote welfare" (9.61, West Publishing, 1983). The New Hampshire Criminal Code similarly declares: "A parent, guardian or other person responsible for the general care and welfare of a minor is justified in using force against such a minor when and to the extent that he reasonably believes it necessary to prevent or punish such a minor's misconduct" (627.6:I, Equity Publishing, 1985). The New Hampshire statute places no explicit limits on the degree of force, and the Texas statute stipulates only that it cannot be "deadly."

In both states the statutes also apply to teachers. However, in New Hampshire the state education department has issued regulations ending corporal punishment in all state-funded schools. The New Hampshire legislature did not object to these regulations, but it rejected bills (in 1988 and again in 1990) to ban corporal punishment in all schools, not just state-funded schools. The Texas legislature defeated a bill in 1992 to forbid corporal punishment by teachers.

To this day, the federal government's National Center on Child Abuse and Neglect seems to give tacit approval to corporal punishment. A 1992 publication, for example, states: "The injury [from physical abuse] may have resulted from over-discipline or physical punishment that is inappropriate to the child's age" (National Center on Child Abuse and Neglect 1992: 2), implying that discipline which is not "over-discipline," and physical punishment appropriate to a child's age, would be legitimate.

Parents can of course be charged with physical abuse if the hitting exceeds the frequency and severity of violence allowed by cultural norms for disciplining children. But in fact, parents are rarely held accountable by the courts for "excessive" corporal punishment. The reason is that child protective services rarely have the resources to attend to such cases, and moreover the norms are not clear.[1]

Despite the general acceptance and widespread use of corporal punishment, there are nonetheless signs that American society may have reached a turning point concerning cultural norms on corporal punishment and the actual use of corporal punishment. There are a number of indications of such a change under way. A decade ago, we would have estimated that it would be at least two generations before the United States arrived at the point that led Sweden in 1979 to make any corporal punishment of children by parents illegal. Now we think that it could occur within the next ten to twenty years because the pace of change is accelerating. Here are some of the small, but cumulatively important, indicators of that impending change:

1. National surveys of children in 1975 and 1985 show that although the overall one-year prevalence rates of corporal punishment did not change (the same percentage of parents spanked in 1985 as in 1975), there were statistically significant decreases in three aspects of corporal punishment: chronicity, severity, and the number of years parents continued hitting.
2. The number of states that prohibit use of corporal punishment by teachers has been growing exponentially.
3. In 1992, the Task Force on Corporal Punishment was established by the American Psychological Association, Division of Children and Youth Services; a similar task force was established a year earlier by the American Academy of Pediatrics.

4. A national advocacy organization devoted solely to eliminating corporal punishment — EPOCH (End Physical Punishment of Children) was established, also in 1992. Actually, it is EPOCH-USA, because it is an affiliate of a new international advocacy organization with affiliates in many countries, including the United Kingdom (long a bastion of corporal punishment).

However these developments play out over time, they are likely to stimulate research in the meanwhile on corporal punishment — much as growing disquiet over the discovery of child abuse in the late 1960s spurred a flurry of research on battered and abused children. Given the near universality of corporal punishment in the socialization experience of children, one might think that it would be a familiar and well-researched topic in the literature. Ironically, however, relative to its importance, corporal punishment has been broadly neglected. It likewise receives scant attention in textbooks and books of advice to parents. Straus (1994), for example, examined ten of the leading child-development textbooks and found they devoted an average of only half a page to corporal punishment.

The most important reason for such neglect, we believe, is an unrecognized "selective inattention" to corporal punishment. Deeply embedded cultural norms have led almost the entire population, including most social scientists, to believe that corporal punishment is "sometimes necessary" for the welfare of the child (Straus 1991, 1994).

The aim of this book is to focus concerted attention, from a variety of theoretical perspectives, on corporal punishment, and thus to help fill a significant lacuna in the research literature. The lack of adequate theoretical grounding for research has undoubtedly hampered study of corporal punishment. A theory-based approach to corporal punishment is needed because it is likely to stimulate more creative and fundamental research than the ad hoc approach that now prevails. Theoretically grounded research is also needed because it provides meaningful ways of organizing and interpreting research findings. Probably the main exception to the theoretical vacuum is social-learning theory (Bandura 1973), which suggests broadly that children learn behaviors through trial-and-error conditioning and also through vicarious learning, observing the behavior of others and the positive or negative consequences it brings. Valuable as the social learning approach has been, it is not sufficient to cope with the phenomenon of corporal punishment. It deals with only limited aspects of what leads parents to hit their children and with only limited aspects of the consequences for children of being hit by their parents. To complement social-learning theory it is important also to examine corporal punishment by parents through the lenses of a number of other theories, such as attribution theory, exchange theory, social-stress theory, family-systems theory, and social-control theory. Hence our aim in this book to assemble and juxtapose a wide array of theoretical perspectives on corporal punishment.

We solicited contributions from leading scholars in a number of disciplines and theoretical traditions and asked each to apply a given theory to the task of explaining the causes and consequences of corporal punishment by parents. In each chapter, our contributors define corporal punishment from the perspective of a particular theory, identify those aspects of corporal punishment that the theory is most adequate to explain, and relate the theory at hand to other theories. Many of the chapters also review empirical research on corporal punishment informed by the given theories, explore methodological issues, and suggest avenues for further research.

We hope that this book will stimulate further research by psychologists, sociologists, and other social scientists concerned with child development and parent behavior. Given the recent and growing concern with corporal punishment, we believe that the book appears at an opportune moment, when it might be the catalyst for more systematic and coherent research.

Note

1. However, the law does not give specific guidelines, and, as a result, there is tremendous ambiguity concerning the line between physical punishment and physical abuse. See Gelles and Straus (1979) and Straus (1990a) for a discussion of the concept of abuse.

2

Corporal Punishment in Ecological Perspective

JAMES GARBARINO

An ecological perspective on corporal punishment in childhood directs our attention simultaneously to two classes of phenomena. The first is the interaction of the child as a biological organism with the immediate social environment as a set of processes, events, and relationships. The second is the interplay of social systems in the social environment that shape the experience of the child.

While all students of animal ecology must accommodate to the purposeful actions of the organism, the human ecologist must go further and seek to incorporate the phenomenological complexity of the organism-environment interaction — the social and psychological maps that define human meaning, the social "geography and climate" (Garbarino and Associates 1992). This is particularly important in understanding something as culturally "loaded" as corporal punishment, where the very choice of terms plays a crucial role in establishing or obscuring meaning. If, for example, we substitute "violence in the name of discipline" in place of "corporal punishment," we go far toward illuminating the issues at stake in any assessment.

From an ecological perspective, it would seem that risks to development can come both from direct threats and from the absence of normal, expectable opportunities. Besides such obvious biological risks as malnutrition or injury, there are sociocultural risks that deprive the developing individual world of essential experiences and relationships and thereby threaten development.

Certainly one goal of this book is to assess the status of corporal punishment as a risk (and opportunity) factor in the lives of children.

This chapter considers the concept of developmental risk and opportunity through the sharpened focus of a systems approach to childhood experience. Such an approach will help to clarify the complexity we face in attempting to understand the interplay of biological, psychological, social, and cultural forces in that particular form of violence against children defined as "corporal punishment."

An ecological or systems approach may help us discover the connections among what might at first seem to be unrelated events, for example, patterns of oppression directed at adult women and the level of violence deemed normal in adult-child relations. It also can help us see that what often seems like an obvious solution may actually only make the problem worse. For example, the "commonsense" idea that allowing people to hit children will "get it out of their system" may prove to reinforce rather than diffuse further violence.

Individuals and other actors in their environments negotiate their relationships over time through a process of reciprocity. Neither is constant; *each* depends on the other. When asked, "Does X cause Y?" the answer is always, "It depends." We cannot reliably predict the future of one system without knowing something about the other systems with which it is linked. And even then it may be very difficult.

For instance, we see this when we ask, "Does early day care enhance or harm development?" We answer, "It depends on the child's age, the quality of parent-child attachment, the day-care provider's relationship to the child's parents, and the day-care provider's motivations and training, as well as the more obvious question of what *exactly* constitutes the experience of day care. In short, it depends" (cf. Belsky 1986).

We see the individual's experiences as subsystems within systems within larger systems, "as a set of nested structures, each inside the next, like a set of Russian dolls" (Bronfenbrenner 1979: 22). In asking and answering questions about development, we can and should always be ready to look at the next level of systems "beyond" and "within" to find the questions and the answers (Garbarino and Associates 1992). What is the social significance of corporal punishment? To answer such a question we will need to look at its psychic function as well as its cultural meaning.

Consider the case of child abuse. We need to look at the community that establishes laws and policies about child abuse as well as at the families that offer a powerful definition of reality for the next generation. We should look also at the culture that defines physical force as an appropriate form of discipline in early childhood.

But we must look, too, within the individual as a psychological system affected by conscious and changing roles, unconscious needs, and motives, to know why and how each adjusts in ways that generate conflict. In addition, we must look "across" to see how the several systems involved (family, social services, social network, and economy) adjust to new conditions.

Interaction among these social forces is the key to an ecological analysis of child development. These forces exist as linked social systems, implying that intervention can take place at each system level *and* that intervention at one level may well spill over to others. Our primary research agenda in expanding our understanding of childhood is to explore — systematically and empirically — the paths and consequences of these linkages.

This systems approach examines the environment at four levels beyond the individual organism — from the "micro" to the "macro." These systems have been catalogued in detail elsewhere (Bronfenbrenner 1979, 1986; Garbarino and Associates 1992). The goal here is to introduce them briefly in order to provide a framework for outlining what we need to know about corporal punishment in childhood.

The dual mandate to look both *inward* to the day-to-day interaction of the child in the family, the school, the neighborhood, and the peer group and *outward* to the forces that shape these social contexts is both the beauty and the challenge of human ecology. It demands much of us *intellectually* if it is to be more than merely an academic exercise and *personally* if it is to lead to social reform (Garbarino and Bronfenbrenner 1976).

Like the biologist who learns about an animal by studying its habitat, sources of food, predators, and social practices, the student of child development must address how children live and grow in their social environment. Unlike the animal biologist, the human ecologist must go further and seek to incorporate the phenomenological complexity of the organism-environment interaction. Reviewing existing research tells us we have far to go in fulfilling this agenda. Too often, limitations of time, of resources, and of vision have preempted the more significant ecologically oriented study of childhood in favor of circumscribed and ecologically invalid investigations.

A Science of Childhood Opportunities and Risks

Children face different opportunities and risks for development because of their mental and physical makeup *and* because of the social environment they inhabit. Moreover, social environment affects the very physical makeup of the child, what Pasamanick (1987) calls "social biology." In contrast to sociobiology, which emphasizes a genetic origin for social behavior (Wilson 1978), social biology concentrates on the social origins of biological phenomena (for example, the impact of economic conditions and social policy on brain growth and development).

These effects are often negative (for example, the impact of poverty and famine on mental retardation and birth weight or the mutagenic influence of industrially produced carcinogens). But they may be positive as well (for example, intrauterine surgery or nutritional therapy for a fetus with a genetic disorder). When these social influences operate in psychological or sociological terms we refer to them as sociocultural opportunities and risks.

When we refer to "opportunities for development" we mean relationships in which children find material, emotional, and social encouragement compatible with their needs and capacities as those exist at a specific point in their developing lives. For each child, the best fit must be worked out through experience, within some very broad guidelines of basic human needs, and then renegotiated as development proceeds and situations change. As Dunst's recent work (1992) reveals, moreover, understanding developmental opportunities helps to explain the variance in outcomes left unaccounted for in models that simply address "risk." This suggests, for example, that in studying corporal punishment in childhood we should seek to document its relation to all aspects of parent-child relations, including its impact on modeling the parent's behavior in other domains besides violence.

To explore this complex field, it is useful to begin with recent findings regarding the "accumulation of risk." For example, Sameroff and his colleagues (1987) report that the average IQ scores of four-year-old children are related to the number of psychological and social risk factors present in their lives — risk factors that include socioeconomic conditions, as well as intrafamilial psychosocial factors, such as rigid and punitive child-rearing style.

But this research reveals that the relationship is not simply additive. Average IQ for children with none, one, or two of the factors is above 115. With the addition of a third and fourth risk factor the average IQ scores drop precipitously to nearly 85, with relatively little further decrement with accumulation of the fifth through eighth risk factors. An ecological perspective on corporal punishment warns us that as a risk factor its impact will be different for children for whom it is the sole risk factor, in contrast to children who are already "on the edge" as a result of the socioeconomic and demographic facts of their lives. We have found this in our study of the impact of community violence on Palestinian children; the effects of exposure are mediated by the nature of discipline within the home, with those exposed to more punishing styles more adversely affected by violence outside the home (Garbarino and Kostelny 1995).

What is more, "windows of opportunity" for intervention appear repeatedly across the life course, and what may be a critical threat at one point may be benign or even developmentally enhancing at another. For example, Elder's classic analyses (1974) of the impact of the economic crisis of the 1930s in the United States reveal that its effects were felt most negatively by young children. By contrast, some adolescents (particularly daughters) actually benefited from the fact that paternal unemployment often meant special "opportunities" for enhanced responsibility and status in the family.

Analyzing research by Rutter and others, Bronfenbrenner (1986) confirmed that the stress of urban life associated with "family adversity" (Rutter's term) is most negative and potent for young children (whereas it may even stimulate some adolescents). High on our agenda for future study should be a more complete elaboration of this hypothesis in answer to the question, "Under what circumstances and conditions are the challenges of adversity 'growth-inducing'?" Naturally, efforts to understand the impact of corporal punishment must address this issue was well (and a study of Palestinian children offers some models for doing this; see Garbarino and Kostelny 1995).

Forrester (1969) concludes that because systems are linked and therefore influence each other ("feedback"), some of the most effective solutions to social problems are not readily apparent and may even be counterintuitive. According to Hardin (1966) the First Law of Ecology is, "You can never do just one thing." Intersystem feedback ensures that any single action may reverberate and produce unintended consequences.

In the late 1940s and early 1950s, American parents reported in surveys that their motivation in purchasing television sets was "to bring the family together" (Garbarino 1972). The irony of what television has meant for family interaction is apparent. This feedback issue underlies some concern that any simple measures to reduce corporal punishment *may* lead to unanticipated negative side effects (for example, a compensatory increase in verbal attack), although existing research suggests that this concern is largely unfounded (Straus 1994).

As our research implements this approach we can see the reality of contextual influences in all aspects of development. Thus, for example, the link between early developmental delay and later IQ deficit appears to differ across social-class groupings in the kind of social system present in most U.S. communities. In one classic study, 13 percent of the lower-social-class children who were developmentally delayed at eight months showed an IQ of 79 or less at four years of age. In contrast, only 7 percent of the middle-class children who were delayed at eight months of age were retarded at four years of age.

For the upper-class children the figure was only 2 percent (Willerman, Broman, and Fiedler 1970).

Does developmental delay predict IQ deficit? It would seem that it depends upon the family and community environment in which one is growing up. We might hypothesize that the social-class effect linked to family status would be exaggerated in some communities, while it might also be diminished in others. Indeed, this hypothesis is supported by existing research (Bronfenbrenner 1986; Garbarino and Kostelny 1992). We might also predict that the effects of corporal punishment will be greater in some contexts than in others, particularly if there are other elements of the culture that stimulate and reinforce aggression — for example, mass-media imagery.

Is IQ influenced more by genetics or by environment, by nature or by nurture? It depends. For example, a reanalysis of twin study data reveals that when identical twins were separated at birth and reared in *similar* communities the correlation between their adult IQs was strong (.86). When identical twins were reared in *dissimilar* communities the correlation between their adult IQs was weak (.26) (Bronfenbrenner 1975). Which is more important, nature or nurture? It depends.

This certainly has applications for the study of corporal punishment in childhood. For example, we might expect that the impact of early corporal punishment would be greater in some settings than in others. Is it too much to expect a reversal in the directions of effect (that is, for the effects to be positive in some settings and negative in others)? This may be stretching things too far. A study by Baldwin and his colleagues (1993) does reveal that although hitting children has generally negative effects, in high-threat inner-city environments a more directive and tough parenting style does seem to have protective effects, whereas the same style is counterproductive in a more benign community setting. We might expect that corporal punishment as a feature of the community environment could be decisive in exacerbating organismic risk.

From Microsystems to Macrosystems

Having outlined the range of issues included in an ecological-systems perspective, we can turn to an inspection of the four levels of systems in the human ecology of childhood. This process of mapping the social environment provides a useful conceptual structure for efforts to sort out the influences of corporal punishment as a factor in child development, and it includes four elements: microsystems, mesosystems, exosystems, and macrosystems (Bronfenbrenner 1979; Garbarino and Associates 1992).

Microsystems are the immediate settings in which individuals develop. The shared experiences that occur in each setting provide a record of the microsystem and offer some clues to its future. Microsystems evolve and develop much as do individuals themselves, from forces generated both within and without. It has become commonplace to emphasize the need for longitudinal research, but it is a valid concern nonetheless; we must understand the biographies of the child's microsystems. In the case of corporal punishment it means that we need to understand how a pattern of hitting children evolves in a family, and how this evolution affects outcome. For example, most child-abuse experts agree that the onset of hitting prior to six months of age is a powerful risk factor for ultimate involvement in physical child abuse.

The quality of a microsystem depends upon its ability to sustain and enhance development, and to provide a context that is emotionally validating and developmentally challenging. This in turn depends upon its capacity to operate in what Vygotsky (1986) calls "the zone of proximal development," that is, the distance between what the child can accomplish alone (the level of actual development) and what the child can do when helped (the level of potential development). Too little research focuses on this crucial teaching process; child development is a partnership.

And what does corporal punishment mean for that partnership? Many parents seem to believe it adds a tool for influencing the child's behavior. Many child-development specialists have come to understand that this tool is actually of very limited effectiveness, and that it carries with it many unproductive side effects. Thus, the value of hitting as a positive teaching strategy is quite limited, and its costs as a negative teaching strategy quite high. It certainly diminishes the partnership nature of the socialization process and may lead to the extremely costly "error" of psychological maltreatment (Garbarino, Guttmann, and Seeley 1986).

It is important to remember that our definition speaks of the microsystem as a pattern *experienced* by the developing person. Individuals influence their microsystems, and those microsystems influence them in turn. Each participant acts on the basis of an emergent social map — a phenomenological record and projection.

We have only begun to study the formation of the child's social maps — from an appropriately ecological perspective, and from the child's point of view (Garbarino, Scott, and Associates 1989). But we do have an inkling that exposing a child to corporal punishment creates a negative emotional experience of the family regardless of the overt cognitive definition offered by the child. That is, hitting children creates negative feelings despite the fact that the child may come to rationalize the hitting as "normal," "necessary," and "for he child's own good." In the extreme case of physical child abuse, research shows that cognitive interventions which assist the child in exploring the meaning of hitting can bring about a realignment of belief in which the negative feelings aroused are now matched by an appropriate cognitive evaluation (Herzberger 1986) — that is, that hitting children is wrong, that it leads to adverse developmental outcomes, and that the responsibility lies with the parent, not the child.

Mesosystems are relationships *between* microsystems, in which the individual experiences reality. These links themselves form a system. An important issue for present purposes is the impact on the child of mesosystem consistencies and discrepancies in the normativeness of corporal punishment.

Does it help the development of a child who is hit at home to be hit also at school? Does this consistency across systems enhance development? Or is the child who is hit at home better off in a school that avoids hitting because this contrast gives the child "a second opinion" and therefore a chance to model nonaggressive behavior? Does a mesosystem discrepancy on this issue challenge the child to reconsider the model offered at home, or does it simply confuse the child? Practitioners (including teachers) are often unsure about this issue, and there is no clear body of research to resolve it. Studying the issue empirically would be a major contribution.

To complete this mission we need a better understanding of the dynamics of the "linkages" that create and sustain mesosystems. For example, we need to know more about the importance of mesosystems in intervention programs. Research suggests that the strength of the mesosystem linking the setting in which an intervention is implemented with the settings in which the individual spends the most significant time is crucial to the long-term effectiveness of the intervention, and to the maintenance of its effects (Whittaker, Garbarino, and Associates 1983). This implies that interventions to reduce corporal punishment in one setting (for example, school) may not endure if efforts are not made to create support for those interventions in other systems into which the individual may enter (for example, family). Gaining the power to affect these other systems in a coordinated way is a matter of public policy, a matter for exosystems.

Exosystems are settings that have a bearing on the development of children, but in which those children do not play a direct role. For most children, the key exosystems include the workplace of their parents and such centers of power as school boards, church councils, and planning commissions that make decisions affecting their day-to-day lives. Obviously, these exosystems play a crucial role in the status of corporal punishment in the life of the child. Policies regarding corporal punishment made by schools and governments establish the climate in which children and adults will relate to each other around issues of punishment and discipline as students and teachers, children and foster parents, and so forth. Of course, there is often slippage between policy and practice, but the setting of policy remains a force in shaping the experience of children. Corporal punishment is no exception to this general phenomenon.

Note that the concept of an exosystem illustrates the projective nature of the ecological perspective, for the same setting that is an exosystem for a child may be a microsystem for the parent, and vice versa. Thus, one form of knowledge needed concerns strategies and tactics for intervention aimed at transforming exosystems into microsystems, such as by initiating greater participation in important institutions for isolated, disenfranchised, and powerless clients — for example, by getting parents to visit the family day-care home or by creating on-site day care at the workplace. This perspective suggests an important role for parent education in the various microsystems of the parent as a vehicle for altering the experience of the child.

A second area of needed mesosystem research concerns power. Albee (1980) has gone so far as to identify powerlessness as the primary factor leading to impaired development and mental disability. It certainly plays a large role in determining the fate of groups of individuals via public policy and may even be very important when considering individual cases — such as whether or not parents have the influence needed to enroll a medically vulnerable child in a special-treatment program. What is more, the power of children to articulate their experience and have their account validated in public settings may play an important role in changing values and practices with respect to corporal punishment.

In many cases, risk and opportunity at the exosystem level are essentially political matters. And this demands that our knowledge base include a fine appreciation of the politics of childhood as well as its biology, psychology, sociology, and anthropology.

The ecological perspective forces us to consider the concept of risk beyond the narrow confines of individual personality and family dynamics. In the ecological approach, both are "causes" of the child's developmental patterns and "reflections" of broader sociocultural forces. Mark Twain remarked, "If the only tool you have is a hammer you tend to treat every problem as if it were a nail." Inflexible loyalty to a specific focus (for example, the parents) is often a stumbling block to effective intervention. However, the obverse must also be considered: "If you define every problem as a nail, the only tool you will seek is a hammer."

Viewing children only in terms of organismic and interpersonal dynamics precludes an understanding of the many other avenues of influence that might be open to us as helpers, or that might be topics of study for us as scientists.

This message provides a crucial guide to research on intervention and program evaluation, and it reflects the operation of macrosystems of culture and ideology. It tells us to consider a multiphase strategy for reducing corporal punishment, one that incorporates educational materials for children and parents, educational advocacy efforts aimed at policy makers, work with spiritual leaders to deal with the core ethical and philosophical issues involved, and intensive efforts to get the mass media to address the role of cultural images in stimulating and reinforcing changed attitudes and values concerning hitting children as a "normal" activity.

Macrosystems are the context within which micro-, meso-, and exosystems are set—the broad ideological, demographic, and institutional patterns of a particular culture or subculture. These macrosystems serve as the master "blueprints" for the ecology of human development that reflect a people's shared assumptions about how things should be done, as well as the institutions that represent those assumptions. Macrosystems are ideology incarnate. They help provide a vantage point for asking if corporal punishment is "normal," "natural," "inevitable," or "inconceivable."

Macrosystem refers to the general organization of the world as it is and as it might be. Historical change demonstrates that the "might be" may become quite real, and may occur either through evolution (many individual actions guided by a common reality) or through revolution (dramatic change introduced by a small cadre of decision makers). The fact that some nations (six at last count: Sweden, Norway, Denmark, Finland, Austria, and Cyprus) have outlawed corporal punishment and others are considering doing so is testimony to the possibility of macrosystem change (and to the role of exosystems in child development).

Societal blueprints differ on important dimensions, dimensions that find their fundamental institutional expressions in such ideological issues as a "collective versus individual orientation." The implications for discussions of corporal punishment are important. For example, in a collective-oriented society the fact that corporal punishment may severely impair the development of a small minority of children may be acceptable if it also enhances the obedience and cooperative behavior of the majority. In an individualistic society, however, this rationale might be inadequate because of the greater emphasis placed upon the rights of the individual.

This sort of macrosystem issue challenges cross-cultural analyses to be clear about the ideological foundations of such comparisons and not to assume universality. International child-development initiatives like the U.N. Convention on the Rights of the Child face this issue directly. In the case of the U.N. Convention, the attempt was made to negotiate a global consensus (at least among educated-elite representatives from each society and region). While not barring corporal punishment in a absolute sense, the spirit of the U.N. Convention is clearly progressive on this score and supports efforts to reduce and ultimately eliminate universally the hitting of children.

Religion provides a classic example of the macrosystem concept because it involves both a definition of the world and a set of institutions reflecting that definition — both a theology and a set of roles, rules, buildings, and programs. Religious support for corporal punishment is a central issue in any cultural analysis of the topic, to wit the title of Straus's (1994) book *Beating the Devil out of Them.*

Conclusion

An ecological perspective has much to contribute to the process of understanding corporal punishment in childhood. It gives us a kind of social map for navigating a path through the complexities of research. It aids us in seeing the full range of alternative conceptualizations and points us in the direction of multiple strategies for intervention.

It provides a kind of checklist to use in thinking about what is happening and what to do about it when faced with developmental problems and social pathologies that may be associated with corporal punishment. It does all this by asking us always to consider the micro-, meso-, exo-, and macrosystem dimensions of developmental phenomena and interventions. It constantly suggests the possibility that context is shaping causal relationships. It always tells us "it depends" and stimulates an attempt to find out "on what."

PART **II**

Comparative Theories

3

Parent-Offspring Conflict and Corporal Punishment in Primates

LYNN A. FAIRBANKS AND

MICHAEL T. McGUIRE

The baboon mother forages with a small group along the edge of the stream; her infant son rides ventral. Suddenly she grabs his arm and tries to pull him off her chest. The infant screams but retains his hold and slides lower onto his mother's stomach. The mother struggles with her son for a few seconds and finally succeeds in pushing him off onto the ground. The infant screams and gecks, his hair standing on end, and climbs onto his mother's back. She gives a slight jerk; he drops off and throws a brief tantrum, crouching on the ground, screaming and making small jerky movements with his entire body. He starts to climb onto his mother's back again; she hits back at him with a hand and knocks him off. (Ransom and Rowell 1972: 122)

Primate mothers form close, long-lasting affiliative bonds with their offspring. Nevertheless, instances of corporal punishment, such as that described above, are not uncommon. Early field studies provide numerous examples of primate mothers pushing away, hitting, and biting their infants. More recent quantitative studies have established that the highest rates of aggressive handling in primate social groups are typically displayed by parents against their own offspring (for example, Jay 1963; Nash 1978; Kurland 1977; Horrocks and Hunte 1983; Bernstein and Ehardt 1986). Theories of life-history strategies and parent-offspring conflict derived from the general perspective of evolutionary biology help to explain why this is so.

This chapter will argue that corporal punishment is the result of an essential conflict between parent and offspring, as parents try to balance the competing demands of their lives. We begin with a brief overview of parental-investment theory, which predicts that parent-offspring conflict will occur as a consequence of the parents' attempts to maximize their reproductive success by distributing parental care across all of the offspring they can produce in their lifetime. Conflict of interest between parents and offspring produces attempts by the parent to limit offspring behavior, resistance by the offspring, and escalation to corporal punishment. Parent-offspring conflict theory is then used to explain variation in the form and frequency of punishment by primate mothers according to the age and sex of the offspring, the presence of siblings, and the mother's reproductive opportunities and socioeconomic circumstances. Empirical findings on the nature, timing, context, and consequences of corporal punishment in primate societies support the conclusion that corporal punishment most often serves the best interests of the parents, and not necessarily those of the offspring. In a final section, we ask if data from nonhuman primate studies can inform our understanding of human corporal punishment.

Definition of Corporal Punishment

Corporal punishment is defined as pushing away, slapping, hitting, or biting of immature animals by their parents, as it occurs in normal parent-offspring relationships. A typical circumstance in which corporal punishment occurs is during a mother's rejection of her infant's attempts to suckle or ride. Primate parents also hit, threaten, or bite their older juvenile offspring, particularly when they are interfering with the parents or are harassing a younger sibling. The data on the rate of corporal punishment that are discussed here have been derived from direct observations of behavior of socially living primates in naturally composed captive or free-ranging groups. Abusive parental aggression caused by early experimental deprivation or spontaneously occurring pathology has been covered in depth elsewhere and will not be included in this discussion (Ruppenthal et al. 1976; Troisi et al. 1982; Reite and Caine 1983; Maestripieri and Carroll 1998). We will also not include aggression toward immature animals by unrelated individuals.

Evolutionary Biological Theory

The central organizing principle of evolutionary biology is Darwin's theory of natural selection (Darwin 1859). Conceptually, the basic process of natural selection is simple: there is variability in populations of living organisms; some of this variability is heritable; and certain individuals, by virtue of their characteristics, are more likely than others to survive and reproduce. This process leads to genetic changes in populations across generations as the descendants of some individuals outnumber the descendants of others. The physical and behavioral traits of individuals who do not leave descendants will die out, while the traits that help aid an individual to survive and reproduce effectively will continue to be passed on in a population. Each new generation inherits this history, its sensory and behavioral predispositions, and its physical and behavioral constraints.

Life-history theorists have taken this basic process and developed logical and mathematical models to explore the consequences of different patterns of reproduction (Stearns 1993). The first assumption guiding life-history models is that individuals within a species have a limited amount of energy to expend within their lifetime. Some of this energy will go to growth and development, some to maintenance of basic body functions, and some to reproduction (Fisher 1930). Reproductive effort is divided between offspring production and parental care; parents who produce more offspring will have less time and energy left to care for each one, while those who provide more parental care will not be able to produce as many. The problem which parents must solve is that of balancing offspring quantity and offspring quality to maximize the total number of offspring they produce that are likely to survive to adulthood and to reproduce successfully (Pianka 1976; Clutton-Brock 1991).

In order to make an optimal parental-care decision, a parent must have some way of calculating how much the care will benefit the offspring, and how much it will cost the parents in terms of decreasing their ability to invest in other offspring. For example, when a primate mother carries her newborn infant she pays a relatively small energetic cost in exchange for a large increase in her infant's chances of survival. Thus the benefit of parental care is relatively high compared to the cost. As the infant grows and becomes more self-reliant, the relative benefit to the infant of increased parental care declines, while the energetic cost to the mother of providing care increases. If the mother carries a large juvenile offspring, her cost will be high, while the benefit to the juvenile will be relatively small. Under these conditions, the mother is better off using her energy for other purposes. According to parental-investment theory, a parent should provide care to one offspring so long as the benefit to the parent's lifetime reproductive success from investing in that offspring is greater than the benefit from switching the care to another offspring (Trivers 1972).

A key implication of parental-investment theory is that there will be conflict between parents and offspring over the optimal amount of parental care (Trivers 1974). The theoretical rationale for this conflict is based on differences in the degree of relatedness among parents, offspring, and siblings. Since a parent is equally related to all of its offspring, from the parent's perspective the benefit of parental care given to one offspring must simply outweigh the cost in the parent's ability to invest in other offspring. The offspring, on the other hand, is more closely related to itself than to its present and future siblings. As a result, the cost of parental care from the perspective of the offspring is discounted by the degree of relationship among the siblings. For full siblings, who share one-half of the same genes by common descent, the optimal equation from the offspring's perspective would be to continue receiving care until the benefit to itself exceeded twice the cost to the parent. The optimal point for the parent to shift its energy to other offspring is always earlier when calculated according to the parent's optimum than when calculated according to the offspring's. This conflict of genetic self-interest is manifested in behavioral conflict between mothers and their offspring, and in competition among siblings for the attention of their parents.

The parental-investment strategies described here have evolved through natural selection to promote reproductive success. To say that an animal follows a strategy in biological terms does not imply that it is consciously aware of its own motivations, or that it is able to conceptualize the costs and benefits of its acts. We assume that animals will use the sensory information available to them, and that many of the basic emotions, such as anger and fatigue, have evolved to serve as the proximate cues to trigger evolved behaviors.

The Timing of Corporal Punishment in Primate Life Histories

There are several crucial times in the life span when conflict of interest between a primate mother and her offspring would be expected to be high. The first conflicts should occur as the growing infant becomes increasingly costly to carry and feed. A major peak in conflict is expected when the mother prepares to mate again, and the third point of conflict coincides with the birth of a new sibling. It is at these times, when the self-interest of the mother differs most from the self-interest of her offspring, that we would expect corporal punishment to occur.

EARLY CONFLICT OVER THE MOTHER'S TIME AND ENERGY BUDGET

In the first few months of life, a primate infant is totally dependent on its mother for food, warmth, and transportation. As infants grow larger and more self-sufficient, the costs of infant care for the mother and the benefits for the infant continuously change (Dunbar and Du bar 1988; Altmann and Samuels 1992). Larger infants are heavier to carry and more costly to feed; they are also more capable of walking on their own and feeding themselves.

MATERNAL REJECTION

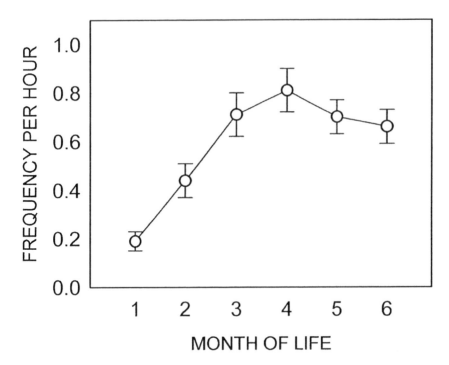

Fig. 3.1a. Maternal rejection.

Balancing these costs and benefits results in an optimal parental style that increasingly restricts the infant's free access to its mother's care and attention.

Figure 3.1a shows how the rate of maternal rejection changes from birth to six months of age. These data come from a longitudinal study of maternal behavior in vervet monkeys (*Cercopithecus aethiops sabaeus*) that has been ongoing since 1980 (for example, Fairbanks 1993a; Fairbanks and McGuire 1985, 1993). The vervet monkeys in our captive colony live in large outdoor enclosures, in stable social groups that have been managed to approximate natural social conditions. As figure 3.1a indicates, the frequency per hour of maternal rejection is extremely low during the first two months of life when the infants are still small and totally dependent on their mothers. The frequency of rejection then increases rapidly with infant age to a peak at four months of age. As rejection increases, the amount of time that infants spend in ventral contact with their mothers declines (figure 3.1b). By the time an infant

VENTRAL CONTACT

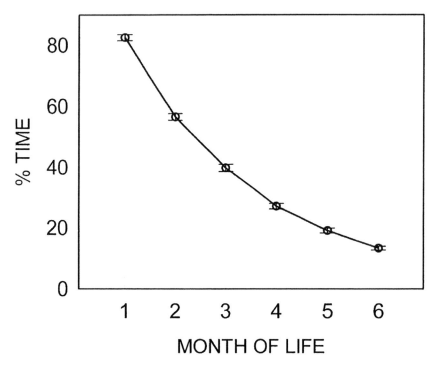

Fig. 3.1b. Ventral contact.

is six months old, it is observed in ventral contact with its mother about 20 percent of the time, and the mother controls when this contact will occur. Adjusting the frequency per hour of rejection for the amount of time infants spend in ventral contact reveals that the rate of rejection per contact hour continues to rise from birth to six months (figure 3.1c).

Maternal rejection takes a variety of forms during this period, from simple shielding of the nipple to prevent suckling, to overt conflict that involves pushing, hitting, and biting by the mother accompanied by tantrums and increased attempts to maintain contact by the infant (Jay 1963; Ransom and Rowell 1972; Nash 1978). In our vervet monkey colony, the younger the infant, the more traumatic the response to maternal rejection. When a mother tries to push off a three-month-old infant, the infant will scream and hold on

REJECTION RATIO

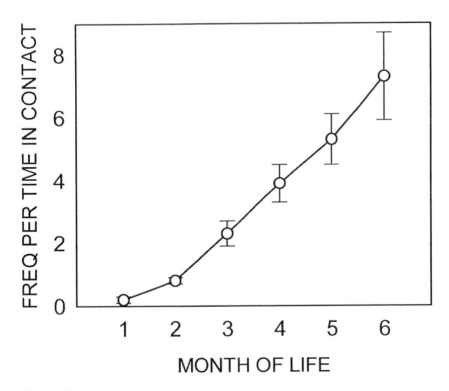

Fig. 3.1c. Rejection ratio.

even tighter. If the mother continues trying to remove the infant from her ventrum, both mother and infant will typically get more and more agitated and the process is likely to escalate to hitting and biting. Sometimes during these episodes a juvenile female will rush over and carry the infant away. At other times, the mother will give in and allow the infant to continue clinging.

CONFLICT OVER THE MOTHER'S MATING BEHAVIOR

These early disputes between mother and infant are followed by a more acute phase of conflict when the mating season begins. Most primates are seasonal breeders, and if the mother is not cycling and ready to mate when her infant is about six months old, she will sacrifice her chances of breeding for the coming year. If the infant is strong and healthy at the beginning of the mating season, the mother will increase her chances of conceiving again by reducing access to the nipple (McNeilly 1979; Lee 1987). Reduction of nursing time entails some risk to the health and welfare of her current infant. Yet, from the mother's perspective, the risk is offset by the opportunity to produce another infant. A number of empirical studies have demonstrated this trade-off between care to the current infant and future fertility by showing that primate mothers who are more rejecting toward their infants are able to conceive again sooner and are more likely to produce an infant in the following year (Simpson et al. 1981; Fairbanks and McGuire 1987; Gomendio 1991; Berman et al. 1993; Johnson et al. 1993).

During the mating season, females of many primate species suspend normal activities and spend time consorting with adult males (Berman et al. 1994). There is a dramatic change in the mother-infant relationship during these periods. Consorting females usually separate themselves from the rest of the group and focus their attention on their male partners. For the infants, the mating season is a time of acute distress. They are abandoned by their mothers and are likely to be afraid of her adult male consorts. The presence of an infant from the previous birth season has an inhibitory effect on the mother's mating activity, thus increasing the conflict between mother and infant to an even greater degree (Eaton 1972; Takahata 1980; Small 1983).

As parent-offspring conflict increases, so does the likelihood of corporal punishment. It is not surprising, therefore, that the rate of maternal rejection and punishment is at its highest point during the mating season (Worlein et al. 1988; Collinge 1991; Berman et al. 1994). Infants will use a variety of means to regain access to their mothers, but the more the infant persists, the more punishment it receives. Some infants respond by chasing after the mother. Others spend more time grooming her in an attempt to remain in contact. A few infants, by virtue of their increased tenacity, actually manage to increase the amount of time they spend in ventral contact, while others experience relatively long periods of separation and neglect.

MATERNAL REGULATION OF SIBLING RIVALRY

The next major transition in the mother-infant relationship comes with the birth of a younger sibling. At this point, the mother shifts most of her attention to the new infant, and the older sibling is no longer allowed to suckle or cling. This creates a conflict of interest among the siblings and signals the beginning of sibling rivalry. In our colony, we have seen yearlings attempt to push their new sibling aside and gain access to their mother's nipple. Others jump on their mother and harass her with play invitations or demands for attention. Similar behavior has also been reported for vervet monkeys in the field, as well as for other primate species in both captive and free-ranging settings (Kurland 1977; Hooley and Simpson 1983; Lee 1983; DeVinney et al. 2001). If a new infant dies shortly after birth, a yearling sibling may return to a more infantile relationship with its mother, with some mothers tolerating an extended period of ventral carrying and nursing that can continue for several months (Holman and Goy 1988). This tendency to regress after the death of an infant sibling is consistent with parental-investment theory and demonstrates that, in the absence of the younger sibling, the yearling will both seek and receive more maternal care than it is otherwise able to get.

Parental-investment theory predicts not only that sibling rivalry will occur but also that parents should intervene to minimize any harmful effects of sibling conflict. Mothers typically respond to harassment of new infants by rebuffing, threatening, or hitting the older sibling. In conflicts among family members, mothers will side with closer kin against more distant kin, and with younger offspring against older sisters and brothers (Bernstein and Ehardt 1985). After the offspring's first year of life, parental regulation of sibling conflict becomes a major reason for corporal punishment of young primates by their mothers.

PUNISHMENT DECLINES WITH AGE

As juvenile primates grow and develop, they place fewer demands on their mother's time and energy, and as a result the incidence of maternal punishment steadily declines. Figure 3.2 shows the frequency per hour of maternal aggression to offspring at one, two, and three years of age in the vervet colony. The rate of maternal punishment drops by half each year, and for three-year-old offspring, maternal threats are rarely observed. While the frequency of punishment declines, the reasons for punishment remain essentially the same. Mothers punish their offspring primarily for behavior that directly interferes with the mother or with younger offspring (Bernstein and Ehardt 1985, 1986).

The juvenile period marks the beginning of a major divergence between mother-daughter and mother-son relationships. Daughters continue to spend time in close proximity to their mothers, while sons direct their attention elsewhere, to play partners and male peers (Fairbanks and McGuire 1985; Fairbanks 1993b). Juvenile daughters show an active interest in their infant siblings and make frequent attempts to touch, hold, and carry them (Fairbanks 1990). Greater involvement of mothers and daughters leads to continuing sources of conflict, and comparison of the rate of aggression toward sons

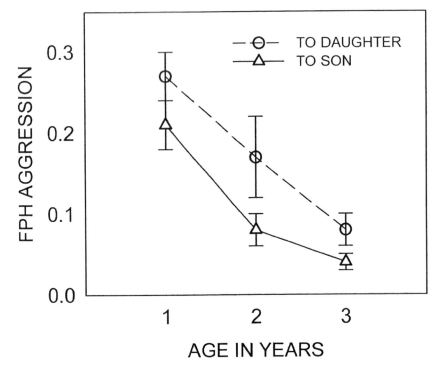

Fig. 3.2.

versus daughters demonstrates that mothers threaten their juvenile daughters significantly more often than they threaten their juvenile sons (figure 3.2).

The form of maternal control of offspring behavior changes with age as mothers are able to increase the effectiveness of punishment while minimizing the costs to the offspring. With very young infants, mothers use physical means to prevent or punish unwanted behavior (Bernstein and Ehardt 1986). They escalate to more intense forms of physical aggression, such as biting, only after continued resistance by the infant. For older offspring, noncontact threats play a larger part in mother-offspring aggression. A noncontact threat is a facial expression that is analogous to a very stern face with lips pursed and eyes intently focused on the recipient. This expression is usually accompanied by a sudden jerking motion of the head or body toward the offender. When mothers are trying to restrict the activity of their juvenile offspring, they use a combination of contact aggression and noncontact threats. For adolescent offspring, noncontact threats usually convey enough information, and they are rarely ever followed by contact aggression.

The Economics of Corporal Punishment

Parental-investment theory predicts that the level of parent-offspring conflict should be related to the disparity between the cost/benefit functions for parents and offspring. This disparity is related to the condition of the parents and the offspring, but it is not a simple function of the parent's status or access to resources. The economic circumstances of the parents affect the level of conflict through their influence on the parents' alternatives (Lee et al. 1991).

At the worst extreme of economic deprivation, a mother might be in such poor condition, and so deprived of resources, that she has no energy to spare to care for her offspring without severely jeopardizing her own survival. A primate infant can't survive without its mother, and the fitness of older immature offspring would also be reduced by the mother's death. In such a case, the best strategy for the mother is to abandon her youngest and most dependent infant and save herself. This would result in the most severe form of conflict and the likely death of the dependent infant.

The prediction for a mother in better condition, but still strained by lack of resources, would be completely different. In this case, the mother's best strategy for promoting her own reproductive success would be to extend the period of care for her current infant. If she tried to wean her infant too soon so that she could breed again within the next year, she would stand a good chance of damaging her own health and losing both infants. By continuing care, she is likely to produce at least one surviving infant during a two-year period, and would also increase her chances of being fit and ready to reproduce in the third year. Under these circumstances, we would expect minimal mother-infant conflict, and the rate of maternal rejection and punishment should be low.

Finally, the mother in the best condition with the greatest access to resources can successfully wean her current infant and produce two infants in two years. From the perspective of the infant, however, this means greater withholding of maternal care at six months of age instead of eighteen months, and cessation of ventral contact and nursing at twelve months instead of twenty-four. Thus, greater parent-offspring conflict is predicted in the more prosperous family than in the moderately deprived family described above.

The nonlinear relationship between maternal resources and the quality of maternal care is illustrated in a recent study of vervet monkey mother-infant dyads from our captive colony (Fairbanks and McGuire 1995). Mothers from the colony were classified as being in marginal, average, or prime reproductive condition at the time their infants were born. Females in marginal condition for reproduction included adolescent females, very old females, and females who were below a critical body weight. Successful reproduction in vervet monkeys is related to age, and mothers who are very young or very old have reduced fertility and higher rates of infant mortality than prime-aged mothers. The mothers who have the most difficult time producing surviving offspring are the adolescent females. A three-year-old vervet monkey is not fully grown but is still capable of conceiving. In the first seventeen years of breeding records from the vervet colony, the majority of pregnancies of three-year-old mothers resulted in failure. Pregnant three-year-olds are more likely to have problems with delivery, more likely to produce a stillborn infant, and more likely to lose a live-born infant in the first few months of life (Fairbanks and McGuire 1984; Fairbanks 2003). If an adolescent mother succeeds in delivering a live infant, she is often noticeably physically depleted. In these cases, when a mother is in marginal condition for reproduction, we would expect her to limit the amount of care she gives to her infant so she doesn't jeopardize her own survival and possibilities for reproduction in the future.

Females in the best condition for reproduction in the colony are the high-ranking mothers of prime reproductive age. High-ranking females have preferential access to resources and are able to control the behavior of other group members (Silk 1987). They also have higher fertility and reproductive success compared to lower-ranking females (Fairbanks and McGuire 1984; Harcourt 1987; Silk 1987). The counterintuitive prediction from parental-investment theory is that these mothers who are in the best condition for reproduction should be more rejecting than mothers in average condition.

Figure 3.3 shows the rate of maternal rejection for vervet monkey mothers in marginal, average, and prime reproductive condition (Fairbanks and McGuire 1995). Maternal rejection was higher for mothers in the poorest condition for reproduction and also for mothers in the best condition, when compared to average mothers. Marginal and prime mothers were also more likely to leave their infants with caretakers, and played a smaller role in maintaining mother-infant contact. Average mothers, in contrast, spent more time in contact with their infants and were more nurturant and protective. Data on infant survival rates indicated that mothers in marginal condition limited maternal care to restore their own health, often at the cost of infant mortality. Mothers in prime condition were able to use rejection to increase their own fertility without suffering higher rates of infant mortality than average mothers.

A similar relationship among maternal resources, fertility, and mother-infant conflict was found in a comparison of vervet monkeys living under different ecological conditions in East Africa (Cheney et al. 1988; Hauser and Fairbanks 1988). Mothers living in wild troops with better access to high-quality food resources did not provide more care for their current infants but

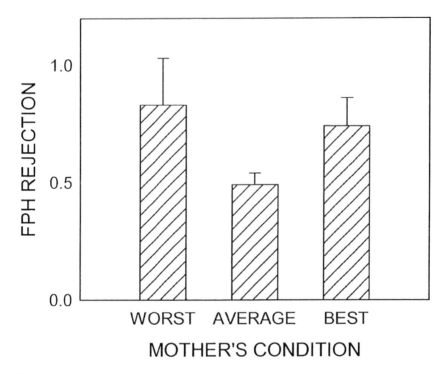

Fig. 3.3.

instead used their surplus energy to increase their fertility in the next season. These mothers were more rejecting toward their infants, and they had shorter interbirth intervals compared to mothers living in troops with a less reliable water supply and a poorer-quality food supply.

The effects of maternal condition, social rank, and adolescent mothering on maternal punishment of offspring are consistent with a U-shaped function of the effects of socioeconomic conditions on the rate of punishment and neglect (Lee et al. 1991; Fairbanks and McGuire 1995). Mothers will be most punitive when conditions are extremely bad, but they will also be relatively punitive when the mother is able to take advantage of favorable conditions to increase her reproductive success. In effect, the level of maternal punishment and rejection depends on the mother's options and opportunities. If a mother can increase her own lifetime fitness by rejecting her current infant, she should do so. In the worst case, this involves sacrificing the current infant so that the mother can survive and reproduce in the future. In the best case, the mother is able to take advantage of her greater opportunity to produce more surviving offspring in a shorter period of time.

Common Situations in Which Primates Rarely Use Corporal Punishment

Physical punishment of offspring by primate mothers is generally restricted to situations that involve direct interference with the mother's body or protection of younger siblings. Two situations where corporal punishment is commonly used in human families, to teach children to avoid dangerous places and not to eat toxic or inedible foods, are only rarely observed in primate societies.

Monkey mothers use restraint or retrieval, not punishment, to teach their offspring about danger. When an infant is attempting to approach a threatening individual or a risky situation, the mother will prevent it from proceeding by holding its leg or tail. If a mother hears an alarm call when her infant is out of contact, she will immediately retrieve it and carry it away from danger. Cues of the mother's distress are readily transmitted to the infant who is in close ventral contact. Experimental tests of squirrel monkey mother-infant dyads have demonstrated that infants show the same intensity of physiological stress response as their mothers when they are in a dangerous situation (Weiner and Levine 1992). When confronted with novel and potentially dangerous situations in our captive vervet colony, older infants stayed near their mothers and matched their mothers' degree of boldness or caution (Fairbanks and McGuire 1993). Young monkeys appear to be very sensitive to their mothers' level of alarm and respond appropriately without being punished.

Predation is a serious threat to infant and juvenile monkeys in the wild (Cheney and Wrangham 1987; Isbell 1990), but field reports of the use of physical punishment to teach offspring to avoid danger are rare. Vervet monkeys have distinctive alarm calls that designate an aerial or a ground predator (Struhsaker 1967; Seyfarth et al. 1980). The appropriate response to the leopard alarm call is to jump into a tree, while the best response to the eagle alarm call is to seek cover on the ground. Young vervets learn what to do by observing the response of their mothers and other adults in the group, and adults may positively reinforce their offspring's production of the correct alarm call by repeating the call (Seyfarth and Cheney 1986). In addition to this positive response, Caro and Hauser (1992) report four occasions when mothers were seen to punish their offspring physically for producing an erroneous alarm call. The punishment occurred after the mothers had initially responded with flight but then, after realizing the error, returned and bit or slapped the infants. Punishment in this context is rare, however, and in their general review of teaching in animals, Caro and Hauser (1992) found no other instances reported in the literature.

Food selection also involves learning between mothers and their young. The foraging environment often includes toxic foods that can harm naive infants and juveniles, but research on the development of food selection in primates has generally led to the conclusion that infants and immatures learn which foods to eat by copying older animals or by direct trial and error, not by social punishment (Galef 1976; Milton 1993). An infant monkey stays close to its mother during its early attempts to forage on its own and will frequently sniff at her mouth. This provides the infant with ample opportunity to learn by example. The value and importance of using the mother as a model for food choice has been underscored in a study at a vervet monkey field site in East Africa, where infants who spent more time foraging with their mothers were more likely to survive than those who foraged on their own (Hauser 1993).

As in the case of predation, monkey mothers appear to teach their young about food through positive example, not through punishment. In thousands of hours of observation of free-ranging vervet monkeys on St. Kitts, only one instance of food-avoidance teaching through punishment was observed (McGuire 1974; Fairbanks and Bird 1978). The home range of one of the vervet troops contained a grove of mancineel trees (*Hippomane mancinella*) which bear fruits that look and smell like small apples but are highly poisonous. The monkeys would sit under the trees for shade from the midday sun and would forage in the clammy cherry vines that wound through the mancineel branches. One day, when an infant picked up a mancineel apple and was about to take a bite, its mother rushed over and hit it, knocking the apple out of its hands. In addition to this instance, there are a few anecdotal accounts of mothers removing food from their infant's mouths, but no other reports of mothers hitting or punishing their offspring to teach them not to eat a particular food. In food-avoidance experiments, mothers will even allow their offspring to eat a food that they have personally learned to avoid without punishing them or warning them away (Fairbanks 1975; Cambefort 1981).

Consequences of Corporal Punishment

CONSEQUENCES FOR THE MOTHER

The evolutionary biological model makes clear predictions about the consequences of corporal punishment for the mother. Mothers should use rejection and punishment when they can increase their lifetime reproductive success by limiting the behavior and the demands of individual offspring. Observations from our vervet monkey colony and from the studies of other primate species cited above are consistent with this point. A vervet monkey mother who rejects her infants more often has a significantly shorter interval to the birth of her next infant (Fairbanks and McGuire 1987). Similar results have been reported for free-ranging vervet monkeys, as well as for other primate species in both captive and field environments (Altmann 1980; Simpson et al. 1981; Lee 1984; Nicolson 1987; Hauser and Fairbanks 1988; Gomendio 1991; Berman et al. 1993). From the mother's perspective, maternal rejection and corporal punishment allow her to regulate the behavior of one offspring so that she can distribute the energy she has available for parental care optimally across all the offspring she can produce in her lifetime.

CONSEQUENCES FOR THE INFANT

Parent-offspring conflict theory predicts that the short-term response of offspring to rejection by the mother will be to protest (Jay 1963; Rosenblum 1971; Strusaker 1971; Ransom and Rowell 1972; Nash 1978; Worlein et al. 1988; Collinge 1991; Berman et al. 1994). The infant who is acting in its own self-interest should try to extract more care from its mother than its mother is typically willing to give. From a functional viewpoint, the infant should not respond to punishment by simply reducing its demands. If it is strongly motivated by its need for maternal care, its initial response to punishment should be to increase its attempts to maintain access to its mother. As the infant clings even tighter, it becomes more costly for the mother to remove it. When an infant throws a tantrum, it further disrupts the mother and threatens its own safety. The mother doesn't want to endanger her infant, so she often gives in to the tantrum and allows the infant to cling and suckle. The resulting behavior of the mother seems inconsistent, sometimes punishing and sometimes rewarding the infant's demands. This inconsistency can be explained by the fluctuating costs and benefits to the mother and the infant for their actions. The outcome of this process is a compromise between what the offspring demands and what the mother wants to give, with behavior of each influencing the costs and benefits of the other.

Evolutionary theory makes no specific predictions about the long-term consequences of punishment for the offspring, but empirical data from our colony and from other primate studies suggest that there is consistency in maternal style toward offspring across generations of the same matriline (Fairbanks 1989; Berman 1990; Maestripieri et al. 1997). In the vervet monkey colony, factor analysis of maternal behaviors consistently produces a maternal-protectiveness factor and a maternal-rejection factor (Fairbanks and McGuire 1987, 1993). Each matriline has a characteristic level of maternal rejection, and significant differences are observed among matrilines (Fairbanks 1996a). Figure 3.4 shows the mean maternal-rejection factor scores for thirty-four

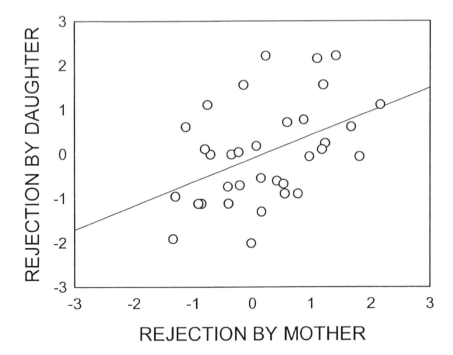

Fig. 3.4.

vervet monkey mothers by the mean maternal-rejection factors for their adult daughters ($r = 0.44$, $p < 0.01$). Part of this consistency in parenting style between mothers and their adult daughters can be explained by the similarities in the social circumstances of females in the same family. In vervet monkey society, a daughter usually inherits her mother's dominance rank, and dominance rank is a significant predictor of the level of maternal rejection. High-ranking mothers are more likely to be rejecting toward their infants, and when mothers rise in rank, their level of maternal rejection also rises.

To what extent is family consistency in maternal rejection a direct result of punishment experienced in infancy, as opposed to shared circumstances in adulthood? Do mothers who reject and punish their infants more often produce daughters who use the same rejecting style when they become mothers? When the level of maternal rejection that each female received as an infant was compared to the average level of maternal rejection she exhibited as an adult, the correlation of $r = 0.30$ was positive but not statistically significant. The same pattern of results has also been reported for free-ranging rhesus monkeys; Berman (1990) found a significant correlation between mothers and daughters in overall rate of maternal rejection and a positive, but not significant, association between rejection experienced in infancy and adult mothering behavior. More research is needed on this important issue before any definitive conclusions can be drawn.

Contrary to expectations, there has been little evidence of harmful effects of early maternal rejection on later behavior and adjustment for nonhuman primates (Fairbanks 1996). In our research with vervet monkeys, we have identified a consistent relationship between the degree of early maternal protectiveness and later individual differences in temperament along a bold/cautious dimension (Fairbanks and McGuire 1988, 1993). Individuals with highly protective mothers tend to be more cautious when faced with novel and potentially threatening situations later in life, compared to individuals with less protective mothers. Rejecting mothers, in contrast, have offspring who are more socially assertive as infants and relatively fearless as adolescents when confronted with a social stranger. In other species, relatively high levels of early maternal rejection within the "normal" range have also been associated with increased resourcefulness, boldness, and ability to cope with stressful situations later in life (Simpson and Datta 1991; Fairbanks 1996; Schino et al. 2001).

Implications for Understanding Human Behavior

Can these insights from the evolutionary biological theories of parent-offspring conflict, and data on primate mother-offspring relationships, tell us anything about corporal punishment in human families? As primate observers, it is impossible for us not to compare the behavior of the monkeys with that of our own species, and to notice the similarities and differences in family relationships. There are similarities in the context and patterning of parental punishment, but there are also fundamental differences in how monkey and human parents punish their offspring. One of these differences is in the ritualization of punishment. When a monkey mother punishes her infant or juvenile offspring, she generally uses a motion that is appropriate to stop or prevent the particular unwanted behavior. There seems to be no monkey analog to more the stylized forms of corporal punishment that are commonly used with human children, such as spanking on the buttocks. Another fundamental difference between monkeys and humans is in the ability to generalize the effects of punishment across time and space. Punishment by monkey mothers is restricted to behavior that occurs in the present, and most punishment is in response to actions that directly interfere with the mother or with younger siblings. We have not observed any instances of delayed or protracted punishment of offspring by monkey mothers. In contrast, humans often use punishment as a tool to control behavior that is distant in time and space, and they will hit their children to teach them about environmental dangers or relationships outside the immediate family.

The greater cognitive sophistication of our own species has allowed us to think about corporal punishment, to intellectualize its use, and to extend its functions beyond the basic mammalian process described here for monkey mothers. In spite of these differences, there are still many similarities in the way humans and nonhuman primates use corporal punishment to control offspring behavior. For example, the change in the rate of corporal punishment with offspring age found in the National Family Violence Survey (Wauchope and Straus 1990) is remarkably similar to that shown here for vervet monkeys. In both studies, age was the strongest and most consistent predictor of the rate of corporal punishment. The incidence of corporal punishment started low in early infancy, rose to a peak at the transition between infancy and childhood, then declined gradually with age. The peak for the monkeys was at the point when the mother was preparing to breed again. Interestingly, the peak at the age of two in the National Family Violence Survey also matches the typical interbirth interval between successive siblings for modern American families. Insights from parent-offspring conflict theory would suggest that the high level of conflict observed at this time reflects the differing self-interest of parent and child, with the parent trying to promote maturity and self-control sooner than the child would like.

Parent-offspring conflict theory can also help to explain the seemingly inconsistent effects of social class and mother's employment on corporal punishment (Straus and Gelles 1990). A simple model of environmental stress does not predict the incidence of corporal punishment in human families very well. In vervet monkeys, the nonlinear effects of ecological and social variables, such as habitat quality and dominance rank, can be explained by looking at the available options and focusing on how a mother can benefit from controlling and limiting her infant's behavior. Monkey mothers in strained circumstances are less punishing when a little more maternal indulgence can make a large difference in the welfare of the infant, but they are more punishing when maternal care compromises their own future health and welfare. A similar approach might also be applied to predicting variation in human use of punishment. For example, Gelles and Hargreaves (1990) found that working outside the home did not influence the rate of mother-to-child corporal punishment, but working mothers who reported that they had more responsibility for supervising and disciplining their children than they could handle used corporal punishment more often than mothers who did not feel they had excess childcare responsibilities. A mother's perception that her child-care burden is too heavy is an indicator of parent-offspring conflict and would be expected to lead to overt behavioral conflict and the use of corporal punishment.

Parent-offspring conflict theory also points to several relatively unexplored variables that would be expected to influence parental solicitude and the rate of corporal punishment in human families (Daly and Wilson 1988; Hrdy 1992). For example, close birth spacing should increase both sibling rivalry and parent-offspring conflict, and thus increase the incidence of corporal punishment. Divorce and remarriage would be likely to increase mother-offspring conflict, as mothers must balance the needs of their current children with the opportunities created by new relationships. Stepparents would also be expected to be more punitive than genetic parents. The mother's age should be a factor in mother-offspring conflict because the costs and benefits of parental care change over the life span. Higher rates of corporal punishment would be expected for adolescent mothers, who could improve their long-term prospects for social and economic security by greater restriction of their current infants. All of these variables can be predicted to influence the level of parent-offspring conflict, and consequently the rate of corporal punishment, if we consider that maternal care has been designed by natural selection to maximize lifetime reproductive success.

In monkeys, as in humans, physical aggression is more common within families than between families, and the mother is the most likely perpetrator of aggression against her own offspring. This fact is difficult to explain from the perspective that, in its ideal form, maternal behavior should be devoted solely to the benefit of the individual child. Evolutionary theory explains this apparent anomaly as an attempt by the mother to maximize her reproductive success by effectively limiting and distributing her reproductive effort and parental care across her life span. Parent-offspring conflict theory recognizes that the interests of the parents and their offspring overlap but are not identical, and that a complete understanding of why and when parents use corporal punishment must take into account an understanding of this essential source of conflict. We believe that many of the basic motivational systems underlying parental behavior are still with us, and that recognition of the reasons for parent-offspring conflict will help us to understand the causes of corporal punishment in human families.

Note

We would like to thank Karin Blau, Jill Kusnitz, Michaela Heeb, Dan Diekmann, Grenville Morton, and all of the past observers and research assistants who made this research possible. Funding was provided by National Science Foundation grants BNS 84-02292, BNS 87-09765, and BNS 91-108017 to Lynn Fairbanks and by Veterans Administration Merit Review grants to Michael McGuire.

4

Putting Corporal Punishment of Children in Historical Perspective

MICHAEL DONNELLY

The history of the family and, as a complement and offshoot, the history of childhood have burgeoned in the past several decades, producing a wealth of documentation and new interpretations about family life in the distant and recent past. Few of these studies have focused intensively on corporal punishment of children by parents, but many broach the subject. Indeed, discipline and punishment often figure as key themes in historical accounts of the family, since punishment is typically assumed to be a central and enduring means of child rearing. How parents punish children, moreover, is frequently taken as a way to indicate, symptomatically, something of the subjective tenor of family life.[1]

There are a number of special problems involved in interpreting this historical literature and in making it accessible and familiar for researchers in the social sciences.[2] Like other areas of "private life" in the past, the patterns of relations within families are by their nature difficult to recover and to document.[3] More difficult still, reevoking the tone of sentiments in family life of times past may involve long chains of inference, in effect wringing wider significance out of what may be only anecdotal information. In fact the evidence on which (sometimes sweeping) generalizations in this field have been based may on examination appear to be scant, patchy, partial, and, not infrequently, plainly unrepresentative.[4]

There is also a fundamental conceptual problem involved in approaching the history of the family, since its basic objects of study — parents, offspring — are at once biological and cultural categories. "It is easy to assume," says the historian Pat Thane, "that definitions and expectations of age groups — infants, children, adolescents, adults, the aged — are fixed and unchanging, determined principally by the biological facts of physical and mental development and decay" (1981: 6). And yet the cultural definitions given to, and the expectations attached to, basic developmental stages (infancy, childhood, adolescence, adulthood, old age) have changed and varied considerably. Historians have done much to document this variability, but they may nonetheless also be prone occasionally to echo uncritically certain familiar, apparently timeless, commonplaces about child rearing and parent-child relations. It is similarly easy to lapse into an implicitly functionalist set of assumptions about the family and its roles, taking "the family" to be a quasi-natural, elementary social unit. The form of the family may vary across, and even within, cultures; but on a functionalist view "the family" as an institution essentially represents society's response to a set of relatively invariant biological and social exigencies.[5] Historians of the family are by no means immune to the appeals of functionalism, notwithstanding a training that tends to induce them in general to historicize (rather than to naturalize) the phenomena they study. Even as the history of the family has become increasingly recognized as a distinctive sub-field, a debate still simmers as to just what is historically variable about the family and, in particular, to what extent the larger developments in society across time are likely to affect and alter child-rearing practices. While many historians have in effect stressed "the huge differences in the way children are treated and expected to behave at different periods" (Tucker 1977: 15), others have argued forthrightly a quite different standpoint, that "there is no reason to assume that parental care must vary according to the developments and changes in society as a whole" (Pollock 1983: viii).

However historians try to resolve these conceptual problems, they tend to construct their narratives of family history along, broadly speaking, two tracks. One strategy involves mapping out trends in the development of the family over time, thus placing the family as an evolving object in a more or less long stream of history. In such inquiries the present serves at least implicitly as a terminus, and the organizing question is to understand how and why the evolution of the family followed the course it did: How was it before, what changed, when, and how? Identifying trends over time is key here, since it suggests to the historian how to narrate a history of change and development, with the family over time becoming more this, less that, and so forth. This perspective also opens to the historian a possible normative standpoint. If the family in the present is thus represented as the continuation of trends stretching back into the past, then the reconstruction of past history offers a baseline against which the trends in progress can be evaluated. Given some set of principles on which the performance of families might be judged, are the trends in course better or worse, good or bad?

The second broad strategy historians deploy makes use of the past as a foil, or rhetorical counterpoint, against which the novelty and distinctiveness of the present (or some other delimited period) can be brought into relief. Rather than charting a trend across time through which the family as an institution can be tracked, this second, alternative way of putting the family into history brings into focus some particular historical moment. It aims to establish in detail a specific, time-bound cultural context in which distinctive family-role sets are defined, experienced, and (possibly) contested. The second strategy involves in effect highlighting in the foreground the distinctive setting that gives particular meaning to the experience of family life, while pushing to the background some other (often enduring, familiar) aspects of family patterns.

The two tracks can be called roughly "evolutionist" and "contextualist." Often they do not emerge as fully explicit strategies. Nor are they necessarily mutually exclusive—indeed, they are not infrequently combined in different parts of a broader analysis. But the strategies can be usefully distinguished because they tend to contain and to rest on different assumptions. They tend, moreover, to mobilize or induce different reactions to, and suggest different implications about how to regard, the contemporary family. Schematically, to represent the family as an enduring, if evolving, institution usually means to conceive it in basically naturalistic (and often implicitly functionalist) terms, as that set of social arrangements which performs biological reproduction and the rearing and nurturing of offspring. By contrast, the so-called contextualists are more likely to emphasize the constructed, and hence possibly contestable, character of cultural roles, and the specific meanings of family experience in a given sociopolitical setting.[6]

Evolutionist Histories of Childhood and the Family

In broad outline, there is a familiar and by now rather conventional account of the evolution of childhood—what one critic describes as the "monotonous regularity" of the received view (Pollock 1983: 1). It is based principally on intellectual history, deepened at some points by research that is more social-historical; what it charts are principally shifts in parents' attitudes toward children, from which historians try to infer how children were likely to have been treated.[7]

The bald claim of Philippe Ariès that in medieval Europe "the idea of child-hood did not exist" (1962: 125) functions as a starting point and stimulus for much of this historiography. Even where Ariès has been challenged and crit-icized, there is still a reasonably broad consensus that childhood as we know it was largely an invention of the past three or four centuries. As Ariès himself pointed out, this should not be taken to imply that earlier children were "ne-glected, forsaken or despised." Ariès's argument is rather that in the medieval period the specific nature of children as children was ignored, and that children (beyond the stage of infancy) were likely to be regarded as little adults. As the notion of childhood gradually emerged, it came to entail the eventual removal of children from the everyday world of adult society and fostered new attitudes toward children based on their newly perceived needs and special nature.

Critics were quick to point out that Ariès had not so much established that there was *no* medieval conception of childhood as that the *modern* conception was absent (see, for instance, Wilson 1980). But this was enough to stimulate widespread curiosity about the historical variability of the family and of child rearing. What much of the subsequent historiography traces, again following Ariès's lead, is a series of changing or evolving conceptions of childhood. If, once, "the [modern] idea of childhood did not exist," by what stages did it emerge? The key shift, as registered in this historiography, appears to be con-ceptual: once differentiated in its nature from adults, the child became an object of inquiry in its own right, and moralists set themselves the task of explaining and justifying appropriate relations between adults and children, between parents and their offspring. The child's perceived difference thus pro-vided an original and fundamental rationale for formal education, in the large sense, focused on children and designed to counter their difference and imma-turity. Education is also the presumed link between conceptions of childhood and parents' actual treatment of children (the link between attitude and be-havior), since to each conception of childhood corresponds an appropriate pedagogy. Lacking information for the most part about the actual behavior of parents, historians hence turn their attention to cultural conceptions of child-hood, and to the doctrines of education that presumably translated those conceptions into practical maxims.

As a rough periodization, historians of the modern Western (or more nar-rowly, Anglo-American) family typically highlight a series of discrete stages and watershed periods in the perceptions of childhood:

1. In the sixteenth and seventeenth centuries, in contrast to the medieval pe-riod, the emerging conceptions of childhood may well have required a greater surveillance of children and a growing strictness in disciplining

them. The Calvinist notion of the infant's inborn depravity was widely diffused: infants were "sprigs of old Adam whose wills had to be broken" (Plumb 1975: 70). This doctrine, since it so stressed the moral distance and psychological difference of children from adults, also laid on adults the responsibility to correct their offspring's nature, in the familiar and endur-ing phrase, "to break their will."

2. The early eighteenth century, according to a number of interpreters, initi-ated a sea change of attitudes, opening in Plumb's (1975) phrase, a "new world" for children. The Puritan-Evangelical view of children was still strongly present, represented notably in the teachings of John Wesley (see Greven 1990); but there was a greater variety of attitudes, and elements of debate about what was appropriate treatment of children. There were also notable signs of a change in sensibilities and a growing sentimentality about children, originating among elite groups but gradually diffused among other social strata. John Locke's conception of the child as a *tabula rasa* (a blank slate), and therefore innocent and ignorant, suggested a pedagogy quite different from that of the Calvinist conception; it too, however, placed a clear onus on adults to educate children. Rousseau's *Emile* represented yet another, quite different conception of the child as "a little human animal destined for the spiritual and moral life" (Boutet de Monvel 1963: vii), and hence to be nurtured and trained accordingly.

3. Historians have discerned a shift in family sentiments in the 1830s, begin-ning particularly in middle-class educated households in America, to what has been called "child nurture" (Wishy 1968), with the mother supplanting the father as "the most powerful agent in developing a child's character," and with "less emphasis . . . placed on physical punishment, while corre-spondingly more importance was given to psychological methods of disci-pline" (Pleck 1987: 39).

4. Finally, from the late nineteenth century onward, psychology, social work, and the other social sciences have become an increasingly significant source of expert opinion about children, and thereby a palpable influence on their treatment. The systematic study of children, pioneered notably by G. Stan-ley Hall, has led to a more "empirical" view of their development.

What can one infer from such apparent changes in the conception and understanding of childhood about actual patterns of behavior and, in particu-lar, about the use, frequency, severity, and purposes of corporal punishment inflicted on children? Again here, notwithstanding some dissenting voices, many historians appear to have reached a rough consensus.

In the seventeenth century, as Lawrence Stone has insisted, "there can be no doubt whatever that severe flogging was a normal and daily occurrence in the . . . grammar school"; similarly, "whipping was the normal method of discipline in a sixteenth- or seventeenth-century home" (1977: 164, 167). Plumb has likewise claimed that "harsh discipline was the child's lot, and they were often terrorized deliberately, and not infrequently, sexually abused" (1975: 66). In the American colonies, parents were particularly concerned with "breaking the will" of the child (Illick 1976). As John Demos has argued, a child asserting his or her will would have appeared to devout Puritan parents as "a clear manifestation of original sin. . . . Such being the case, the only appropriate response from parents was a repressive one" (1970: 136).

Many historians identify signs of a shift in the period around the beginning of the eighteenth century, away from cruel and repressive methods of child rearing toward more kindly methods. This was, in Plumb's phrase, the "new world" for children opening up: "Books, games, clothes especially designed for children" as well as amusements and educational endowments were newly available (Pollock 1983: 18). The shift seems to reflect a new sensibility and increasing attention to children as potential moral subjects: "Will breaking and physical discipline began to decline, and efforts to instill conscience and guilt began to replace the use of shame to reprove inappropriate child behavior" (Stearns and Stearns 1986: 31). The new ideals may first have appealed to elite groups, but apparently they were progressively diffused to other social strata. In the Stearnses' metaphor, "The long campaign to control anger, launched in the eighteenth century, grew to the proportions of a steady war in the Victorian era" (1986: 36). With time, this "war" (carried on through a wave of advice manuals about child rearing) brought more and more consequences for parents' behavior. In mid-nineteenth-century America, as the Stearnses have interpreted the changes in progress, "outright physical abuse was on the decline. Physical punishment for childhood transgressions became increasingly infrequent, and even in the schools corporal punishment began to abate in frequency" (1986: 58). To put the point sharply, "a generation or more of parents had broken with the disciplinary styles of their own parents. . . . The impression of a distinct, if incomplete and sometimes inconsistent, transformation in parental style is inevitable," and the transformation was essentially achieved from the 1870s to the 1920s (Stearns and Stearns 1986: 99).

While historians of evolutionary bent may disagree about the timing of such stages, and about their respective weight and scope as cultural influences, there is, again, reasonable consensus about the direction of change. The pattern evident through successive conceptions of childhood is a gradual softening of sentiments toward children, a shifting away from largely instrumental attitudes, a strengthening of emotional ties. It is in many respects a special case of the growing humanitarianism, and the related declining intensity of punishment, that Durkheim (1978) described as a secular trend in organically solidaristic societies. The idiom in which authoritative opinion about children has been expressed has likewise shifted in a consistent direction, from initially religious to medical and eventually to psychological terms. The consequences of these changes have been to raise children's status, from the bottom of the social scale at the very margins of adult society to the center of sentimental concern in the modern family.

On what varieties of evidence have historians sought to base their conclusions? The available evidence is largely literary, from a variety of manuals advising parents on child rearing to occasional personal documents, like memoirs or diaries, in which individuals recollect the circumstances of their own childhoods or report on children they observe and interact with. Both sorts of evidence present difficult problems of interpretation.

Some historians take advice manuals as straightforward statements of the dominant values and attitudes of a culture; on that assumption, what manuals advise on the subject of corporal punishment can be taken as a reflection of prevailing practice, perhaps somewhat idealized. Other historians have been far more cautious about interpreting advice manuals — they remain key sources, perhaps, but ones to be read with great care. The hortatory tone typical of manuals may reflect, for instance, not an injunction to conform to conventional practice but actually an effort to criticize current practice and to recommend superior alternatives — in other words, an effort to change behavior. In a carefully argued reflection on the use of advice manuals as historical sources, Mechling (1975) has suggested that there are two basic sorts of advice literature. One sort tends to "reflect" current practice, while the other represents the "vanguard" of change (1975: 46); few historians, she complains, note the difference, which bedevils their interpretations of what such advice meant in context (see also Brobeck 1976). The potential or presumed audience for manuals presents a similar sort of problem: Have manuals typically come from, and been addressed to, status-conscious middle-class audiences (unlikely to be representative of the population as a whole)? Are they works of opinion leaders whose influence is eventually diffused down through the social hierarchy? Most problematically of all, how can one infer actual behaviors (and the array or variety of actual behaviors) from a set of prescriptions about what parents should strive to do? To what extent, the skeptic might ask, do parents learn how to parent from reading advice books?

Memoirs and diaries seem at first glance to be more tractable sources; at least they appear to report observations and thus to require less tortuous inferences on the part of the historian interpreting them. On the other hand, personal documents present other difficulties in their own right. The lives of the great majority of children are not represented in written accounts. The observations about childhood that tend to be recorded are more often than not about remarkable children. And what is reported tends not to be daily patterns, the routine and the typical, which would likely be taken for granted and thus hardly seem noteworthy. Even the best-publicized childhoods are likely to be selectively reported and biased. In biography or autobiography generally, what is typically recalled about an individual's childhood is selected in hindsight, usually because of its connection to, or relevance for, some trait evident later in the person's development; childhood is interesting, in other words, insofar as it can be seen as indicative of, or as influencing, what came later.[8]

Even if the varieties of evidence available may limit historians of the family to rather impressionistic interpretations, the narratives that historians construct may carry a powerful rhetorical message. Perhaps the clearest example is Lloyd de Mause's bald claim that "the further back in history one goes, the lower the level of child care, and the more likely children are to be killed, abandoned, beaten, terrorized and sexually abused" (1974: 1). This grim picture is at least partly relieved by the sharply upward trend in recent history finally to nurture children. Edward Shorter (1975) describes a similar evolutionary track, arguing that before modernization adequate or good mothering of children was scarcely possible. Again, whatever the merits of such an argument, its force is clearly to vindicate the present against the past, and to represent a course of progress. Interestingly, the drafters of Sweden's progressive law banning corporal punishment drew explicitly on the same image of development: the ban is presented as if it were simply taking the next step in social development ("a natural historic development"), anticipating the course that historical evolution would otherwise take (Herman 1985: 10). In this respect, how historians plot the evolution of the family may indeed put the present into perspective. The "trend of history," even when that phrase is little more than careless shorthand, carries a powerful rhetorical charge, as if history had a momentum, dynamic, and direction of its own.

Contextualist Histories of the Family and of Childhood

The alternative, contextualist strategy for placing the family in history tends to work on a smaller canvas; for that reason alone contextualists tend to be skeptical about the long-term, upward course of historical evolution portrayed by other family historians. Contextual history is, to shift the metaphor, telescopic in its focus rather than panoramic. The interpretive watchword of the contextualist is to embed the family in its particular time and place, to place it against the background of its contemporary and environing culture and social arrangements. "The family," to put the point extremely, does not exist, at least "not as a point of departure, [not] as a manifest reality"; it must instead be conceived "as a moving resultant, an uncertain form whose intelligibility can only come from studying the system of relations it maintains with the sociopolitical level" (Donzelot 1979: xxv). Such synchronic contextualizing is particularly important for understanding the more subjective aspects of family life, since individuals' experience of families is necessarily time bound and culturally specific. What the experience of family life means to a given individual is mediated by the cultural frames available to that individual, and by other aspects of his or her contemporary social experience. Parents raise children generation after generation, encountering many of the same existential predicaments and social dilemmas. And yet the individuals who experience these events do so not only through their roles as parents or children but also through other social roles they play, and through the culturally constructed and time-bound perceptions of those roles. To draw the implications of this point of view, the historian cannot casually speak of "corporal punishment" as if it were recognizably the same phenomenon across time. The very meaning of the act of corporal punishment has itself changed, and needs to be interpreted within specific contexts. Likewise, standards for evaluating interpersonal force and violence have shifted; what might have been acceptable levels in one period would appear at later times extreme and abusive.

Given such interpretive maxims, contextualist historians are likely to offer a perspective on corporal punishment in the family rather different from that of the evolutionists. To begin with, they are likely to note that the phenomenon of corporal punishment appears to interest historians of some periods (and cultures) notably more than historians of other periods (and cultures). Why so? It may be that corporal punishment has been a highly charged issue at certain periods in the past (as it is currently) but far less so, apparently, at others. While over the long term corporal punishment may appear to have been a perennial theme in family dramas, acted out generation by generation, it has been more salient, problematic, or anxiety producing at some times than at others. Evolutionist historians would not necessarily disagree but might be more inclined to interpret the evident tensions in such periods as signs of change or as the very means by which transitions from one phase in a course of evolution to another are worked out. Evolutionists, in other words, tend to weave such signs of change into the broader cloth, and thus to smooth out the path of development—as in Stone's (1979) description of "steady linear change." For contextualists, on the other hand, the question of why then, why more at one time than at some other time, is likely to move to the foreground. Moreover, contextualists are likely to suggest that what historians can discover about corporal punishment in the past may itself be a function of periodically heightened sensitivity to the issue.[9]

The waxing and waning of interest in corporal punishment is also likely to suggest a different strategy of comparison across time, leading the historian to ask if there might be some general pattern evident in those periods when corporal punishment was more, rather than less, problematic or anxiety producing. In fact, contextualist historians have noted a number of intriguing parallels among such periods, at least as regards the past century and a half of U.S. history. If the current phase of concern with corporal punishment is dated from the late 1960s onward, there were earlier, comparable peaks of interest in the 1830s and 1840s, and again in the period from the mid-1870s to the 1920s.

In the antebellum period, a broad-gauged movement of social reformers organized campaigns against corporal punishment focusing variously on "prisoners, sailors, women and children" (Glenn 1984). The so-called House of Refuge movement was one branch of this campaign, whose aims in some respects paralleled the contemporary "cult of domesticity" described by cultural historians. The 1870s and immediately after have been described as an era of "child saving" (Platt 1965), "the beginning of a massive national crusade against child abuse" (Hiner 1979: 234), which later broadened into a campaign not merely against abuse but against the very use of corporal punishment on children.

In each of the periods there appear to have been precipitating events, on which social reformers successfully focused public attention, meanwhile mobilizing campaigns to combat the identified "social problem." In 1874, a highly publicized case of child maltreatment led directly to the establishment of the New York Society for the Prevention of Cruelty to Children (SPCC), modeled in part on societies for the prevention of cruelty to animals (SPCA) and soon imitated in a number of other cities and states. Somewhat similarly, the 1962 publication of an article entitled "The Battered Child Syndrome" in the *Journal of the American Medical Association* quite quickly led to a national campaign against child abuse and to legislation in all fifty states against caretakers' abuse of children (Pfohl 1977).

None of these reform campaigns initially focused on corporal punishment; indeed, the campaigners were careful to draw a clear line between (extreme and illegitimate) cases of abusive treatment and (presumably appropriate and legitimate) conventional uses of corporal punishment. It is noteworthy, how-ever, that in each of the cycles of reform the apparently clear line between abuse and proper use began over time to blur. What initially gave scandal were, presumably, relatively rare events; in time, however, the campaigns raised protest not only against the abuse of children (including physical abuse through excessive, extreme, or severe corporal punishment) but also against the very use of corporal punishment itself. It is as if it were difficult to draw and maintain a firm line between physical abuse and "normal," "acceptable" corporal punishment: hence a gradual broadening of focus beyond extreme cases of child abuse to more widespread, common, and even conventional practice. Indignation about scandalous events raised, over time, perplexities about what had been accepted practice. Was corporal punishment in fact not different in kind but merely in degree from physical abuse? As Hiner notes, describing campaigns against corporal punishment in early twentieth-century America, "Many parents and professional educators began to conclude that it was impossible to make a rational distinction between legitimate corporal punishment and child abuse" (1979: 241). Corporal punishment came to seem too "closely related in both logical and emotional terms to the physical abuse so roundly condemned by the reformers" (241).

Once targeted as a social problem, corporal punishment has moreover been criticized in the different periods in quite similar terms; in the 1830s, the early twentieth century, and the 1980s, virtually the same arguments appear and reappear. The reformers' repeated themes represent corporal punishment as (1) a form of violence, however well intentioned, focused, and controlled it may be; that tends moreover to be (2) counterproductive, in that it produces resentment in the child rather than thoughtful reflection on his or her con-duct (children remember the beating but not why they were beaten); and that (3) demeans the child, rather than promotes his or her moral autonomy and growth. The perennial alternative to corporal punishment appears similarly to be reasoning with the child and using moral suasion, which reformers have long claimed, and continue to claim, can be both less deleterious and more effective.

In contrast to the evolutionists' smooth upward curve of social progress, the contextualists suggest a different image of historical movement: a series of cycles of reform, in which the periodic waxing of indignation is followed by waning interest and some interval of lull before the next cycle begins, and so on.

The final contribution of the contextualists may be to put into relief the dynamics of the current cycle of reform. If there are noteworthy similari-ties with earlier reform movements, there are also significant (and perhaps decisive) differences. In the current campaign, child-care professionals have occupied the forefront of advocacy; they are far more numerous than their earlier amateur counterparts; and more significantly still, they have the power of established institutional positions. Moreover, while the current campaign repeats the arguments of past campaigns, it also echoes the rhetoric and the claims for recognition of other "oppressed groups" (notably those of the women's movement). "Children's rights" are akin to the "human rights" claimed by other groups (the United Nations Convention on the Rights of the Child makes the equation explicit). In the current context the campaign against corporal punishment of children may still appear to be a single-issue movement; nonetheless, it draws also on the unprecedented groundswell of other contemporary claims for human rights.

Conclusion

There is in the end no choice to be made here between evolutionist and contextualist approaches. The two tracks plainly each have their value and are perhaps most useful of all in combination, with each operating as a corrective on, or complement to, the other. To take a case in point, family law has undoubtedly evolved since the eighteenth-century formulations of Blackstone, for whom children still fell "within the empire of the father." Children, like wives before them, now have a quite different standing (albeit still controversial) in law. Talk of "children's rights" may have begun in the early twentieth century as rhetoric, but it has come to influence court practice and legal reasoning. At the same time, even as the evolutionist historian looks back retrospectively to the late eighteenth century and recounts the changing (doubtless improving) status of children in law, the contextualist colleague can still point to the discontinuous cycles of reform and agitation through which historical agents struggled to articulate and give substance to the new "rights." The contextualist's role in this division of labor is significantly to play up the activity of social critics and reformers — of agents of change — whose numbers, zeal, and capacity to mobilize support appear to rise and fall cyclically. This is a key insight to recall as one tries to examine corporal punishment in historical perspective. The current day may, on one hand, represent the recent stage in a centuries-long path of evolutionary change, but it needs equally to be located, on the other hand, within cycles of social reform and cultural change.

Notes

1. I wish to thank members of the Family Research Laboratory, University of New Hampshire, for thoughtful comments and suggestions on an earlier version of this chapter.

2. For a thoughtful reflection on the value, and on the difficulties involved, in bringing historians and social scientists together in a joint project on child development, see Glen Elder et al., *Children in Time and Place: Developmental and Historical Insights* (Cambridge: Cambridge University Press, 1993), "Epilogue: An Emerging Framework for Dialogue between History and Developmental Psychology," pp. 241–49. See also in the same volume, the less sanguine remarks by Michael Zuckerman, "History and Developmental Psychology, a Dangerous Liaison: A Historian's Perspective," pp. 230–40.

3. "Private" here can be understand in two senses, as referring to the ordinary, everyday domestic sphere, which tends to go undocumented; or as referring to what is hidden and unavailable to public view. In the second sense, the contemporary family is likely to be more "private" than earlier families. As Laslett (1973) argues, the greater privacy of the contemporary family in this latter sense involves a lessening of social control over the relations of family members with each other.

4. An egregious example is Ariès's *Centuries of Childhood* (1962), which relies extensively on the early seventeenth-century diary of a Dr. Heroard. Heroard kept the diary as physician to the dauphin of France, the future Louis XIII. Ariès comments simply on the usefulness of the source: "Thanks to the diary . . . we can imagine what a child's life was like at the beginning of the seventeenth century" (1962, 62).

5. The reaction to Ariès's book (1962) is an indirect indication of just how widespread this conventional view was. It was as if Ariès opened up a new topic, whereas previously historians had assumed that there was little to investigate.

6. Such contextualism is not limited to historians. For similar approaches in the social sciences, see Kessel and Siegel 1983 and James and Prout 1990.

7. The historiography summarized here deals for the early period with northwestern Europe (especially England) and its colonial extensions, and then for the early nineteenth century onward principally with the United States.

8. Despite such limitations Linda Pollock has argued that personal documents still provide the best evidence available on the actual behavior of parents. On the basis of a systematic analysis of 416 diaries and autobiographies, drawn from Britain and America from the sixteenth century to the nineteenth, she reaches some startling conclusions: reporting on the period 1850–99, she notes, for instance, that "the lack of information on discipline in the American texts is striking. It seems that American parents of this epoch were not concerned with regulating the behavior of their sons and daughters to any great extent" (1983, 187). Her general conclusion reads similarly: "The sources used reveal that there have been very few changes in parental care and child life from the sixteenth to the nineteenth century in the home, apart from social changes and technological improvements. . . . It is also clear that the majority of children were not subjected to brutality. Physical punishment was used by a number of parents, usually infrequently and when all else had failed" (1983, 268). It is noteworthy that Pollock reaches the surprisingly unhistorical conclusion that not much had changed, that parents continued to rear children more or less as they had always done. The conclusion is suspiciously close to the initial assumption that Pollock acknowledges launched her revisionist study: "I believe there is no reason to assume that parental care must vary according to developments and changes in society as a whole. . . . I am of the opinion that changes should be investigated against this background of continuity" (1983, viii).

9. This has a direct bearing, in the view of many contextualists, on the status of the

evidence available about corporal punishment. As a number of feminist historians have pointed out, in a related area, it is quite difficult to track the incidence over time of domestic violence. The evidence available about domestic violence is far more abundant in some periods than in others, which may reflect not necessarily greater incidence but better or more complete recording; the very evidence to which historians have access may be an artifact of heightened (but transient) awareness of a social problem. Similarly, the historian's interest in such phenomena may reflect something in his or her own context. Some contextualists would maintain further that much of the evidence (especially literary evidence) available to historians about family life is similarly culturally laden, and hence temporally specific. What literary sources about family life reflect, in other words, are not the perennial themes of family drama but the specific experiences of culturally and socially located individuals.

5

Grid-Group Theory and Corporal Punishment

JEAN GILES-SIMS AND CHARLES LOCKHART

Family-violence researchers explain parental use of corporal punishment in a variety of ways. Many existing explanations rely heavily on personality characteristics, family and social context, stress, and sociobiology (Daly and Wilson 1987; McCord 1991; Turner 1994). A few researchers have drawn in varying ways on explanations involving culture, some focusing on violent subcultures (Wolfgang and Ferracuti 1967), others showing how violence in other areas of social life spills over into families (Baron and Straus 1987; Baron, Straus, and Jaffee 1988; Campbell 1992; Levinson 1989; Straus 1985, 1991, 1994).

In this chapter we demonstrate the utility of one specific theory of culture—grid-group theory—for explaining variations in parental disciplinary practices. Accordingly, we: (1) introduce grid-group theory, (2) derive profiles of four distinct parenting orientations from grid-group theory, (3) explore empirical support for these distinctive cultural orientations toward corporal punishment, (4) briefly discuss the policy implications of grid-group theory with respect to reducing parental use of corporal punishment, and (5) suggest priorities for future research.

Grid-Group Theory

Grid-group theory (Douglas 1970, 1978, 1982a, 1982b, 1986; Thompson, Ellis and Wildavsky 1990) offers a means for deriving a diverse but limited number of cultural types based on persons' answers to basic social questions, such as: Who am I, what do I do, how does the world work, what are humans really like, to whom am I accountable, and how do I hold others accountable to me? (Wildavsky 1994).[1] It is, in short, a means for explaining the origins of social preferences (for example, preferences for using corporal punishment). Grid-group theorists argue that persons' answers to these questions depend on their beliefs and values with respect to two fundamental social dimensions: the need for and legitimacy of external prescription to control behavior (grid) and the desirability of affiliation with others (group). Grid-group's theoretical power hinges on its claim that only four general ways of responding to these issues are socially viable.[2] Preferences with respect to various patterns of social relations generate supporting justifications or cultural biases, and vice versa. Together the preferences and justifications form four distinctive ways of life or cultures: individualism, hierarchy, egalitarianism, and fatalism (see figure 5.1).

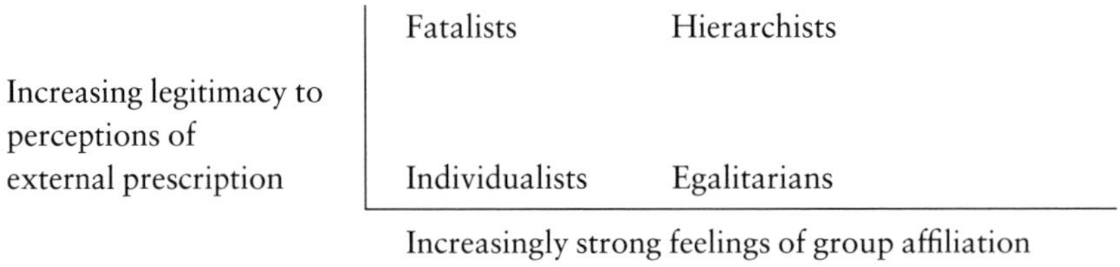

	Fatalists	Hierarchists
Increasing legitimacy to perceptions of external prescription	Individualists	Egalitarians

Increasingly strong feelings of group affiliation

Fig. 5.1. Grid-Group Theory's Dimensions and Cultures.

FOUR WAYS OF LIFE

Low tolerance for external prescription, reinforced by weak feelings of group membership, yields individualistic preferences emphasizing self-regulation among voluntary, shifting, contract-based networks of persons. Individualists assume that persons are self-interested, with roughly equal broad competencies, such as rationality. The beliefs characteristic of this culture are exemplified by Smith's *Wealth of Nations,* and the orientation is fundamental to capitalist societies.

Increasingly strong feelings of group affiliation together with extremely weak beliefs in external prescription characterize a way of life that grid-group theorists call egalitarian. This way of life assumes that humans are broadly equal and unmarred by natural flaws destructive of social harmony. Egalitarians prefer to organize into small groups that reach consensus on collective decisions through discussion. These beliefs and preferences are reminiscent of Rousseau's descriptions of the social ideal in *The Social Contract.*

High feelings of group affiliation in conjunction with perceptions legitimizing strong external prescription create a cultural pattern emphasizing hierarchy. Adherents of this culture view humans as inherently unequal. Further, they perceive shortcomings of varying seriousness as naturally afflicting persons. So for hierarchists society is appropriately organized vertically, with the best and the brightest directing schools, churches, and so forth, and thus integrating the activities of others into institutions that provide sound lessons in the correct way of living. The ideal polis portrayed by Plato in *The Republic* illustrates this way of life.[3]

Grid-group theory's fourth cultural pattern, fatalism, combines weak feelings of group affiliation with strong beliefs in external prescription. The unhappy combination of recognizing a need for social constraint but not feeling part of any broader social collective and thus of the constraining institutions predisposes fatalists to avoid social interaction beyond the family whenever possible. One manifestation of avoidance is that fatalists do not construct works of political theory; others have attempted to describe their views (Banfield 1958), although descriptions of fatalists are often criticized on the basis of racial or class bias.

These characterizations represent central tendencies found in these four cultures, although individual differences exist among persons adhering to specific cultures. Persons adopt particular cultures in response to experience with the world, and early developmental experiences are especially important in forming cultural orientations. So persons facing similar environmental circumstances (for example, children of a certain social class educated in a particular fashion) are apt to develop similar cultural orientations as a consequence of experiences that foster a fairly narrow range of reactions.

RIVAL BELIEF SYSTEMS

Each way of life's cultural bias includes distinctive beliefs about nature, human nature, and appropriate forms of social institutions. Individualists see nature as a resilient cornucopia. In the individualists' vision humans are naturally self-seeking and strive to improve their lives through voluntary contracts with others involving the exploitation of natural resources (not pejorative, given nature's resilience and bounty). They also believe that humans are roughly equal in broad general capacities, such as rationality. These views produce individualists' distinctive preferences with respect to social institutions. Because they believe that the world is composed of self-interested, equal, capable persons operating in an environment of plenty (see Locke's *Second Treatise,* ch. 5; Nozick 1974), they also believe in self-regulation and thus in limited external control (for example, limited government). For individualists, then, persons can reasonably be held responsible for their own fates.

In contrast, egalitarians perceive a delicate, ephemeral nature. Exploitation of the natural environment represents a threat rather than a virtue for them. Egalitarians tend, moreover, to view humans as equal and without natural social flaws: they assume humans' natural inclinations to be benign, thus meshing with a delicate environment. For egalitarians, trouble is introduced into human relations as a consequence of the ubiquitous stratifying influences of hierarchies and markets. These undo natural human equality and pervert natural human goodness in the process (Nagel 1973). Thus egalitarians favor sharing a limited bounty roughly equally; for them "small is beautiful" (Schumacher 1973), or to cite the lesson on a popular bumper sticker persons should "live simply so that others may simply live." Egalitarian groups in the feminist (Joreen 1973) or environmental (Downey 1986; Zisk 1992) movements typically have little formal structure. Instead they require participation by all in time-consuming, group decision making aimed at achieving consensus. In contemporary, large-scale societies, egalitarians frequently compromise their small-scale ideals by forming coalitions with hierarchists that selectively seek to reduce differences among persons through, for instance, a combination of progressive taxation and extensive social programs (for example, social democracies, such as Sweden).

Hierarchists perceive a more complicated nature. Within certain limits, they agree with individualists that exploitation of nature is beneficial. Beyond these limits, however, hierarchists tend to side with egalitarians and view more ambitious assaults on nature with suspicion. This conception of nature as tolerant or perverse elicits beliefs in the need for experts who are capable of discerning crucial boundaries of human activities as well as modes of behavior appropriate for living within these boundaries. Since crucial limits are not visible to all, this perspective leads inevitably to the conception of important inequalities among humans. And belief in human inequality in turn requires the organization of the social collective into a series of vertically arrayed institutions that allow relevant experts to guide the lives of their followers or constituents. Deviating from established social norms is, for hierarchists, dangerous both for individuals and—more important—for the social collective.

So while hierarchists share the frequent penchant of some contemporary egalitarians for an active governing body, they view its purpose more sternly as a dual project of education and social control.

Persons who are fatalistic in the grid-group sense perceive nature as random and humans as capricious. They thus have little faith in the hard work advocated by individualists, the collective deliberation and shared exertion of egalitarians, and the disciplined expertise of hierarchists. Good things may come of such practices, but according to the fatalist, only through luck. Consequently, with respect to large-scale society, fatalism is a culture of avoidance; the trick is to stay out of harm's way, reducing social interaction with large-scale society to a limited range of crucial instances.

Grid-group theorists argue that all four ways of life are typically found in varying proportions in all long-standing, large-scale societies. Akin to the interaction of different amino acids in biological systems, each cultural group provides services for the others that they cannot provide for themselves. This is similar to the "organismic" society described by Durkheim. Were it not for the ubiquitous stratification of hierarchies and markets, for instance, egalitarians would have no source of distress and thus no rallying cry. And if environmental concerns were taken as cavalierly by everyone as they are by individualists striving for market success, various forms of ecological depredation would be even more extensive than they are now. Egalitarians typically raise the profile of this sort of threat to society. Hierarchists and individualists characteristically focus their attention on other societal threats, such as social disorder and economic decline, respectively, toward which egalitarians are less likely to direct their perceptions (Dake and Wildavsky 1990). So most societies are "multicultural" in the sense of being composed of adherents of these four ways of life. Societies themselves differ in part in the proportions in which these cultures are found among their populations and additionally as a consequence of the varying historical contingencies and social structures in their environment. Varying contingencies can prompt different institutional responses from similar cultures (Hall 1986; Katzenstein 1984, 1985). And particular institutional choices at one point typically reduce the flexibility of subsequent choices with respect to alternative institutions as the relative influence of rival cultures varies over time. Additionally, specific persons in relatively pluralistic contemporary societies may be socialized by parents and others representing multiple cultures. They may retain sympathies for these cultures by adhering to their disparate practices in distinctive domains of social life (Hochschild 1981; Walzer 1983). Practicing egalitarianism in the family and applying a more hierarchical or individualistic perspective in the workplace is one common contemporary manifestation of the effects of social context on culture (Lockhart and Coughlin 1992).

Profiles of Culturally Derived Parenting Orientations

Distinctive cultural beliefs about how the world works and how we hold others accountable to ourselves are likely to influence parental disciplinary practices toward children. As we suggested in the previous paragraph, culture is not the only source of variance in these practices. Aspects of social structure influence facets of culture, and vice versa, with specific variables in each broad category having distinct consequences. But we are not concerned in this chapter with the various social structures that foster the different cultures that we have introduced. Rather, we wish to explore the consequences of these cultures for parental disciplinary practices, the use of corporal punishment in particular. We are aware that parents of specific families may not always share a culture. Nonetheless, in this section we will apply grid-group theory to parents without considering the complications raised by dual-culture families.

HIERARCHICAL PARENTS

Hierarchists' penchant for expertise translates into faith that there is a correct way of doing everything. Accordingly, hierarchical parents perceive their roles primarily in terms of teaching their children *the* correct way of living. The rules of different hierarchical traditions vary of course, but common to all specific traditions is the conception of one correct way. This correct way is known to and revealed by experts — church officials and other authorities, including parents themselves. Persons with this perspective rely less on carrots or positive reinforcement in rearing children than on various forms of punishment. They believe that, as Plato suggested, children should *want* to follow the prescribed path because it *is* the right way. The proper reward for good behavior is then intrinsic, and for parents to apply other external rewards would be inappropriate. Instead, hierarchical disciplinary practices focus on the threat and application of punishment. Children are, from this perspective, socially flawed in that they know less well than authorities how to behave or are less responsive to discipline with respect to their misguided egoistic urges (Dake et al. 1993: 13–14). And since the right way of doing things is already known, there is from the hierarchical perspective little benefit to having children, many of whom have only limited abilities, attempt to discover the right way by trial and error.

Instead, hierarchical parents strive to assure the health and safety of the social collective by training their children in appropriate behaviors. They frequently rely on corporal punishment to enforce rules and sometimes require transgressors to make restitution to their victims, thus reaffirming social bonds (Hamilton and Sanders 1988). Hierarchical parents may also seek to shame their children into compliance with ridicule (Wilson 1993: 154). But the association of pain — physical or psychological — with deviance is justified by the need to teach children the discipline needed to avoid tempting deviations from socially sanctioned norms (Nietzsche, *On the Genealogy of Morals*). This parenting orientation is frequently associated with blue-collar child-rearing practices in the United States (Kohn 1977). Greven (1991) shows, moreover, that the admonition "spare the rod and spoil the child" is widely followed among fundamentalist Christians, who tend to be adherents of hierarchy. Similar views have historically supported widespread disciplining of children through corporal punishment in societies with preeminent hierarchical cultures, such as Germany and Japan (Peterson, Less, and Ellis 1982). "The more a society [we would say culture] values the inculcation of conformity or obedience in children, the more it is typified by the use of coercive socialization" (Ellis and Peterson 1992: 52). Across broad stretches of time and geography, the hierarchical family has been more common than other types of family and so has acquired the label "traditional" (Goode 1982; Tucker 1988).

EGALITARIAN PARENTS

Egalitarian parents follow sharply different practices. While often exhibiting some hierarchy in their orientations toward infants and very young children, egalitarians minimize this approach as quickly as possible. Since they believe in essential equality among humans and in natural human virtue, egalitarian parents have little reason to dissuade their children from developing their own ways of perceiving, evaluating, and behaving.[4] Instead, they value their children as distinctive and, as the children develop self-direction, increasingly coequal persons. For egalitarians, one's family is a potentially important basis for group affiliation, and children thus represent for them vital resources as lifelong companions and friends. Since they hold these views, disciplining in the hierarchical sense is an unlikely activity for egalitarians (Robertson 1988). Even if they find punishment necessary on a few occasions, egalitarians are not apt to resort to threats, abusive language, or corporal punishment. Egalitarians and hierarchists (the high-group cultures) do share some ground, however, in that they both ultimately punish through social ostracism those who will not conform to the group or the social collective (Wilson 1993).

As in other social relations, egalitarian parents try to use the quality of their relations with children as a means to attaining accountability from them.

High-quality parent-child relationships are achieved through lengthy, non-threatening discussion that ideally leads to common understandings but also allows self-direction to develop. Among egalitarian parents hard and fast rules, and their associated punishments, are limited to affirming procedures that teach children to respect other persons. This is the basic philosophy of much contemporary, particularly Rogerian, therapy (Kirshenbaum and Foster 1991). In contemporary America, this egalitarian parenting orientation is most commonly found among white-collar, professional households (Kohn 1977). The increasing prevalence of egalitarian parenting practices since the 1960s, as leveling of power between parents and children occurred, is one of the most notable facets, along with increasing gender equality, of the contemporary American cultural landscape (Franzwa and Lockhart 1994).

INDIVIDUALISTIC PARENTS

Given its basic characteristics, family life is more likely to elicit high-group rather than low-group perspectives; most parents tend to follow hierarchical or egalitarian orientations even if they might behave more individualistically in other spheres of social life. Nonetheless, families with individualistically oriented parents exist. Because individualistic parents perceive persons as generally capable of mastering their own fates, they will, similar to their egalitarian counterparts, be less concerned than hierarchical parents that their children follow social conventions. But in contrast to egalitarian parents, individualists, who conceptualize life in terms of actions and accomplishments rather than discussion and feelings, are apt to be more concerned with the practical achievements of their children than with the intimacy of their long-term personal relations with them (Zelizer 1985). Disciplinary practices are apt to be ruled by pragmatism, by what works. Carrots and sticks will be applied as specific contexts appear to warrant. Since voluntary contractual relations are fundamental to the individualistic perspective, individualistic parents are apt to be predisposed toward bribing their children to act in desirable ways and generally to prefer carrots to sticks (Anderson 1971: 129, 135). Individualistic parents also differ from their egalitarian counterparts in that they will be less opposed to using corporal punishment if carrots fail. Individualists shrink from involuntary emotional ties to groups, preferring the openness of freely chosen, mutual, and frequently shifting networks of associates. They thus see friendship as a voluntary, replaceable form of human interaction that is distinct from, though not necessarily incompatible with, family. So when children's behavior cannot be successfully adjusted through the application of carrots, individualistic parents have no principled objection to applying sticks in the form of corporal punishment. Their penchant for bidding and bargaining is apt, however, to keep the severity of the punishments they apply in line with the gravity of the offense.

Overall, the families of individualistic parents are characteristically more loosely structured than their hierarchical or egalitarian counterparts. Kantor and Lehr (1975) would probably classify families with such parents as "random."[5] Their discipline might be labeled permissive (Baumrind 1971), even neglectful. Thus while families in which individualistic parents are dominant tend to generate fewer memories of terrible childhood trauma among their offspring than do families dominated by hierarchical parents, the former are also apt to elicit less extensive feelings of warm affection than families with egalitarian parents. Individualistic parents may provide less structure and support than some children need, and their discipline (including corporal punishment) may be erratic. While individualistic parenting is not limited to the United States (Arnold 1864: 62, 124), Americans — unsurprisingly, given their "exceptional," dominant individualistic culture — probably have a higher proportion of individualistic parents than other societies. We see evidence of this in the frequent claims of school teachers and others who work with children and adolescents that many parents of these youngsters are relatively self-absorbed and uninterested in at least some of the developmental difficulties of their children.

FATALISTIC PARENTS

Fatalists distinguish between social relations within the immediate family and those in broader society, hence Banfield's concept of "amoral familism" (1958: 10–11). Supportive interaction is appropriate within the family; social avoidance is appropriate in broader social relations. As in the case of the other cultural biases, fatalistic parents have characteristics similar to those of the two other cultures with whom they share grid and group positions. But since the mixture of grid and group is unique for each corner of figure 5.1, so too will be the resulting orientations. Their high grid position, for instance, means that fatalists share with hierarchists a sense of human inequality and inherent character flaws, and when they do interact with others — in the family or in other unavoidable situations in broader society (Mars 1982) — they frequently favor practices similar to those of hierarchists, who strive to obtain order through a structure of rules and punishments designed to achieve universal adherence to one correct way. But fatalists also share a low-group orientation with individualists. They thus do not sense membership in the broader social institutions that devise and administer these rules, and they consequently lack faith that these "alien" institutions can successfully devise and apply remedies for overcoming human inadequacies.

Fatalistic culture accordingly creates difficulties for parenting by posing a dilemma between preferences for stern, one-right-way discipline and beliefs that any specific source of guidance is apt to be flawed. Fatalistic parents are thus likely to be inconsistent disciplinarians, moving back and forth between the application of a discipline similar to that which we associated with hierarchy and the relative indifference that we mentioned with respect to individualistic parents. This discontinuity is bound to be frustrating, and perhaps as a consequence of frustration fatalistic parents use corporal punishment more impulsively. They are also apt to be less clear about the aims of such punishment and less consistent in its application. Thus fatalistic parents are more likely than those of other cultures to engage in seriously abusive forms of corporal punishment in the disciplining of their children (Viney et al. 1982). This punishment may be accompanied by verbal, psychological attacks on the children. Because fatalism results from lack of opportunities for control and repeated negative experiences, children in fatalistic families are likely to suffer from multiple social and family problems. Those conditions both exacerbate corporal punishment and the consequences for children.

Empirical Support for Cultural Patterns of Corporal Punishment

Typically, each of these four ways of life appears along with the three other cultures in what are thus "multicultural" societies. If, as we believe, adults' dominant cultural patterns influence their parental practices, then societies composed of varying proportions of these four cultures will exhibit variations in the use of corporal punishment. A limited amount of evidence exists in support of our view.

Levinson (1989) analyzed ninety small-scale societies representing all inhabited regions of the world. He found some corporal punishment in 74 percent of these societies, but regular parental use of corporal punishment occurred in only 13 percent (Levinson 1989: 28). According to Levinson sharp differences in reliance on corporal punishment of children correlate with variation in two factors: gender hierarchy and societal complexity (Levinson 1989: 81–97). A particular manifestation of gender inequality — polygynous single-parent (cowife) households — was an exceptionally good indicator of corporal punishment. Levinson's portrayal of the cowives' situations is bleak, suggesting that these women commonly adhere to fatalism because they have so little control over their faces in this extreme form of patriarchy. One of the societies Levinson refers to in which severe physical punishment of children is routine, the "Rocky Road" Jamaicans, is further described by Cohen (1966) in a way that leaves little doubt as to its predominantly hierarchical character. Levinson's study supports our view that corporal punishment is most likely to occur when parents adhere to either fatalistic or hierarchical cultures.

Societal complexity appears in Levinson's work as another correlate of corporal punishment of children. Both individualists and hierarchists build complex societies. However, Peterson, Lee, and Ellis (1982) argue that it is a concern for conformity rather than complexity itself that leads to more corporal punishment as societal complexity increases. Social conformity, a crucial element of social stability in the hierarchical perspective, becomes more difficult to assure as social complexity grows. Accordingly, hierarchists turn to more stringent measures — for example, corporal punishment — to achieve it. Using a sample of cultures from the Standard Cross-Cultural Sample and the Human Relations Area Files, Peterson et al. (1982) related cross-societal use of corporal punishment to differences in the importance of conformity and self-reliance — characteristics that we would associate with hierarchical and individualistic cultures, respectively. They examined such factors as closeness of supervision in political, economic, religious, and family realms and also coded scales for conformity and self-reliance. Their data included as well a five-point scale measuring the extent to which corporal punishment was threatened or used to control children. In cultures valuing conformity, they found that corporal punishment is regularly used to correct rule violations. In cultures that value self-reliance and independence in children, corporal punishment is less likely. Their model — the variables mentioned above, including supervision and orientations toward conformity and self-reliance — explained 30 percent of the variance in the practice of corporal punishment (Peterson et al. 1982: 138). This work also appears to support our earlier suggestions as to how culture influences the use of corporal punishment. Further, Ellis and Peterson (1992) have replicated these findings using broader, more recently coded data. They find that corporal punishment, lecturing and overall control are all used more in cultures valuing conformity.

Levinson (1989: 103–04) also identifies characteristics of societies relatively free from various sorts of family violence. These characteristics are, without exception, unequivocally egalitarian, particularly in terms of gender issues. Phillips's (1966) thick description of one of these societies, the Bang Chan of central Thailand, reinforces this identification. Levinson's data also support grid-group theory's predictions that parents who adhere to an egalitarian culture are relatively unlikely to use corporal punishment in disciplining their children.

Swedish experience, along with that of other Scandinavian societies, provides a related affirmation of grid-group theory's predictions in this regard.

Sweden has made exceptional efforts to reduce corporal punishment of children through legislation and education about alternatives, and it has an exceptionally high incidence of egalitarians in its population (Grendstad 1990).

In their path-breaking cross-societal study Almond and Verba (1963: 275–81) compared early and adult socialization in the United States, the United Kingdom, West Germany (FRG), Italy, and Mexico. They investigated the degree to which respondents from different societies participated in family and school decisions as children, as well as in consultations relating to their adult jobs. Their results show that children in the United States participated much more than in the other four societies, with Italy trailing in participation in all categories.[6] In general, these results match what we would expect in comparing notably pluralistic, liberal societies (the United States and the United Kingdom) with the less obviously pluralistic societies exhibiting dominant hierarchical political traditions. The case of the Federal Republic of Germany is particularly interesting. German parental expectations in the 1950s and even early 1960s were typically hierarchical. Parents were concerned about their children love order and industriousness and exhibit obedience and deference to authority (Conradt 1980: 252). These preferences are strikingly similar to those of the obviously hierarchical Jamaican parents described by Cohen (1966), who routinely engage in corporal punishment. But Western, individualistic influence on the Federal Republic's hierarchical tradition was pervasive during the cold war. By the late 1960s and 1970s German parents were expressing much more concern that their children exhibit independence and free will, and they were losing interest in obedience and deference (Conradt 1980: 252). Grendstad's (1990) data also suggest that the Federal Republic has grown much more individualistic and egalitarian in recent decades and is now far less similar to the hierarchically dominated societies of Mediterranean Europe than it was in the 1950s. While we have nothing more than impressionistic data, German parental disciplinary practices across this period appear to have changed to reduce corporal punishment, as grid-group theory predicts.

A few other "outcroppings" of data also support the predictions of grid-group theory with respect to parental disciplinary practices. In a historical analysis of childhood, including references to dominant cultural values, de Mause (1988) discusses several forms of childhood maltreatment and parent-child relations. His analysis links individualistic values to child abandonment, and fatalism to incidents of infanticide. De Mause also associates hierarchy with child abuse, and egalitarianism with mutuality in parent-child relationships. Additionally, in an analysis of data on children age1 three to five, from the National Longitudinal Survey of Youth, Giles-Sims, Straus, and Sugarman (1993) found that African Americans and Native Americans reported significantly more corporal punishment (prevalence = 69 percent and 68 percent, respectively) than Hispanics and Anglos (prevalence = 62 percent and 60 percent, respectively.)[7] One possible explanation of these differences is that the relative lack of social opportunities and influence among African Americans and Native Americans may produce greater rates of fatalism and thus corporal punishment as well. Finally, regional differences in attitudes toward corporal punishment also contribute empirical evidence in support of grid-group theory's predictions. Some data indicate that Southern residents accept corporal punishment of children in families and in school more — by 71 percent — than residents in the West, the North Central region, and particularly the Northeast — which vary from 59 percent to 56 percent in acceptance rates (Giles-Sims, Straus, and Sugarman 1993; Flynn 1993; Hyman 1990). Grid-group theory's explanation of this regional variation rests on suppositions that egalitarians make up a greater proportion of the population in the Northeast and that individualists form larger sections of the populations in the West, North Central, and Northeast, compared with a greater prevalence of hierarchical and fatalistic cultures among the population of the South. While this explanation needs to be rigorously tested empirically, it is consistent with well-known characterizations of regional cultural variations across American history (Ellis 1993) as well as recent empirical evidence on regional cultures of relevance to grid-group theory (Lieske 1993).

Grid-Group Theory's Policy Implications

There are now many studies identifying negative side effects of corporal punishment. Disciplining children in this manner increases the chances that they will become physically aggressive and delinquent (Kandel 1991; Straus 1991) and that they will experience social, economic, and psychological problems (Straus and Gimpel 1992; Straus 1991, 1994; Straus and Kaufman Kantor 1994). Given these findings, it would appear sensible for policy makers to try to reduce parental use of corporal punishment.

Grid-group theory suggests that a direct approach, for instance, new legislative prohibitions on corporal punishment or more funds for parent effectiveness training, is not apt to have much effect on parental behavior in this regard. While a few hierarchical parents might accept the authority of new societal laws prohibiting corporal punishment, surely many would recognize that government had fallen into the hands of the cultural adversaries and would be unlikely to comply with the new rules in the privacy of their homes. Individualistic parents, while perhaps being more open minded about research explaining what works among parenting techniques (Day and Roberts 1983), are unlikely to support legislation constraining parental freedom of action. Practices that fit with persons' cultures may well be sustained in spite of what others regard as empirical demonstrations of their ineffectiveness.

This prognosis is discouraging. Why it is that the Swedes appear to be able to do better? In our view their success is contingent on an unusually high proportion of egalitarians in their population. These persons prefer to use alternatives to corporal punishment in disciplining their children. For better or worse, we do not currently know how to manipulate the relative proportions of rival ways of life in our population. This means that sharp reductions in the use of corporal punishment lie beyond what public policy can currently accomplish. Egalitarians in the United States should take heart, however, that their influence and thus presumably their numbers appear to have grown substantially over the past few decades.

Future Research Priorities

Our claim that the cultural biases derived from grid-group theory offer powerful tools for explaining parental choices with respect to disciplinary practices requires — and we think merits — more extensive and rigorous analysis drawing on appropriate empirical data. We suggest three specific projects. First, we recommend that measures for grid and group (Boyle and Coughlin 1994; Grendstad 1990) be included in surveys that also query respondents about their parenting practices. The necessary data could be acquired with roughly twenty items added to surveys serving other purposes. Surveys generalizable to the whole society would be more useful than those sampling narrow subsectors of society. While daunting in their complexity, cross-societal surveys would be even more useful. The general aim here would be to ascertain whether those who adhere to the four ways of life that we have delineated actually follow the parental disciplinary practices that we have associated with them for the reasons that we have proffered.

Second, we have argued that culture changes — slowly — with societal circumstance (Eckstein 1988; Inglehart 1990); it would be useful to have panel data — again of samples generalizable to the whole society — on grid, group, and parenting practices. Such data would allow us to ascertain whether personal parenting practices change as culture changes and — at the cost of additional questions — would give us better ideas as to the nature of the forces behind cultural change.

Third, we would like to further develop grid-group theory so as to form a more effective bridge with existing social structural and social-psychological theories of the family. Grid-group theory's most typical applications to date have involved explaining why individuals differ in their preferences on one or another broad-ranging issue of contemporary public life: the welfare state, affirmative action, zoning, and so on. When we apply grid-group theory to a social institution as small as the family, it is possible that the dimensions could be redefined in more productive ways familiar to theorists of the family — for example, control and warmth (Maccoby and Martin 1983). If this were feasible, it would not only create a theoretical bridge between grid-group theory and existing work on a specific, small-scale institution, the family, it would also create additional incentives to search for similar linkages with work on other specific institutions and offer hope of integrating more of what we know about social life.

Finally, any future research efforts could be made policy relevant by assessing relative group support for strategies to change corporal-punishment practices. Given the increasing research on the negative side effects of corporal punishment, we expect a mounting social-policy and possibly public-health agenda for training in alternative, effective means of disciplining children without the use of physical force.

Notes

1. For the deeper roots of grid-group theory see Durkheim (1951) and Evans-Prichard (1940).

2. This claim is controversial, but it is obviously less limiting than the widely accepted notion that variations on only two ways of life — hierarchy (tradition) and individualism (modernity) — are socially viable; see Lindblom (1977). Additionally, similar claims have been derived independently by Fiske (1991, 1992). These claims are as well consistent with other psychological research on grid (Cloninger 1987; Higgins 1990) and group (Cloninger 1987; Triandis 1990). Technically, grid-group theory admits a fifth, non-socially interactive way of life — the hermit's (Thompson 1982) — that we do not consider here.

3. Strictly speaking, Plato, whose practical reason is directed toward a limited range of specified ends, is — along with Kant — "off the map" (figure 5.1) of grid-group theory. See O'Neill (1991). But the polis portrayed in *The Republic* is clearly an example of hierarchy.

4. Egalitarian orientations sometimes appear as well in larger-scale collectivist form, in kibbutzim and the like. In this guise egalitarian intentions are apt to be mixed with hierarchical organizational practices (Dake et al. 1993).

5. Relatedly, see de Mause (1988: 34–35) on various forms of abandonment as practices of individualistic parents.

6. The United States was edged out of the lead on job consultation by the United Kingdom (Almond and Verba 1963: 281) but was far ahead in participation on the other two indices involving children.

7. Straus and Camacho (1993) report Hispanics as having slightly lower rates than Anglos.

PART III

Psychological Theories

6

The Origins of Physical Punishment

An Ethological/Attachment Perspective on the Use of
Physical Punishment by Human Parents

PATRICIA M. CRITTENDEN

"I've told you twice already. . . . Now that's it!"

"If you don't listen to me, I'm going to have to spank you!"

"Don't you *ever* use that tone of voice with me!"

"I told her over and over again not to do it and I explained that it was dangerous.

She stuck her face in mine and told me that what she did was her business.
That's when I smacked her."

"Now, every time I try to control him, he threatens to call the child-abuse line.
If the government lets kids do that, it's my not fault if they grow up
without respect for the law!"

As her pups tumbled about in the sunshine, their mother suddenly growled
deeply in her throat. The pups paused, then resumed their play. But
when she snapped her teeth and nipped at them, they scrambled into the
den behind her.

Physical punishment of children is an almost universal behavior among
human parents (Gelles 1978; Straus 1991). Across historical periods and varied cultures, it has been widely, almost universally, accepted as a natural and
unquestioned aspect of parenting behavior. Although exceptions exist, they,
too, are informative to the theory being developed here. Periodically, and

especially recently, the appropriateness of physical punishment has been questioned (Greven 1991; Peisner 1989). In this chapter, I explore the use of physical punishment from the perspective of evolved biases to human behavior as they affect the functioning of the parental caregiving system.[1] This perspective places *homo sapiens* in the context of other social mammals and explores aspects of parental behavior that may reflect genetically biased and adaptive responses selected during our period of evolution. Their adaptiveness among humans today is then considered. Because my argument represents a blend of theory with empirical findings drawn from many species, its conclusions are tentative.[2] They may, however, provide a basis for valuable empirical research.

A Theoretical Perspective

The relationship between parent and child is a complex and changing one. On the surface, we think of it as a relationship defined (a) by the parent's love for the child and (b) by the responsibility to protect and nurture him or her. Put another way, the parent functions as a wiser, stronger, and protective attachment figure with regard to the weaker, less experienced, and vulnerable child (Bowlby 1969).

Two points are important to note. First, the parent-child relationship is not egalitarian; to the contrary, it represents a dominance hierarchy in which the dominant member is both stronger and also responsible for the welfare of the weaker member. It differs from dominance hierarchies among adults in that there is no dispute over the dominant role — at least not in early infancy. Second, in spite of loving their children, parents are often so angry with their children that they hit and spank them. In other words, our behavior at times is both unloving and potentially dangerous to our children. Is this consistent with loving them? How are parental love and anger related? When the hitting is so extreme that it abusively endangers children, how can it be considered protective? Moreover, even when it does not result in injury, physical punishment may have negative psychological effects (Weiss, Dodge, Bates, and Pettit 1992; Straus 1991, 1993). How can this be consistent with nurturant child rearing? A developmental perspective that emphasizes the changing relationship between parent and child and the origins of this behavior in our evolved genetic inheritance may be relevant to understanding the prevalence of, and the occasions that elicit, physical punishment among human parents.

The Function of Physical Punishment in Children's Development

EARLY INFANCY

A neonate has no awareness of its position in the social world of humans and contributes nothing purposefully to the relationship with its caregivers. Nevertheless, the physical features and behavior of neonates are powerful elicitors of parental caregiving in adults (Eibl-Eibesfeldt 1979). This is true for adult humans as well as adults of other mammalian species (Lorenz 1973). When species-specific communicative signals based on appearance and behavior are distorted or absent, the risk of abandonment, abuse, or distorted caregiving by adults of the species increases (Field, Sostek, Goldberg, and Shuman 1979). Thus, neonates passively and without consciousness or intent contribute to the parent-infant relationship in ways that promote or endanger their survival (Bell and Harper 1977). In human neonates, the critical features, that is, species-specific characteristics, include a large head with disproportionately large eyes, certain odors, and particular behaviors, including rooting, crying, looking, and sinking in and relaxing when held (Klaus and Kennell 1976). These behaviors function to increase the probability that the infant will be held, which in turn promotes feeding and protection (Bowlby 1969).

Mammalian neonates, including human neonates, are rarely punished physically (Lebra 1976; Straus 1991). For humans, this is especially true among nonindustrialized human cultural groups in which infants are in physical contact with their mothers during most of the first several months of life (Brazelton, Robbey, and Collier 1969; Konner 1972; Takahashi 1986). The most frequent exception occurs among those human mothers in industrialized countries who fear spoiling their children by holding them too much. Unfortunately, lack of holding increases infant crying (Bell and Ainsworth 1972). Mothers of infants who cry persistently sometimes spank even small infants, rather than picking them up. This, in turn, sometimes results in injury to the infants.

The use of physical punishment increases when infants are able to grasp objects. At that time, some, but by no means all, mothers slap their babies' hands to prevent them from putting dangerous objects in their mouths. Nevertheless, up to about seven months of age, there is no way in which infants can endanger themselves without their parents' having first permitted it.

LATE INFANCY AND ATTACHMENT

With the onset of crawling, however, the relation between parental caregiving and infant safety changes. Infants' emerging ability to crawl, and later toddle and run, away from the safe haven of their parents to explore a beckoning world presents new dangers to infants, dangers that infants cannot predict or understand. Although the danger could be resolved by keeping children confined, in reality such a solution would endanger children in the long run by preventing them from learning to adapt to the world.

A change in the parent-infant relationship ensues that enables parent and infant to function in a communicative system with the goal of promoting development by (a) enhancing exploration whenever it is safe and (b) providing protection otherwise. This relationship is commonly referred to as attachment of the infant to the caregiver (Ainsworth 1979; Bowlby 1969). Its importance, however, is tied to the use of communication to regulate infants' and attachment figures' behavior in ways that promote both development and protection of infants.

In the last quarter of the first year of life, the nature of mother-infant communication changes in ways that permit exchange of messages about intentions and about authority. With looks, pointing, and directed gaze, infants are able to communicate their desires and intentions (Bruner 1975). Caregivers, on the other hand, use tone of voice, facial expression, and gestures to convey approval or disapproval of the infant's intention. A reciprocal dialogue based on communication and feedback is thus enjoined. So long as agreement is reached, the system works smoothly. Infants and toddlers venture forth eagerly to explore the world, and mothers watch and encourage unless the venture appears dangerous (Blurton-Jones 1972). If something reduces the probability of infants' being safe, for example, the infant strays too far away or an unfamiliar person approaches, either the infant will seek the mother (by call or approach) or the mother will call or actively fetch the infant.

Mothers who call their children back to them expect a rapid and certain response from their children. Indeed, their vocal signal is as clear as the growl of a canine. The mother's sharp voice is entirely unlike her voice when she is playful or soothing. It is a command, clear and unambiguous, that both tells the child what to do and establishes a hierarchy of authority: the mother is dominant and expects the child to obey. This communication of the relative status of the members of the dyad (Watzlawick, Beavin, and Jackson 1967) is as important as the actual content of the command because it determines the negotiability of the command. Given the limited understanding of children and the substantially greater ability of attachment figures to assess children's safety, the dominance of attachment figures is important to children's survival. Developmentally, this change in the pattern and purpose of communication corresponds both with children's ability to locomote independently and with the appearance of fearful wariness in regard to new things (Bronson 1972).

Together, these new, species-specific behaviors function to regulate the balance of exploration with protection.

Most of the time, this new, hierarchically organized relationship functions smoothly as a communicative system, with feedback between the members of the dyad. As was true in early infancy, mothers ordinarily use infants' signals as one source of information about infants' needs and desires. Mothers' behavior on any specific occasion is, however, the result both of a transaction with their children and also of their attitudes toward punishment. These attitudes represent adults' mental combination of the unique characteristics of the current situation with what they have previously learned from experience as well as with cultural values and beliefs (Belsky 1984; Sigel 1986). Maternal behavior, therefore, is not reflexive but highly probabilistic and transactional (Patterson and Reid 1984).

Sometimes, however, the communicative exchange fails. Mothers expect their children to remember and obey prior limitations, or infants refuse to obey maternal demands. In such cases, confrontation occurs. Two things are at issue: what the child will actually do and the dominance relation between the parent and child.

The importance of affect as a means of mediating the resolution of such conflicts cannot be underestimated. Affective signals both elicit parental nurturance and communicate messages about dominance. These, in turn, promote protection. Fear and anger are especially important for protection. When children feel fearful, they seek closeness with their parents. The more anxious they are, the more comfort they seek. The ultimate comfort is, of course, close bodily contact. Sometimes only close body-to-body touching will calm a frightened child.

When contact is denied by a preoccupied or rejecting parent, the child's response is anger. Expression of anger by angry vocalization, aggressive hitting, and so on, functions as punishment of parental unavailability. Consequently, it increases the probability that the attachment figure will respond promptly with physical contact the next time the child signals a desire for closeness. For this reason, children's angry behavior is among the most powerful of their attachment behaviors.

Similarly, when parents are concerned for their child's safety, they seek closeness. The more concerned they are, the more effort they exert in regaining proximity to the child and the closer they desire to be when they are reunited. Indeed, when they have been very worried, most parents pick up and embrace their children immediately upon being reunited.

PRESCHOOL-AGE CHILDREN AND THE GOAL-
CORRECTED PARTNERSHIP

Children are more frequently physically punished during the preschool
years than at any other age (Holden and West 1989; Lytton, Watts, and Dunn
1988; Straus 1991). Moreover, punishment of preschoolers more often results
in injury or death, that is, child abuse, than at any other age (Crittenden and
Craig 1990). Consequently, changes in the nature of the parent-child relationship at that age are of considerable importance.

At the end of the second year of life, there is a period of rapid neurological
growth in children's brains (Geschwind 1964). Out of this come new skills,
including the ability to remember sequences of events, to use language to
describe past and future events, and to realize that other people have different
goals, desires, and plans. In motor skills, children gain physical coordination
that permits them to move about with enough speed, agility, and endurance to
exceed the range of adult supervision and protection. Finally, new ways of
using affect appear; in particular, preschool-age children display coy behavior
(Eibel-Eibesfeldt 1979). Together, these skills enable children to move independently into the world outside their families, to negotiate with their parents
about this process, and to disarm conflict that might arise because of differences in child and parent plans (Crittenden 1992a).

Needless to say, differences in plans are frequent in the preschool years.
Children desire to explore widely and feel competent to do so. Indeed, if their
parents have managed infancy well, children are largely unaware of their
actual vulnerability (Crittenden 1992b). Nevertheless, preschool-age children
are vulnerable and their parents are only too aware of it. This engenders
considerable conflict between parents and their young children. Some of the
conflict can be neutralized by the preschoolers' ability to talk, negotiate, and
accept compromises, that is, to establish a goal-corrected partnership with
attachment figures (Bowlby 1969; Marvin 1977). Preschoolers are not able,
however, to understand the logic behind parental prohibitions. Without that
understanding, the parent must prevail on the basis of dominance. Hence the
many conflicts over both children's desires and also their "respect" for adults.
(See Holden and Zambarano 1992 for empirical evidence supporting this
general conclusion.)

Parent-child disputes resemble immature versions of adult disputes; there are
verbal and nonverbal threats, and physical aggression may be used in an effort
to win the battle of wills. Not understanding their limitations, children are the
most likely to initiate physical aggression. The response from parents is usually
swift and unerring. Aggression of children toward parents is not permitted.

Under these circumstances children would appear to be at serious risk from parental aggression. Conflict and aggression are not, however, either unusual or lethal behaviors among social mammalian species. To the contrary, many species, including all primates, use ritualized aggression that leads to submission displays before injury is inflicted, in order to establish or change dominance (de Waal 1989; Seyfarth 1981).

The patterns of behavior among other species are relevant to preschool-age children's behavior. Intraspecies conflict generally involves a dispute over dominance and the rights and prerogatives of dominant animals, for example, to food or mates. When two animals battle and one appears to be losing, the losing animal exhibits a set of submissive and disarming behaviors that function to terminate the battle. These behaviors are of two sorts. One type defines the dominance hierarchy by making the losing animal vulnerable to destruction, for example, baring the belly and the neck. The other reestablishes the relationship, with the losing animal seeking nurturance from the dominant animal. Examples of this sort of behavior include smiles with the teeth covered, that is, with no toothy threat, and eye contact displayed as sideways glances too brief to be possibly misinterpreted as threatening stares (Argyle and Cook 1976; Murray 1977). With these signals, the submissive animal demands, through the "bribe" of sweetness, the universal right of the dominated — the right to be protected by the dominant leader (Hold 1976). These behaviors appear to be the result of preprogrammed maturation occurring at the end of infancy (Sackett 1966).

Among preschool-age human children, it is noteworthy that when preschoolers initiate conflict with parents and lose, as they almost inevitably will, they too show "coy" behavior. Coy behavior, however, has the components listed above for terminating aggression and eliciting nurturance (Eibl-Eibesfeldt 1979). Thus, preschoolers are protected from parental aggression by coy behavior that disarms parental anger. At the same time, the parent has "won" the battle and reestablished both his or her power to rule and also the obligation to protect the child.

The battle of wills is not, however, always fought face to face. Often it involves forbidden behavior on the child's part that occurs when the parent is not present. The control systems just described would appear to be ineffective under such conditions.

Anger may be the critical form of communication regarding such infractions. When a child is caught doing something that he or she has been told not to do, parents often respond with anger. Consider the example of a little boy who has been told repeatedly not to run into the street. His mother, seeing him in the roadway, becomes terrified that he will be hit by a car. She rushes out and safely retrieves him. When he is clearly safe, however, she may explode in anger. Shaking him by the shoulders, she may first thrust her face in his while she tells him never, never to do that again. Then, she may turn him about and spank him — to ensure that he understands and remembers the importance of her message.

To an observer, the anger may seem inexplicable and inappropriate. On the other hand, anger has a very high communicative value and is a very powerful motivator of future behavior (Bowlby 1969; Crittenden 2000). In this example, the mother may reason with her son after his return. This reasoning may be effective. Common sense, however, tells us that many children are likely to repeat their unthinking behavior. Maternal anger, however, carries an additional "punch" which increases the probability that the child will remember his mother's message. The child who might forget or discount the importance of his mother's words is less likely to forget or dismiss her anger.

If anger is a powerful stimulant to memory and future behavior, how best might anger be expressed? Simply telling a child that you are angry is likely to be ineffective. Indeed, discussion of anger distances one from the feeling state and is antithetical to the state of being angry (Crittenden 1994). The anger itself must be expressed, and this is most effectively done nonverbally. The mother's tone of voice, facial expression, and behavior must signal anger. These, in turn, must elicit fear in the child. If the mother does not see an effect from her words and nonverbal expressions, she will be likely to intensify the message. As with signals of fearfulness that lead to increasing needs for body contact, the ultimate expression of anger is communicated through physical contact, in this case, through hitting or spanking. Physical punishment, in other words, can be considered a culminating form of the communication of anger to be used when other forms have failed to elicit the desired response. As with hugging, touch is the ultimate communication.

So the mother spanks her wayward child. Doing so reinforces her message, and thus protects her child. In addition, it reestablishes the dominance hierarchy, with the mother once again dominant. However, with little children, spanking causes them to seek comfort from their attachment figure, that is, the person who spanked them. This giving of comfort usually reestablishes the nurturant aspect of the mother-infant relationship.

CULTURE

Parental behavior in infancy is relatively similar across cultures. With children's increasing age, however, cultural differences become more apparent. Although it is beyond the scope of this chapter to explore the nature of these differences, it is important to note that cultures vary regarding the nature of enforced behavioral standards, degree of permitted negotiation with children, and extent of independence required of children. Further, there is probably a relation among these factors that reflects the need for balance between exploration and safety. Where children are encouraged to explore widely and independently, there will be a need for firm parental discipline that can be readily internalized. With young children, this will often be expressed as high rates of physical punishment. Where firm discipline is not used, young children must necessarily be kept in close contact with protective parents or live in relatively safe contexts. Cultural patterns like these become apparent in the preschool years.

SCHOOL-AGE CHILDREN

The most important developmental change associated with the period of rapid neurological growth between five and seven years of age is children's ability to use logic mentally and verbally. With this ability, they become able to understand, at least partially, adults' reasons for demanding compliance with specific rules and to negotiate meaningfully about these demands (Holden and West 1989). So powerful is this new mental ability that school-age children devote considerable effort to learning and applying rules in school, home, and play contexts. This leads to considerable synchrony between parents and children. This period of joint attention to dominance hierarchies and rule-based regulation of behavior is reflected in greater use of verbal control of behavior and lowered rates of physical punishment and serious child abuse (Wauchope and Straus 1990).

On the other hand, children are testing their newly learned understanding of dominance relationships with peers. During the school years, some children engage in bully-victim relationships (Bowers, Smith, and Binney 1992) as well as in the more healthy selection of peer leaders. In both cases, however, the species-specific behaviors for instigating and terminating aggression, as well as for eliciting nurturance from dominant children, are used.

A second important accomplishment of the school years is children's initial mastery of prosocial behavior. In addition to learning what not to do so as to avoid danger, school-age children learn how to interact with others and how to care for themselves under a wide range of ordinary circumstances. It is important to note that although punishment can teach children to inhibit undesirable behavior, it is of limited effectiveness in teaching them new behavior and skills (Crittenden, Landini, and Claussen 2000; Holden and West 1989). In other words, punishment can teach children what not to do, but not what to do. Further, learning what to do involves experimentation and error. When children fear being punished for mistakes, they are hesitant to attempt new behaviors. This, in turn, interferes with important learning.

ADOLESCENTS

Adolescence denotes the transition from childhood to adulthood. Like other periods of marked behavioral change, the transition from the school years to adolescence is precipitated by rapid neurological change with accompanying change in cognitive abilities and affect. Cognitively, adolescents are able to use formal logic, that is, reasoning using abstractions and symbols (Piaget 1952). Affectively, adolescents experience sexual feelings. Both of these developments change adolescents' behavior with regard to their parents. Knowledge regarding acceptable behavior and rule-based systems (gained in the school years), together with formal logical thinking, create the potential for adolescents to develop broad understandings of ethical and moral behavior (Erikson 1959; Kohlberg 1978; Piaget 1965). This, in turn, paves the way for adolescents to make personal and independent judgments regarding their own appropriate and inappropriate behavior. Adolescents, in other words, seek increasing independence from parental control and guidance.

Like preschool-age children, adolescents often challenge the dominance of adults, especially parents. The outcome of that challenge, however, is very different. First, adolescents lack the physical features that elicit nurturance. To the contrary, they now have features of adults, including features indicative of sexual maturity. These features mark them as equal contestants for intra-species dominance. Second, unlike preschoolers, adolescents have many skills and competencies and are only slightly more in need of protection than adults. Third, because of adolescents' mental and physical competencies, neither arguments nor physical fights between adolescents and adults have predetermined outcomes. Both their intelligence and their physical strength make adolescents potential winners of dominance disputes.

It is no wonder that many parents find adolescence such a difficult period. Their almost-adult children want nurturance and need protection, often from their own overestimation of their skills. At the same time, parents can no longer simply dominate their children and must earn respect from adolescents who offer little generosity regarding the wisdom of older people. Finally, adolescents use all the nonverbal signals of challenge without the physiological features of immaturity.

Nevertheless, adolescents also use their new mental abilities to negotiate disagreements without resort to physical violence. Especially when parents and children have previously developed reciprocal and egalitarian relationships, the interpersonal skills for managing disputes without resorting to physical aggression are already well developed. In that case, the adolescent years serve to refine these skills and broaden their scope. On the other hand, if parents have continued to count on physical and intellectual dominance to control children, neither parent nor adolescent will be well prepared to cope with the challenges of adolescence.

As a result, in some cases, challenges to parental authority become serious disputes that may result in adolescents' facing parental aggression and, potentially, forfeiting parental nurturance and protection in order to gain independence. Although parents and adolescents are not equals on matching characteristics, they are fairly well matched across the range of competencies tied to dominance. That is, adults have greater wisdom and essential resources, whereas adolescents have greater physical strength and a willingness to accept risk. The issue becomes when, not if, adolescents will demand full independence.[3]

Maintenance of parental authority becomes tied to parents yielding power gracefully in cases where adolescents are in fact competent, and earning respect from adolescents where adolescents are not prepared to do without nurturance and assistance. Most parents do yield; only half of American adolescents and parents of adolescents report any use of physical punishment in adolescence (Bachman 1967; Steinmetz 1971; Straus and Donnelly 1993). Nevertheless, among the half who are physically punished at least once, there are some for whom physical punishment by parents is the usual way of solving disagreements. For these families, the rate and severity of parent-child violence may increase in adolescence (Crittenden, Claussen, and Sugarman 1994). Some of this violence is reported as abuse of adolescents or delinquents' aggression against parents (Garbarino 1989). More of this violence, however, is unreported accidental injury to both adults and adolescents.

Beyond the challenges provided by adolescents are the problems of reestablishing relationships in a new dominance hierarchy. Among other species, a submissive animal that cannot reestablish a working relationship with the dominant animal will either be fatally attacked or be expelled from the social group (Barnett 1975; Maxim 1981). Adolescent humans face similar issues. Even while they are challenging parental authority, they must retain a relationship with their parents. Failure to do so often results in their being kicked out of their home prematurely or being subjected to parental tyranny. Neither outcome fosters the transition to relatively egalitarian relationships or to independence.

Individual Differences in the Use of Punishment

There are important individual differences in how physical punishment is used by parents. Four aspects of such differences are most important: the developmental appropriateness of parental expectations, the severity of punishment, the predictability of punishment, and parental developmental history.

DEVELOPMENTAL APPROPRIATENESS

With regard to developmental appropriateness, some parents make demands that are beyond their children's ability to meet, for example, expecting an infant to inhibit crying or not to mouth objects. No amount of punishment will extinguish these behaviors. Similarly, preschool-age children may be asked to remember complex directives or too many directives. In addition, they may be asked to induce related rules from known prohibitions — a task that is beyond the mental abilities of children under the age of seven or eight (Piaget 1952). Parents of school-age children may both underestimate their children's abilities, by choosing not to discuss rules and the reasons for them, and overestimate their abilities, by presuming greater logical ability and memory than children have. They may also discount the sometimes conflicting influence of peers and alternative interests on school-age children's behavior. Finally, in adolescence, some parents fail to acknowledge and foster their children's emerging ability to offer reasonable alternative perspectives.

When parents cannot yield authority and cannot flexibly change their relationship with their adolescent children, they risk trapping their adolescents in struggles that cannot be terminated without the destruction of, or injury to, one of the parties. Even in less extreme cases the struggle may result in premature ejection of the adolescent from the protection of the family unit. Alternatively, adolescents who give up the struggle and submit meekly to parental domination may limit their future ability to function as independent adults. In addition, unduly rigid and domineering parents may fail to prepare their adolescents for relationships between equals and, in particular, for *intimate* relationships between equals. Regardless of whether the adolescent selects the dominant or submissive role, this inflexibility may affect the quality of future spousal and parental relationships (Crittenden, Partridge, and Claussen 1991; Erlanger 1979; Feshbach 1970; Owens and Straus 1979).

SEVERITY

When parents punish infractions very severely, they terrorize children (Brassard, Germain, and Hart 1987; Garbarino and Garbarino 1986). If enough severe physical punishment is used in the early months of life, children can learn to inhibit all behavior; that is, infants who experience a terrorizing environment can become frozen, rigid infants unable to interact with their environment. This reduces greatly their ability to learn to adopt to new experiences. Older infants can learn selective inhibition of the punished behaviors (Crittenden and DiLalla 1988). If, however, punishment is frequent and severe, children may learn to comply too readily. Out of fear of punishment, they may limit exploratory behavior and focus their attention on anticipating and complying with parental demands. Although this has protective value, both in terms of external threats and threats of parental attacks, it limits children's ability to learn to cope independently (Crittenden and DiLalla 1988; Crittenden 1992b, 1994). In the school years, some children maintain compliance with powerful adults while nevertheless exhibiting aggression over weaker peers. Such a child is considered a bully rather than a leader.

Severe physical punishment also interrupts the parent-child dialogue regarding dominance. This dialogue is an essential component of children's learning to accept responsibility for themselves and, ultimately, for their own children. When relationships become nonnegotiable and dominance is based only on power and not on competence, there is the potential for rigidity in both character and relationships and, in extreme cases, for either despotic or submissive behavior. This can be expected to have ramifications both for spouses and for children of the severely punished person.

PREDICTABILITY

If punishment occurs without fail, it will effectively extinguish the prohibited behavior. If, however, the forbidden behavior occurs and is not punished, it may recur at high rates and be relatively impervious to punishment. Finally, if punishment is directed in an inconsistent and unpredictable manner to many behaviors without a logical rule structure that can be discerned by children, they will, in the case of mild to moderate punishment, learn nothing about restrictions and behave in an unruly and often provocative manner. If, on the other hand, the unpredictable punishment is very severe, children may learn to inhibit almost all behavior and to maintain a watchful, wary stance. This outcome, labeled "compulsive compliance," is common among abused children (Crittenden 1992a; Crittenden and DiLalla 1988; Lynch and Roberts 1982; Ounsted, Oppenheimer, and Lindsay 1975).

Parental Developmental History

Possibly the most important variable in differences in how parents use physical punishment is parents' own developmental history. Although specific childhood experiences and cultural contexts are relevant, I refer not to these "external" features but rather to how adults have learned to use the information available to their minds.

In the developmental section of this chapter, I have implicitly differentiated affective and cognitive information. Here I argue that, in their development, parents learn how to integrate (a) affectively derived information, that is, preconscious, genetically biased feelings, with (b) cognitively constructed rules regarding behavior. The most adaptive pattern of mental functioning is a flexible balance that integrates both sorts of information, such that each regulates, informs, and moderates the other. Many children, however, learn to distrust and discard one or the other source of information. Adults also differ in terms of the types of feelings experienced most often (for example, satisfaction, anger, and fear) and the content of the behavioral rules learned (for example, be seen but not heard, or be respectful but state your case). (See Crittenden 1994, 2002 for a fuller discussion of this approach to individual differences in mental functioning.)

In complex ways, these mental orientations affect how parents respond to children's affective signals and whether they permit children to express negative feelings. Where such feelings become the primary focus of parental attention and, therefore, the motivation behind parental behavior, there is risk of indiscriminate and inconsistent overuse of physical punishment. Where such feelings are experienced but not allowed to be displayed, especially in the context of certain, severe, and socially condoned punishment of infractions, there is risk of rigid, rule-based behavior that, at its extreme, can involve systematic, cruel, and terrorizing aggression.

Effects of Physical Punishment on Children

There are few studies of the effects of physical punishment on children that adequately control for developmental appropriateness, severity, predictability of the punishment, and parental developmental history. Psychological maltreatment, such as a parent's expression of disgust for the misbehaving child, may accompany corporal punishment and be compounded in its effects. (See Claussen and Crittenden 1991 for discussion of the relation between psychological and physical maltreatment in infancy and the preschool years and Crittenden, Claussen, and Sugarman 1994 for a similar discussion of school-age children and adolescents.) These correlates of physical punishment will greatly affect the way in which the punishment is experienced by children as well as its effects upon them (Brassard, Germain, and Hart 1987). Unfortunately, most evidence of the negative effects of punishment is confounded with these factors (Straus 1991).

Because the argument regarding the evolutionary function of parental aggression against children presumes an advantage to the species from the use of physical punishment, such carefully controlled experiments may be important. An evolutionary approach, however, does not presume that the genetically biased behavior patterns (in this case, patterns using physical punishment and coy behavior) necessarily favor the development and survival of *every* individual child. To the contrary, it is clear that infants and children whose physiognomy or behavior is atypical do not elicit caregiving as effectively as more normative children and may actually elicit neglect and abuse. In addition, parents whose own developmental history was skewed may use physical punishment in ways that injure or kill their children or distort their psychological development. These risks to individuals, however, may not be reflected in our genetic evolution; natural selection functions to perpetuate behaviors that promote the survival of the species as a whole, without regard (or mercy) for individual cases of failure to survive or thrive.

Nevertheless, technological cultures are extremely sensitive to the welfare of individuals. Over our history as a species, this may be an anomaly that reflects the unusual circumstances of our current situation. Technological countries have resolved most of the external threats to survival, that is, starvation, attacks by predators, exposure to weather, and disease. Under these circumstances, the survival of children is largely ensured — unless we ourselves threaten it. Consequently, we have become more aware and concerned regarding the risks to some children of harsh use of physical punishment.

In addition, given our luxury of access to life-sustaining resources and our ability to combat disease, we have turned our attention from maintaining life to ensuring its quality. This includes a concern for the psychological effects of punishment. There can be no question that under at least some circumstances physical punishment is detrimental to individuals' personality, mental health, happiness, and ability to raise children (Jean-Gilles and Crittenden 1990; Claussen and Crittenden 1991).

Conclusions

SUMMARY OF AN ETHOLOGICAL APPROACH TO PARENTAL USE OF PHYSICAL PUNISHMENT

The argument offered here is that physical punishment of children represents the ultimate communicative signal that parents can give regarding both prohibited behavior and the dominance relationship between parent and child. Further, it is argued that physical punishment is usually the end point of a communicative process that did not successfully elicit, in its earlier stages, either child compliance or acceptance of the parents' dominance, that is, "respect" for the parents.

The origins of this nearly universal communicative pattern between parent and child can best be understood in the context of the need of mammalian young to be nurtured and protected from danger while still being able to explore. Protection is accomplished by the maintenance of a dominance hierarchy between parent and child in which the dominant individual, the attachment figure, incurs the obligation to nurture and protect the weaker person, the child.

Various physical characteristics of children and nonverbal signals from both attachment figures and children function to clarify the roles of attachment figure and attached person. Of these, touch is the strongest signal — whether it is used with affection or anger. These feelings may reflect a rapid and adaptive appraisal system, operating at the preconscious limbic level, that yields protective behavior in less time and with greater certainty than learned information. Thus, the parental anger that accompanies physical punishment may not be inherently irrational or inappropriate; to the contrary, it may reflect the probability of protecting children from imminent dangers. The argument, then, is that affect, including negative effect, is not "bad" or dangerous; rather, it reflects an evolutionary function that tends to promote survival.

Children, however, do mature and learn the skills necessary for self protection. Consequently, children and parents are constantly redefining their relationship (Watzlawick, Beavin, and Jackson 1967). The two critical periods with regard to physical punishment appear to be tied to the changing parent-child relationship in the preschool years and adolescence.

As a consequence of situational variation and children's developmental change, parents must tailor genetically biased behavior to each unique circumstance (Eibl-Eibesfeldt 1979). In humans, more than any other species, affective regulation of behavior need not be a reflexive, stimulus/response directive. Rather, humans learn to integrate affectively derived information with cognitive information to achieve a flexible balance of situation-specific regulation of behavior. Moreover, humans learn to use signals and language to represent behavior, characteristics that allow individuals to define their relationships without physical combat (Goffman 1966).

Learning to integrate information occurs both in children and adults. Infants and parents of infants tend to respond more affectively, whereas adolescents and parents of adolescents show more integration of cognition with affect. Not all learning, however, is unique to individuals; culture passes the cumulative wisdom of previous individuals to each new generation of parents, thus moderating the influence of biology in ways that are suited to each cultural setting. Because children have both less experience from which to learn varied responses and less mental experience with the process of integrative regulation of behavior, they are less likely to take cultural and situational variables into account. Parental guidance is, therefore, critical to their survival. At crucial moments this must be displayed as unambiguous dominance.

FUTURE DIRECTIONS

Much of this chapter has been theoretical in nature. As such, it can be used to generate hypotheses that can be tested empirically. For example, the theory presented here suggests that most physical punishment will be tied to danger or respect for parents. This hypothesis can be tested; its outcome is relevant to intervention to modify patterns of parental use of physical punishment. Similarly, differing patterns of parent-child relationship have been proposed for different age levels; the proposed relations between danger and the punishment of young children and between respect and the punishment of older children may be particularly informative. If empirical work supports the influence of genetic predispositions on parental use of physical punishment, it will be important to describe in detail the eliciting conditions in varied cultures. In addition, research should explore means of modifying eliciting conditions as well as the extent of malleability of human behavior at different ages and under different conditions. Finally, distorted forms of punishment are hypothesized to be associated with bullying behavior, spousal violence, and parents' own experience as children. Specifically, inconsistent punishment is hypothesized to be associated with bully/victim behavior, and extreme and severe punishment with compliance and submission or, occasionally, with covert bursts of serious aggression.

Theory, by its nature, necessarily exceeds empirical certainty. Nevertheless, when well constructed, theory suggests plausible relations among important aspects of experience; these relations should be both novel and intuitively useful in explaining aspects of experience that were previously less well understood. In addition, good theory is internally consistent; its postulates are believable and lead logically to the hypotheses and conclusions offered by the theory. Finally, good theory is testable.

I have tried to keep these criteria in mind as I have applied evolutionary, attachment, and systemic thinking to the use of physical punishment among humans. Some of what I have proposed may not be philosophically or ethically acceptable to all. The theory I offer, however, is not a treatise on what *should be* but rather a discussion of *how things may have come to be as they are*. The achievement of the human mind is that it can observe its own functioning and decide if, when, and how to change. Change, however, is best undertaken when survival is not at risk and when current functioning is well understood. I have argued that, in technological cultures, we have the first of these. This chapter, together with the other perspectives in the volume, is an attempt to achieve the latter and, thus, free us to choose, within the range of genetic malleability, how to organize our parental behavior in the future.

Notes

1. I wish to thank George W. Holden for his helpful comments on an earlier draft of this chapter.

2. Although cross-species comparisons are insufficient to determine the meaning of behavior in any given species, they can be used, and are used here, to develop an argument regarding the source and function of commonly observed behavior. The ubiquity of parental physical punishment lends itself to this method of hypothesis development.

3. There are, however, substantial cultural and historical variations in whether egalitarian relationships apply to both genders or only to males.

7

Behavioral Theory and Corporal Punishment

SCOTT W. POWERS AND

ROBERT E. LARZELERE

Children *learn* how to behave. Significant adults in children's lives, especially parents, are their primary teachers. Behavioral theory is based upon principles of learning derived from empirical investigation. The application of learning principles to assist people in living more adaptively is often termed behavior therapy. A discussion of how behavioral research and its application can inform us about the causes of corporal punishment and its effects on children, families, and society is of great utility. This chapter discusses the topic of corporal punishment of children from a behavioral-theory and behavior-therapy perspective. Basic principles of learning theory will be presented, followed by information based upon the work of behavioral clinicians. The goal is to address the question, How can we better understand the causes and consequences of corporal punishment and utilize this knowledge in an objective way to assist families in the important process of raising their children to be secure, adaptive, and productive people?

Basic Principles of Learning Theory

OPERANT PRINCIPLES

The principles of *operant conditioning* (Martin and Pear 1983; Skinner 1938, 1953) are fundamental to the role of behavioral theory in furthering understanding of corporal punishment of children. Many of the principles of operant conditioning were derived from research in the animal laboratory. These principles were then generalized to human studies, and they have been widely applied as behavior-change technologies in numerous settings (for example, schools and workplaces; Powers and Rickard 1992).

Observable events are the focus on an analysis of operant behavior. Unobserved internal states are of interest only to the extent that they can be measured objectively and used to increase prediction of observable behavior (for example, rules that govern behavior; Hayes 1989). Thus, a well-defined observable behavior in the stream of ongoing behavior is selected as the operant or target behavior to be explained. For example, in the course of a typical day of ongoing child behavior, a child comes in from outside and hangs up his coat. Major concepts used to explain the rate of the target behavior include *antecedent events* (parental reminders to hang up the coat) and *consequent events* (the parent smiles and pats the child on the shoulder immediately after the child has hung up the coat). From an operant-theory perspective, the rate of target behavior is explained primarily in terms of the effect of antecedent and consequent events on the subsequent likelihood of the recurrence of that behavior.

Operant principles are usually defined on the basis of *function,* that is, the effect on the recurrence of the operant behavior. Assessment designed to understand the dynamic interplay of antecedents, operants, and consequences is called a *functional analysis of behavior.* If the probability of the recurrence of an operant behavior *increases* following a consequence, the consequence is called reinforcement. In our example, if the child hangs up his or her coat the next time after coming in from outside, the prior smile and pat by the parent (consequent event) can be viewed as reinforcing. *Positive reinforcement* occurs when the addition of an event (usually pleasant) contingent upon the occurrence of an operant behavior increases the likelihood of the recurrence of that behavior. *Negative reinforcement* occurs when an event (usually aversive) that is removed contingent upon the occurrence of an operant behavior increases the probability of the recurrence of that behavior. For example, a child begins to scream and yell at the store because he or she wants a candy bar (antecedent event). In an effort to stop the screaming, the parent lets the child have the candy (operant behavior). The child immediately stops screaming (consequent event). If in the future the likelihood of the parent giving in to the child in order to remove the aversive event (that is, screaming) increases, negative reinforcement of giving in his occurred. Also, there is an illustration of positive reinforcement in this example. The child's screaming (operant behavior) was followed by the child receiving a candy bar from the parent (consequent event). If in the future the probability of the child screaming in the store to obtain candy increases, that behavior has been positively reinforced.

By functional definition, punishment *decreases* the probability of an operant behavior occurring in the future. That is, a punisher has a *reductive effect* upon behavior. For illustrative purposes, punishment can be divided into two forms: presentation of an aversive event contingent upon the occurrence of an operant behavior ("positive" punishment, of which corporal punishment is an example) or removal of a positive event contingent upon the occurrence of an operant behavior ("negative" punishment). For example, a child hits his or her sibling in order to obtain a toy (operant behavior). The parent says, "No hitting," physically separates the children, and makes each one do a five-minute house chore (consequent event). If in the future the probability of physical fighting by the siblings over toys decreases, the consequences imposed by the parent were punishing. In this example, the parent added aversive events; hence, "positive" punishment. This example can be changed to illustrate an instance of the parent removing a positive event contingent upon the occurrence of sibling aggression ("negative" punishment). Specifically, the parent could have taken the controversial toy away until the next day or prevented the children from engaging in a preferred activity that day (for example, having dessert or watching a movie). If in the future the probability of hitting between the siblings over toys decreases, the parent's imposed consequence was punishing.

From the functional perspective of operant conditioning, the *outcome* of antecedent and consequent events is the key issue, not necessarily whether or not the events appear aversive or pleasant. Specifically, if the probability of a behavior does not decrease in the future, the event cannot functionally be considered a punisher. The functional definition of punishment can be confusing, because it differs from the conventional lay definition and from definitions of punishment from most other perspectives. According to the functional definition, it is meaningless to ask whether corporal punishment is effective, because punishment is effective by definition (that is, it reduces the subsequent rate of the immediately preceding behavior).

To approximate the usual definition of punishment, some behavioral authors define punishment as an aversive stimulus (for example, Reynolds 1975;

Walters and Grusec 1977). Using this definition allows an investigator to ask whether corporal punishment (as an aversive stimulus) is effective in reducing the target misbehavior: That is, does an aversive discipline response effectively reduce the subsequent rate of the target misbehavior? Unless otherwise specified, "punishment" will denote the functional definition in this chapter. To clarify which definition is being used, "reductive" technique will be used to describe a punisher in the functional sense; and "aversive" will be used to describe a punisher in the aversive sense.

In either case, what might appear aversive and be intended to be reductive may actually function as a reinforcer for a child. For example, a parent's repeated nagging and yelling at a child to put away his or her toys might appear to be aversive. However, if nagging is one of the few occasions on which the parent pays attention to the child, it could actually increase the likelihood of the child not putting away the toys. In this case, the nagging and yelling are reinforcers of noncompliance; they were intended as punishers but function as reinforcers.

The nagging and yelling can also serve as a *discriminative stimulus* (S+ or S−). A discriminative stimulus is an event or condition that signals that a particular operant behavior is likely to be reinforced or punished. An example of a discriminative stimulus is a telephone ringing. Given that stimulus, picking up the receiver and saying "Hello" will usually be reinforced by a conversation with a caller (phone ringing is an S+). If the typical phone conversation is not reinforcing, then people become less likely to answer the telephone, perhaps screening callers with an answering machine or getting an unlisted telephone number. When phone conversations are experienced negatively, then the phone ringing may be an S−, signifying that answering the phone is unlikely to be reinforced.

In a similar way, parental nagging and yelling may serve as a signal that continued child aversive behavior (for example, noncompliance) will get the parent to quit complaining, which would negatively reinforce the child's aversive behavior in response to subsequent parental nagging. In contrast, a clear, effective parental warning is a signal that continued noncompliance will result in negative consequences.

Different situations may elicit different behavior patterns in children through stimulus-discrimination learning. For example, a child may misbehave more in public or around grandparents because he or she has learned that the contingencies of reinforcement and punishment are different in those situations. Similarly, discrimination learning may explain parental use of corporal punishment, in that such parental behavior may be reinforced in private (for example, by terminating sassing) but be punished in public situations from bystanders'

negative feedback. If so, then a private situation would be an S+ for corporal punishment, whereas a public situation would be an S− for corporal
punishment.

A clear, effective warning may also become a *conditioned punishment*. A
conditioned punishment is a response that did not have punishment qualities
originally but came to have punishment qualities by being paired with another
punisher (for example, the negative consequence following the warning if
compliance failed to occur).

The interplay between punishment and reinforcement during ongoing behavior interactions of people is a key aspect of the functional perspective. The
dynamics of such interplay are highlighted by the following discussion of
coercion theory.

COERCION THEORY

Coercion theory (Patterson 1982; Snyder and Patterson 1995) may be
the most comprehensive behavioral theory for explaining the interaction between parents and children in discipline encounters. Coercion theory was
developed primarily to account for processes within the family that make it a
training ground for aggression. The central thesis of coercion theory is that
family differences in parental and child use of aggression are shaped and
maintained by reinforcement and punishment (operant principles). Negative
reinforcement is especially important in aggression training, for example,
when the child's aggression is effective in turning off aversive parental actions,
such as control attempts. Patterson (1982) and colleagues (Snyder and Patterson 1995) have documented that negative reinforcement of aggressive tactics
is highly predictive of subsequent use of such aggressive tactics.

Snyder and Patterson (1995) successfully extended the explanatory power
of coercion theory in three ways: First, they showed that, in conflict situations,
negative reinforcement accounts for the subsequent selection of nonaggressive
as well as aggressive tactics. Second, they showed that negative reinforcement
accounts for the parent's selection of tactics during conflict as well as the
child's selection of tactics. Third, they showed that the theory predicts intrafamily choices of conflict tactics more directly than it predicts interfamily
differences in conflict tactics. Coercion theory was able to predict the relative
rate with which a family member chooses a particular conflict tactic, not the
absolute frequency of choosing that tactic compared to other families.

Coercion theory shows that a reductive effect of an aversive response is
always accompanied by negative reinforcement of that aversive response. For
example, when a parent spanks a child and successfully terminates the child's
noncompliance, then the spanking has a reductive effect on noncompliance

(punishment). In addition, the termination of the child's noncompliance negatively reinforces the parent's choice of spanking, thereby making spanking a more likely response to noncompliance in the future.

Coercion theory holds that this works bidirectionally between the parent and child. For example, when a child's tantrum causes parents to drop their bedtime demands, then the tantrum has reduced the parents' demandingness (punishment), and tantrums are negatively reinforced by successfully turning off parental demands. Such negative reinforcement working in both directions can produce the *negative-reinforcement trap,* with aversive tactics being negatively reinforced in both partners over time. This increases the likelihood that both partners will escalate their aversive tactics until one backs off, once again negatively reinforcing the aversiveness "winner" in that episode. Consistent with this, aggressive families escalate their aversiveness more frequently than do other families. The average aversiveness increases at every step of conflict, with physical aggression most likely at the end of a long conflict episode (Snyder, Edwards, McGraw, Kilgore, and Holton 1994; Snyder and Patterson 1995).

Kadushin and Martin (1981) showed that most incidents of physical child abuse occur in situations perceived by parents as discipline episodes. Coercion theory provides an account of the process of such escalation within discipline episodes and across such episodes over an extended period of time. An accurate understanding of the escalation process is necessary to design effective interventions, whether from a prevention or treatment perspective.

One implication of coercion theory is that an ounce of prevention is worth a pound of cure. It is better to prevent a discipline incident than to attempt to handle it appropriately. Strategies to prevent discipline incidents include reinforcing appropriate behaviors (Forehand and McMahon 1981), making clear, age-appropriate commands (Roberts and Powers 1988), using strategies to facilitate appropriate behaviors (Holden 1983), and limiting control attempts to more important misbehaviors (Forehand and McMahon 1981; Patterson 1975). However, preventive strategies are rarely effective enough to avoid discipline incidents altogether (Baumrind 1971), especially after a coercive cycle has been established (Patterson 1982).

Coercion theory also has implications for the potential effects of alternative strategies for preventing the escalation of aggression within parent-child conflict episodes. One counterproductive tactic is for parents to back off from their control attempts in the face of child aversiveness. Instead, parents need to persist in their control attempts until children either comply or use nonaversive tactics (for example, compromise) to resolve a discipline incident. Snyder et al. (1994) found that mothers of nonaggressive four-year-old boys do this by responding to an aversive child behavior with a slightly less aversive response, and by reinforcing the child's de-escalation of aversiveness with ending the conflict. In contrast, mothers of aggressive boys matched their sons' aversiveness and were more likely to respond to the child's de-escalation with renewed escalation of aversiveness.

Parental persistence is important because effective punishment must clearly signal that the misbehavior must stop. When threats or other parental responses are not backed up, they become signals for eliciting aversive acts from the child, which in turn are negatively reinforced when the parent does not persist in the control attempt (Patterson 1982). Research needs to specify the conditions under which persistence maximizes effectiveness of the control attempt and minimizes the risk of escalation to abuse.

Empirical and Practical Work of Behavioral Clinicians

The process of teaching children how to behave has often been called discipline (Christophersen 1992; McCormick 1992). Christophersen (1992: 397–98), in advising pediatricians, notes that parents may have a variety of reasons for using discipline, including to terminate undesirable behavior, to teach the child a lesson, to teach desirable behavior, and to help children internalize society's values. Based upon our understanding of learning principles, the purpose of punishment, as a component of the discipline process, can only be to decrease undesirable behavior. Punishment *does not* serve the purpose of teaching desirable behavior. If a child does not learn desirable behavior, decreasing undesirable behavior will be useless. Therefore, behavioral clinicians first focus on how to teach children desirable behavior, then focus on decreasing undesirable behavior (Forehand and McMahon 1981). Notably, for discipline to be effective, parents must focus on both increasing desirable behaviors and decreasing undesirable behaviors, and they must view discipline as a teaching process that evolves over the long term. Because punishment (functionally defined) is a necessary component of effective discipline, behavioral clinicians emphasize the importance of the *effectiveness* of discipline responses. Effective punishment is characterized by being used contingently for targeted misbehaviors and by parental persistence in the discipline episode rather than giving in, to avoid negatively reinforcing aversive child tactics. Patterson and other behavioral parent trainers (Forehand, Eyberg, Roberts) have made the effective use of "time-out" an essential component of parent training (Patterson 1982: 111). Further, behavioral parent-training programs emphasize maximizing the effectiveness of mild punishment, such as time-out, in contrast to more severe punishers, such as corporal punishment. Mild punishers are preferred over severe punishers for humane reasons and to mini-mize the effect of habituation (that is, the tendency for a frequently repeated punisher to decrease in effectiveness with repetition).

The optimal discipline response is both effective and mild, with more severe discipline responses reserved for backing up time-out if resistance occurs (that is, refusal to stay in time-out), thereby increasing its effectiveness. Most be-havioral parent-training programs for children from two to six years of age advocate a carefully prescribed spanking (for example, two spanks on the bot-tom with an open hand) to be used only as a backup for time-out resis-tance (Barkley 1987; Christophersen 1988; Dangel and Polster 1984; Eyberg and Boggs 1989; Forehand and McMahon 1981; Roberts and Powers 1990). Other behavioral parent-training programs, especially those for older chil-dren, limit backups for time-out resistance to noncorporal consequences, such as chores or withdrawal of privileges. Some behavioral parent trainers have abandoned the use of corporal punishment as a backup for time-out resis-tance and used a holding procedure instead (for example, McNeil, Clemens-Mowrer, Gurwitch, Funderburk 1994). However, it would be difficult for most parents to learn such alternative backup procedures for time-out without individualized training (personal communication, P. C. Friman 1993).

Published research comparing the effectiveness of alternative backups for time-out resistance in two- to six-year-olds has found that a short, room backup procedure is the only contingency as effective as the carefully pre-scribed spanking procedure (Roberts and Powers 1990). In a room backup procedure, if the child does not comply with time-out on a chair, then the child is taken to a room for time-out backup and the door is held closed for one minute, after which the child is returned to the chair for time-out. Not only is a room backup as effective as the prescribed spanking in achieving time-out compliance, but either the room backup or the spanking procedure can serve as an alternative to the other in those few cases where time-out compliance is not achieved after six repetitions of the original backup procedure (Roberts and Powers 1990).

Note that, although other theories state that mild discipline responses are preferable to severe responses, the behavioral perspective is relatively unusual in documenting a systematic process to *increase* the effectiveness of mild disci-pline responses. Paradoxically, a more severe discipline response used solely as a backup is a key to increasing the effectiveness of a mild discipline response, such as time-out. The role of effective backup procedures operates for other discipline tactics as well. For example, Roberts (1982) studied the effect of a single warning versus no warning in a behavioral parent-training program for teaching child compliance to parental instructions. The group with a time-out warning (that is, after an initial instruction followed by noncompliance, a warning in the form "If you do not do——, then you will go to time-out") decreased noncompliance as much as the no-warning group (that is, an initial instruction with immediate time-out contingent on noncompliance), but they accomplished this with 74 percent fewer time-outs. Thus a single warning was often effective in achieving compliance *if it was backed up by the effective use of time-out*. In a nonexperimental study, Larzelere, Sather, Schneider, Larson, and Pike (1998) found that the effectiveness of a reasoning response to toddlers' misbehavior was greater when it had recently been combined with an aversive punishment, such as time-out or spanking. In all three studies, a mild discipline response became more effective by itself after being backed up by a more severe discipline response. Moreover, over the long term, the increased efficacy of mild discipline will likely decrease the potential for coercive escalation and reduce the need for more severe discipline altogether (for example, once a preschool child learns not to resist time-out, the need to use corporal punishment drops to zero; Roberts and Powers 1990).

USEFUL ASPECTS OF A BEHAVIOR PERSPECTIVE FOR INVESTIGATING
CORPORAL PUNISHMENT

Behavioral theories, such as coercion theory, have already proven useful for explaining the development and maintenance of aggression in children. Moreover, Kazdin (1987) considered behavioral parent training to be the intervention of choice for treating aggression in children. As such, behavioral perspectives seem equally applicable to the understanding and treatment of inappropriate parental aggression.

Coercion theory and the interrelatedness of behavioral concepts highlight the complexities involved in discipline interactions. Behavioral perspectives have emphasized systematic methods for increasing the effectiveness of mild discipline responses, with the byproduct of decreasing the use of corporal punishment by most parents. One implication of research on effective discipline is that more aversive punishers should be used mainly to back up less aversive discipline responses, thereby increasing their future effectiveness.

Another use of behavioral theory is to suggest both positive and negative effects of proposed changes in parental discipline procedures. For example, merely getting parents to stop using spanking may undermine the reductive effect of mild discipline responses that had been backed up by spanking. The net effect may be to increase problem behaviors in the children and perhaps increase the risk of child abuse due to increased parental frustration. In contrast, training parents how to increase the effectiveness of mild discipline responses may do more to decrease subsequent use of corporal punishment than merely persuading them to stop spanking.

METHODOLOGICAL IMPLICATIONS

The only randomized comparison studies of parental corporal punishment are those conducted by behavioral psychologists to analyze the effectiveness of spanking as a backup to time-out. Any comprehensive view of corporal punishment must take into account that researchers using robust research designs have found a carefully prescribed spanking to be at least as effective as any alternative. Such methodological sophistication should be a primary goal of future interdisciplinary efforts to study parental corporal punishment.

While true experiments are often impractical or unethical, nonexperimental studies should attempt to do a better job of controlling for variables that findings could be confounded with. For example, studies could compare the effectiveness of corporal punishment versus alternative discipline responses while equating the severity of the problem behaviors. Another way of improving on the typical correlational study would be to ensure that the discipline response systematically precedes the measure of the problem behavior. Although some causal ambiguities remain, this methodological strategy could be adopted by studying the probability of misbehavior recurrences (or delays until their recurrence) following corporal punishment versus alternative discipline responses.

Without these methodological refinements, correlations of corporal punishment with other variables may be misleading due to the intervention selection bias (Larzelere, Kuhn, and Johnson 2004). The intervention selection bias is the tendency of any intervention to be positively correlated with the very problem for which it is intended as a treatment. For example, prior inpatient psychiatric treatment is positively associated with subsequent suicide risk. Before concluding that such correlations indicate the ineffectiveness of hospitalization or of child spanking, inherent confounds must be controlled, such as the severity of the presenting problems.

An interesting methodology was developed by Snyder et al. (1994). They analyzed conditional probabilities of aversive behaviors within observed parent-child interactions. The analyses showed how the probabilities of escalation or de-escalation during conflict episodes differed systematically between dyads of aggressive versus nonaggressive four-year-olds and their mothers. In aggressive families, mothers and sons were more likely to cycle between escalation and de-escalation, whereas in nonaggressive families de-escalation was much more likely to lead to an end of the conflict. Further, mothers of aggressive boys showed an increased likelihood of matching their sons' level of aversiveness, whereas mothers of nonaggressive boys tended to respond at slightly less aversive levels than their sons' preceding behavior. Thus, mothers of nonaggressive boys seem to be better than mothers of aggressive boys at de-escalating conflicts in a systematic way, perhaps thereby teaching self-control to their sons. They are also less likely to abandon the conflict as a response to their sons' escalation of aversiveness.

INTERRELATIONSHIPS WITH OTHER THEORIES

A behavioral perspective can be usefully integrated with other empirically supported viewpoints and theories. For example, cognitive theories of socialization complement a behavioral perspective nicely on several issues. First, Parke's (1974) series of studies showed that the addition of reasoning to a mildly aversive punishment changes the conditions under which an aversive punisher is maximally effective. For example, the timing and intensity of the punisher were not nearly as crucial when punishment was combined with reasoning as when punishment was used by itself.

Second, attribution theory is a cognitive theory with some interesting implications for the effects of alternative discipline responses on moral internalization. Lepper (1983), for example, argues from attribution theory that mild discipline responses elicit more internalization than severe discipline responses, so long as both are effective in obtaining the child's compliance. Thus, like behavioral perspectives, attribution theory implies that mild but effective discipline responses are optimal. Attribution theory further implies that mild, effective discipline responses become particularly important by the age of seven, when children begin making attributions in the same way adults do (Grusec and Dix 1986; Perry and Perry 1983). A strength of behavioral research compared to attribution research is behaviorists' development and documentation of procedures for improving the effectiveness of mild discipline responses.

The role of more severe punishment as a backup for less aversive discipline responses may thus be particularly important between two and six years of age, the age range where the effectiveness of corporal punishment as a backup for time-out resistance has been documented. Milder punishment responses, such as reasoning and time-out, should then be effective by themselves when children begin making adultlike attributions around the age of seven. This developmental progression should reduce the need for severe punishers later, which would be less effective at older ages anyway, according to attribution theory. Consistent with this progression, Larzelere et al. (1998) found that reasoning was effective in delaying the next misbehavior recurrence in two- and three-year-olds to the extent that it had recently been combined with a negative consequence, such as time-out or spanking.

Conclusion

A behavioral perspective has much to contribute to furthering our understanding of the causes and consequences of corporal punishment. Behavioral parent training is the best-documented treatment for antisocial aggressiveness in children, and a behavioral treatment has the potential to be equally effective for curbing inappropriate parental aggression. Strengths of a behavioral approach include its contribution to understanding the microsocial interactions between parents and children that underlie potential escalations in aggression. A second strength is the systematic development and evaluation of interventions to make discipline responses both mild and effective.

How can we better understand the causes and consequences of corporal punishment and utilize this knowledge in an objective way to assist families in the important process of raising their children to be secure, adaptive, and productive people? Behavioral theories and the applications derived from them help us begin to answer this question. However, as this book demonstrates, there are many challenges for future research. Some of these challenges include: documentation of techniques that make discipline efforts by parents optimally effective; integration of various theoretical perspectives into the development and design of research studies; methodological advancements in research to ensure objectivity; and successful application of the objective findings of research in the everyday lives of families.

8

Behavior Analysis, Evolutionary Theory, and the Corporal Discipline of Children

WILLIAM M. BAUM AND ANNE S. KUPFER

A scientific understanding of human behavior has progressed to the point where corporal punishment is no longer necessary in child rearing. Children's behavior can be shaped with reinforcement and noncorporal punishment. Progress toward establishing these socially acceptable approaches has been slowed because of a lack of distinction among three different types of hitting, all of which tend to be labeled "corporal punishment." We distinguish among conventional corporal discipline, impulsive aggression, and true corporal punishment. Of these, impulsive aggression presents the biggest problem, because our evolutionary inheritance makes everyone susceptible to it, to one degree or another. Since impulsive aggression toward children is induced and maintained by environmental conditions, it can be treated and prevented by proper intervention. Traditionally, advocacy of conventional corporal discipline derived from the notion that "bad deeds" arise from free will and that children have to be taught to "be good." A more deterministic view of behavior encourages a more compassionate attitude toward wrongdoing. Seen in the perspective of evolutionary theory, socially unacceptable behavior is natural rather than wicked and may be approached with a view that is practical, rather than moralistic. In the behavior-analytic view, both the tendency to impulsive aggression and to punishable behavior may usually be understood as contingency traps. Contingency traps are avoided by two types of methods:

commitment and social contingencies, usually called "education," combined with rules. Applied-behavior analysts have developed a variety of powerful reinforcement-based methods for treating undesirable behavior. They find true corporal punishment to be necessary only as a method of last resort in rare circumstances. Establishing reinforcement and noncorporal punishment as alternatives to conventional corporal discipline and impulsive aggression will require educating both parents and children.

This chapter examines the use of corporal punishment of children as a cultural practice from the combined perspective of behavior analysis and evolutionary theory. In this perspective, behavior, including human behavior, is seen as a function of three types of variables: genetic dispositions, current environmental situations (including cultural practices), and individual conditioning histories. According to this synthesis of behavior analysis and evolutionary theory, behavior depends entirely on environmental events, some going back to childhood and some going back over many generations of natural selection. An individual's actions today cannot be understood without reference to history, both ontogenetic and phylogenic. A complete account includes a careful specification of the behavior itself, of the conditions under which it is likely to occur, and of the overt consequences of the behavior. An account omitting any of these three elements is incomplete and may lead to important oversights.

Our discussion will focus on: (1) misunderstandings about the use of the word *punishment* in general and the phrase *corporal punishment* in particular, (2) how this misunderstanding has impeded progress toward eliminating the use of corporal disciplinary practices in our culture, (3) how traditional views of human nature foster the use of corporal disciplinary practices, (4) the provenance of corporal disciplinary practices and the concept of "punishable" behavior, and (5) how alternative disciplinary strategies will decrease acceptance of and reliance on corporal discipline.

What Is Meant by Corporal Punishment?

The behavior-analytic use of the word *punishment* differs from the common use of the phrase *corporal punishment*. To most people, punishment means corporal punishment and refers to the use of slaps or spankings to stop children's behavior that is considered inappropriate. The main goal of hitting is the immediate termination of the child's actions. Often, hitting the child is called punishment even if it is ineffective. This view of corporal punishment, because it fails to make such key distinctions as to whether and why it is effective and why it occurs in the first place, interferes with our understanding it as a cultural practice and product of our evolutionary history. To gain this understanding and, with it, to eliminate corporal disciplinary practices from our culture, we need a clearer idea of what we mean by "corporal punishment" and a clearer definition of punishment in general.

A FUNCTIONAL DEFINITION OF PUNISHMENT

The definition we offer of punishment is derived from laboratory studies. Behavioral research has identified a number of factors that determine the effectiveness of punishment. They include: a careful specification of the behavior to be punished, including the situations in which it is likely to occur and particularly the reinforcement that maintains it, a careful description of the punisher and whether escape from it is possible, and a specification of when the punisher is to be presented — that is, the schedule of punishment (see Azrin and Holz 1966 and Walters and Grusec 1977 for reviews).

Azrin and Holz (1966) offered a *functional* definition of punishment, which may be paraphrased thus: Punishment is a reduction of the future probability of an action as a result of delivery of an event for that action. The event that accomplishes the reduction in future probability is a *punisher*. A functional definition casts punishment as a procedure (delivery of a punisher contingent upon an action) and emphasizes the behavioral effects of that procedure (reduction of future probability).

This definition differs from others that might be given, in at least three ways. First, it omits subjective terms, such as feelings or states of mind. It emphasizes the event's effect on behavior, rather than what a person might feel or say about the event. Although what a person feels or says might be important for some purposes, there is no reason to assume that a person's reports about punishment should replace the observation of its actual effects.

Second, emphasis on reduction in future probability avoids the possible misconception that would equate punishment with immediate suppression of unwanted behavior. Immediate suppression of a child's behavior may have nothing to do with punishment. More likely, a slap elicits a host of physiological responses, such as crying and passivity, which are incompatible with the unwanted behavior. Even if hitting immediately suppresses it, if the behavior remains just as likely to occur again, it cannot be said to have been punished.

Third, the definition helps us to avoid being trapped by our prejudices about which events should be punishing, based on our own experience. An adult observer who would find it terribly aversive to be hit and would avoid doing anything that resulted in being hit cannot assume that therefore being hit will punish any child's behavior. Our own subjective impressions are no guide at all. Indeed, in many situations hitting not only turns out to fail as punishment but actually functions as positive reinforcement. For example, if hitting is associated with other physical and verbal contact (that is, "attention"), it may strengthen the behavior that produces it. True punishment is recognized by its reducing the probability of the unwanted behavior's being repeated.

A functional definition helps us to separate punishment from aggression and to understand the reasons behind both. Instead of suggesting that punishment occurs because of a parent's "frustration," we are drawn to examine the circumstances surrounding punishment and aggression. The factors that promote the use of punishment may differ widely from the factors that promote aggression. We turn now to defining this distinction more carefully.

Parents hit or otherwise inflict pain on children for a variety of reasons. We shall focus on three types of hitting, distinguished by the environmental circumstances that established and maintain them. The first, *true corporal punishment,* we shall discuss only briefly near the end, because it applies to situations that are relatively rare. The two types of greater concern, neither of which constitutes true punishment, we shall call *conventional corporal discipline* and *impulsive aggression.* These two together we shall refer to as *corporal discipline,* preferring the word *discipline* to value-laden words like *abuse* and *violence.*

CONVENTIONAL CORPORAL DISCIPLINE

Cultural traditions may dictate that when a child misbehaves, the child should be hit, regardless of how the parent may feel. It is the parent's duty. The hitting is not impulsive but planned in advance and may even be reluctant. In William Faulkner's novel *The Reivers,* a boy, having misbehaved, is taken by his father to the place where he would usually be strapped for a misdeed, but his father withholds the whipping because the enormity of the boy's transgression precludes its being expunged by a mere whipping. He trusts instead to the boy's guilt and shame to mete out justice. The incident illustrates both the conventional aspect of the corporal discipline and the environmental circumstances of its occurrence. Justice, as understood by the culture, must prevail.

As time goes by, however, conventions change. Like all cultural practices, the disciplinary practices that go with talk about justice and paying for sins are passed from generation to generation, but usually with some modification, depending on changes in other practices in the culture. The current public debate over "corporal punishment" (loosely defined), of which this book is evidence, is likely to decrease the frequency of conventional corporal discipline, particularly as more effective noncorporal methods increase in frequency. Being relatively susceptible to education and social pressure, conventional corporal discipline is of less concern than impulsive aggression, which is rooted in the biology of our species.

IMPULSIVE AGGRESSION TOWARD CHILDREN

When people speak of "corporal punishment," the main problem of concern is *impulsive aggression of parents toward children.* Who objects if parents try to shape the behavior of their children? We only object when that worthy goal is used to try to justify parents' aggressive behavior toward their children.

Aggression is "impulsive" when it constitutes an immediate, emotional reaction that is maintained by immediate reinforcement. This immediate reinforcement is of two sorts. First, as is true of much "emotional" behavior, engaging in aggression is itself reinforcing. Second, the aggression is reinforced by the immediate suppression of the child's unwanted behavior. Impulsive aggression is *not* maintained by any long-term reduction in the future probability of the child's inappropriate behavior.

In our view, the so-called problem of corporal punishment is more usefully seen as two problems: conventional corporal discipline, which will yield to cultural change, and impulsive aggression toward children, which is less tractable. This leaves true corporal punishment as a possible way to reduce or eliminate inappropriate behavior in children, although we shall argue that it is an undesirable method, at best a method of last resort. We shall be concerned primarily with impulsive aggression toward children: where it comes from, its likely effects, and how to prevent it.

Progress in Understanding Human Behavior

Formal attempts to explain human behavior go back at least to Greek thinkers like Plato and Aristotle. In modern times, Skinner (1953, 1957) was a leading proponent of recasting this endeavor in scientific terms. Many advances have occurred since the 1953 publication of his *Science and Human Behavior.* Journals like the *Journal of the Experimental Analysis of Behavior, Journal of Applied Behavior Analysis, Journal of Behavioral Education, Journal of Organizational Behavior Management,* and *The Behavior Analyst* attest to the increasing application of behavior analysis to human behavior. Areas of successful application include choice and decision making, self-control, verbal behavior, child development, cooperation, quality management, education, and treatment of deviant behavior.

In comparison with the ancient Greeks, we know a lot today about the sources of human behavior. Due both to basic and applied research, we know enough to modify many sorts of problem behavior. The methods involved, which are not only powerful but also socially acceptable, depend on skillful use of positive reinforcement and noncorporal punishment. As a general rule, to change behavior, we introduce new contingencies of these sorts into the person's environment.

With the alternatives available today, there is no longer any justification for advocating corporal discipline as a general means. Removing this justification also removes any possible excuse for aggression toward children.

Traditional justifications of conventional corporal discipline and impulsive aggression toward children rest on the notion of free will. According to tradition, children are punished for evil so that they may choose good. The more we identify genetic and environmental contributions to mental retardation and hyperactivity, effects of television violence on children's aggression, and so forth, the less we speak of free will, the less we resort to corporal discipline to control behavior, and the more we treat behavioral problems with compassion, as practical problems with behavioral solutions.

Similarly, if the genetic and environmental sources are clarified, instead of impulsive aggression toward children being seen as parents' free choice of evil, it may be seen as the practical problem of getting parents to use effective behavioral techniques. What if parents were taught that their tendency toward aggression arises naturally from evolution and environmental factors and, because of this, is a practical problem that can be treated by behavioral methods?

BEHAVIOR AND ENVIRONMENT

It is often said that, in contrast to the relatively fixed behavior of other species, human behavior is highly malleable. There is some truth to this, in the sense that many of our essential skills, such as speaking and caregiving, seem to depend on experience. Our remote ancestors, however, grew to adulthood in a more stable environment than the one we experience today. Probably our environment has changed more in the past five thousand years than it did in the previous five million years. In the perspective of evolutionary theory, five million years provide scope for genetic change. In a relatively stable environment, genes that relinquish some control to the environment can be selected, particularly if they increase the possibilities of adaptation to whatever variation occurs in the environment.

When control over development is delegated to the environment, it becomes possible for behavior to change as the environment changes. A person can learn to wear different clothes in winter and summer.

The malleability of behavior, however, is an outcome of changes in the environment, changes that often themselves result from human behavior. People have displaced other species, aggregated into enormous settlements, and changed the landscape, all in too short a time for any significant genetic change in our collective genes.

When environmental change outstrips genetic change, many behavioral tendencies, even behavioral tendencies that depend on experience, are likely to be appropriate for the environment in which genetic evolution took place, an environment that no longer exists, and inappropriate for the highly modified environment in which we live today. As a result of our history of evolution, we are left with tendencies to develop unhealthy dietary practices, substance abuse, and aggression toward our fellows.

THE ORIGINS OF PUNISHABLE BEHAVIOR AND PARENTAL AGGRESSION

On the one hand, one may look at conventional corporal discipline (as defined here) and the justification of parental aggression in the name of punishment as practices of our culture, and ask how they arose and are maintained. On the other hand, one may seek the origins in individual human nature, which directs us toward our species' evolutionary history.

Cultural Perspective

VALUES, RESPONSIBILITY, AND FREE WILL

Historically, Western civilization has focused on the problem of evil and the notion of free will. If God is good and just, why is there evil in the world? The answer has often been, "Because people, having the freedom to choose between good and evil, often choose evil." Punishment offers the means to discourage bad behavior while preserving at least the appearance of free choice of good.

In such a view, flogging adults or children might even be a service, whether the miscreants are actually grateful or not. Severity in chastisement might thereby appear a virtue. If a parent beats a child, it could be for the child's own good. Charles Dickens and other writers have shown how readily such a view leads to abuse.

When children (or adults) are credited with their good deeds, they will be blamed for their sins and punished. Perhaps paradoxically, for those who believe that denial of free will would remove people's dignity, the notion of free will, because it holds the child to blame for sins, has been the cause of much misery.

DETERMINISM AND COMPASSION

Instead of blaming misdeeds on the perpetrator, one may blame them on the environment. In the United States, practices in our justice system have shifted dramatically in this direction. Pleas of temporary insanity and mitigating circumstances have become common. Criticism of capital punishment often hinges on the injustice of severely punishing someone who grew up in a disadvantageous environment. If one teenager kills another in a gang war, where should the blame be assigned? More and more, it is assigned to the availability of guns and drugs and to the absence of alternatives to gang membership.

The more we assign blame to the environment, the more we adopt the view opposite to free will, determinism. Since the more we assign blame to the environment, the more we seek alternatives to punishment, it is fair to say that determinism makes for compassion. To understand is not necessarily to condone, but the youngster who murders may be seen as a victim and treated as someone in need of help.

That recognizing the influence of environment makes for compassionate treatment of misbehavior has two sorts of implications for parental aggression. First, it suggests that caregivers who have been trained to look for environmental sources for misbehavior will be less inclined to punish by hitting and perhaps less inclined to hit at all. Training parents to see when a child is tired or under stress might go a long way toward discouraging parental aggression and replacing corporal punishment (not without training in alternative methods, however, a point to which we shall return).

Second, if we regard aggression toward children, whether or not intended as punishment, itself as misbehavior, we may seek for its environmental origins. If we understand why adults are likely to strike children, we may be able to take steps to prevent such striking. This would require new cultural practices that allow more intervention in families, particularly families in which the parents are at risk of engaging in aggression. If parents were trained in ways to avoid aggression, beginning before or soon after the birth of the first child, the incidence could be reduced. Such training would focus on the environmental origins of aggression. These may be understood in the light of the evolutionary history of our species.

EVOLUTIONARY PERSPECTIVE

Evolutionary sources for aggression may be separated into two sorts. First, our bodies are so constructed that some environmental circumstances tend to make us aggressive. Behavior analysts say these factors *induce* aggression and call their effects *induction* (Segal 1972). Second, the course of early development opens a child's nervous system to certain types of environmental influence, particularly from other humans, essential to the child's success of an adult (Hinde 1983; Petrovich and Gewirtz 1991). If these early experiences usually promote success, their genetic base is selected, but the openness of early development may be hazardous for a minority of the population, producing untoward effects that, like the beneficial ones, persist into adulthood. For example, viewing aggression on television may enhance aggressive tendencies in some people, but only the susceptible minority (Wilson and Herrnstein 1985).

Induction is something like mood. The idea is that some repeated environmental events make certain classes of behavior likely just by their repetition. A subset of such behavior, called *adjunctive* behavior, occurs when an important resource is finished, removed, or omitted when it usually would appear (Falk 1961, 1971, 1977). For example, if a creature is fed occasionally but predictably, a variety of activities become likely following each feeding or omission of feeding. Different species show different adjunctive behavior, but in some species it often takes the form of aggression.

The sorts of events known to induce aggression are: withdrawal or omission of resources and physical discomfort, particularly pain. If one pigeon is allowed to eat for several seconds periodically (for example, once per minute) in the presence of another pigeon, after a while each time the food is removed the one being fed will often attack the onlooker (Staddon 1977). If two rats are sitting peacefully in a cage together, delivery of just a few electric shocks suffices for one to attack the other (Azrin, Hutchinson, and Hake 1967). A monkey confined to a chair and given electric shocks to the tail will bite any object within reach, for example, a piece of hose or a rubber ball (Hutchinson 1977). Induced aggression varies from one individual to another and from one species to another. For example, aggression is rarely induced in rats by removing food, probably because rats rarely fight over food in their natural habitat.

Human beings appear to be susceptible to both sorts of induction (Kelly and Hake 1970; Hutchinson 1977). Medical personnel testify to the aggressiveness of people in pain. People also tend to become aggressive when some accustomed good is no longer forthcoming. When a vending machine fails to deliver, a likely response is to hit or kick the machine. A spouse withholding affection or a child withholding cooperation constitutes a situation in which a person may become aggressive. People vary a great deal in this regard; it takes remarkably little to induce aggression in some individuals, but almost everyone has limits beyond which aggression becomes probable (for example, threats to one's children). It may be modified by the training of one's culture, but the tendency always remains; it is the way our bodies are organized.

Parental aggression toward a child may be induced by the child's behavior, or the child may function only as the target for aggression induced by other pain or deprivation. If the parent is suffering from a headache or a hangover, or has lost job or spouse, the parent may "lash out" at the child. If the child causes the parent discomfort by loud noise or wild behavior, that may suffice to induce aggression. If the child impedes the parent's progress toward a goal (reinforcer), such as leaving a store and getting home, that may suffice to induce aggression. These instances when the child's behavior itself induces the aggression are most likely to be misidentified as corporal punishment. That the child's behavior induces the aggression is only incidental; as with lashing out, no punishment is intended and usually none is achieved.

From an evolutionary perspective, the genes that make for such induction must, on average, in the environment in which our species evolved, have made for higher reproductive success. Aggression under the right circumstances might lead to access to resources vital to health and survival or to opportunities to reproduce. It might increase fitness also when a child's welfare is threatened not only by a stranger but even by the child's own dangerous actions.

The tendency toward induced aggression might have been advantageous in the environment in which our species evolved, but today parental aggression toward children constitutes an unfortunate by-product. Its drawbacks may have been minor in comparison with the overall benefits to fitness, particularly if that environment included fewer factors that might induce aggression to-ward children (that is, less "stress"). Rapid change in our environment over the past five thousand years, having outstripped genetic evolution, may have bequeathed to us a frequency of aggression that would have been unaccept-able even five thousand years ago. On top of this, civilization also has devel-oped views and means (for example, methods of behavior modification) that render aggression even less appropriate now than five thousand years ago. If all this is so, and culture tends to evolve so as to preserve fitness, we should expect cultural practices to evolve that curb the tendency to aggression, par-ticularly toward children. This line of reasoning explains the existence of the present volume.

Induction of aggression, like most traits, is subject to individual variation. Variation in genetic disposition and in history of reinforcement for aggression probably accounts for a lot of the variance among parents, but some portion of the variance is explained also by early experience. Anyone might be driven to aggression, but people who were themselves hit as children may be par-ticularly prone. It is as if the early experience of being hit makes it seem appropriate, perhaps even loving, to hit one's own children. This possibility can be understood in the light of the way genes and environment interact during development.

When genes are selected that lead to structures in the nervous system that require environmental stimulation for further development, behavior is in a sense malleable, but only for a while; it may subsequently be extremely difficult to change. Early experience has powerful and lasting effects because even a small effect early in life changes the whole course of development for the rest of life — what may be called a "cascading" of effects. One cannot go back and change the course of development. If the effects are dysfunctional, for example, a heightened susceptibility to induced aggression, then the adult's behavior has to be retrained.

REINFORCEMENT

Research on aggression indicates that induced aggression is reinforcing. This is evidenced by an organism's willingness to engage in some action in order to have the opportunity for aggression. A pigeon will learn to peck at a button when the only result of its pecks is the opportunity to act aggressively toward another pigeon (Cherek, Thompson, and Heistad 1973). Monkeys will learn to pull a chain that lowers a ball to bite on (Azrin, Hutchinson, and McLaughlin 1965). Although ethical considerations prevent this sort of research with humans, much anecdotal evidence suggests that aggression can be rewarding. People report that aggression "feels good," and expressions like "letting off steam" and "venting frustration" also testify to this. For some people, aggression-inducing situations may render hitting a child immediately reinforcing.

Immediate reinforcement for parental aggression also comes from the child. If the child ceases yelling and becomes docile after being hit, the removal of an aversive state (yelling, intransigence, and so on) reinforces the parent's aggression. Seen this way, the parent's aggression functions like escape, as when covering one's ears is reinforced by reduction of a loud noise.

Such extrinsic reinforcement increases the frequency of the action that produces it. As parental aggression is reinforced by its effects on the child, it shifts from being purely induced to being operant behavior. Aggression that was initially induced, perhaps only rarely, becomes more and more probable as the history of reinforcement builds; it becomes the most likely, perhaps the only, response to the child's misbehavior.

The way to treat parental aggression, and the way to prevent it, is first to understand it as a problem in self-control. In the next section we try to characterize the problem with an eye to intervention.

Parental Aggression and Self-Control

CONTINGENCY TRAPS AND SELF-CONTROL

People call bad behavior irrational or maladaptive. The terms suggest an alternative that would be rational or adaptive. If squandering money is irrational, saving would be rational. If overeating is maladaptive, dieting would be adaptive. If hitting a child is irrational and maladaptive, using other means is rational and adaptive.

The alternatives are labeled this way because of their consequences. The ultimate consequence of squandering money is loss of long-term goods, such as the ability to make a down payment on a house. The ultimate consequence of overeating is long-term disaster, in the form of discomfort and illness. The ultimate consequences of parental aggression are of both types: long-term loss of control over the child's behavior and long-term disaster in the form of a fearful and angry child. The long-term nasty consequences lead to the labels of "irrational" and "maladaptive." People who have no problem saving, dieting, or using nonaggressive techniques with children look upon people who do have problems as behaving foolishly because they bring ruin upon themselves.

The problem, of course, is that eating, spending, and hitting tend to be rewarding in the short run. Were it not for the relatively immediate payoff, anyone could avoid improvidence, overeating, or aggression.

Figure 8.1 shows the effects of delay on effectiveness of consequences. Any reward's power over behavior decreases rapidly with short delays, then more slowly at longer delays. The value of an offer of $100 remains greater than the value of an offer of $10, so long as both are to be received immediately or after ten days. But the offer of $10 immediately may outshine the offer of $100 ten days from now. A larger reward, if delayed enough, is less effective than an immediate small reward. Therein lies the source of many sorrows.

When relatively immediate consequences conflict with long-term consequences, people say the situation calls for self-control. To behavior analysts, self-control means behaving according to long-term consequences. Its opposite, impulsiveness, means behaving according to short-term consequences (Baum 1994).

A person who behaves impulsively is caught in a contingency trap. A contingency trap is a combination of two choice alternatives, each with some contingent consequences. One way of behaving (impulsiveness; eating ice cream or hitting a child) produces minor but immediate (and hence potent) reinforcement, whereas the other way (self-control; dieting or using nonaggressive methods) leads to major but deferred (hence weak) reinforcement.

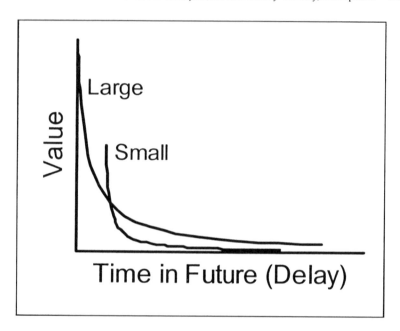

Fig. 8.1. The decrease in value or effectiveness of a consequence as it is delayed or removed into the future relative to present behavior. A small, relatively immediate reinforcer or punisher may be more effective than a large, relatively delayed reinforcer or punisher, although both decline rapidly with increasing delay. When both are delayed, the smaller consequence always has the smaller value.

Figure 8.2 diagrams a contingency trap (Baum 1994). Impulsive behavior, B_I, produces two sorts of consequences: relatively minor reinforcement (small S^R) at once or with a short delay (symbolized with a short arrow) and relatively major aversive consequences (symbolized by large S^P, for punisher, on the presumption that if the consequence were immediate, it would punish the impulsive behavior). Even though the ultimate consequences may be extremely aversive, the delay of perhaps months or years (long arrow) before their realization prevents them from punishing the impulsive behavior. The behavior identified as self-control, B_C, also produces two sorts of consequences: relatively minor punishment (small S^P) relatively immediately (short arrow) and relatively major desirable consequences, symbolized with large S^R on the presumption that they would reinforce self-control if they were not so delayed (long arrow).

Most of the challenges of our lives fit the paradigm in figure 8.2. Overeating is impulsiveness maintained by short-term oral reinforcement, but it would be punished if only the long-term discomfort could somehow be made equally

Choices:

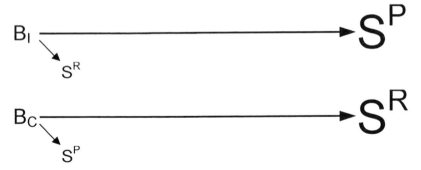

Fig. 8.2. A contingency trap. B_I and B_C denote impulsiveness and self-control, the two choices. S^R and S^P denote reinforcer and punisher, desirable and undesirable consequences. Short arrows indicate immediate consequences. Long arrows indicate long-term consequences.

immediate. Dieting constitutes self-control because it entails foregoing tasty delights (immediate punishment, S^P) and produces desirable results (large S^R) only after long delays. Once someone's behavior has fallen into a contingency trap like this, self-control remains improbable without some change in these contingencies. A parallel argument applies to impulsive aggression; there, too, self-control remains improbable without some sort of intervention.

PARENTAL AGGRESSION AS A CONTINGENCY TRAP

Parental aggression toward children is impulsive behavior, the result of a contingency trap. When an adult hits a child, the short-term results are rewarding to the adult; he or she "lets off steam," and the child immediately stops resisting or quiets down. The long-term results, however, will eventually be unwelcome. In general, the child will fear, resent, and avoid the adult and will ultimately achieve less success on growing up. The trouble is that these deleterious effects, because they are remote, may pall beside the immediate gratification of venting, compliance, or quietude.

Figure 8.3 diagrams corporal punishment as a contingency trap, in analogy to figure 8.2. The parent's alternatives are shown at the left; the impulsive behavior is labeled "Hitting," and the behavior constituting self-control is labeled "Noncorporal Means." Hitting produces immediate reinforcement (short arrow), both intrinsic (that is, "venting") and from the child's reaction (that is, "compliance" or quietude), but in the long run (long arrow) it leads to undesirable consequences in the child, such as fearing, avoiding, and resenting the parent. Noncorporal means achieve appropriate behavior on the part of

Choices:

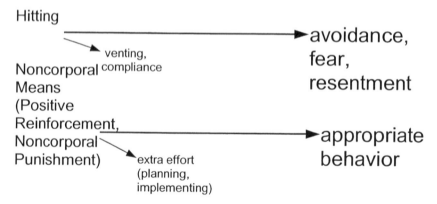

Fig. 8.3. Impulsive aggression as a contingency trap. Hitting, as impulsiveness, produces short-term reinforcement (venting and compliance) but leads to undesirable results (avoidance, fear, and resentment) in the long run. Noncorporal means (that is, positive reinforcement and noncorporal punishment) have the disadvantage that they require extra effort in the short run, but they lead to desirable results (appropriate behavior without avoidance, fear, or resentment) in the long run. Compare with figure 8.2.

the child in the long run without the adverse consequences but require extra effort, a punisher, in the short run. This short-term punishment may constitute one of the biggest obstacles to using noncorporal methods, because positive reinforcement and noncorporal punishment may require the parent to go to some trouble, depending on the magnitude of the problem presented by the child. For the normal range of behavioral problems, parents can rely on handy reinforcers, like smiles, hugs, and praise, and handy noncorporal punishers, like frowns and moderate disapproval, and even these sometimes require patience for the parent to implement them; for severe behavioral problems, much more planning and effort may be required. Shaping appropriate behavior in a child with a developmental disability or a child growing up surrounded by crime and drugs is likely to take special training.

Although not all parents fall into it, the contingency trap shown in figure 8.3 is a part of every parent's world. The temptation to aggression is ever present in the form of induction by discomfort and thwarted reinforcement. Once hitting has occurred and been reinforced, it increases in frequency and becomes established; the parent has fallen into the contingency trap. Seen this way, the problem of rejecting corporal discipline becomes the problem of avoiding or, having succumbed to it, escaping from the contingency trap shown in figure 8.3.

SOLUTIONS TO CONTINGENCY TRAPS

Everyone has to contend with some contingency traps, because no one is perfect. Anyone who has a bad habit or wishes to cultivate a good habit is dealing with a contingency trap. Different people fall into different contingency traps, because each person has a unique history of reinforcement and because a powerful reinforcer for one person's behavior may be weak for another's, but everyone falls into some contingency traps.

Broadly speaking, two types of solution apply to the problem of encouraging self-control: (1) commitment and (2) added social contingencies, which we shall discuss in connection with rules and education.

COMMITMENT

Commitment focuses particularly on the choice between impulsiveness and self-control. It consists of acting in advance of the choice situation to render impulsiveness impossible — that is, to prevent the choice from even arising. Someone who might be tempted to turn off an alarm clock and remain in bed when it is important to get out of bed engages in commitment by placing the alarm clock across the room. Someone who tends to squander money engages in commitment by joining a payroll-deduction savings plan. Requiring car manufacturers to conform to emissions standards is a commitment strategy in that it prevents air pollution by making it impossible for motorists to pollute.

The possibilities for promoting self-control by commitment are often limited. Many contingency traps offer no possibility to remove the impulsive alternative. What strategy should be used to help someone be more assertive with members of the opposite sex? How might a government increase the use of public transportation? Parental aggression falls into this category. Commitment would require making hitting somehow physically impossible, and this generally cannot be done.

As an alternative to commitment, we turn to added social contingencies. In the terms of figure 8.2, we add small immediate consequences, reinforcers for self-control or punishers for impulsiveness. This occurs when other people, such as therapists, teachers, and government officials, get involved in helping someone to make the right choice. These helpers offer approval, disapproval, and token reinforcers and punishers, trying to modify their subjects' behavior (that is, to "educate" them), and they typically rely on exhortations like "Just say no."

RULES AND "EDUCATION"

The behavior-analytic use of the word *rule* differs from everyday use of it. It includes everyday usage, but is more general. A rule is a verbal discriminative stimulus that is occasioned by a long-term contingency (Baum 1995). It could be a statement like "You shouldn't smoke; it will kill you one of these days" or a sign on the wall saying, "Thank you for not smoking." The long-term contingency that occasions speaking out or hanging the sign is the relation between breathing smoke and poor health.

The rule itself, however, is part of a socially arranged short-term contingency. The statement or sign about smoking indicates that smoking here will result in disapproval and possibly unpleasantness or even a fine.

The rule signals a short-term social contingency that encourages or discourages the same behavior that enters into the long-term contingency (Baum 1995). The long-term contingency between smoking and poor health may fail to affect behavior by itself, but the added social contingency between smoking and disapproval, combined with the overt rule, because of its relative immediacy, may do the job.

"Education" about contingency traps consists of practice with rules and short-term social contingencies. Children in drug-awareness programs hear as much or more about the social unacceptability of taking drugs as about the likely bad long-term consequences. Even if it is occasioned by the relation that taking drugs will result in poor health and loss of social status in the long run, "Just say no" signifies that saying no will result in approval and saying yes in disapproval in the short run.

In such education, modeling and role-playing should be more helpful than exhortation by itself. When children see other children saying no to offers of drugs and they say no themselves in classroom simulations, they get to practice the behavior that the education program seeks to strengthen. Behavior therapists get clients to practice adaptive behavior like assertiveness with the aim of increasing its likelihood outside the therapy situation; the greater the similarity of the simulation to the real situation, the better. The strengthening effects of practice may be the key to understanding the power of so-called covert reinforcement, in which a client repeatedly imagines engaging in the desired behavior with pleasant consequences (Cautela, personal communication).

Such training results not only in the strengthening of specific desirable acts of self-control but also in the establishment of whole patterns of behavior that encompass various forms of self-control and preclude various forms of impulsiveness (Rachlin 1995). The person who has incorporated dieting as a pattern not only turns down a second dessert but also chooses low-fat entrées and requests salad dressing to be "on the side." The person who has incorporated noncorporal means as a parenting pattern also engages in a variety of behaviors, all of which provide consequences for the child's behavior while also excluding both corporal discipline and impulsive aggression.

Like any contingency trap, the tendency to parental aggression can be lessened by added social contingencies combined with rules, particularly if these are practiced. Parents who are susceptible could be educated, very much as children are educated about drugs or therapy clients about assertiveness. They might benefit particularly from simulations in which the temptation is presented but the parent withholds aggression and substitutes other means. The comparison to assertiveness is particularly instructive, because assertiveness is the desired alternative to an undesirable behavior pattern, such as passivity. The desirable alternative to corporal discipline, the "other means" to be encouraged by education, is the use of positive reinforcement and noncorporal punishment to shape children's behavior. We turn now to noncorporal techniques.

The Power of Reinforcement

Reinforcement refers to an increase in the frequency of some behavior as a result of either the occurrence of a pleasant event following that behavior or the termination of an unpleasant event following that behavior. The behavior-consequence dependency that reinforces the behavior is called a reinforcement *contingency.*

The power of reinforcement lies in three features. First, reinforcement contingencies maintain large amounts of behavior relative to the number of reinforcers. Initial training requires frequent reinforcers, but, once established, reinforced behavior remains robust with just occasional reinforcers. Second, reinforcement not only strengthens the specific behavior reinforced but also increases the frequency of related behavior that is desirable and, therefore, also worthy of reinforcement. For example, if a parent rewards his child for sharing her cookie, the child may begin sharing toys with her playmates. Third, positive reinforcement produces side effects in the form of positive emotions. The excitement of children when receiving praise or a pleasant surprise attests to the power of reinforcement as a preferred method for management of behavior.

The behavioral approach to child rearing and education stresses the management of individuals' behavior by arranging contingencies of reinforcement and, when necessary, noncorporal punishment. Throughout their development, children require frequent feedback on their progress. They need to be praised for appropriate behavior, and, just as important, they need to be guided toward alternatives to inappropriate behavior, alternatives for coping with unpleasant occurrences in their environment. For example, if a toy is removed from a child, the response given by natural selection (that is, induced by removal of an accustomed good) is to grab the toy back, perhaps hit, kick, or bite, or perhaps to cry vigorously and fall to the ground. These responses are deemed unacceptable by society and, in addition, cannot guarantee the desired outcome, recovery of the toy. Parenting should include teaching desirable behavior that is an alternative to behavior given us by the evolutionary history of our species.

BEING GOOD VERSUS BEHAVING WELL

Children are not born "good" or "bad." Nor are children born good and then "choose" to be bad. Such conceptions confuse the *child* with the *behavior*. Failure to separate the behavior from the child renders parents less effective in managing the child's behavior. If behavior is assumed to emanate from within the child, then bad behavior is blamed on something in the child, and remedial efforts aim at "fixing the child." This is exactly the sort of view that has maintained overreliance on the use of corporal discipline and has encouraged both conventional corporal discipline and impulsive aggression toward children. Even if the child's physiology were readily accessible (and it is not!), the lack of knowledge of what to "fix" renders this approach to child rearing and education ineffective. A child's behavior results from genetic dispositions modified by current environmental arrangements and individual learning history, of which parents and other caretakers are a part. Children may be predisposed to have tantrums in the sense that any child will cry if hurt or frustrated, but the child that has a tantrum whenever denied a treat reflects a history in which parents or other caretakers reinforced having tantrums. The behavioral approach stresses seeking solutions by environmental arrangements.

Children *are* born different from each other, however. No matter how much humans share by virtue of a common phylogeny, natural selection depends on individual variation, and individual variation remains a feature of any species. From an evolutionary perspective, individual variation is both necessary and good. Children will engage in a variety of behaviors with varying intensities or frequencies and will require varying degrees of imposed societal intervention to shape their behavior. Children differ with respect to their general level of activity, the amount of time they are able to remain working on a task, their general responsiveness to environmental events, such as distractions, novel situations, reinforcers, and punishers, the extent to which they are able to control their own behavior, how quickly their behavior falls into routine patterns, and probably many other dimensions. It is a mistake to try to gloss over such differences by classifying them or grouping them into "syndromes" or "disorders." Rather, the individual differences point to an important societal change needed in our culture, an acceptance and appreciation of individual variation that will lead to an individualized approach to parenting and educating children.

In the behavioral approach, we first specify our goals, the behavior we consider desirable, and then consider various teaching strategies to help children master these skills. Rather than classify children according to what is "right" and "wrong" with them, a more useful classification system is based on different teaching and management strategies. Such an approach avoids value statements about children's learning differences that often cause embarrassment for the child and guilt for the parents.

This emphasis on individual variation in no way denies the importance of similarities across children at a more general level. Basic research on behavior has revealed some general principles that apply in a great many situations. For example, we know that behavior is affected by its consequences. If something pleasant follows an action, that action is more likely to occur again. If something unpleasant follows, the action is less likely to occur again. Previously neutral environmental events, such as the word *no,* occurring at the same time the parent is frowning or removing a toy from the child will eventually gain similar control over the child's behavior as the frown or the removal. Other environmental events, in the presence of which consequences follow behavior, become *discriminative stimuli,* or cues, and control the future likelihood of the behavior. For example, if a child is given a bath every day after dinner, completion of dinner will signal time for a bath. If the child likes baths, the bathing will occur right after dinner with no problems. If the child dislikes baths, we should expect some dawdling toward the end of dinner and perhaps some acting up after dinner every day. Once the relationship between the completion of dinner, acting up, and baths is understood, a parent can alleviate the problem in a number of ways, such as making the bath more reinforcing, scheduling a fun transition activity from dinner to bath, or scheduling a highly reinforcing activity routinely only after baths.

Basic research has shown that individuals allocate time and effort to different activities as a function of the frequency and amount of reinforcement associated with those activities (Baum 1973; Baum and Rachlin 1969; Herrnstein 1970). These data indicate that differences in the rewarding values of the different activities in which a child engages will lead to differences in likelihood of engaging in those activities. For example, watching television might be a highly rewarding activity. A child might comply immediately and raise no fuss when told to go and watch television. Toothbrushing, however, might be a relatively unrewarding activity. We should expect avoidance behavior in response to a parent's request for toothbrushing. The problem is further exacerbated if we request toothbrushing when the child is watching television. In the behavioral perspective, the child's lack of response to the instruction "go and brush your teeth," far from being attributed to uncooperativeness or considered bad, is considered an expected outcome (Hineline 1984). Adults behave similarly if told to perform an undesirable activity while engaged in a highly desirable one. Knowledge of these and other experimentally derived principles paves the way for positive methods of child rearing and education.

The task at hand is teaching children to "behave well," to behave optimally within acceptable societal norms. Stating the goal this way focuses attention on what constitute "acceptable societal norms" and "optimal behavior," and not on the child's physiology or soul. The goal of parenting then becomes to shape behavior and bring it under proper environmental control, not only with respect to short-term consequences but also with respect to long-term consequences. An extensive technology exists for meeting such behavioral goals. Once parents are educated in this technology and have a general understanding of child development and the norms of the culture, they are in a position to teach their children to behave optimally in their environment without using conventional corporal discipline or succumbing to impulsive aggression.

Unfortunately, at present society prepares parents badly for this difficult task. Parents are left to their "instincts," often with disastrous effects. What children need to know and how children need to behave to be effective in this culture has changed greatly in the past few decades and will continue to change in the decades to come as the environment changes. Our notions about "good" and "bad" become subtler as our understanding of human behavior improves and technology advances. There is perhaps no better time and perhaps there was never a greater need for a major cultural change in our approach to child rearing than now.

TEACHING CHILDREN TO BEHAVE WELL

When a child is punished for "behaving badly," it is left up to the child to discover how to behave well (Skinner 1971). The absence of positive guidance illustrates the erroneous belief that children are born with or developmentally acquire knowledge of what is appropriate and only need to be discouraged from bad behavior (typically by punishment) or wait to mature in order to engage in appropriate behavior. Nothing could be further from fact. All behavior produces some kind of effect on the environment. Individuals vary greatly in their sensitivity to the effects of their behavior, but learning cannot occur without a consistent interplay between behavior and environment. Parents, therefore, need to structure a child's environment to give the consistency needed to shape desirable behavior. What follows is a short catalogue of basic preventative strategies, based on general reinforcement principles, for decreasing undesirable behavior. They might be thought of as skills or parental actions that should help parents to avoid contingency traps. Prior to all of these, of course, should be recognition that child rearing is an important and time-consuming job.

VIEWING EACH CHILD AS AN INDIVIDUAL

The importance of accepting a child as a unique individual cannot be overemphasized. Parents need to learn to appreciate their child's individual behavioral characteristics. Just as parents delight in knowing the color of their child's hair and eyes or which relatives their child resembles physically, so parents need to delight similarly in discovering their child's characteristic activity levels, responsiveness to environmental events, such as sounds, colors, shapes, and textures, responsiveness to other people, general likes and dislikes, and predominant learning style. These characteristics should direct parents to the particular procedures needed to teach and manage their child without engendering alarm or anger. The child's behavior may respond well to natural and inconspicuous contingencies in one area (for example, athletics) and might require repeated exposure to more salient contingencies in another area (for example, reading). This should not be seen as dysfunction, only as individual variation.

Knowing their child's behavioral tendencies allows parents to predict the environmental conditions that give rise to unacceptable behavior, particularly by identifying antecedents and behavior that presages real trouble. Parents can then prevent the unacceptable behavior by manipulating the antecedents or avoiding a potentially troublesome situation.

Figure 8.3 illustrates that such parental care incurs a short-term cost in time and effort. Research needs to be done on the extent to which this cost contributes to parental impulsive aggression. Experiments with pigeons reveal that one pigeon attacks another pigeon more often under schedules of reinforcement that require a large number of responses than under less costly schedules (Sicignano-Kupfer 1981). If both parents are working or there is only one parent in the home, the added response cost (removal of reinforcers as a consequence of inappropriate behavior) of child rearing may seem overwhelming. The willingness of parents to incur the response cost entailed in individualized approaches to child rearing will determine its success. Parents need to be taught to accept the response cost for the sake of long-term benefits of generating appropriate behavior and preventing undesirable behavior from arising in the first place.

ESTABLISHING STRUCTURE AND DELINEATING BOUNDARIES

Establishing structure means clearly delineating boundaries—that is, clearly delineating which behavior is considered acceptable and the situations in which it is expected, which behavior is considered unacceptable, and consequences for both. Although most parents engage in this practice to some extent, all parents should be taught to do it explicitly, even establishing structure in the form of written rules, if necessary. Written rules ensure consistency across time and across parents. The child's ability to retain the rules determines whether they need to be publicly posted and how often they need to be reviewed with the child (Samalin and Hogarty 1994). Such codification may be one of the best ways to prevent impulsive aggression, because it prepares the parent as well as the child; no one is surprised; tendencies to emotion (adjunctive behavior) are mitigated.

Parents might also be taught to provide structure by establishing daily routines, such as a fixed sequence of events during shopping or at bedtime (for example, Ferber 1985). The routines specify the allowable activities during a specific period of time, the duration of which depends on the amount of time the parent has to devote. As always, rules about violations of the routine need to be clarified, consistently implemented, and, for the sake of clarity and consistency, written down.

By referring to the rules during occurrences of unacceptable behavior, parents reduce tension in parent-child disagreements and confrontations, because the parent stands apart from both the stated requirement and the upcoming consequence. This method reduces the overall aversiveness of the interaction for the parent, thereby decreasing the probability of impulsive aggression.

Rules should take the form of positive guidance statements that remind a child of what behavior is correct, instead of pointing to what the child is doing wrong. For example, rather than saying "Don't slam doors" if a child slams a door, the parent says, "Remember to close doors gently." This may be combined with having the child repeat or practice the correct behavior.

USING REINFORCERS EFFECTIVELY

Parents often have difficulty selecting reinforcers and delivering them properly (Hall and Hall 1980). They need to be trained first of all to identify reinforcers appropriate for their child. What is reinforcing for one child may not be for another. Further, what may be reinforcing in one context may not be reinforcing in another. For these reasons, a child's preferences are usually the best guide to picking reinforcers. Parents should include the child in the selection process whenever possible and frequently present options from which the child can choose. For example, parent and child may visit a toy store solely for the purpose of identifying various reinforcers.

Another aspect to this skill is selecting the correct magnitude of a reinforcer relative to the behavior required. The magnitude should correlate with the amount of behavior or effort required from the child. Errors may occur in both directions, too much of a reinforcer for too little behavior or too little of a reinforcer for too much behavior. Either mistake deters efforts to increase future occurrence of the behavior.

Parents need training particularly in delivering reinforcers contingent upon the behavior to be maintained. Parents sometimes deliver reinforcers for the absence of undesirable behavior or without regard to the child's behavior at all (for example, to make up for a child's loss of something nice). Neither will increase the desired behavior. It is essential to teach the correct behavior explicitly.

Each reinforcer should be delivered as immediately as possible following the desired behavior. The longer the delay between behavior and reinforcer, the less likely the behavior will be maintained. The parent's verbal behavior helps to bridge the gap, and the older the child the less bridging may be required (Baum 1995).

Other aspects of this skill concern how often to deliver reinforcers and ensuring that reinforcers vary. In the early stages of training, reinforcers need to be delivered frequently, and if one loses effectiveness another needs to be substituted. Once desirable behavior is established, it can be maintained by less frequent reinforcement. After an activity has been reinforced for a period of time, engaging in that activity (for example, solving math problems) may itself become reinforcing. The child may take satisfaction in a job well done without the need for conspicuous reinforcers. Such transitions may result from shifts of reinforcers, for example, from material reinforcers, such as food, clothes, and toys, to social reinforcers, such as approval, recognition, privileges, and social activities.

Left to their own devices, parents cannot be expected to learn how to use reinforcers effectively, but there is nothing abstruse or magical about the skill. Parents could readily be trained to be effective in this way with their children.

CONSISTENCY

Perhaps the most important aspect of behavior management is consistency. Intermittent reinforcement causes behavior to persist. This is fine for behavior we want to maintain but disastrous for behavior we wish to eliminate. Parents often fail to realize how they inadvertently maintain undesirable behavior by reinforcing it intermittently. As with the other skills we have discussed, consistency is trainable, and any course in behavioral management would emphasize the power of consistency as a deterrent to impulsive aggression.

TREATING INAPPROPRIATE BEHAVIOR WITH REINFORCEMENT

Although the strategies mentioned so far tend to minimize undesirable behavior, they cannot prevent it from occurring and cannot be relied on to eliminate it. Children exhibit predisposed behavior that is socially unacceptable at every stage of development. Parents need to know that these undesirable actions are to be expected, that they will persist until acceptable alternatives are taught, and that their own initial responses to the children's behavior determine future occurrences. The following are some basic interventions for eliminating inappropriate behavior that is not considered life threatening without the use of punishment (for example, La Vigna and Donnellan 1986; Meyer and Evans 1989).

DIFFERENTIAL REINFORCEMENT AND IGNORING

Training parents to reinforce behavior differentially, by attending to appropriate behavior and ignoring inappropriate behavior, is a first step in training parents to deal effectively with undesirable behavior. Although the concept might seem obvious, consistent application requires skill. The earlier discussion of effective reinforcement implied the importance of simultaneously reinforcing desirable behavior by looking at, touching, and expressing approval contingent upon that behavior while extinguishing undesirable behavior by carefully omitting any such reinforcement for it.

Maximizing the effectiveness of differential reinforcement, however, requires careful specification of both the behavior to be strengthened and the behavior to be eliminated. This becomes important, for example, when the parent wishes to eliminate undesirable behavior by reinforcing some appropriate behavior that is incompatible with the undesirable behavior. This is technically known as differential reinforcement of incompatible or alternative behavior (DRI or DRA). For example, if parents wish to eliminate "whining," they must first be clear as to what constitutes a "whiny" tone of voice and what is an acceptable tone. For DRI to work, the two need to be specified in such a way that they cannot occur at the same time; then reinforcers need to be delivered only when the child speaks in an acceptable tone of voice.

Two other differential reinforcement schedules are differential reinforcement of other behavior (DRO) and differential reinforcement of low rates (DRL). DRO schedules are widely used for eliminating undesirable behavior because they are easy to implement. An undesirable behavior is specified, and then a reinforcer is delivered periodically contingent on the nonoccurrence of the specified behavior. Although DRO schedules usually reduce undesirable behavior, they have the drawback that they teach no alternative behavior. DRL schedules are effective for dealing with behavior that is acceptable at a low rate but unacceptable if it occurs too frequently. For example, when traveling with a child on a long trip, a parent may accept the child's asking occasionally, "How long till we get there?" Only when the question repeats every few minutes does it become undesirable. A DRL schedule specifies a minimum interval that must elapse between occurrences; early occurrences go unreinforced. A timer can be used to help the child wait out the interval. The length of the interval is increased gradually, and eventually the timer can be omitted.

Extinction refers to the procedure of omitting any reinforcement for some specific behavior. The parent who elects to extinguish by ignoring some behavior, however, must be prepared to persevere. Otherwise, the ignoring will not only fail to reduce the undesirable behavior but may even produce something worse. The reason for this cautionary note is that when extinction begins, the undesirable behavior typically intensifies at first. During this initial increase, the child may not only engage in the familiar undesirable behavior more often but also exhibit new undesirable behavior, such as aggression. Such escalation represents "emotional" behavior or, as described earlier, adjunctive behavior, which is induced by omission of reinforcement in many species, including our own. The method backfires if the parent interprets this increase in undesirable behavior to mean that ignoring is failing and gives up. The parent may then end up providing attention to more severe forms of inappropriate behavior than before (for example, aggression), thereby having made the overall situation worse. Many failures of behavioral management can be traced to this sort of unintentional reinforcement of escalation.

If parents are to be trained to ignore undesirable behavior, they need to be taught to expect and persist through the period of escalation, waiting for the decrease that will eventually follow. Parents can be trained in specific strategies (for example, looking away or leaving the room) to cope with an initial increase in, for example, tantrums (Hall and Hall 1980). Of course, the parent must ensure the safety of the child. Ignoring should be used only with behavior that is ignorable. Dangerous or highly intrusive behavior, such as aggression or property destruction, cannot be treated by ignoring.

The Use of Punishment

Grouping corporal discipline and impulsive aggression together with corporal punishment has given punishment a bad name. Failing to draw these distinctions leads to the position that punishment is unacceptable in any form (for example, Sidman 1989; LaVigna and Donnellan 1986). When we separate corporal discipline and impulsive aggression from punishment, it becomes possible to distinguish corporal from noncorporal punishment. As with positive reinforcement, noncorporal punishment, when applied consistently, reduces unwanted behavior and may be socially acceptable. Corporal punishment, in contrast, is generally unacceptable, except in certain special circumstances.

Noncorporal Punishment

REPRIMANDS

Although caregivers often use expressions of disapproval, verbal or otherwise, to try to decrease behavior, such reprimands are of limited utility unless they are consistent, immediate, brief, delivered in close proximity to the child, and paired with other behavior-decreasing procedures (Van Houten 1980). Even when all of these factors apply, however, reprimands may still be ineffective (Pfiffner and Barkley 1990; Rosen, O'Leary, Joyce, Conway, and Pfiffner 1984). They are persistent only because they require so little effort, but persistent reprimands may actually engender more inappropriate behavior when they turn into nagging and scolding. These not only serve as inappropriate models for a child's verbal behavior but, if they are aversive enough, may also engender impulsive aggression in the child. Used sparingly, however, reprimands may be effective punishers.

RESPONSE COST

More effective than reprimands is response cost, which refers to the removal of reinforcers as a consequence of inappropriate behavior (Kazdin 1972). Reinforcers, such as privileges or allowance, are removed in specific amounts and for specific duration. The effectiveness of response cost depends on the efficacy of the reinforcers. If a child throws a toy at a sibling, an initial consequence might be to remove the toy for a specific period of time. Once the child is engaging in appropriate behavior, the toy can be returned. If the toy is not a potent reinforcer, the child will simply pick up another toy and throw it.

When response-cost procedures fail, it is usually because their implementation was inconsistent. Parents and other caretakers require training with procedures like response cost because consistency is a skill. When response cost is applied very soon after undesirable behavior and is applied every time the undesirable behavior occurs, it will usually be effective. When behavior seems uncontrollable, the reason lies less in the complexity of the behavior than in an inconsistent and changing environment.

TIME-OUT

Since its initial demonstration (Wolf, Risley, and Mees 1964), time-out from positive reinforcement has proven an effective technique for eliminating undesirable behavior. Time-out resembles response cost in that it entails removal of reinforcement contingent on inappropriate behavior, but it differs from response cost in that all reinforcers are removed instead of a certain amount of a specific reinforcer. Time-out also means a distinctive stimulus situation — a place or other distinctive cue that defines the time-out. Variants of time-out include nonexclusionary time-out, such as having the child remain in place while removing materials, removing social attention by moving others away from the child, and exclusionary time-out, which is moving the child to another place without reinforcers, possibly while allowing the child to observe others behaving appropriately. Once time-out has begun, release from time-out requires fulfillment of a specific criterion, usually being quiet and cooperative for a specific period of time. It is essential that time-out be implemented with minimal attention from the caregiver.

Time-out procedures work best to decrease inappropriate behavior that is maintained by attention or positive reinforcement. Time-out fails, however, when the goal of the undesirable behavior is escape from what the child is being asked to do or if the child generally seeks to be alone in the first place. In such situations, use of time-out may actually increase the frequency of undesirable behavior. Sending a child to another room will work as a time-out only if the environment the child is leaving is more reinforcing than the other room.

Is Corporal Punishment Ever Necessary?

The answer to the question of whether corporal punishment is ever necessary is yes, under certain extreme circumstances. The amount of training necessary to make this decision will never be attained within the general culture, by parents and other general caretakers. Several years of formal training coupled with extensive practical experience are required. Just as surgery may be performed only by trained specialists, so the use of corporal punishment should occur only under the supervision of trained specialists. Specifying the training and experiential requirements is the responsibility of state- and academic-accreditation bodies.

METHOD OF LAST RESORT

Corporal punishment as defined here refers to the planned and systematic presentation of stimuli, such as slaps, that impinge directly on the sensory receptors of the individual, that are contingent upon each occurrence of undesirable behavior, and that produce a decrease in the future probability of that behavior. In general, corporal punishment should be reserved for dangerous and potentially injurious behavior and only after other procedures have failed to produce clinical results (Lovaas and Favell 1987). The ongoing debate over use of corporal punishment in clinical settings stems more from concern over moral and ethical issues than from any question over the effectiveness of the procedures. Confusion arises when punishment is defined in personal or subjective terms, blurring the distinctions we have tried to make here.

Quick reduction of injurious behavior prevents harm to the child and others and allows more time spent on teaching appropriate behavior. Head banging or eye gouging, for example, or other severe aggression toward others or toward property cannot be ignored. Physical or chemical restraint may seem to be required, but the child learns nothing from them. In these situations, it may be appropriate to rely on our innate disposition for certain aversive stimuli to decrease any behavior that produces them. Natural selection has ensured the rarity of such inappropriate behavior as jumping from high places or placing a hand on a hot stove with minimal intervention from others. There is nothing particularly social about physical discomfort or pain; as consequences, they are usually mediated by the functioning of our bodies. When used in the extreme situations that call for corporal punishment, the less these stimuli are associated with caregivers the better.

When used properly, corporal punishment produces lasting success. Matson and Taras (1988) reviewed 382 studies, over a twenty-year time span, involving the use of corporal punishment on individuals with developmental disabilities. They concluded that the use of corporal punishment was not only more effective in reducing inappropriate behavior but also resulted in reductions that lasted. Lovaas (1987) reported fifteen-year follow-up data on nineteen autistic children who had received a program that included slaps for inappropriate behavior. Nine children had achieved normal educational functioning, eight were able to function in classes for mildly mentally handicapped individuals, and only two remained seriously handicapped. Treatments without corporal punishment have yet to demonstrate any such long-term success.

In a position paper on the use of behavior-reduction strategies with children who have behavioral disorders, the Council for Children with Behavioral Disorders (1990) endorsed "the right of qualified educators and other professionals to employ appropriate behavior reduction procedures when such methods are undertaken with suitable planning and adherence to the guidelines offered" (1990: 255). Trying to avoid the subjectivity and strong emotional reactions generated by the terms *punishment* and *aversive control*, the council made a distinction between corporal punishment and behavior-reduction strategies. They defined corporal punishment as a procedure "which is used as a general measure to discipline youngsters" (1990: 250). They considered behavior-reduction procedures to refer "to a continuum of strategies employed by practitioners to decelerate the rate or probability of behavior that is judged inappropriate in a particular situation" (1990: 245). Although we agree that a distinction must be made between the layperson's definition of corporal punishment and the scientific and clinical definition, we doubt that substituting a new term, such as behavior reduction, is helpful. If we want to eliminate hitting as a parenting practice from our culture, we need to define the term correctly and then indicate in as many ways as possible that it is no longer an acceptable parenting practice and is to be used only under the guidance of trained professionals (for example, Sulzer-Azaroff and Reese 1982).

There is no question that corporal punishment is effective and necessary in these exceptional circumstances, but this would in no way justify corporal punishment in more usual circumstances. Therefore we, as a society, need to seek ways to eliminate conventional corporal discipline and any possible excuse for impulsive aggression.

Summary

First and foremost, society needs to approach child rearing and education with a preventive model. Many behavior modification and therapy approaches exist for the treatment of children's deviant behavior (for example, Patterson and Reid 1970; Stuart 1971; Burchard and Harig 1976; Lovaas and Newsom 1976; Wahler 1976; Barkley 1990). To prevent parents' inappropriate behavior in response to their children's deviant behavior, however, requires education for parents and children in the general understanding of behavior, the role of evolutionary history in dispositions to undesirable behavior, and the role of culture in specifying what we consider correct behavior and acceptable rearing practices.

The chapters in this book exemplify one way to support the efforts of professionals and parents who are working to generate nonaversive treatments for undesirable behavior. Since some of these programs will be more effective than others, they must all be carefully evaluated. This means putting aside personal beliefs and theories, specifying procedures clearly, and measuring outcomes. Evaluation should be based on data.

Our culture is in the midst of a restructuring of practices connected with child rearing. Current views of such matters as corporal punishment, causes of children's behavior, and the role of an inner self in the control of behavior are being challenged, clarified, and reframed. To move away from corporal discipline, there must be changes in our basic beliefs about the control of human behavior—a shift, for example, from control by an inner agent to control by the environment. This sounds like a tall order, but it has probably already begun.

We have given examples of some preventive strategies that minimize the frequency of undesirable behavior and some strategies for dealing with established undesirable behavior, all of which exist as alternatives to conventional corporal discipline and impulsive aggression. The examples are not exhaustive; there are many other techniques and many variations of the ones mentioned. As our new patterns of parenting and child rearing develop, such skills will be essential in the twenty-first century.

9

Spare the Rod and Spoil the Child
Lay Theories of Corporal Punishment

ADRIAN FURNHAM

How many children have acquired a bad habit as a result of having it attributed to them!
— *Michael Burn*

The irritating thing about badly behaved children is that they so often make as orderly and valuable men and women as the other kind.
— *Mark Twain*

Before I married I had six theories about bringing up children, but no children; now I have 6 children and no theories
— *Anon.*

The refined punishments of the spiritual mode are usually much more indecent and dangerous than a good smack.
— *D. H. Lawrence*

In nature there are no rewards or punishments; there are consequences.
— *H. Vachell*

My object all sublime
I shall achieve in time —

To let the punishment fit the crime —
The punishment fit the crime.
— Gilbert and Sullivan

The object of punishment is prevention from evil; it never can be made
compulsive to good.
— H. Mann

He who truly loves will chastise well.
— French proverb

Lay Theories

Over the past decade there has been a considerable research effort aimed at understanding ordinary, lay, or folk theories of human behaviour. Furnham (1988) examined lay theories of issues from the separate disciplines of psychology, psychiatry, medicine, economics, statistics, law, and education.

Many issues determine the quality, quantity, range, and diversity of lay theories on any particular issue, which in turn influences the extent of research into the topic. Thus, while there exists evidence for a number of interesting lay theories for the cause of schizophrenia (Furnham and Rees 1988; Furnham and Bower 1992), the fact that relatively few people have personal contact with schizophrenia means that their beliefs, ideas, and theories are largely derived from popular media accounts of schizophrenics. On the other hand, because everybody experiences periods of ill health there has been considerable research into this topic, which has revealed both the complexity and power of lay theories (Helman 1984; Vincent and Furnham 1994).

This chapter is concerned with lay theories of corporal punishment. Despite the fact that the issue of such things as the efficacy of punishment and the morality of corporal punishment in particular have been discussed and debated by lay people for centuries, there remains relatively little research on their lay theories. There may be a number of reasons for this surprising paucity of research literature. The first is that the topic is highly political, with both experts and lay people being influenced as much by sociopolitical values as by disinterested evidence. This is often not the best atmosphere in which to conduct research. Second, it appears that neither experts nor lay people have sophisticated or complex specific theories as to why corporal punishment should or should not be implemented. On the other hand, there are many polls and surveys that simply look at attitudes per se rather than the nature, structure, and function of lay theories of punishment.

The study of lay theories is interesting because it enables social scientists to compare and contrast lay theories with scientific theories. But the study of lay theories is also important because they are, in part, predictors of behavior. Thus, presumably, if one holds a theory that corporal punishment discourages "naughtiness" and installs "self-discipline," it would be advocated by the holder of the theory, whether parent, teacher, or psychologist. It has been argued and demonstrated that lay theories or belief systems serve psychological functions.

Much of cognitive social psychology is concerned with how people make sense of the social world. That is, various belief systems (locus of control, just world) are said to serve to make the world a stable, orderly, and predictable place. The function of these beliefs is probably to establish a cause-and-effect relationship between phenomena that in turn enables one to apportion blame, praise, or responsibility. For instance, Lerner (1980) argues that just-world beliefs are functional and essential; in fact, they are ways of adapting to a world in which one feels relatively helpless by attributing absolute virtue to the legal system. He notes:

> Much of the previous discussion portrays the "belief in a just world" as inextricably bound up with the person's motives and goals. People want to and have to believe they live in a just world so that they can go about their daily lives with a sense of trust, hope and confidence in their future. If it is true that people want or need to believe that they live in a world where people get what they deserve, then it is not surprising that they will find ways, other things being equal, to interpret events to fit this belief. (1980: 14)

Similarly, Gans (1972) has proposed a functional analysis of poverty which implies that the existence of, and explanations for, poverty fulfill a number of important functions. For instance, the poor may be labeled and punished as deviants in order to uphold the legitimacy of dominant social norms. Also, poverty helps to guarantee the status of the nonpoor, in that they remain a relatively permanent measuring rod for status comparison.

More important, lay beliefs in part reflect and drive social behavior. Lay beliefs — like attitudes and explanations — do have consequences for the development of other beliefs and for behavior. Central to a great deal of the early psychological work on attitudes is the concept of balance. Balance, congruity, and dissonance each assume that people are motivated to be, and to appear, consistent, while an awareness of imbalance or inconsistency is tension producing and not easily tolerated, so that attitude change is a principal tool for resolving inconsistencies. Thus, if one major core belief changes, for whatever reason, others related to it are also likely to change. For instance, Furnham and Bland (1983) found, as predicted, that the Protestant work-ethic beliefs are closely related to more general conservative social attitudes. They also argued that if work-ethic beliefs are on the decline one might expect conservative social attitudes to change likewise, and since there is not evidence of the latter one should not necessarily infer the occurrence of the former.

Lay beliefs, moreover, have behavioral consequences. As Furnham and Lewis (1986) have noted, lay economic beliefs can actually affect economic variables just as much as economic beliefs. Consumer sentiment has consequences for consumer demand, in that if people believe high inflation is likely to continue they may spend rather than save and have high wage demands, which partly accounts for the continuance of high inflation. Similarly, Katona (1971) found that public pessimism about the economy showed a sharp decline about six to nine months before a major recession. Of course, it is impossible to tease out cause from correlation when examining lay beliefs and behavior, and it is possible that some form of reciprocal determinism operates.

Attitudes to Punishment and Discipline

This chapter concerns lay theories about the efficacy and morality of corporal punishment particularly with respect to children and adolescents. It is an area that has not attracted a great deal of good research (Straus 1994). These beliefs and theories, however, are no doubt related to much broader beliefs about punishment in general.

Both the American public and the British public rate school discipline as a major educational problem and have done so for years (Ziegler and Smith 1984). It seems that for many lay people the terms *discipline, punishment, control, order,* and *retribution* are closely associated.

The role of punishment in learning or controlling behavior has been of interest not only to psychologists and sociologists but also to philosophers and ethicists. Of course, lay people have also debated the efficacy and morality of punishment, and proverbs reflect this. Thus we have "spare the rod and spoil the child" and "an eye for an eye, a tooth for a tooth." For many years arguments have been put forward as to the efficacy of punishment. Walters et al. (1972) offered the following conclusion:

> The evidence suggests that moderately intense consistently administered punishment can be effective in suppressing undesired behavior and that . . . side effects of punishment may even be facilitating via increments in attention to elements of the task at hand. Moreover, the absence of punishment is frequently taken as tacit approval of behaviour. Thus in attempting to use non reward to eliminate undesired behaviour the agent may be inadvertently strengthening these behaviours. Furthermore, the use of indirect methods

such as withdrawal of attention or redirection of attention may not provide as clearly the important information upon which to base subsequent choices. Thus direct punishment may have the advantage of promoting the child's ability to make a conscious choice relative to direct techniques of discipline. (1972: 383)

The lay arguments in favor of punishment as an effective way of shaping behavior are essentially threefold. First, punishment is an effective way of eliminating undesirable behaviour if (and only if) alternative behavioral responses are available and rewarded. Second, because avoiding a threatened punishment can be rewarding, in that it is a reduction of anxiety, a symbol of actual threatened punishment, such as a policeman, can be very effective. Third, punishment can be informative, in that it can provide useful feedback on behavior.

On the other hand, some have argued that punishment is not only morally wrong but also an ineffective way of controlling behavior. Often punishment does not prescribe an alternative behavior; it simply tries to suppress an existing one. Thus, it is feasible that an even more undesirable behavior may be substituted for the punished one (Deese and Hulse 1967). Second, it has been established that punishment can "fix" or encourage a behavior (such as bed wetting) rather than punish it. This may be due to the fear or anxiety induced by the punishment or fear of punishment. Third, certain by-products of punishment, such as the hatred of the inflictor or a phobia about the place of punishment, may result that are, in themselves, highly undesirable. Furthermore, various psychological studies seem to indicate that punishment often temporarily suppresses behavior but does not weaken them, and that as soon as the punishment ceases the behavior returns.

Hogarth (1971) has suggested that there are essentially three punishment philosophies (or sentence strategies) widespread among lay people, philosophers, and lawyers:

> 1. Punishment (retribution): The attempt to impose a just punishment on the offender in the sense of being in proportion to the severity of the crime and his culpability, whether or not such a penalty is likely to prevent further crime in him or others. 2. Reformation (rehabilitation): The attempt to change the offender through treatment or corrective measures, so that when given the chance he will refrain from committing crime. 3. General deterrence (deterrence): The attempt to impose a penalty on the offender before the court sufficiently severe that potential offenders among the general public will refrain from committing further crime through fear of punishment. (1971: 70)

In a study using measures of this system McFather (1978) found: "Deterrence sentences were the most severe for all crimes, whereas the rehabilitation sentences were the least severe for serious crimes only. Surprisingly, the re-habilitation group subjects consistently blamed the victim of the crime more than did the other groups" (1978: 41).

As well as general beliefs about the efficacy and morality of punishment there have been various surveys of public attitudes to specific crime and appropriate punishment. In a study of more than three thousand members of the British public, Hough and Mayhew (1985) found that recommended punishments varied as a function of the crime, but they also found a fair degree of congruence between the courts and the public in terms of views on imprisonment.

A number of attempts have been made to examine specific psychological belief systems and attitudes to punishment. For instance, Vincey et al. (1982) believed that general beliefs about free will versus determinism would predict attitudes to punishment. Specifically, they hypothesized that libertarians (those who believe in free will) would consistently recommend more punitive measures for behavioral deviations than determinists. They found the precise opposite, however, and suggested that this may be due to the burdensome moral responsibility that punishment represents to those who believe in free will and hence demand it be administered with scrupulous attention to fairness and justice. However, they concluded that "there is no empirical basis for believing that libertarians are categorically more punitive than determinists; the opposite is also true" (1982: 945–46).

Similarly, Ryckman et al. (1986) did not find that high, as opposed to low, authoritarians endorsed the use of harsher strategies for *all* crimes, but they did find that authoritarians were more likely to endorse higher crimes like murder, rape, and manslaughter—not for lesser crimes like burglary and robbery.

It seems, then, that laypeople's beliefs about the efficacy and desirability of punishment are multidimensional. Nevertheless, there appears to be a general dimension of pro- versus antipunishment. It seems intuitively reasonable that conservative beliefs are associated with punishment and retribution and liberal beliefs with education, though, as the literature has shown, this intuition may be too simplistic.

In other areas of research, such as lay theories for the origin of things like alcoholism, depression, and schizophrenia, it is apparent that laypeople are influenced by the "grand theories" or schools in psychology, such as psycho-analysis, behaviorism, and humanistic theory. Furthermore, laypeople also occasionally endorse sociological, even sociopolitical, theories of psychological phenomena. However, the same does not appear to be true of lay theories of punishment and discipline. Clearly the most obvious theoretical foundation for beliefs about the effectiveness of punishment is learning theory, be it classical or modern. However, equivocal results and the implications of findings for parental or teacher behavior lead both experts and laypeople to be either pro- or antipunishment based as much on personal experience and *other* beliefs and values, not specifically on lay theories of punishment.

The School Debate

For generations one of the most popular topics in high-school debates has been that of corporal punishment. It is chosen no doubt because of the personal experiences of young people (in the home, the school, the club) and the topic's apparent salience to their lives. What is noticeable is that the same arguments are used again and again, suggesting that they are presumably part of the folk consciousness, particularly that of young people. These arguments are of course highly politicized. Further, one cannot ignore the fact the schools themselves inculcate theories and practices of punishment.

These debating positions are frequently reiterated. Curiously, the academic debate is not much different, and although marginally more sophisticated and filled with jargon, much the same points are made in it. But the school debate is also between teachers and parents, parents and educational psychologists, and so forth. Ziegler and Smith (1984) gave elementary- and secondary-school teachers a twenty-item likert-type attitude survey with all items derived from the extant psychological literature. Interestingly, elementary-school teachers with least experience agreed with the psychologists' conclusions most and secondary-school teachers with most experience agreed with them least.

Strongest agreement was noted on statements about pedagogical approaches to discipline problems. Teachers agreed that, "to be effective, disciplinary decisions must be made quickly, firmly" and that "disciplinary problems in school are extensions of out-of-school problems." They also strongly agreed that "firm control techniques prevent more effectively than tentative ones," "a first step toward good classroom discipline is a clear, commonly agreed on functional list of rules," and teachers should "focus more on students who are behaving themselves than on those who break the rules."

Teachers registered the strongest disagreement with statements from the behavioral or human relations views that dealt specifically with punishment: notably, that "punishment fails to provide motivation"; that "punishment results in shame, guilt and sense of sin"; and that "misbehaviour and punishment breed and reinforce each other." Strong disagreement was also noted on two other statements regarding punishment: "Punishment usually succeeds in moving a child to hostility and making him unreceptive to education," and "punishment usually does not cancel misconduct, it reinforces it."

The authors conclude: "Nearly all the psychologists contended that punish-

Table 9.1 Means, standard deviations and factor loadings on the ten items

Statements	Scale*		Loading factor 1	2	3
	Mean	SD			
3. Spanking is needed as a last resort when all else fails	2.74	1.58	.80		
6. If you can't spank, children will be spoiled, run wild, etc	2.19	1.42	.75		
1. Spanking works better than other methods of controlling children	2.21	1.49	.76		
10. It is unrealistic to expect parents never to spank	4.22	1.96	.67		
2. Spanking is needed as a last resort when all else fails	4.00	2.01	.67		
4. One or two instances of parents spanking their children are not going to cause any permanent damage	4.55	1.73	.63		
8. By the time a child is a teenager, spanking has usually stopped	5.31	1.49		.85	
7. Most parents spank only rarely or only for serious problems	4.23	1.56		.83	
5. Parents can't stop spanking unless they get training in alternatives	3.28	1.82			.85
9. If parents don't spank they will verbally abuse a child	3.26	1.66			.55
Eigenvalue			3.72	1.24	1.10
Variance			37.3	12.4	11.0

* Agree 7 6 5 4 3 2 1 Disagree

ment is the least desirable method of managing behaviour or misbehaviour, yet the practising teachers expressed the strongest disagreement with statements involving the efficacy of punishment. It appears that teachers emphasize 'practical' control techniques" (1984: 839).

More recently Furnham (1995) looked at correlates of attitudes to spanking children. A simple ten-item questionnaire was derived from Straus (1994), who listed what he called "Ten Myths about Spanking Children." This were presented to subjects, who rated them on a seven-point agree-disagree scale.

Table 9.1 shows the means and standard deviations per question. Given that

4 on the 7 point scale was neutral it seemed that subjects agreed with four items: 4, 7, 8 and 10 while disagreeing about all others except 2 on which they were neutral. A varimax factor analysis was performed on the items to reveal their underlying structure. Three clear factors emerged which accounted for 60 per cent of the variance. The first factor expressed *pro-spanking* sentiments and accounted for a third of the variance. The second factor which accounted for a sixth of the variance referred to the comparative *rarity of spanking,* while the third factor considered *alternatives to spanking.*

Further analyses showed that there were no sex differences on any of the factors. Number of children, religion, and religiousness also failed to yield any significant differences. There were however, various *age* and *political-belief* differences. Younger subjects tended to endorse factor 2 more strongly (r = 30, p < .001). A one-way ANOVA looking at the relationship between political beliefs and spanking attitudes showed that two or three F levels were significant. Right-wing (and center) supporters tended to be more prospanking than left-wing supporters. Compared to those on the left and the right, centralists believed more that parents need training in alternative methods other than spanking.

Alas, fewer studies appear to have been done on the theories of parents who, for obvious reasons, may have among the best reasons to hold the ideas they do.

Academic Disagreement

Since the Second World War, various groups in Britain have commissioned reports from Working Parties on corporal punishment. Most have attempted to define corporal punishment and then ascertain its prevalence. Many have also attempted to review the salient literature as well as canvass other groups.

In 1979 the British Psychological Society (BPS) commissioned such a report. The review covered the effectiveness of punishment with respect to laboratory animals; social, cultural, and educational uses of corporal punishment; psychopathology and corporal punishment; and attitudes to punishment. The writers of the report canvassed various bodies as well as reviewing the salient literature. For instance, they noted that the Association for Behavioural Modification with Children had this to say:

> Corporal punishment is only one form of punitive management and it is suggested that it needs to be considered in a broader context. The prevailing view in this Association is that, in general, corporal punishment can and should be avoided. The following broad reasons have been put forward by members to justify this view:

1. It is generally ineffective. More than one commentator has emphasised the way in which school punishment books show the same small band of pupils being caned regularly throughout their school careers. Though the majority of pupils may behave acceptably under a system which includes corporal punishment, it is felt that they would be equally amenable to milder approaches. . . .

2. It is unnecessary. There are many countries in the world where corporal punishment in schools is either banned, or simply not used, without apparent ensuing chaos. . . . Commentators have, moreover, paid tribute to schools in this country where the staffs have rejected corporal punishment and have achieved excellent morale.

3. Corporal punishment is a bad example. There is evidence that children imitate the actions of their elders, and that methods of child-rearing depending heavily on punishment of a physically aggressive kind produce children who themselves behave in a physically violent fashion. Children who are beaten tend in their turn to beat and bully.

4. It may contribute to poor teacher-pupil relationships. Pupils who are punished physically may develop feelings of resentment or revenge which lead to anti-teacher behaviour which, in turn, may provoke more hostility from the teacher. Better-behaved pupils may also be alienated by such behaviour in the teacher, so that they sympathise with and support the disruptor rather than influencing him to behave acceptably. Alternatively they may become afraid of the teacher.

5. It can exacerbate difficult behaviour. For pupils unaccustomed to achieving recognition as significant individuals by approved methods, corporal punishment provides an alternative route to this end. The pupil then behaves disruptively so that the teacher will, by punishing, signify that he has noticed him. It may also help the pupil acquire significance in the eyes of his fellows in the situation where the teacher's reliance on corporal punishment has prejudiced a class against himself.

6. It is logically incompatible with the ideas of a community based upon mutual respect and care for the welfare and dignity of the individual. . . . Many of those misdeeds held to warrant corporal punishment, such as bullying, destructiveness, dishonesty, truancy, rudeness and persistent laziness, are indicators of problems needing help if the pupil is to lead a satisfying life in the community. Corporal punishment does not contribute to the kinds of relationships and atmosphere most likely to promote such help.

7. To sanction corporal punishment in schools may be to deny teachers the guidance and support which they might otherwise seek in relation to other modes of operation. (1979: 11)

They add:

While the principles of learning mentioned so far, and the techniques of behaviour modification based on those principles, are very helpful in promoting appropriate social learning in children, they are unlikely to solve all the problems encountered in their schools. Unfortunately, some forms of anti-social behaviour are rewarded by various consequences in the school principles — by the attention or approval of peers; by the attention, even though disapproving, of the teacher; by the interest and stimulation the pupil derives from his success in disrupting a class or upsetting a teacher he does not like or respect, and so on. Sometimes it is hard to think of rewarding consequences for more desirable behaviour which, alone, will compete effectively with those which encounter the disruption (though it is easy to jump to the conclusion that there is none). Punishment may then be needed to discourage the disruptive behaviour while the more desirable behaviour is being rewarded. The use of positive consequences should then improve teacher/pupil relationships to a point at which it is no longer rewarding to be disruptive.

Research has shown that appropriate planned punishment can improve behaviour and has thrown light on some of the ways in which it can be made most effective. It should be devised so that it is:

1. Applied consistently. The same kind of misbehaviour should be predictably punished by the same consequence, rather than according to the mood of the teacher. Most often, consistency will require that a misdemeanour is punished in the same way every time it occurs. It would be difficult to justify *corporal* punishment with such frequency.

2. Applied as a natural consequence of particular misbehaviour rather than as condemnation of the individual as a worthwhile person. The latter approach can lead to a lowering of self-esteem, and there is evidence that such a decrement leads to a lowering of moral controls.

3. Applied by somebody who is warm and caring rather than hostile or punitive in attitude.

4. Not so severe that the pupil is strongly motivated to avoid detection as a possible alternative to improving his behaviour.

5. Not an example of aggressive behaviour which we would not wish to see in the pupil himself, that is, not a bad example.

6. Fair and reasonable, so that it does not provoke retaliation and can be seen as constructive by the pupil himself.

7. Accompanied by guidance in, and reward for, the alternative behaviour desired.

8. Accompanied, where necessary, by explanation of the reasons for it.

9. Applied soon after the misbehaviour rather than some time later.

10. Applied, where possible, to the intention, rather than to the misdemeanour itself, since this has been shown to be more effective. Plainly, it would be hard to justify the use of *corporal* punishment in this way.

Where some physical intervention is necessary to prevent a child harming either himself or others, it may be necessary to restrain him physically. This, however, is quite distinct from corporal punishment and has a different purpose. We believe that the positive measures outlined above will make the need for such restraints very rare. (1979: 12–13)

The BPS research led it not to a particular conclusion but rather a detailed list of the various opinions about, arguments in favor and against, and belief about the effect of corporal punishment. Because this remains both comprehensive and up to date, it is summarized below.

OPINIONS ABOUT THE USE OF CORPORAL PUNISHMENT

1. Children often prefer corporal punishment to alternative sanctions.
2. Parents display a diversity of opinions about the use of corporal punishment.
3. Although a majority of teachers appear to favor the phasing out of the use of corporal punishment, there is an active minority in positions of authority who hold strong retentionist views.
4. The teachers' unions are concerned that their professional judgment should not be questioned and that the issue of abolition of corporal punishment should be left for them to decide.
5. Institutions that train teachers do not approve of the use of corporal punishment and would prefer to see it abandoned.
6. In general it seems to be agreed that the use of corporal punishment is not easy to justify with girls and with handicapped and emotionally damaged children.
7. Nearly all professional organizations concerned with the welfare of children favor the abolition of the use of corporal punishment.
8. Sanctions operate in all aspects of normal life. The question is not whether they should be used but rather which sanctions are most effective in which circumstances once the goals have been agreed.

ARGUMENTS IN FAVOR OF THE USE OF CORPORAL PUNISHMENT

Maintenance of order in the classroom is a universal concern and a major source of anxiety for teachers. All means of meeting this problem should be made available to them. Corporal punishment is the only effective sanction for some pupils. Parents, pupils, and teachers all tend to favor the retention of the use of corporal punishment, although for different reasons.

ARGUMENTS AGAINST THE USE OF CORPORAL PUNISHMENT

There is no evidence to suggest that corporal punishment is a more effective means of controlling behavior than any of the alternatives available. Effective alternatives to corporal punishment exist, such as the techniques of applied behavior analysis, which emerge as a promising recent development bringing psychological principles to bear on the problems of shaping behavior in the school and classroom. The use of corporal punishment betrays far too simple an approach to complex problems that have to be analyzed in terms of human relationships set in the particular social context of the school. In order that physical punishment may be optimally effective, a number of conditions have to be observed that cannot obtain in a normal school setting. In those countries where corporal punishment has been officially abandoned, teachers are opposed to any suggestion that it should be reintroduced.

THE EFFECTS OF CORPORAL PUNISHMENT

Corporal punishment as used in schools may carry with it certain undesirable side effects. Among these are:

1. A blocking of further communication.
2. Alienation of the child from the school situation in particular and the educational process in general.
3. Corruption of the good human relationships between teacher and child that are necessary for a love of learning to be fostered.
4. The provision of an unfortunate model of successful violent behavior, particularly when exhibited by a figure representing authority.
5. A risk of introducing a sadomasochistic element into the procedure.

When physical punishment is administered by another person, social aggression appears to be a common result. However, this also appears to occur when rewards are withdrawn in the absence of good behavior.

There appears to be a positive link between vandalism and other forms of delinquency, on the one hand, and the amount of corporal punishment, on the other. Although it is not possible to demonstrate a causal connection, other evidence suggests that corporal punishment might increase rather than decrease such behavior. Where corporal punishment has been abandoned an important decrease in such behavior is often reported.

It should be noted that the above opinions are arguments that were supplied not by laypeople but by organizations involved with teaching and research. To the extent that not all the people from those organizations were social scientists, it may be assumed that they were a lay but involved population.

The passion regarding this debate, however, does not die. In May 1993 Penelope Leach published a paper in the BPS monthly magazine, *The Psychologist*. The paper was entitled "Should Parents Hit Their Children?" and she in fact considered lay theories of punishment. She is particularly scornful of what she sees to be the misinterpretation and hence application of learning theory via the media: "Pseudo-science thus lends credence to common sense, parental statements such as 'if he gets a slap every time he does it, he'll soon learn not to' " (1993: 120). She concludes:

> While psychologists may consider it inappropriate to involve themselves in moral debate, their profession has a unique contribution to make to the pragmatic aspects of this discussion and a responsibility to ensure that its body of knowledge is available, without distortion, to policy-makers. Data from psychology, very briefly exemplified here, suggest that physical punishment is unlikely to be effective in helping parents to shape their children's behaviour as they themselves wish, or in building the self-discipline society requires of all socialized citizens. On the contrary: the use of physical punishment frequently provokes or exacerbates behaviours parents and others wish to minimize; *may be harmful to children* in a number of ways and increases their vulnerability to physical abuse. Literature from psychology and related professions provides clear evidence, and suggests some explanations for the inter-generational continuance of physical punishment. It suggests that, despite evidence of the greater effectiveness of non-punitive disciplinary methods, the use—and abuse—of parent physical punishment is unlikely to end without external intervention such as legal change. (1993: 220)

Eysenck (1993) felt the need to respond. His letter, in full, went thus:

> Penelope Leach, in her article on "Should parents hit their children?" in the May 1993 issue of *The Psychologist,* raises a number of intractable problems. She concludes her argument by saying that "the use of physical punishment frequently provokes or exacerbates behaviours parents and others wish to minimise." How can we know this? The correlation between physical punishment and unacceptable child behaviour may be granted, but what is suggested is a causal relation. There are three major possibilities: (1) Parental punishment causes juvenile behaviour. (2) Genes which cause parents to inflict punishment are inherited by the child and cause his or her unacceptable behaviour. (3) The unacceptable behaviour of the child, however caused, makes parents adopt a punitive strategy. Any or all of these hypotheses may be used to predict the observed correlation; there is no way that is socially acceptable to discriminate between them. Leach opts for (1), without even considering (2) or (3) seriously; this is not acceptable scientifically, in view of the very strong evidence for strong genetic determination of individual differences in behaviour. There is the added complication that identical parental behaviours may have differential effects depending on the genetic constitution of the child—the flame that melts the wax tempers the steel. Leach's account is too one-sided to form the basis of responsible recommendations to law-giving bodies.

She argues that "social policy cannot always await rigorous research evidence." Perhaps that is the reason social policy is so ineffectual! Certainly psychologists should be chary of giving advice not based on rigorous research evidence. Our sole justification for being taken seriously in the field of social policy is precisely that our advice is based on rigorous research evidence; if it is not we are no different from the usual run of lay commentators making contradictory suggestions. Psychiatrists arguing vociferously on opposite sides in court have brought the profession into disrepute; we should avoid similar disasters. Both the APA *Monitor* and *The Psychologist* have been inclined to adopt positions on public matters where rigorous experimental evidence was quite clearly lacking; this is clearly wrong from publications of what purport to be scientific societies. When the evidence is in we should certainly speak up; to do so when the evidence is uncertain, confused and contradictory is not the best interest of psychology as a science.

Eysenck's reply evoked two further responses, both of which criticized him for falling into the same trap by emphasizing biological or genetic factors rather than environmental factors.

Although most popular magazine articles on the subject of corporal punishment tend to be partisan and zealously advocate one position over another, it is quite probable that laypeople have been exposed to both sides of the argument. Clearly there is no consensus from the academic community on the efficacy of punishment, though the majority appear to be against the idea. Hence it is not surprising that laypeople are equally divided.

Furthermore, many academics disparagingly talk about the commonsense view that advocates, tolerates, or condones corporal punishment. The argument of laypeople tends to be that they experienced punishment as a child and it did them no harm, even good; that as parents, teachers, or minders they "dished out" physical punishment and that it was effective; and that the alternatives are ineffective. Scientists attempt to contradict this "personal-experience" approach sometimes by patronizing others but occasionally with data. But they neglect to add that it is equally commonsensical to those who reject corporate punishment.

Frequently it is possible to "compare and contrast" lay and scientific theories to show how the latter are significantly more coherent, consistent, explicit, and so on, than the former. Also, it is often possible to point to different, clearly identifiable, specific, and theoretically based models or explanations for a phenomenon like anorexia (Furnham and Hume-Wright 1992) or rape (Harbridge and Furnham 1991). The same cannot, however, be said of this area of research.

Parental Beliefs

One related area of research that has attracted a fair amount of attention is the literature on parental beliefs and concepts that have been demonstrated actually to influence parental behavior (Simmons et al. 1993).

There have been a number of studies on parents' beliefs about child rearing, parental and educational, as well as studies on parents' knowledge of behavioral principles (McLoughlin 1985; Stevens 1988). Some have been concerned mainly with preschool children, where, for instance, Lawton, Schules, Fowell, and Modser (1984) found that parents appear to be more certain of their actual parenting and its relation to their children's social development, less certain of its relation to their intellectual development, and least certain of its relation to their physical development. Others have been interested in how parental beliefs (particularly about sex-typing) influence behavior toward the child or toward particular types of education.

"Naive" or lay theories of child development are, however, culture specific. Keller, Miranda, and Ganda (1984) found numerous differences between German and Costa Rican mothers' beliefs about child development and optimal parenting. For instance, German women expect infants to see, think, understand words, and identify pictures or objects earlier than do Costa Rican women. Parental ideas of development (and education) would thus appear to be culture specific and also class specific. No doubt the explanations are affected not only by demographic differences of nationality and class but also by situational or contextual features.

There are a number of reasons why the study of parental beliefs has been considered important. Goodnow (1981, 1984) argued that parents' beliefs illuminate effects of culture and class but, more important, that parental beliefs relate to child-rearing practices, which in turn have developmental outcomes for the child. Holen (1988) found, as one might predict, that the parent's sex and caregiving experiences influence how individuals solve child-rearing problems.

There is also evidence for a systematic bias differentiating parents' and children's explanations. For instance, Compass, Adelman, Freude, and Taylor (1982) showed that when asked to explain behavior, parents made more attributions than their children to the characteristics of the child than to the environmental factors. More interesting, however, was the finding that parents and children differed in their locus of attributions when interviewed individually, but that these differences were not present when families were interviewed with both parents and children present. This suggests that attributes, attitudes, beliefs, and theories are expressed and formulated quite differently depending on the context in which they are required (Furnham 1988).

Less work has been done on the lay theories of people with and without children, before and after they have children, and on parents from different socioeconomic groups. There is sufficient evidence from studies on social mobility to suggest that parents' beliefs and responses are the major determinants of the education outcomes of their children. More important perhaps is the literature that suggests that parenting practices are transmitted across generations via social environmental processing. However, in most studies it has not been possible to determine whether behavior is transmitted directly through modeling or indirectly through such things as well-being or parental beliefs. Work in this field, however, has tended to describe different typologies applicable to parents, namely, permissive, authoritarian, and authoritative (Buri 1991). As one might expect, disciplinary attitudes are closely associated with parental styles, thus authoritarian parents are more likely to believe in and actually carry out corporal punishment, while permissive parents are mostly unlikely to do this. Furthermore, one may predict on the basis of this literature that the children of authoritarian parents are themselves likely to be authoritarian parents, and hence a preference for corporal punishment is transmitted from one generation to the next.

Assuming that laypeople hold lay theories — as opposed to simple beliefs — about the efficacy of, and therefore the necessity for, corporal punishment, the question remains as to where they acquired such theories. They probably come from two major sources — personal experience in the home and classroom and books, magazines, and program on parenting. It is not uncommon to hear adults approve of spanking on the ground that they were spanked and it did them no harm, even some good. However, the trauma of corporal punishment for some children at school has meant that they have reacted to it very strongly as adults and oppose it vehemently. Much must depend not only on the regularity and severity of the punishment but also on the perception of its just and unjust implementation at the time and retrospectively.

The second source of theories, in popular books, family-oriented magazines, and media discussion program on effective methods of parenting, by experts, others by journalists, appear of late to be fairly consistent in their recommendations not to smack or spank children. These are usually aimed at a literate, middle-class parent population who are in any event less likely to use any form of physical punishment. Indeed, it would be an interesting historical study to collect references to corporal punishment in guide books for parents published over the past century or so. These publications and other ethnographic works are no doubt important sources of lay ideas on the subject.

Conclusion

Because of both their own direct experience (at home, in the classroom) and their exposure to the old debate (through popular media), most laypeople hold strong beliefs about corporal punishment. Most of these beliefs concern the efficacy and morality of spanking versus its alternatives. To suggest that these beliefs constitute a theory may be something of an exaggeration, but they nearly all constitute a coherent belief system. To a large extent it seems people's attitude to, and beliefs about, corporal punishment can be plotted on a single pro versus anti dimension. Furthermore, the more extreme the view, the more coherent it is, and the more it may be related to other well-known belief systems like conservatism, the just world, the work ethic, authoritarianism, and so forth. Thus, those who score high on social conservation, believe in the just world, and endorse the work ethic are more likely to be in favor of corporal punishment. Although this hypothesis awaits empirical proof, it fits in with the previous research in this field (Furnham 1986).

It also seems from the literature that there is some evidence that attitudes to, and beliefs about, corporal punishment of children are, along with other parental beliefs and styles, transmitted from one generation to another. Despite the fact that the "mechanism" of this transmission remains obscure, a number of feasible hypothesis can be put forward and tested.

Perhaps one of the more surprising features of this literature is the paucity both of good theory and of research on the topic. Whereas in other applied areas in the behavioral sciences there are a plethora of distinct theories of the aetiology, development, and even cure of (where appropriate) specific problems, this appears to be less true for the area of corporal punishment. Although the language and concepts from learning theory can be borrowed and applied to classroom or other behavior, there seem to be few specific theories of the efficacy of consequences of corporal punishment. Indeed, the same supposedly disinterested scientists appear to be so zealous about the topic that their passion for their cause overcomes their need for evidence.

Difficulties of Making Rational Choices Concerning Corporal Punishment of Children

SCOTT FELD

A rational-choice perspective on behavior focuses attention on the goals of an actor and the choices that actor makes to further those goals. Understanding parents' use of corporal punishment of children, in particular, requires attention to parents' goals for the behaviors of their children, and their beliefs about whether corporal punishment helps them reach those goals. Parents may have widely varied behavioral goals for their children. Some parents may believe that obedience to authority is an important goal, in and of itself, while others may believe that children should internalize moral values and learn to make personal decisions in accord with those values. Whatever the goals of particular parents, a rational-choice theory suggests that parents will tend to use corporal punishment to the extent that it is effective in achieving the parents' goals relative to the other available strategies of parenting.

The relative effectiveness of any particular parental strategy is likely to vary depending upon the goals, the environment of the family, and the availability of other resources. For example, parents whose goal is for their child to be obedient to authority may find that the strategies effective for them are different from those of parents whose goal is for their child carefully to think through moral choices. Parents who live in crowded neighborhoods, subject to multiple unwanted influences in the neighborhood, in school, and on television, may need to use strategies different from those who have less competition for influence over their children. Parents who are very busy may not find that time-intensive behavioral strategies (for example, "time-outs" and/or careful explanations) are alternatives as viable for them as for other parents.

The central problem with applying a rational-choice perspective to the use of corporal punishment is to understand how parents determine their most effective strategies. This is the central problem from the perspective of a parent making the decisions, from the perspective of an observer predicting or explaining the decisions, and from the perspective of a policy maker seeking to affect those decisions.

The General Problem of Determining Rational Choices

The problem may be characterized as the problem of "bounded rationality" (Simon 1957: 1983). In human decisions, there are generally many possible strategies. The ideal type of rational choice involves making the best choice from a well-defined set of alternative strategies. If individuals are unaware of many of the alternatives, they may not be able to choose the best.

A further problem of "limited information" is that individuals find it difficult to determine the likely outcomes of their use of various strategies. Clear knowledge about the consequences of corporal punishment under various conditions does not exist, and even partial information is not readily available. In practice, each parent needs to use particular strategies in context and observe the consequences.

Experimenting with one's own life is highly problematic for many reasons, including the lack of controlled comparisons, the small number of children, the relative uniqueness of each set of circumstances, the wide variations in results to similar strategies for similar situations, and the long-term nature of many of the goals.

In practical decisions, people rarely attempt controlled experiments by contrasting different strategies but instead tend to try a promising strategy and evaluate whether the results are adequate (Simon 1957). Simon coined the term *satisficing* to refer to the tendency to search for a strategy that produces outcomes that are "satisfactory," rather than to attempt to find the strategy that produces the "best" outcomes. In this context, a parent tends to try out a promising strategy and continues to use that strategy if it produces acceptable results. If the results are unacceptable, then the parent presumably searches for other strategies that might produce satisfactory results.

The determination of "acceptable" is itself an imprecise and somewhat unscientific process. Presumably, parents have notions of acceptability derived from such sources as their own childhoods, the behaviors of other children they observe, and idealized images from others. What is acceptable to one parent may be unacceptable to another. Even the interpretation of the situation might be subject to social influence in the way that Becker (1963) suggests that people learn to be marijuana users; that is, associates may help them to interpret the ambiguous results as positive or negative.

Punishment as Strategy in Interaction

A further degree of complexity in decisions to use corporal punishment is introduced by the "interactive" aspects of a situation. A parent presumably tries to create a reward structure in which a rational child will choose to behave appropriately and desirably. The use of corporal punishment is intended as an application of deterrence theory; the more certain and severe the punishment, the more effectively will unwanted behavior be discouraged.

However, focusing on certainty and severity of punishment neglects the social and interactive aspects of the process. Deterrence theory suggests that a parent can best obtain compliance from a child by making it clear that non-compliance will certainly be followed by severe punishment. But children do not limit their considerations to responding to contingencies structured by parents — they also structure contingencies to influence the behaviors of their parents.

A sophisticated child may recognize that implementing punishment is often costly to parents, especially in terms of their empathetic response to a child's pain. While the typical parent's claim that "it hurts me more than it hurts you" may be exaggerated, most parents probably do experience some pain from the sufferings of their children, even when it is "deserved." A sophisticated child might use the understanding that a parent prefers *not* to punish a child to his or her advantage in a process of "negotiation" with the parent.

A sophisticated child may also recognize that he or she has the power to create rewards or costs in response to the parents' actions. For example, nonpunitive parents may find that their children reward their niceness with "good" behavior, while unduly punitive parents may find that their children punish their hurtfulness with their own misbehaviors.

A simple game matrix, shown in figure 10.1, can illustrate the situation. The particular values are arbitrary, but they illustrate the nature of the situation when there are simultaneous interdependent rewards to both parties.

This matrix indicates the values of each of the outcomes of different combinations of parent and child behaviors. For example, if the child conforms (the first horizontal row) and the parent does not punish (the first vertical col-

PARENT

		Not punish	Punish
	Conform	+1/+2	−6/−1
CHILD			
	Misbehave	+6/−3	−1/−6

Fig. 10.1.

umn), then the outcome (at the intersection of the first row and first column — at the top left) is valued +1 by the child and +2 by the parent.

For simplicity of exposition in the present context, the parent will be referred to as "she" and the child as "he." Suppose that the child begins by conforming, and the parent by not punishing (top left). The child can improve the value of the outcome to himself by misbehaving (second row, first column) instead of conforming (first row, first column); he values this outcome (bottom left) as +6. However, this change of child's behavior is costly to the parent, who values this outcome (bottom left) as −3. The parent cannot move to an outcome that is more valued to her by directly changing behaviors, but she can cause the child to suffer by inflicting punishment (second column, second row) instead of not punishing (first column, second row). While this change is costly to the parent, it is very punishing to the child. Although the parent cannot directly improve her own outcome, this punishment (or threat of it) may encourage the child to change his behavior in a direction that would benefit the parent.

It bears repeating that the particular values are arbitrary; nevertheless, it should be noted that the specific values in the matrix were systematically determined from a minimal number of separate assumptions, as follows: (1) The parent receives two points, and the child receives one point when the child conforms and the parent does not punish. (2) The child gains five points from misbehaving. (3) The parent loses five points from the misbehavior of the child. (4) The child loses seven points by being punished by the parent. (5) The parent loses three points by punishing the child.

The analysis of this example illustrates the nature of difficulties in predicting behaviors and outcomes in interactive situations. In this situation, the parent has the option of costing the child seven points by punishing the child, but the child has the option of costing the parent five points by misbehaving. From this "mutual fate control" (Thibaut and Kelley 1959), it would appear that the parent has greater control over the child than vice versa. However, the parent can only punish the child with a cost to self of three points, while the child punishes a parent by benefiting itself by five. The child finds it easier to punish the parent than vice versa; but it is costly for the child to reward the parent.

Given these countervailing considerations, it is difficult to conceptualize and measure the relative power of the participants.

However, power may not be the central issue; each participant has a "dominant" strategy, that is, a strategy that is preferred irrespective of what the other does. The child prefers to misbehave; misbehavior secures him five points more than conforming, whether the child is punished or not. The parent prefers not to punish; not punishing secures her three points more than punishing, whether the child conforms or misbehaves. Thus, except for the deliberate manipulation of the behavior of the other, there is a stable equilibrium outcome of this situation when the child misbehaves and the parent does not punish!

Most parents would probably find this result to be unacceptable; they would feel that accepting and tolerating the misbehavior of a child would be irresponsible. As a result, parents try to *commit* themselves to punishing a child for misbehavior, even though it is costly to them in the short run.

As Schelling's (1960) discussion of commitment and conflict indicates, if the parent can credibly "commit," then the child is confronted with a choice between conforming with no punishment or misbehaving with punishment. Given that choice, a rational child chooses to conform, and the parent is satisfied.

However, "commitment" is not merely the province of the parent. A child may be able credibly to commit to punishing the painful and humiliating behavior of a parent. If a child can effectively commit to misbehaving whenever a parent punishes, and to conforming some of the time when a parent does not punish, then a parent may be induced not to punish. Even without much deliberate rationality, there may be some evolutionary tendency for people (including children) to reciprocate — that is, to reward rewarding behaviors and to punish punishing behaviors (cf. Axelrod 1984). To the extent that a parent recognizes that the child will respond to punishment with further misbehavior, the parent might rationally choose to accept occasional misbehavior from the child without punishing in every instance. This should be a familiar outcome to many parents.

What happens when a committed parent meets a committed child? They either cooperate with one another from the start or become enmeshed in a mutually destructive cycle of noncooperation. If such a cycle ends at all, it may only end when one of them submits to the presumably greater commitment of the other.

One hopes that the anticipation of the outcome of a potential conflict determines the outcome without having actually to engage in the conflict. To the extent that one participant recognizes that the other is more committed, there is no need for the destructive conflict to intervene before accepting the ultimate equilibrium. Thus, the participants have incentives to use negotiations to determine what would be the ultimate outcome of a destructive conflict without having actually to undergo and experience the costly consequences of the mutually destructive behaviors.

Factors Affecting the Strength of Commitments

We may consider the nature of some of the factors that enter into the strength of the participants' commitments, especially the bases upon which they evaluate their own and the others' outcomes.

Specifically, if a parent believes that any misbehavior cannot be accepted, then the parent's commitment to punish wrongdoing is credible. A strong commitment may arise from such factors as: (a) other parents in the immediate environment having highly valued outcomes (that is, well-behaved children), (b) public association of the parent's identity with success of the child, and (c) public association of the parent's identity with the commitment to punish wrongdoing. Theoretically, these arise from the parent having a high comparison level (Thibaut and Kelley 1959), such that lesser outcomes are unacceptable, and/or having rewards derived largely from fulfilling commitments rather than from the direct outcomes of the actions (cf. Schelling 1960).

Analogously, if a child feels that punishment cannot be tolerated, then the child's commitment to respond uncooperatively to punishment is credible. A strong commitment may arise from such factors as: (a) other children in the immediate environment having high outcomes (that is, frequent misbehavior without being punished), (b) public association of the child's identity with being able to misbehave without punishment, and (c) public association of the child's identity with the commitment not to yield to punishment.

Thus, it should be apparent that the reference communities of both parents and children have significant effects on the outcomes of the negotiations between parent and child. A reference community of other parent-child pairs tends to produce a self-fulfilling prophecy. The outcomes of other parents and children determine the comparison levels for both the parent and the child.

Also, to the extent that a community emphasizes the outcomes of children in the evaluation of parents, it becomes recognizably more important to parents to secure high levels of conformity from their children and more credible that they will be committed to punish children for misbehavior. In contrast, a community in which parents do not care about the outcomes of children makes it very difficult for a parent to establish a credible commitment on this issue.

Finally, to the extent that a child can make a public commitment (presumably to a particular group of age peers) not to tolerate parental control, it may become impossible for the parent to impose control without leading to destructive war. It may be more reasonable for the parent to compromise as a concession to the child's commitment.

In its most essential form, the issue generally comes down to a negotiation between parent and child about how much conformity is required of the child to avoid punishment by the parent. Since punishment by the parent is worse than some other outcomes for *both* participants, it stands to reason that any effective negotiation would minimize the occurrence of that outcome. However, the misbehavior of the child has countervailing consequences for parent and child; that is, they cannot agree on the extent of child misbehavior on the basis of their conflicting interests. Reaching some agreement is in the interest of both participants so long as the agreement is better than the state of full conflict; however, there are multiple possible points of agreement that could meet this condition, and it is indeterminate which one will be chosen in a particular situation.

At the same time, one might wonder why parents actually administer as much punishment as they do, considering that it is in the mutual interest of parents and children to avoid such parental punishment. I suggest that: (1) It is difficult for both parties to interpret the actual outcomes as consistent with any (other than the most extreme) agreement — that is, the two parties may disagree on whether the agreement has been violated. (2) The particular forms and consequences of the child's misbehaviors and the parent's punishments are always changing. The negotiation must be over the general levels and conditions of tolerated misbehavior, but those conditions are always new and different. (3) The parent threat must remain credible — if the child continues to "press at the envelope," then a parent may feel the need to discourage such experimentation. In fact, it would seem that most punishment is not the extreme form but is more often symbolic, relatively incidental punishment indicating that the parent is willing and able to do more if further provoked.

In fact, the frequently inconsistent implementation of punishment by parents may indicate the nature of a breakdown in negotiation. Nonpunishment may indicate to the child that a certain level of misbehavior is tolerated; the child is then surprised, disturbed, and angry when that "agreement" is violated by the parent in the form of unexpected, and especially severe, punishment. The maintenance of any agreement requires the responsible commitment of both parties — otherwise, the interaction is likely to deteriorate into a mutually destructive conflict.

From this perspective, whether a parent punishes in general or uses corporal punishment in particular is the outcome of the process of negotiation. Given the complexity of even the simple type of situation just represented in the game matrix, and the additional complexities introduced by variations in the reward structures depending upon the particular community, family, time, and immediate situation, it is impractical for parents systematically to analyze their entire situations. Instead, they are likely to adopt some type of practical "heuristic" for reaching decisions that are as rational as possible under the circumstances.

Practical Heuristics and Rational Resistance to Evidence

Ironically, although rational-choice processes lead parents to use their experience to understand the consequences of their own strategies, it is very difficult for them to gain much understanding from their own experience. For example, consider that a parent has had generally good relationships with her own parents, was spanked as a child, has good feelings about herself, and has no particular resentment about having been spanked by her parents. It seems likely that she would adopt spanking as part of her own parenting repertoire, since it appears to have "worked" in her own case.

Her experience gives her strong preconceptions that spanking, as used by Mom and Dad, is a good strategy for her to use with her own children. If her child behaves "well," then the experience reinforces her preconceptions, and she has little reason to change her strategy. If her child does not behave well and/or her use of spanking seems to be associated with unwanted consequences, then she may reconsider; but her most likely approach to change will be to consider how her use of spanking might not have been implemented properly — she might decide to spank more, harder, or differently. If "improvement" follows, then the parent can attribute that to her strategy. Otherwise, there are many other changes that she can try before she considers eliminating spanking. Also, even "unsuccessful" outcomes may be rationalized to result from influences beyond parental control — parents often attribute child problems to the influences of peers, teachers, television, neighbors, and so on. Finally, even if a parent concludes that her own strategy of spanking is unsuccessful, she might still think that the "radical" change of eliminating spanking is too dangerous to consider — however unsuccessful a particular strategy is, other strategies could make the situation worse. No one wants to risk extraordinary failures with one's own few precious children, and any serious departure from experience and conventional wisdom is likely to be considered high risk.

Even if a parent has a more open mind about effective parenting strategies, she is likely to find it very difficult to isolate the impact of any particular part of a parenting strategy, or even to determine the impact of an overall strategy.

The many sources of variation in outcomes other than the parent's strategy make it difficult to attribute particular outcomes to a particular strategy, particularly when there are few independent cases to examine. Consequently, any parental strategy can be associated with any outcome in a particular instance. In my own studies of parenting, I found all types of patterns, including parents who used little physical punishment with a very physically aggressive child and parents who used much physical punishment with a very gentle child. Thus, it should not be surprising that most parents would be unable to discern clear connections between using spanking and promoting desired behaviors.

Even if a parent notices a positive correlation between the physical aggressiveness of other parents and their children, like that often found in large cross-sectional scientific studies, that association would not necessarily imply a causal impact of parental physical punishment. Parents and their children share many characteristics that could lead them to similar levels of aggressiveness; the coincidence can arise from sources as diverse as levels of activity, general styles of physicality, a shared social milieu, shared or similar experiences with television and other media, high general levels of conflict, weak verbal skills, and so forth.

Considering that scientists have difficulty ascertaining these causal processes, even using information from large systematically designed studies, it should be apparent that parents cannot isolate these types of cause and effect. Consequently, it is "rational" for parents to rely upon presuppositions and to resist changing those presuppositions, when the only possible contradictory evidence (their own experience) is so far from definitive.

Intervention and Change

As discussed above, the inability of parents to analyze situations sufficiently to determine the best strategies implies that they will typically rely upon role models and implicit assumptions, and that there will be strong inertial tendencies in parenting strategies. To the extent that corporal punishment is an established aspect of parenting, it may be difficult to change or replace. Nevertheless, to the extent that parents are trying to be rational, there are possibilities for intervention and initiation of change.

First, much of the previous discussion is based upon the premise that parents feel that their own experiences were successful. There are large numbers of people who are critical of their own upbringing, either because they were unhappy with their own experiences as children, or their own outcomes, or both. Once those parents reject their own parents as role models, they leave room for the substitution of new role models and approaches.

Second, some of those people who recognize their own lack of success as parents may find new authorities with new solutions—for example, psychotherapists, college professors, religious leaders, charismatic television personalities, popular authors, and even personal friends and relatives. To the extent that those new authorities seem sufficiently trustworthy, some parents will experiment with other approaches.

Third, to the extent that negotiation with children reflects the social context of other parents and children, parents may come to recognize that what worked in another time and place will not necessarily work here and now. They may recognize that adapting to the policies and practices of others in the immediate environment may be more successful.

To the extent that one wants to influence parental strategies, one presumably needs to: (1) make parents aware of the ways in which their current approaches are undesirable and/or unsuccessful, (2) suggest that the lack of success is not likely to be the result of their particular implementation but may be the result of the general approach, (3) suggest that there are other feasible strategies that offer the possibility of greater success with relatively little risk, and (4) offer them information and models that facilitate the implementation of those alternative strategies with maximum likelihood of success.

For parents to accept the intent of any or all of these communications, parents must have great confidence in the sources of the information. None of the content of the communications is likely to be self-evident, and all require that the parents take risks that they would rather avoid. Parents would prefer to think that (1) their parenting *is* successful, (2) a simple modification of a strategy is all that is required for improvement, (3) they are already using the only feasible and correct approach, and (4) they need not even consider any serious departures from their current approaches. Thus, intervention and its requirement of change are likely to be resisted, unless parents see both the need for and likelihood of success of their own change.

While scientists and practitioners may believe that parents are continuing to use suboptimal and even harmful parental strategies, they should expect it to be difficult to convince parents. Parents have reason to expect that their own values and circumstances may be different from those assumed by those who wish to change them, and that those others may value different outcomes.

Conclusions

In conclusion, parents acting rationally in pursuit of certain goals for their children necessarily find it difficult to determine how best to parent their children based upon their own experiences as parents. Consequently, it is rational for them to rely heavily on their own preconceptions (often drawn from their own childhood experiences) and reasonably resist any influences and efforts to change them. Practitioners who wish to change parental behaviors might benefit from understanding the nature of "bounded rationality," whereby people continue to use the same strategies so long as they are "satisfactory." Effective intervention in the context of bounded rationality is likely to require simultaneously communicating that the current strategy is unsatisfactory, and that a particular alternative strategy is readily available and easily and successfully implemented.

PART **IV**

Sociological Theories

Unintended Consequences of Punishment

JOAN McCORD

Because punishments are intended to control children's behavior, many people assume that the major — and perhaps the sole — consequence of punishment is teaching children to behave as they ought to. Yet the use of punishment is (I will argue) counterproductive. Furthermore, the use of punishment has additional unintended consequences. I will attempt to demonstrate how children perceive punishments and what those unanticipated consequences are. These illustrations rest on the nature of reasoning itself, though they are bolstered by empirical evidence.[1]

Although this book is about the use of corporal punishment, most of what I have to say applies to using any type of punishment — including, of course, physical punishment. First, punishments give pain and therefore teach children that, at least under some conditions, it is all right to give pain to others.

The law of the excluded middle asserts that things must be either of one class or not of that class. I believe this law is fundamental to rational thought. Even very young children come to understand it and can therefore reason that parents are either good or not good.

Let me begin with the assumption that children believe their parents are good. If good people do good things, then if they punish, it must be good to give pain. If good people do bad things, then even if giving pain is bad, it is all right to do some bad things. That is, if a parent uses punishments, then either the parent is doing something right and it is right to give pain or the parent is doing something wrong and it is all right to do something wrong. In either case, the use of punishment appears to permit giving physical or mental pain to others.

The above reasoning rests on the typical view that children believe their parents are good. The alternative would be for children to believe that parents who punish are not good. If the parents are not good, however, the child has reason not to do as the parents say he ought to.

Empirical evidence shows a consistent correlation between the use of physical punishment and misbehavior, suggesting that even if some punishment is generated by the misbehavior, its use has failed to curtail the misbehavior. Evidence from a longitudinal study suggests that punishment actually increases the likelihood of conduct problems among children. Cohen and Brook (1995) retraced children ten years after their parents' discipline had been measured. They summarized their study by noting that "the magnitude of the estimates and the fact that the influence begins so early in life lead us to conclude that the predominant influence is from punishment to conduct problems. Once begun, punishment has a more potent negative effect on the temperamentally vulnerable" (1995: 162).

Second, punishments reduce the ability of punishers to influence the behavior of children. Other things being equal, children prefer to be in pleasant surroundings. To the extent that fear of punishment makes an environment unpleasant, children will attempt to escape that environment. Often, punishments are effective only in teaching children not to misbehave "in full view" of the punishers. Parents have a difficult (if not impossible) task if they hope to teach a child that what they are punishing is an action rather than getting caught for an action. If a child who will be punished for, say, breaking a lamp has broken other things for which he was not punished, it will be hard to show the nature of what it is that differentiates the two classes other than that he was caught by a punisher for one.

Parents who punish their children for aggression may be successful in moving aggression outside the home but not in stopping the aggression itself.

Evidence about delinquency shows both that delinquents have received a good deal of punishment from their parents and that they spend more time unsupervised than do their nondelinquent peers (McCord 1979; Sampson and Laub 1993). Children who are punished frequently can be expected to try to escape their punitive home environments, thereby making it more difficult for parents to supervise them or teach them the kinds of behavior parents would like to promote.

Third, punishment enhances the value of what is being punished. It is reasonable to assume that what requires punishment must be attractive. The use of punishment signals the value of something that is being punished, thereby teaching children to want what is prohibited. During the process of learning about the environment, children learn that punishment is used to try to make people stop doing something they would like to do (even as rewards are used to try to get people to do what they might not otherwise do). Children see that no one is punished in order to stop one from doing unpleasant things. For unpleasant things, a warning about unattractive features is typically sufficient.

If a parent wants to stop a child from eating a bitter fruit, he or she need only be sure the child understands what being bitter means and point out that the fruit will not taste good. Adding a punishment to forbidding eating the fruit implies that there would otherwise be grounds for eating it. Punishments are used to stop people from doing attractive things.

Children, who are beginning to form appetites and tastes, can be influenced by punishment to desire forbidden objects. An experiment shows how this works. Aronson and Carlsmith (1963) asked children in preschool to rank five toys. After a child had done so, the experimenter put the toy that child had ranked second on a table. The children had been randomly assigned to one of two groups. If the child was in the first group, the experimenter said, "If you play with this, I'll be annoyed, but you can play with this and this." If the child was in the second group, the experimenter told the child not to play with the toy on the table and said, "If you played with it, I would be very angry. I would have to take all of my toys and go home and never come back again. You can play with all the others . . . but if you played with the —— , I would think you were just a baby." All children were asked to rerank the toys approximately forty-five days later. Whereas only a minority of the children who were merely told not to play with their second preference (or the experimenter would be annoyed) increased the ranking of that toy (four of twenty-two children), a majority of those who were threatened with punishment had done so (fourteen of twenty-two).

Conversely, what is used for punishment is likely to take on a negative valence in the eyes of a child. Children as well as adults know that punishments are designed to give pain. Children therefore learn what adults believe to be painful by noting what is used for punishment. Information about values is conveyed when children are given schoolwork, chores, or isolation as punishments. Unfortunately, the use of valuable activities as punishment diminishes the value of those activities in the eyes of children who have been punished.

Deprivations, too, affect values. Thus, parents who take away dessert as punishment enhance the value of eating dessert. Those who forbid watching television increase the desirability of television.

Fourth, the use of punishment introduces an option or alternative to the action that is desired. When punishments are used in training, they must be linked to forbidden behavior. The link sets up a conditional relationship such that the child is taught that if he or she does *x* (the forbidden act), he will receive *y* (the punishment). This conditional relationship is equivalent to "don't do *x* or *y* will happen." That is, the statement means that if a boy does what he has been told not to do, he will be punished. Alternatively, he will be punished unless he refrains from doing *x*. This equivalence has undesirable consequences.

In the first instance, parents who intend to teach children not to *x* are teaching them, instead, to choose between taking a *y* or not doing *x*. Let me use an example. Suppose that parents want to teach Jimmy not to tease his sister Susie. If he teases Susie, they say, Jimmy will not be allowed to go to the movies. Jimmy can scan his choices. Perhaps: "I could tease Susie and watch television instead of going to the movies." Or "I wonder if the movie is as much fun as teasing Susie." In other words, introduction of a punishment has allowed Jimmy a legitimate choice that includes doing what is putatively forbidden.

In the second instance, Jimmy may figure out ways to avoid painful consequences from what is deemed by the punisher to be painful. He may well accept the choice of teasing Susie and not going to the movies. That is, Jimmy may find attractive alternatives to going to the movies.

Another option for Jimmy is to become accustomed to punishment so that such punishment will not hurt. This he could do by deciding not to like movies. If punishments include being sent off alone, he could decide to enjoy solitude. Children learn to repeat behaviors that result in "reinforcement" through such negative attention as being told they are wrong (Gallimore, Tharp, and Kemp 1969; Witte and Grossman 1971).

Physical punishments are not an exception. Children can learn to ignore physical injuries (Goldfarb 1958). In fact, pain-giving consequences seem to acquire positive value through exposure (Aronson, Carlsmith, and Darley 1963; Shipley 1987; Solomon 1980).

There is reason to believe that those who expect to receive pain may actually seek it. For such children, punishments may enhance the attractiveness of forbidden behavior. Some experimental evidence lends credence to this possibility. Walster, Aronson, and Brown (1966) randomly assigned students to one of two conditions. In one, they were led to believe that they would be required to eat terrible foods consisting of caterpillars, grasshoppers, and squid. In the other, the students were led to believe they would be fed cream puffs, pie, cookies, and fruit. Individually, the students participated in an experiment during which they gave themselves shocks. Those assigned to the painful food condition administered more shocks to themselves.

A consequence of punishment, then, seems to be that children come to expect pain and become immune to its deterrent effects. That immunity seems to make them care little about pain, whether it is their own or that of others.

Fifth, the use of punishment teaches children to be egocentric. Punishments can be effective only if children are taught to care for consequences to themselves. A parent who uses punishment in teaching children implies that the children should be concerned with avoiding their own pains.

Hoffman (1963) found negative correlations between the use of power-oriented punishment and consideration of others. My own longitudinal study, which was based on retracing, as adults, adolescent boys for whom there had been direct observations of families decades before, indicates that those whose parents used physical punishments were least likely to be altruistic and most likely to be self-centered (McCord 1988).

Let me summarize my main points:

1. An unintended consequence of punishment includes the fact that punishment serves as an endorsement for giving pain. Though children may know that they cannot give pain under all circumstances, if they accept the punisher's legitimacy, they must acknowledge that giving pain to control others is sometimes acceptable.
2. An unintended consequence of punishment includes the fact that punishment reduces the probability of influencing a child by example or discussion. Yet we know that a good deal of socialization is carried out by showing children how to act and by helping children understand what is expected of them.
3. An unintended consequence of punishment includes making the forbidden more attractive. Punishment adds covert value to misbehavior.
4. Punishments also reduce what might have been prohibited to behavior that can be chosen. By providing choices, rather than enforcing desired actions, the use of punishment dilutes the messages parents would like to convey.
5. Egocentrism, too, is an unintended consequence of punishment. This fact makes it particularly difficult to teach children to be considerate of others while using punishment in the process.

Note

1. I included this evidence in my paper prepared for the American Academy of Pediatrics conference, "The Short and Long Term Consequences of Corporal Punishment," Elk Grove Village, Ill., Feb. 9–10, 1996.

12

Moral Development and Corporal Punishment

JOHN MARTIN RICH

Moral development refers to the growth of the individual's ability to distinguish right and wrong and to develop a system of ethical attitudes and values. It is generally recognized today that moral development is studied from three leading theoretical perspectives: social-learning theory, psychoanalytic theory, and cognitive developmental theory (Irwin 1982).

As other chapters in this book examine these theories in greater detail, this chapter provides a brief summary in terms of the theories bearing on moral development, followed by an application of each theory's findings to corporal punishment. It discloses similarities and differences among the theories and their findings. Finally, it presents other pertinent research findings that do not fit neatly into these theories.

Social-Learning Theory

Bandura (1965), while recognizing that learning occurs through direct experience, emphasizes that learning can take place by observing the example of others. Based on the principle of modeling and imitation, a child who observes a person (model) perform an act is more likely to behave in a similar manner (imitation). Repeated trials may be unnecessary; the child can learn the behavior merely through observation. If a child watches a dummy being kicked and is placed in the room with the dummy, it is more likely that the child will kick the dummy than if she or he had not seen it kicked, even if the child is not rewarded for kicking it and has not seen the model rewarded; however, reinforcement of the model or the child, while it created no new learning, did increase the frequency of the child's performing the act. The child needs to be attentive to what the model does, admire the model, and have the capability of performing the modeled act. Other than parents, the model the child is most likely to emulate is one who can provide rewards and control the consequences of behavior, and who possesses high status. Modeling fosters learning of different kinds of behaviors, such as play patterns, aggression, language, and many social behaviors. Modeling may also create such undesirable responses as overaggressiveness, dishonesty, and deceitfulness.

Social-learning theory emphasizes social situations as the context in which behavior is learned. The mediation of other people is a critical requirement for needs satisfaction. Bandura (1971) concludes that behavior changes that occur through classical and operant conditioning are mediated by processes of cognition and self-regulation.

Mischel and Mischel (1976) hold that a comprehensive psychological approach to morality should include the individual's moral judgments as well as the moral conduct and self-regulatory behaviors needed to achieve moral ideals. To understand moral competence, the concept of cognitive and behavioral construction competencies is offered. The latter term refers to the diverse cognitions and behaviors that the individual is capable of constructing. Every person constructs a highly selective rendition of "reality." Modeling effects have shown that observational learning involves novel organization of information by the individual rather than mirroring observed responses. Age-related cognitive patterns are modifiable when subjects are exposed to relevant cognitive-learning and social-learning experiences designed to alter them (Rosenthal and Whitebrook 1970). Such cognitive skills as linguistic construction and conceptual organization of a set of stimuli are changed through observational learning and rewards. Cognitive competencies related to moral reasoning and conduct can be modified in a similar manner (Prentice 1972).

Moral conduct requires the individual to comply with commitments and obligations under difficult conditions. Such situations require more than problem solving and decision making: they also require the ability to regulate one's behavior for long periods in the face of temptations and social pressures and without the aid of external rewards. With self-regulatory systems the individual adopts contingency rules that specify appropriate behavior, performance criteria, and the consequences of fulfilling or failing to fulfill the criteria. Despite strong countervailing pressures, knowing and utilizing relevant rules to cognitive transformation during self-control efforts may produce considerable self-mastery.

The young child lacks control over behavior and tends to interpret positive and negative outcomes as a result of external rather than internal factors. But the child begins to assume personal responsibility with the growth of cognitive and behavioral competence.

The predictive validity from moral reasoning to moral behavior, in contrast to Kohlberg's claim, is modest, though statistically significant (averaging .30) as typically found in correlational personality studies linking measures from diverse response modes (Mischel 1968). This suggests that overall knowledge of an individual's moral reasoning would enable one to predict no more than 10 percent of the variance in moral behavior.

Little evidence can be found for a superego or a unitary-trait entity of conscience or honesty. Rather, moral action is based on such components as moral judgments, voluntary delay of reward, resistance to temptation, self-reactions to transgressions, and self-reinforcing patterns. Thus this theory emphasizes the specificity of self-control behavior and cognitive and situational variables, thereby encouraging researchers to study specific mechanisms that influence self-regulation and prosocial conduct.

The child develops standards of self-control in three distinctive ways. One is by external monitoring and intervention by authority figures when the child may do personal harm to self or others. Second, the child may anticipate external reward or punishment by those who can reinforce or withhold reinforcement. Third, the maturing child may reach the point where internal control is dominant. Nevertheless, the child continues to accept parental standards as his or her own because of potential feelings of guilt, shame, and self-derogation should the child violate parental judgments (Sears, Maccoby, and Levin 1957). Children develop the ability to depend on themselves, to control themselves, and even punish themselves for transgressions. They reinforce themselves by saying approving words their parents use, control themselves by warning of the consequences of their acts, and punish themselves by self-reproof.

APPLICATIONS TO CORPORAL PUNISHMENT

Social learning is at least one of the factors in the development of aggressive behavior. Children who exhibit high levels of aggressiveness have parents who use corporal punishment. Parents of aggressive children are more likely to use punishment than reward when attempting to shape their children's behavior. The level of a boy's aggressiveness is usually formed by the age of eight (Eron 1982).

Bandura and Walters (1959) compared twenty-six highly aggressive adolescent boys and twenty-six control boys. The aggressive boys were under the supervision of probationary services and had a history of aggressive behavior, whereas the control group was identified by school counselors as neither markedly aggressive nor markedly withdrawn. It was found that the parents of the aggressive boys encouraged their children to be aggressive. Not only did the parents believe that boys should know how to fight and stand up for their rights but the fathers in the aggressive group tended to use physical punishment and deprivation of privileges as disciplinary techniques, whereas fathers in the control group tended to use reasoning more. Additionally, fathers in the aggressive group were less accepting of dependency from the boy than fathers in the control group.

Aronfeed (1968) uses two broad categorizations of the disciplinary measures of parents. The first category is induction, in which the parents seek to transmit their values and also threaten withdrawal of affection as a reaction to the child's transgressions. The second category is sensitization and involves corporal punishment, "screaming" and "bawling out," ridicule, and public shaming. It was found that children would have a more internalized orientation when experiencing discipline of the inductive type than they would from the sensitization type. Additionally, children whose parents use corporal punishment are more likely to be physically aggressive toward their peers than children whose parents who use inductive discipline.

Psychoanalytic Theory

Freud (1932) postulates the id, ego, and superego. The id consists primarily of drives, inherited instincts, or urges, which are like a boiling cauldron of mixed desires, libido, and destructiveness seeking an outlet. But the id, having no sense organs or muscles, has no direct access to the environment and therefore finds its only outlet through the ego, which at first is slightly developed and offers little resistance to the id. But the ego learns the dangers of the environment from experience and recognizes the need to restrain the id and make its instincts conform to the reality principle.

The superego, a third part of the psyche, emerges in early childhood. The ego is split in two: the doer or executive (the ego), and the watcher and moral critic (the superego). Parents and other adults can punish the child and impose rules that must be obeyed. These external rules or commands become internal laws of conduct. As the child grows up, the father's role is carried on by teachers and other authority figures; their injunctions and prohibitions remain powerful in the ego ideal (that is, the child takes them as models) and continue in the form of conscience to exercise moral censorship.

The superego corresponds to conscience insofar as conscience means a blind feeling of right and wrong rather than a knowledge of what is good or socially valuable. Thus the superego says "Thou shalt" and "Thou shalt not" without saying why. It cannot explain its commands because the source of authority is buried in the unconscious. Some neurotic patients are excessively conscientious. They are never satisfied with their behavior and accuse themselves of sins of omission and commission, including going through elaborate rituals of self-punishment. Thus while excessive guilt and conscientiousness may lead to neurosis, without such restraints societal chaos would reign.

A Freudian explanation of children who lack sufficient conscience is the failure to develop a superego, which thereby permits the id to dominate and run roughshod over the ego. Freud believes that a substantial amount of repression is needed to balance id impulses with cultural demands. Sublimation, a form of repression, is a defense mechanism that transforms id impulses into more socially acceptable behavior. Freud (1961) calls upon humans to sublimate aggressive instincts so that civilization can obtain mastery over the dangerous love of aggression. Sublimation serves to build culture in the form of religion, literature, art, and the like. Thus it can be seen that children lacking sufficient conscience are unable to restrain their id impulses and learn to sublimate them.

The Freudian developmental theory assumes a series of biologically determined stages that arise from sexual and erotic feelings. Each stage involves some problem whose resolution determines the personality structures which emerge from that developmental stage, and each stage is a prototype of a major personality component.

Of these stages, the phallic stage is important for our purposes because it is at about the age of four that the superego begins to form. This stage also involves the development of the Oedipus complex, castration anxiety, and sex-role identification. The superego develops in the resolution of the Oedipus complex. The development occurs as the child is able to grasp the parent's values, although children frequently are more rigid and condemnatory of their faults than are their parents. Another reason the superego develops out of the Oedipus complex is that it relieves castration anxiety and the fear of loss of love.

Some neo-Freudians have interpreted the superego and the developmental stages differently. Sarnoff (1976) views the superego's development as encompassing the first three decades of life. Cognitive maturation, psychosexual development, and social expectations contribute throughout this period to superego changes. Sarnoff also holds that the conceptual contents of the superego begin to be acquired as early as six to eighteen months. Before guilt and shame develop to motivate ego functions to enforce superego demands, elation and depression (relating to fear of loss of love) guides the fulfillment of the ego ideal. By the age of six the child is cognitively capable of retaining complex ethical concepts and appreciating and differentiating situations in which they apply.

Erikson (1950) emphasizes cultural factors in the developmental process and gives less weight to purely sexual components in the different stages. Abraham (1954), in his developmental theory, held that there is a linear development of successive phases, in which at each phase one particular erotogenic zone dominates the libidinal life of the child. Pathologies occur because of a fixation at any one stage of development or a regression to such a phase, in which one particular drive freezes the child to that phase.

APPLICATIONS TO CORPORAL PUNISHMENT

Freud postulated driving forces inherent in human nature. He held that not all impulses are based on the seeking of pleasure, for some, as he found in treating traumatic neuroses, are satisfied by the reinstatement of traumatic experiences. Organic matter has a tendency toward the reinstatement of an earlier condition, to return to its primeval inorganic state (Freud 1942). Thanatos is a term for a regressive tendency in organic life, the goal of which is death.

But by postulating thanatos, Freud was faced with the dilemma of accounting for reproductive cells and the sexual instinct for the perpetuation of the race and was, therefore, led to acceptance of instincts for sustaining and enhancing of life processes, which he called eros (Freud 1933).

Freud's dualism centered around the sexual instincts, eros, and the aggressive instincts, thanatos, whose aim is destruction. The opposition of these two forces creates the phenomenon of life, and the two instincts are inherent in all living substances. In the Freudian system humans are faced with the intractable dilemma of either turning the aggressive instincts against others or turning them against themselves. Thus, Freud developed a theoretical position to support his belief in the inherent evilness of humans.

From this conception follows the explanation for sadism and masochism. Sadism represents a fusion of the erotic and aggressive instincts turned outward toward others, while masochism represents the fusion of these instincts turned against oneself for the purposes of self-destruction.

The moral system of the individual is imperiled by aggressive drives. An imbalance may occur because restricting aggression may make the superego more tyrannical. "An increase in the need for punishment beyond its habitual limits will often interfere with the integration of the 'moral system,' and in a variety of ways; for example, in turning a person into a criminal" (Hartmann 1960: 29).

Freud claimed that painful stimulation of the buttocks is one of the erotogenic roots of cruelty. Children who show special cruelty toward animals and playmates usually suggest an intense and precocious sexual activity arising from erotogenic zones. The absence of pity as a barrier creates the danger that the connection may be unbreakable later in life. Corporal punishment, usually applied to the buttocks, should not be inflicted upon children "whose libido is likely to be forced into collateral channels by later demands of cultural education" (Freud 1953, vol. 7: 193).

In speaking of a boy's masochistic tendencies, Freud interpreted deliberate misbehavior as a way of forcing punishment and beatings from his father in order to obtain masochistic sexual satisfaction and satisfying his sense of guilt (Freud 1953, vol. 17: 28). Because of repression, "My father loves me" is turned into "My father is beating me," which now combines the sense of guilt and sexual love. It is not only the forbidden genital relation but also its regressive substitute. The beating fantasy originates in an incestuous attachment to the father (Freud 1953, vol. 17: 198). Freud noticed with his patients that the experience of a child in school witnessing another being beaten aroused in the observing child a peculiar excited feeling of mixed character, with repugnance having a large share. In a few cases the beating was felt to be intolerable (Freud 1953, vol. 17: 180).

Flugel (1945) believes that in the infliction of punishment, sadism and, perhaps to a lesser extent, masochism play a part. But punishment professes to be a moral institution and is exercised by impressive authority figures who stand *in loco parentis* and whose precepts and attitudes we introject to form our superego. Thus the sadism of these authorities and the sadomasochistic relation to which we stand to them, Flugel opines, may be mirrored in the relation of superego and ego in internal life, and the element of cruelty often found in the superego may indicate that the sadism of moral authorities is introjected.

The infliction of vicarious punishment can become a pleasant process because, with the infliction of each blow upon the guilty party, we feel that our own conscience is lightened; and in our righteous indignation we satisfy our primitive aggressiveness, our sadism, and the disapproving superego (which is no longer directed against ourselves). A society whose members are bent on punishing one another for sins will scarcely be harmonious or cooperative. An attempted solution, then, is to project the guilt onto an outside group, but this leads to intergroup conflict and, according to Flugel, is one of the main psychological causes of war. In war there is the possibility that the larger share of the punishment may be enjoyed vicariously through the sufferings of the enemy.

Cognitive Developmental Theory

Research on the cognitive component of morality has proceeded in two directions: a large, unsystematic body of literature; and a more integrated body of literature devoted to the studies of Piaget and Kohlberg on higher values and judgmental processes. It is the latter studies on which I will focus.

Piaget's thought is a form of structuralism. His theory is structured because it abstracts a form of thinking or structure from the function that the thinking is serving. The same function (moral judgment) is served by successive structures of judgment that displace or reintegrate prior structures for serving this purpose. For instance, assimilation is a process common to all aspects of life that give rise to the general schemata we call structures. Schemata are cognitive structures created through the abstraction of previous experience (Piaget 1970).

Piaget's stage theory assumes that cognitive and moral development proceed together. He further claims that the structures and cognitive schemata are innate, invariant, hierarchical, and culturally universal. Piaget's research methodology uses a clinical interview technique whereby the interviewer presents problems to the child, sees how he responds, and probes the limits of his knowledge. His study of morality encompasses only a small sample of male youths from middle-class backgrounds. It focuses on how children play the game of marbles, and how they respond and react to stories of moral events posed by the interviewer.

Piaget holds that morality consists of a set of rules and that all morality is based on respect the individual acquires for the rules. Most rules are developed by adults and then transmitted to children. He recorded observations both of the ideas children of different ages form about the character of game rules and of the way they apply the rules. Piaget referred to the former as "consciousness of rules" and to the latter as the "practice of rules."

Several stages were found in the consciousness and practice of rules. In the earliest stage, which is motor and individual in character, the rules are primarily those that grow out of the child's early neuromuscular development. Between the ages of two and five, children imitate the rules of others, but they either play by themselves or play with others without trying to win. Thus, they imitate rules but practice them in accordance with their own fantasies. Since at this stage the child regards rules as sacred and eternal, any attempted alteration is interpreted as a transgression. Between the ages of seven and eight, a less egocentric and more socially oriented outlook develops. Children now try to win and also show concern for the mutual control and unification of rules — although their ideas about them are somewhat vague.

Mastery of the rules proceeds by degrees; between the ages of eleven and twelve the rules of the game have stabilized, and players exhibit a consensus. At this age children take pleasure in discussing rules and the principles upon which they are based. They recognize that the rules are formed by mutual consent and that, once agreed to, they should be observed in playing the game; nevertheless, they realize that a majority can change the rules. In other words, at this age children's practices and attitudes toward rules closely resemble those of adults (Piaget 1965).

The cognitive moral development theory by Kohlberg (1983) was influenced by Piaget's and Dewey's psychological writings. Kohlberg believes that a necessary, but not sufficient, condition for morality is the ability to reason logically. His theory, he claims, is both psychological and philosophical, and his findings generate a philosophy of moral education designed to stimulate moral development rather than teach fixed moral rules. Kohlberg believes that a philosophic concept of morality and moral development is required, that moral development passes through invariant qualitative stages, and that moral development is stimulated by promoting thinking and problem solving. Justice, Kohlberg holds, is the key principle in the development of moral judgment.

Kohlberg's study yielded six developmental stages allotted to three moral levels:

I. *Preconventional Level*
 Stage 1: Orientation to punishment, obedience, and physical and material power. Rules are obeyed to avoid punishment.
 Stage 2: Naive instrumental hedonistic orientation. The child conforms to obtain rewards.
II. *Conventional Level*
 Stage 3: "Good-boy" orientation designed to win approval and maintain expectations of one's immediate group. The child conforms to avoid disapproval. One earns approval by being "nice."
 Stage 4: Orientation to authority, law, and duty to maintain a fixed order, whether social or religious. Right behavior consists of doing one's duty and abiding by the social order.
III. *Postconventional, Autonomous, or Principled Level*
 Stage 5: Social contract orientation, in which duties are defined in terms of contract and the respect of other's rights.
 Emphasis is upon equality and mutual obligation within a democratic

order. There is an awareness of relativism of personal values and the use of procedural rules in reaching consensus.

Stage 6: The morality of individual principles of conscience that have logical comprehensiveness and universality. Rightness of acts is determined by conscience in accord with ethical principles that appeal to comprehensiveness, universality, and consistency. These principles are not concrete (like the Ten Commandments) but general and abstract (like the Golden Rule, the categorical imperative).

These stages are based on ways of thinking about moral matters. Stages 1 and 2 are characteristic of young children, whereas stages 3 and 4, according to Kohlberg, are ones at which most of the adult population operates. No more than 20 to 25 percent of the adult population have reached the last two stages, with only about 5 to 10 percent at stage 6.

Kohlberg (1969) contends that the stages are "structured wholes" or organized systems of thought. Stages imply qualitatively different modes of thinking. Second, stages form an invariant sequence. Third, stages are "hierarchical integrations."

Stages are defined according to responses to moral dilemmas classified in terms of a scoring scheme. Validating studies include a twenty-five-year study of fifty Chicago-area boys, middle and working class; a six-year study of Turkish village and city boys of the same age; and various cross-sectional studies in Britain, Canada, India, Honduras, Taiwan, and the Yucatan.

Stages are organized systems of thought, as about 67 percent of most subjects' thinking is at a single stage irrespective of which moral dilemma is used to test it. The typology is referred to as "stages" because they represent invariant developmental sequences: all movement is forward and does not omit steps, and the stages arise one at a time and in the same order, even though children move through the stages at varying speeds. The stages are hierarchical insofar as thinking at a higher stage comprehends within it thinking at lower stages. Individuals prefer the highest stage available to them in their thinking because higher stages can more adequately organize the multiplicity of data, interests, and possibilities open to each person. Thus the higher stages are not only more socially adaptive but also philosophically superior because they move the individual closer to basing moral decisions upon a concept of justice (stage 6).

APPLICATIONS TO CORPORAL PUNISHMENT

Stage 1 in Kohlberg's theory is based on punishment, obedience, and physical and material power where rules are obeyed to avoid punishment, whereas stage 2 is characterized by conformity to obtain rewards. Higher stages move sharply away from both punishment and reward and are defined in terms of duties based on contract and respect for others' rights (stage 5), or a morality of conscience that has logical comprehensiveness and universality (stage 6).

One principle to keep in mind: individuals are likely to reject moral reasoning below their level and be unable to assimilate that which is above their level (Turiel 1964). Early stages of morality may need to rely considerably on reward and punishment — though not necessarily corporal punishment. Piaget views this early stage as *heteronomous morality,* where the young child bases his morality on respect for authority figures and the "objective" rules of parents and other adults (Piaget 1965). Children at this stage see rules only as things to be done to avoid punishment or obtain rewards. If children are to develop a more autonomous morality in later years, they require a consistent pattern of rules in their early years. Punishment, however, is less justified in late childhood and early adolescence (assuming moral development is not arrested). Piaget believes that an autonomous morality, or a morality of equity and cooperation, begins by middle childhood or early adolescence. In this stage, social experience — principally peer interaction — becomes the main vehicle for increasing cooperative egalitarian growth.

Related Developmental Studies

Loevinger and Wessler (1979) have inquired into women's experience in constructing their theory of ego development, although they imply that the theory may apply to males as well as females. The study employs a method of psychoanalytic projective testing involving sentence-completion tests that are relatively unstructured and designed to reveal the subject's affective as well as cognitive thought patterns. Subjects are given word stems (for example, "I feel sorry . . ." or "When they avoided me . . .") and are then asked to complete each stem in their own words and thoughts. Loevinger's material highlights emotional dilemmas and conflicts about morality that were not included in Kohlberg's investigations. Loevinger applies the qualitative findings of projective testing to quantitative measures of psychometrics. On the basis of these findings, she has formulated an eight-stage theory of ego development as follows (Kohlberg's analogous stages are noted in parenthesis):

1. Presocial
2. Symbiotic
3. Impulsive (orientation to punishment and obedience)
4. Self-protective (naively hedonistic orientation)
5. Conformity ("good-boy" orientation)

6. Conscientious (transition from authority to contractual orientation)
7. Autonomous (contractual orientation)
8. Integrated (principled orientation)

Loevinger and Wessler place each stage in the context of distinctive dilemmas or conflicts undergone to acquire impulse control in character development. Stages 1 and 2 are characterized by the emergence of the ego or self in a largely undifferentiated state in which the infant and young child must connect their presocial self to social relationships. At stage 3 individual thought and action is governed by anticipation of reward of punishment. The individual begins to develop concepts of "right" and "wrong" or blameworthiness into his or her character structure at stage 4, but feelings of self-control and self-mastery are not resolved at this stage. The *conformist* stage (stage 5) shows that most people reflect the attitudes, beliefs, and values of their group connections. But at the level of *conscientiousness* (stage 6) the individual begins to make self-decisions and establish personal goals. Loevinger finds this stage in late adolescents and young adults and has observed it in college students. It is also a period of tension, since the individual is turning away from more conventional thought. The maturing individual experiences deeper conflict at the *autonomous* stage (stage 7) as he or she becomes more sensitive to many situations and changes, develops respect for others' rights, and seeks self-fulfillment. Not more than 1 percent enter stage 8, in which an integrated reconciliation of previous conflicts and polarization occurs. These individuals are able to handle paradox and ambiguity, to value justice and idealism, to oppose prejudice, to manage inner conflicts, to appreciate relationships, and to manifest both humor and wisdom.

Concluding Observations

Thus the Piaget, Kohlberg, and Loevinger/Wessler theories consider punishment at a childhood or early childhood stage of development. The implications are that those disciplinary or socialization systems that utilize punishment exclusively would arrest moral development; therefore it would only be appropriate to employ these systems during the earliest years of life and only at a minimum in later childhood and adolescence if the individual is to move away from heteronomous morality toward a more autonomous morality.

In contrast, social-learning theory emphasizes self-regulatory systems in which the individual adapts contingency rules that specify appropriate behavior, performance criteria, and the consequences of fulfilling or failing to fulfill the criteria. Since it has been found that parents of aggressive children are more likely to use punishment than rewards in disciplining, that parents of aggressive boys encourage their children to be aggressive, and that children whose parents use corporal punishment are more likely to be aggressive toward peers, it is likely that new parenting skills will need to be learned through improved parental education.

Psychoanalytic theory relates corporal punishment to sadism and masochism based on sexual satisfaction and alleviating a sense of guilt, manifesting an element of cruelty in the superego. Maurer (1981) holds that beating and whipping experiences are closely linked with sexual deviations in adulthood. Because sexual deviants may enter the teaching profession undetected, it is best to remove temptation from those unable to resist it. The problem is compounded by teachers who are seriously maladjusted. It is estimated that there are 180,000 teachers who are seriously disturbed and, by extrapolation, about 4,500,000 students who are exposed to them (Wohlford and Chibucos 1975).

Many countries have banned corporal punishment in public schools. Sweden has passed legislation prohibiting parents from hitting their children. Educators and social scientists should seek to determine the policies, programs, and practices in those countries that have either repealed corporal punishment or never endorsed it in order better to assess social and moral outcomes and promising new alternatives.

13

Corporal Punishment of Children
A Communication-Theory Perspective

DOMINIC A. INFANTE

A traditional view of corporal punishment of children is that using physical force to achieve compliance with parents' wishes is sometimes necessary, especially when children do not respond positively to parents' verbal and nonverbal messages that attempt to influence the child's behavior. In essence, corporal punishment is seen as a social-influence strategy of last resort, used "when communication fails." For instance, a father might give his son a disapproving look along with negative head movements to stop the child from pulling the family dog's tail. If these nonverbal messages do not succeed, a verbal message, followed by another, and perhaps another, might be employed to stop the child's behavior. If the child continues to resist this attempted influence, the parent might conclude that he has no other choice but to spank the child.

According to the communication-theory perspective taken in this chapter, there are at least three major problems with this traditional view of corporal punishment. First, corporal punishment is not a physical act that is apart from a sequence of failed communication attempts. Rather, corporal punishment is one of the messages in the sequence. Physical punishments, such as shoving, paddling, slapping, pinching, and shaking are *tactilic* messages, that is, messages conveyed by touch. Among other things, power and status are communicated effectively by tactilic codes (Leathers 1986). The physical pain produced by corporal punishment can make children vividly aware of their vulnerability to parental power. A technique sometimes used to intensify the effect of the tactilic code is to deliver a verbally aggressive message simultaneously; for example, "You're a real bad boy!" Thus, corporal punishment can involve a "double dose" of pain, the physical pain produced by the aggressive tactilic message coupled with the psychological pain of verbal aggression. Viewing corporal punishment as message behavior suggests we may examine corporal punishment by using standard questions for evaluating messages; for example, How competent was the message and its delivery? What alternative messages could have better accomplished the message source's objectives?

A second problem with the traditional view of corporal punishment is the assumption that meaning of the message is unequivocal; that is, "In order to avoid this pain, comply with my wishes now." However, messages having multiple meanings are more the rule than the exception, and there seems no basis for declaring that corporal punishment is such an exception. At least three additional meanings may be even more salient than the "to avoid the pain, comply now" meaning. Along the lines of Berkowitz's (1962) analysis, the child may conclude, "What I have learned from this is physical aggression is an appropriate and effective way to get people to do things. It sure worked well on me!" Another, no less damaging meaning pertains to one's self-concept: "I must be a bad person to deserve punishment like this." A rather common yet unintended meaning might be: "He must not like me as much as I thought; otherwise, why would he hit me?" A communication-theory perspective focuses upon the meaning of messages, both intentional and unintentional.

The third fault with the traditional view of corporal punishment is that the blame for the speaker's failure to persuade is shifted to the message receiver. This is tantamount, for instance, to saying consumers are to blame if an advertiser spends a great deal of money on unsuccessful ads. It is self-evident that such a claim about consumers' responses is untenable. Yet corporal punishment is sometimes justified by similar faulty logic. I will argue that it is not valid to claim corporal punishment is justified because earlier messages failed. Instead, I will contend the earlier arguments probably were not particularly good and better arguments need to be invented. For instance, if arguments do not appeal to what is important to a child, it would not be surprising if the child does not pay much attention to the message. I will contend that the *argumentative-skill deficiencies* of parents make corporal punishment more likely because these parents come to a very premature conclusion that "there is nothing left to say, other than spanking." I will develop the idea that parents having argumentative skills reduces the tendency to shift blame to the receiver for the failure of a particular verbal message, and hence also reduces resorting to corporal punishment based on the perceived "stubbornness" of the message receiver.

In analyzing corporal punishment of children from a communication-theory perspective, we should bear in mind first of all that there is no "grand theory" of communication, explaining all aspects of human communicative behavior. Instead, "communication theory" is more of a superordinate term for a collection of fairly specific theories about different types of communication. I will utilize several. What this means here is that corporal punishment is viewed as message behavior, especially the tactilic code, reinforced at times by verbal aggression and also nonverbal codes, such as proxemics, kinesics, paralinguistics, and eye and facial behavior. In relating corporal punishment to communication theory, I will first determine what is and what is not communicative behavior. I will then conceptualize corporal punishment as a type of communication termed social influence. Of the several types of social influence, I will conclude, the primary process in effect for corporal punishment is compliance. I will examine the various compliance-gaining strategies, including corporal punishment. The idea of failing to gain compliance will be viewed in terms of communication competence. Parents who use corporal punishment may lack communication competence. The thesis that will guide the analysis is that argumentatively skilled parents who are affirming and low in verbal aggressiveness are more likely to succeed in verbally persuading a child and therefore are less likely to resort to corporal punishment. These ideas suggest parents and also children need to learn how to argue constructively, and parents especially need to talk to children in a style that is affirming and low in verbal aggressiveness.

Relating Corporal Punishment to Communication Theory

WHAT IS AND WHAT IS NOT COMMUNICATION?

In order to establish that corporal punishment is communication, we need to determine first what is and what is not communication. A definition of communication is "when humans manipulate symbols to stimulate meaning in other humans" (Infante, Rancer, and Womack 1993: 10). When there is no use of symbols, there is no communication. Not all human behavior, therefore, is communicative. Meaning may be stimulated by nonsymbolic behavior (for example, a sneeze), but communication is not involved. This is based on Cronkhite's (1986) model of *sign arbitrariness.*

According to this model a sign is anything that stands for something else. There are three types, each varying along a continuum of arbitrariness. One type is a *symptom,* a totally natural occurring sign of something which is nonarbitrary — for example, a high fever is a sign of illness. These signs are not communicative behavior. They can stimulate meaning in perceivers, but they do not do so intentionally and therefore are not message behavior. Thus, people with high fevers are not "telling us" they are sick. By perceiving the fever (via a thermometer) we arrive at meaning about the person's state of health through signs over which the person has no immediate control. A person emitting naturally occurring signs and making no attempt to modify the signs in some way is not engaged in communication.

Symbols are at the other end of the continuum in that they are totally arbitrary. Symbols are created to stand for something else. Verbal signs and some of our nonverbal signs represent communicative behavior because, even if enacted at a very low level of awareness, they involve "doing something" with signs that are designed to refer to something. This is the activity of manipulating symbols, which is the essential characteristic of communication behavior.

Rituals, on the other hand, are intermediate on the arbitrariness continuum. These signs are nonarbitrary in the sense that they occur naturally. However, they are also arbitrary to a degree because they can be manipulated or changed in order to stimulate one meaning rather than another in people who interpret the signs. For instance, if a woman changes the color of her hair so that she is seen as more physically attractive, this would represent communicative behavior because she did something with a naturally occurring sign (hair color) in order to stimulate a particular meaning or impression in people. A symptom is ritualized when it is manipulated to modify naturally occurring meaning.

Cronkhite's (1986) model has clarified the focus and scope of the study of communication. Prior to this model there was confusion because Watzlawick, Beavin, and Jackson's (1967) axiom "You cannot not communication" was commonly interpreted in the communication field to mean that all human behavior is communicative. This was misleading because saying something is "everything" begs the question of what it is.

This model facilitates conceptualizing corporal punishment as communicative-message behavior. A tactilic message uses ritualized touch as a sign to stimulate meaning — for example, a congratulatory slap on the back. Corporal punishment also uses ritualized touch as a sign. A slap as corporal punishment, for example, has been ritualized so that it is not as mild as a well-wishing slap on the back but not so strong as to immobilize a person. Slapping is done in a way to startle and alarm a child by a stinging sensation that usually has a very specific meaning — for example, "Stop that, right now!" Thus, corporal punishment uses the skin as a sensory organ to stimulate meaning by rituals that have been stylized into parent-child messages.

These tactilic messages often are reinforced by verbal and other nonverbal messages. For example, a parent might say while slapping a child, "Listen to me when I say stop it!" and display a menacing facial expression and paralinguistic cues, such as increased pitch and volume and a stern tone of voice.

There is a not so subtle difference between this view of corporal punishment as communication and the idea of corporal punishment as something one must resort to when communication fails. The latter implies that there is little choice but to use corporal punishment once a verbal message has failed to influence a child. The former, however, suggests that since there is no known limit on the messages that we can create, it is not valid to say that we have no choice but to use corporal punishment. The more competent the communicator, the more messages he or she can create, and thus the perception of "no choice" is not likely. This will be shown later to pertain to the idea that communication-skill deficiencies of parents make the use of corporal punishment more likely.

CORPORAL PUNISHMENT AS SOCIAL INFLUENCE

Social influence involves people attempting to effect change in other people. Distinctions are commonly made between two forms, coercion and persuasion. An attempt at influence is coercive when force is applied to receivers so they do not perceive a choice in accepting or rejecting the position in a message. The classic example of this is "Your money or your brains!" delivered at gunpoint. Persuasion, however, involves perceived choice by the receiver. The message source presents evidence and reasons for claims about a position, and the receiver feels free to accept or reject the position.

Corporal punishment may be classified as a coercive rather than a persuasive form of social influence. A parent might attempt persuasion prior to enacting corporal punishment. However, corporal punishment itself is not persuasion, because a tactilic message does not present evidence and reasons for claims about positions. Verbal messages do this best. Tactilic messages communicate certain emotional meanings (Leathers 1986). Corporal punishment is a coercive form of social influence because the receiver does not perceive a choice; for example, "If I continue this behavior that my parents want stopped, I will continue to be slapped."

Distinctions also are made among less coercive forms of social influence. Kelman's (1961) model specifies three processes. *Internalization* is a social-influence process where the receiver accepts the influence attempt because its content is congruent with the receiver's beliefs and values. The message source is viewed as credible, someone whose information can be trusted. The induced change is internalized, becoming resistant to further change, and the induced behavior is performed regardless of the source's presence. This is functionally equivalent to "persuasion," as described earlier.

Identification is a process that depends upon the receiver having a "satisfying self-defining relationship" with the source. That is, the source is seen as attractive, charismatic, a model for the receiver's self-actualization. The receiver is influenced because of this identification, that is, through a desire to "be like" the source. The induced behavior is not necessarily internalized, and its performance depends upon the source being present or the receiver thinking of his or her relationship with the source.

The process of *compliance* involves a source who has the power to reward or punish the receiver. Influence is motivated by the desire for rewards and the fear of punishments. Here also the induced behavior is not internalized but is more utilitarian, performed not for intrinsic value but for reward value or cost avoidance. The source in this case is seen as powerful, which outweighs other perceptions.

Corporal punishment, as a form of social influence, does not involve internalization. Parents who use corporal punishment may hope that the child will realize that the object of influence is congruent with the child's beliefs and values and therefore is accepted as a part of the self. However, this is an unrealistic expectation for corporal punishment, since it is a tactilic message and touch (other than by the system of braille) is inherently incapable of communicating claims along with evidence and reasons. Instead, tactile messages are useful mainly to communicate affect (Knapp 1980) and relationship concepts like power and status (Leathers 1986). Parents who want to achieve internalization in their children need to be persuasive by using argumentative discourse. This idea will be developed later.

The social-influence process of identification can operate when parents use corporal punishment, but not in a particularly constructive manner. If a child has a self-defining relationship with a parent and the parent uses corporal punishment to influence the child, the process of identification may lead the child to "be like" the parent by becoming a person who uses physical aggression to influence people. Thus, aggression can beget aggression. This idea is consistent with evidence on the intergenerational transmission of family violence (for example, Kalmuss 1984).

Of the three processes, then, corporal punishment most clearly involves the process of compliance. Corporal punishment using a tactile message code says rather unequivocally, "Do what I say in order to avoid more punishment."

Touch communicates power clearly (Leathers 1986), and a heightened awareness of parental power created by corporal punishment provides the basis for a child's behavioral change. When punishment avoidance is the sole basis for behavior change, the process in Kelman's (1961) terms is compliance.

Since the contention here is that corporal punishment mainly involves compliance as a social-influence process, a closer examination may provide insights into the use of corporal punishment as a compliance- gaining tactic. A considerable amount of research in the communication discipline has focused on compliance-gaining strategies.

CORPORAL PUNISHMENT AS A COMPLIANCE-GAINING STRATEGY

Communication research on compliance-gaining strategies (see Dillard 1990 for a synthesis) was influenced by Marwell and Schmitt's (1967) study that derived sixteen different compliance-gaining strategies from previous theory and research. Generally, these strategies can be classified as reward oriented (for example, other people will be proud of the individual) or punishment oriented (for example, threatening the individual). These strategies have been utilized to investigate a variety of situations, including family communication (deTurk and Miller 1983).

Hunter and Boster (1987) suggest that the selection process for compliance-gaining messages is controlled by the persuader's threshold of how much negative affect he or she is willing to stimulate in a receiver in order to achieve compliance. According to Hunter and Boster (1987), "The more compliance-gaining messages a persuader finds unacceptable, the higher that persuader's threshold" (1987: 65). Individuals with high thresholds for negativity mainly use only those messages that create a good deal of positive affect because all others create more negative affect than they are willing to stimulate. A person with a low threshold for what is acceptable, on the other hand, finds almost any strategy acceptable and therefore is willing to use a variety of reward-oriented and punishment-oriented strategies, because they are willing to stimulate considerable negative affect in receivers. A recent study (Infante, Anderson, Martin, Herington, and Kim 1992) tested this model and found that supervisors with low thresholds for negativity were seen by their subordinates as having a particular pattern of communication traits — high verbal aggressiveness, low argumentativeness, and low affirming style — and subordinates were less satisfied with such superiors.

A study by deTurk (1987) emphasized that physical aggression, which is not included in the Marwell and Schmitt (1967) typology, also is a compliance-gaining strategy; it uses direct coercion and is more likely to be used when persuaders fail to obtain their goals using verbal strategies.

These ideas may be applied to parent-child communication. Parents use compliance-gaining tactics, such as those outlined by Marwell and Schmitt (1967), when attempting to control children. In fact, several studies (for example, deTurk and Miller 1983; Miller, Boster, Rolloff, and Seibold 1977) have utilized parent-child scenarios with those tactics. Corporal punishment can be classified as a rather mild type of physical aggression. In line with deTurk's (1987) model, corporal punishment is a compliance-gaining tactic, one that is more likely after verbal tactics fail.

If corporal punishment is a compliance-gaining tactic that is used after other tactics fail, an apparent issue is, Why do other tactics fail? As explained earlier, for a message source to blame the receiver for a message's failure is seldom tenable. A more obvious reason for failure usually lies with the competence of the influence attempt. Parents who use corporal punishment because other compliance-gaining attempts failed may not be especially competent communicators.

Communication competence has been investigated rather extensively (for instance, see Rubin 1982, 1985; Spitzberg and Cupach 1984; Weimann 1977). Two basic components of communication competence are appropriateness and effectiveness. Appropriateness entails the use of verbal and nonverbal messages that result in no loss of face for the parties involved. Effectiveness means the creation and delivery of messages that allow individuals to achieve their goals. Thus, if a parent uses several compliance-gaining tactics that all fail to influence a child, the effectiveness criterion of competence would not be satisfied. However, if a tactic succeeds in achieving a parent's goal but in doing so causes a child to lose face, then communication incompetence is indicated by inappropriateness. Negative or punishment-oriented compliance-gaining tactics are particularly likely to produce face loss. This is especially true for corporal punishment when a third party observes the act.

What is competent communication in parent-child control situations? The next section will develop the idea that the use of persuasion (a position supported by claims based on evidence and reasoning) can represent competence. Reward-oriented compliance-gaining tactics, such as positive esteem, which stimulate favorable affect, also can indicate competence.

In the language of Hunter and Boster's (1987) model, parents who use corporal punishment are willing to stimulate considerable negativity in children and therefore are willing to use a variety of compliance-gaining tactics, both positive and negative. A plausible progression in attempting to control a child might be that a parent typically begins with one or two reward-oriented strategies, since, as Hunter and Boster (1987) point out, people generally prefer strategies that produce positive affect. If these fail to obtain behavior change, the tactics might become increasingly negative, culminating in corporal punishment as a compliance-gaining tactic of last resort. Parents with a high threshold for what is an acceptable tactic might also begin with reward-oriented strategies. If these fail, rather than proceed to punishment-oriented strategies that are unacceptable because of their negativity, parents might then attempt persuasion, which is generally more difficult to execute than compliance because persuasion usually entails more complex reasoning and appeals based on the receiver's beliefs, attitudes, and values. I will go into more detail concerning these patterns in the next section.

Aggressive-Communication Competence

Why do some parents use corporal punishment and other tactics producing negative affect to control children? Why do other parents use argumentative discourse to persuade their children? These are all aggressive forms of communication, and to answer these questions we need to determine the nature of aggressive-communication competence. I will present a model of aggressive communication and then relate it to corporal punishment.

A MODEL OF AGGRESSIVE COMMUNICATION

Infante (1987) posited that aggressive communication is controlled mainly by four communication traits that interact with factors in the environment to energize particular message behavior. Two of the traits are essentially constructive and two are destructive. This pertains to the idea that aggression can be good or bad.

The constructive traits are assertiveness and argumentativeness. *Assertiveness* is a more global trait, by which one is interpersonally ascendant, dominant, and forceful and uses this behavior for personal gain while creating positive affect in other people (Infante 1987). An example would be group members being pleased that a particular person emerged as their leader. According to Costa and McCrae's (1980) three-factor model of personality, assertiveness is a facet of the extroversion dimension of personality.

Argumentativeness is the trait of advocating and defending positions on controversial issues while attempting to refute the positions that other people take on those issues (Infante and Rancer 1982). Argumentativeness is a subset of assertiveness because all arguing is assertive, but not all assertiveness involves argument—for example, making a request. A good deal of communication research suggests argumentativeness is a very constructive trait (for example, Infante 1981, 1987, 1989; Infante and Gorden 1985, 1987, 1989, 1991; Rancer, Kosberg, and Baukus 1992).

Hostility is the trait of using messages to express irritability, negativism, suspicion, and resentment (Buss and Durkee 1957). Hostility is a facet of the neuroticism dimension of personality (Costa and McCrae 1980). Like the other traits, hostility interacts with situational and other factors. Thus, an aggressive gesture might provoke a hostile response from the receiver in one situation but not in another where the receiver, for example, might be more concerned with satisfying an affiliation need with a third party.

Verbal aggressiveness is the trait of attacking the self-concepts of other people in order to stimulate psychological pain, such as humiliation, embarrassment, and other negative feelings about the self (Infante and Wigley 1986). Verbal aggressiveness is a subset of hostility, which is the more global trait. The locus of attack distinguishes argumentativeness from verbal aggressiveness, that is, positions on issues versus self-concept. Examples of verbally aggressive messages are attacks on character, competence, background, or physical appearance, threats, maledictions, ridicule, and nonverbal emblems. Research has been rather unequivocal in concluding that verbal aggressiveness is a destructive form of communication (for example, Infante, Chandler, and Rudd 1989; Infante, Sabourin, Rudd, and Shannon 1990; Infante, Riddle, Horvath, and Tumlin 1992; Payne and Sabourin 1990; Rancer, Baukus, and Amato 1986; Straus, Sweet, and Vissing 1989).

The argumentativeness and verbal-aggressiveness models have been used to investigate family communication. Several studies have implications for understanding corporal punishment. These will be reviewed here briefly and the implications presented in the next section.

Low argumentativeness and high verbal aggressiveness of spouses has been related to low marital satisfaction (Payne and Sabourin 1990; Rancer, Baukus, and Amato 1986). Parents who were higher in argumentativeness and lower in verbal aggressiveness were more authoritative in parenting style (using reason and encouraging give and take) while parents low in argumentativeness and high in verbal aggressiveness were more authoritarian in style (unilateral, no reasons given, discouraging disagreement) (Bayer and Cegala 1992). Another recent study found that husbands with verbally aggressive wives were more likely to suffer from depression (Segrin and Fitzpatrick 1992). Interspousal violence was predicted by low argumentativeness and higher verbal aggressiveness of husbands and wives (Infante, Chandler, and Rudd 1989). A related study observed that violent marital disputes contain more verbal aggression, especially attacks on character and competence, when compared to disputes in nonviolent marriages (Infante, Sabourin, Rudd, and Shannon 1990).

A good deal of the argumentativeness and verbal-aggressiveness research has focused on superior-subordinate communication in organizations. Since the parent-child relationship is a superior-subordinate one, this research should be relevant to our topic; so, some results will be reviewed briefly. Generally, this research has found that subordinates are more satisfied with superiors and more committed to the organization when their supervisors are higher in argumentativeness, lower in verbal aggressiveness, and affirming in communicator style (Infante and Gorden 1985, 1987, 1989, 1991). Affirming style is relaxed, friendly, and attentive and is essential to a positive view of arguing. Even if subordinates do not like to argue, they prefer having a superior who encourages argument (Gorden, Infante, and Graham 1988). Subordinates who were judged by their supervisors as successful were higher in argumentativeness, affirming, and lower in verbal aggressiveness (Gorden, Infante, and Izzo 1988; Infante and Gorden 1989). These findings raise the possibility that children, as subordinates, may prefer in their parents a pattern like that found in the superior-subordinate research.

The ideas in this section provide a basis for conceptualizing corporal punishment of children as an aggressive parent-child communication exchange, one that is more likely or unlikely depending upon the parents' communication traits. As a whole, the discussion suggests the use of corporal punishment by parents is more likely when parents lack argumentative skills, are higher in verbal aggressiveness, and are lower in affirming style.

Lower trait argumentativeness has been equated with less argumentative skill (Infante 1981, 1985; Onyekwere, Rubin, and Infante 1990). When parents are unskilled argumentatively they may not attempt persuasion to control children, because successful persuasion involves formulating convincing arguments relevant to the receiver about the object of persuasion. Instead, compliance-gaining tactics (for example, pregiving, threat, negative esteem) that require little or no argumentative competence are employed. If one fails, another is tried, and this is repeated until the parent is frustrated and concludes that a forceful tactile compliance-gaining message is warranted—that is, corporal punishment. The speculation that lower argumentativeness, lower affirming style, and higher verbal aggressiveness are associated with more compliance-gaining message usage was supported in a study of superior-subordinate communication (Infante, Anderson, Martin, Herington, and Kim 1992). The idea that lower argumentativeness and higher verbal aggressiveness in parents is related to an autocratic parenting style that eschews persuasion was observed in the study by Bayer and Cegala (1992) reported above.

The constructive-destructive model of aggressive communication along with the ideas discussed in the previous sections provide a rationale for declaring what is destructive and what is constructive parent-child communication when parents attempt to correct or change children's behavior.

DESTRUCTIVE PARENT-CHILD COMMUNICATION

Parents with low thresholds for acceptable compliance-gaining tactics use a greater variety of tactics because most cross the threshold of what is an acceptable amount of negativity one should evoke in others. Since some of the tactics can cause considerable negativity, unfavorable outcomes are not implausible. For instance, "negative altercasting" (Marwell and Schmitt 1967) basically says that only a person with bad qualities would not comply with a request. This is potentially harmful to a child because if the child does not comply and is unable to refute the altercasting claim, a negative change in self-concept might seem necessary to the child. This type of message is verbally aggressive because it attacks the child's self-concept. That the verbal aggression of parents directed at children is harmful is well documented (Straus, Sweet, and Vissing 1989).

Corporal punishment appears to be a negative affect producing compliance-gaining tactic. If it produces negative affect, the outcomes are usually destructive. Of course, an aggressive behavior can produce negative affect but in the long run result in a positive outcome, for example, forcing someone to stop a self-destructive behavior, such as a drug addiction. It is possible, however, that the positive outcome could have been produced by more favorable means.

According to the aggressive-communication model, assertiveness and argumentativeness are constructive. If corporal punishment can be shown to constitute either of these two forms of aggressiveness, corporal punishment could be called, at times, constructive. It does not seem possible for the latter to be enacted by a tactile message (other than braille). For instance, touch cannot be used to symbolize a message like "There are three reasons why you should stop that; number one. . . ."

Whether assertiveness is possible with a tactile message is not as unequivocal. Recall that for a message to be assertive it must attempt to accomplish the source's goal in an ascendant, dominant, and forceful manner while creating positive affect in the receiver. Whether this is possible with corporal punishment is difficult to imagine because it would have to entail a parent slapping a child, for example, and the child experiencing positive affect, such as acceptance, instead of negative affect. Of course, positive and negative affect can be experienced together. In that case, an issue would still remain as to whether such mixed or confused emotions are constructive for the child.

Corporal punishment fits with greater ease on the destructive side of the model. Hostility involves messages used to express irritability, negativism, suspicion, and resentment. Tactile messages, such as slapping, grabbing, shaking, pushing, and pinching, are particularly able to communicate these ideas.

Other nonverbal message codes, such as facial expressions, eye behaviors, gestures, and posture changes, are delivered to reinforce the tactile message. Of special importance is the fact that corporal punishment is sometimes accompanied by verbally aggressive messages, such as "I can't believe you were so stupid!" "You're a real bad boy for doing that!" The psychological pain of verbal aggression coupled with the physical pain of corporal punishment can be more than the child is able to bear, and destructive outcomes, such as those noted by Straus, Sweet, and Vissing (1989), can result — for example, school discipline problems.

Another way corporal punishment can be destructive is derived from the superior-subordinate research which contends that, in America at least, freedom of speech is valued almost above all else and subordinates resent it greatly when superiors deny subordinates the opportunity to express their views (Gorden and Infante 1987, 1991). Corporal punishment, like the unilateral decision making of the autocratic supervisor who says, "Do it my way or you're fired," can have a chilling effect on motivation to communicate. Resentment similar to that observed in superior-subordinate communication may be stimulated when a child feels that he or she has valid reasons for behaving in a particular manner but is distracted from explaining these reasons by the trauma of corporal punishment. This may have an inhibiting effect on future parent-child communication if the child believes that talk is useless or that the parent does not want to consider the child's reasons for his or her behavior.

CONSTRUCTIVE PARENT-CHILD COMMUNICATION

The ideas developed in this chapter also provide a basis for specifying what is constructive communication when parents attempt to influence children's behavior. From the perspective taken in this chapter, parental influence is accomplished best by persuasion. If a parent thinks a child should start or stop a particular behavior, the parent should provide reasons. If the reasons seem persuasive to the parent, the parent should be able to make them persuasive also to the child. In Kelman's (1961) terms, this represents internalization, the most enduring form of social influence. However, if the child successfully refutes the parent's reasons, the parent should reconsider the validity of the request for behavioral change. This would represent an authoritative as compared to an authoritarian parenting style (Bayer and Cegala 1992).

This formulation follows the basic model of argumentation (Infante 1988) — that is, the person who advocates change has the burden of proof, while the person who receives a prima facie case is obliged to attempt refutation. Advocacy and refutation of positions concerning change are based on the claims that are supported by evidence (data) and reasons. This is considered "rational discourse" because of the emphasis on valid reasoning and a reasonable set of obligations as a communicator. I have contended in this chapter that parents who attempt persuasion with their children by being argumentative are engaging in constructive communication because they are using rational discourse that aims specifically at internalization and avoids negative affect producing compliance-gaining tactics, of which corporal punishment is the most extreme type.

Parents who employ persuasion, besides being constructive in the particular situation, may also have a positive effect in the long run because, just as physical violence as an influence tactic is transmitted from one generation to the next, rational tactics likewise can be learned.

Constructive parent-child communication, as suggested earlier, also employs affirming and low verbal aggressiveness styles. One thing particularly clear from the superior-subordinate studies discussed above is that verbal aggressiveness is greatly disliked. Basically, a communicator who is low in verbal aggressiveness displays an awareness of the other's self-concept and a protective stance toward it.

All of this suggests, then, at this particular stage of theory and research, that the most constructive communicative behavior in parent-child influence situations may be characterized by the parent being relaxed (for example, soft and easy gestures, facial expressions, and voice), friendly (for example, smiling, close proxemics, touching), and attentive (for example, eye contact, nodding, paraphrasing), while arguing with the child in a low verbally aggressive manner. In the optimum case the child would reciprocate this communicative behavior because it was learned from the parents as the manner in which disagreements should be settled. The argument follows the form explained earlier; generally, the parent presents his or her case for the child behaving in a particular manner, and the child is encouraged to speak to the case.

Implications and Future Directions

A communication-theory perspective on corporal punishment says, essentially, that the act of corporal punishment is message behavior and should be viewed in conjunction with other messages in the situation, along with the history of the person's message behavior, that is, his or her traits. Several implications follow from this analysis.

Rejecting the idea of a child's stubbornness as justification for corporal punishment and placing responsibility for a message's failure on the message source suggests that parents' communication competence may be an important factor in understanding corporal punishment as a parenting behavior. While a good deal of research has explored communication competence (see Rubin 1990 for a summary), little research has focused specifically on parental communication competence. We have contended that argumentative skill is part of this; however, whether there are other components needs to be determined. Further, are the criteria for competence different from those in other contexts, such as superior-subordinate organizational communication competence? (For a conception see Monge, Bachman, Dillard, and Eisenberg 1982.)

Perhaps the most obvious implication in terms of alternatives to corporal punishment is that parents and children need to know how to argue constructively in order to make corporal punishment unnecessary. Research is needed to determine effects of argumentative skill and training on parent-child communication. Argumentative-skill enhancement is not unusually difficult to achieve. The discipline of communication has specialized since antiquity in correcting argumentative-skill deficiencies. Numerous books present the principles of argumentation theory (for example, Freeley 1966; Infante 1988; Jensen 1981; Rieke and Sillars 1984). Experimentally, a person's argumentativeness can be manipulated readily, and it has been observed to have a favorable effect on leadership behavior (Schultz 1982) and on perceptions of source credibility (Infante 1985).

That persuasion employing argumentation is superior to corporal punishment in influencing children has been treated almost as axiomatic in this chapter. Although previous models and related research emphatically point in that direction, the contention is an empirical issue that has yet to be tested. Numerous dependent variables appear relevant in comparing persuasion and corporal punishment — for example, short-term and long-term behavioral change, willingness to communicate with parents, school discipline problems, level of life satisfaction, conflict-resolution styles, depression, and so forth. A conceptual framework needs to be developed for determining which of the many potential dependent variables should be examined.

Treating corporal punishment as a message in relation to other messages directed our analysis to the idea that parental verbal aggression may not only precede corporal punishment in the sequence of messages that lead to corporal punishment but may also accompany the physically aggressive tactile message in order to reinforce it by a "double dose" of both physical and psychological pain. Little is known about such verbal aggression. In terms of previous typologies (Infante and Wigley 1986), are the messages primarily character and competence attacks, or are other types, such as ridicule and maledictions, used? Moreover, which type do children view as most hurtful? Do children use verbal aggression that serves as a catalyst for parental aggressive behavior? In light of a recent typology of reasons for verbal aggression (Infante, Riddle, Horvath, and Tumlin 1992), why do parents use verbal aggression with children? How aware are parents of the hurt created by verbally aggressive messages? How do verbally aggressive parents resolve the cognitive dissonance produced by hurtful behavior toward loved ones?

Since verbal aggression appears firmly linked to physical aggression, and perhaps to corporal punishment as a form of physical aggression, more research is needed on the causes of verbal aggression, since methods of control typically derive from knowledge of causes. Although argumentative-skill deficiencies are probably responsible for a major portion of verbal aggression in society, other causes also operate. Some identified by Infante, Trebing, Shepherd, and Seeds (1984) are disdain, frustration, social learning, and psychopathology (transference, where people are attacked with verbally aggressive messages because they remind the source of unresolved hurt). In light of its destructiveness and because less verbal aggression probably corresponds to less corporal punishment, methods of control need to be developed and tested. The outcomes of such research could be particularly welcome.

14

Conflict Theory of Corporal Punishment

RANDALL COLLINS

Conflict operates analogously on all levels, from large-scale warfare, political struggles, and social movements down to intimate personal relationships. Differences in scale are significant only because they affect the strength of the variables, not the shape of the conflict process. Let us consider briefly the main principles of conflict theory. (1) Any resource that affects social interactions produces interests in using that resource to control other persons; and the capacity to control in turn sets up a latent conflict. (2) Three kinds of resources are coercive power, material wealth, and emotional ritual. The third of these is especially important because it creates feelings of group solidarity and symbols of memberships; it can paste over lines of personal conflict but also can greatly intensify any conflict that does break out. (3) Conflict becomes overt to the extent there are resources for mobilizing interests. The winner in the conflict is the one with the most resources. When resources are extremely one-sided, dominants get their way without overt conflict; conversely, when both sides are equal, conflict is stalemated. Conflict is most likely to happen when resources are changing through the middle ranges of inequality or when there is ambiguity in perceiving the resources of both sides. (4) Conflict de-escalates as mobilizing resources are used up. This happens through physical casualties and material destruction, and also through the exhaustion of ritualistic or emotional resources. Because fewer resources are used up, mild conflicts can last much longer than severe conflicts (Dahrendorf 1959; Kriesburg 1982; Collins 1975, 1983).

As we apply such principles to corporal punishment within the family, we should bear in mind that there is continuity from the normal processes of control within the family, through its minor quarrels and disagreements, up to fully mobilized violence. The same conflict principles operate throughout; only the particular variables shift. Love and affection are within the scope of conflict theory too; they are one end of the continuum of emotion solidarity but are also interests around which conflicts break out, which can give family violence a deep-seated emotional and symbolic twist. It is important to see that corporal punishment is part of a two-sided struggle for control. However much the sympathy of the outside observer may be on the side of a child or an abused spouse, no one is purely passive, and it is necessary to see how the process of conflict is built up from both sides. Conflict theory should forewarn us: unequal resources produce conflicts, and conflict itself has a ritualistic quality, which escalates emotionally from small, often symbolic beginnings. Even babies have some resources that contribute to the process of conflict escalation.

Let us consider first how various resourcers within the family generate conflicts, then take up the dynamics of conflict processes. The sources of parent-child conflicts are contending interests: local power, class, and status division, so to speak, within the family.

Coercive Power in the Family

On the level of the small group, coercive power mainly consists in direct physical strength and threat. Parents start out as bigger than their children; this is the reason they can use corporal punishment in the first place. When the disparity is greatest, one would expect that minimal threat or occasional use of token force on the part of the stronger would be sufficient to assure dominance. This of course assumes that other things are equal, which is not always the case; even physically helpless small children have resources or motivations that sometimes bring them to challenge adults to use their superior force. The analytically important point is that, taking coercive power in isolation, as the relative physical strength of parents and children changes, the likelihood of physical confrontation increases. Children grow up; parents grow old. At some point they converge in strength and even reverse positions.[1]

Several things follow. Teenagers have more physical power than smaller children and are more of a threat to parents' control. They need not be as big as the parent before their increased strength shifts the balance of power and brings about confrontations. Because of such shifts fathers are more likely physically to punish teenagers, while mothers are more active in punishing smaller children (if we can infer this from data on child abuse in Garbarino and Gilliam 1980). Moreover, boys become more likely to use their strength than girls, not only for cultural reasons but also because of muscular maturation. This need have nothing to do with any innate masculine drive to use force; it follows directly from the principle of conflict theory that increasing availability of a resource motivates one to use it to gain power.[2]

There is also an indirect route from children's physical force to parents' punishment. As children grow in strength, they change in power relative to each other within the local group — siblings or neighborhood, whatever it may be. This destabilizes the situation, perhaps over and over again, and raises the likelihood of fights. Moving to a different neighbourhood or school, adjusting to a stronger boy coming into the crowd or another one leaving — all these can move the lineup of physical strengths nearer to the point where conflict breaks out, or they can introduce temporary uncertainties where the relative powers are not well known and thus promote challenges and testing. It may be for just these sorts of reasons that "tough" inner-city neighborhoods have so much fighting among the children: not because of a culture of violence per se but because of a higher degree of turnover than is likely to exist in a stable suburb. There is in short a small-scale geopolitics of coercive forces among children; this has not been much studied yet, but one can expect that the principles of conflict theory which determine the outbreaks of warfare operate here as well.[3]

The indirect route to parents' behavior is that adults often intervene to control their children's fighting. Within the home and in relation to smaller children, a frequent instigation of parental use of corporal punishment is a fight between siblings (and in fact sibling violence is the most frequent kind of violence within the family: Gelles 1977). Parents seem especially likely to intervene to take the side of a girl against a brother, or of the younger against the older. Here parents are operating just like a state following the balance of power doctrine in international politics, taking the side of the weaker in order to stabilize resources on both sides. (The general theory of third-party interventions is given in Black 1993: 97–143.) Such interventions are not always successful, especially if there are other destabilizing elements or uncertainties in the situation (such as those described in the previous paragraph). Parents intervening in childrens' conflicts is often like the United Nations intervening to keep the peace in Somalia or Bosnia; the intervention changes the balance of power, but not consistently or efficaciously enough to prevent further outbreaks. And it adds yet further feelings of grievance on one side or another, so that the neutral mediator may end up being a new target of conflict for the punished party. Childrens' conflicts thus escalate into conflicts between parents and children; hence the cycle moving back and forth between fights among siblings (or neighborhood kids) and corporal punishment by parents. This is not merely a learning effect but a full-fledged reciprocal structure of cause and effect.

Material Conflicts within the Family

Material resources in the family consist of livelihood and luxuries that for the most part are controlled by parents. Historically, the control of material resources was most extreme in the patrimonial household organization of traditional societies; there the family was the property-owning unit, and children were valuable workers.[4] This type of structure used to be common in American society among farm families, where a fairly strict discipline was enforced; in effect, the child was an employee of the parent, paid in kind. This kind of family organization carries over in contemporary society to some immigrant families. Persons who come from a low-wage economy are especially willing to take on the highly labor-intensive, long-hours businesses that most natives of a high-wage economy like that of the United States find onerous, such as family-operated restaurants, convenience stores, and the like (Bonacich 1972). Here the labor-management conflict that was always latent beneath the surface of the patrimonial household tends to become overt. Immigrants children are pressed into working, often without remuneration, in the family business; at the same time, they compare themselves to native-born peers whose time after school is free or devoted to paid work outside the family.[5] Rebellion sometimes follows, which may escalate into physical punishment by the parent and violent retaliation by the youngster. Here again we may expect that the most severe conflict will happen when the situation is destabilized, in the transition between the dominant family economy and the taken-for-granted American extrafamilial pattern of work.

Conflict over material resources also exists in the modern sector. More research is needed on the range and frequency of things that parents quarrel about with their children; if quarrels between husbands and wives are any guide, conflicts over how to spend money are likely to be high on the list.[6] In the case of children, conflicts take place over allowances, clothes, toys, and cars. Sometimes, either when children are especially rebellious or when their peer group is into carousing, a conflict can emerge because the children (and their friends) destroy family property — for instance, by having a potlatchlike wild party in the home. All such conflicts can escalate to physical punishment and subsequent retribution.

When are these kinds of material conflicts most likely? Age has contradictory effects; older children acquire greater material desires and hence conflicting interests; on the other hand, as teenagers earn more of their own incomes, material conflicts are mitigated. The family's social class should make a large difference. In the upper class, the family holds out large material resources for children, which make physical punishments largely unnecessary. This does not mean wealthy families do not have fights; the distribution of property as children grow up is often a cause of conflict, all the more so because the younger generation may effectively remain in the condition of dependent children for a very long time (sometimes into their sixties or later) while waiting for their inheritance. It would appear that upper-class family conflicts center on money and are fought out by civil proceedings in the courts. In the upper-middle class, the main family resource is paying for the child's education, as well as passing along cultural capital and professional connections that facilitate entry into high-ranking careers. These resources, doled out incrementally and bringing a sequence of status recognitions, probably contribute to the "well-socialized" behavior of these children, and to a minimum of physical punishment.

Conflicts are most likely where parents demand achievement from the children but cannot contribute much financially or culturally toward their education and their career start; this is most likely in the lower-middle class or among downwardly mobile members of the upper-middle class. A certain amount of family violence may break out from either side, since these conflicts most likely involve relatively larger teenagers or college-age students. A typical scenario is the escalation of punishments and conflicts: taking away driving privileges and the like as punishment for poor grades, followed by further anger and rebellion, leading to violence by either parent or child; some cases of family murder have been the culmination of this pattern (from the author's newspaper files). In the working class, parents have fewer material resources to use in controlling their children and less ability to hold out career prospects through their cultural access to education. Working-class parents are motivated to fall back on physical punishment because it is a cheap resource; even if it is not very effective, it may seem better than nothing when material controls are not available. This pattern is found a fortiori in the lower classes, where the family may provide virtually no subsistence at all; for instance, in the urban black lower class where the family is replaced by a loose, sharing network of relatives and friends centered on adult women (Stack 1974), children may not depend on a particular parent consistently for daily subsistence, and hence material control is virtually absent. Here violence is common because there are few other controls. The violence that takes place in lower-class gangs is structurally continuous with the violence of the household — not because this is a self-sustaining culture of violence but because coercion is one of the few means of control available anywhere.

Emotional Ritual and Social Solidarity

We have been treating the foregoing patterns analytically and in isolation. This no doubt will give some readers the sense that conflict theory is unrealistically harsh and interest oriented, as if parents and children coldly calculate their coercive and material resources like states at war. In real life, everything operates simultaneously; the emotional and symbolic aspect of the family overlays material and power relations. This does not mean that conflicts go away. The overall balance of control among family members is made up by their relative resources on all three dimensions. If the processes that produce family solidarity are strong enough, they can submerge raw conflicts on the other dimensions; but family solidarity can also rise and fall as the result of other forms of conflict and control.

Social solidarity in the family is usually experienced as love, affection, or respect. These feelings do not merely happen; they are produced by people putting attention and emotion into their interactions. Attention and emotion are scarce resources, to the extent that various persons and situations inside and outside the family compete for them. Conflict theory is very far from attempting to be brutally hard-boiled on this point; love and affection are good things, highly desired by children and perhaps by everybody. Precisely because love is so much in demand, it is subject to competition and can lead to very intense conflicts.

Very small children generally are given a great deal of affectionate attention for a time. Once they have had this, they come to expect more of the same; inevitably, the honeymoon of early infancy is followed by a comedown as parents resume their normal round of sharing out their attention among the other persons and concerns in their lives. Similar fluctuations can happen throughout childhood and adulthood too. New siblings come, others depart; there are divorces and remarriages; parents' careers, sex lives, athletic interests, and the like all affect how much time and energy there is to devote to their children. With enough information about the network of interactions, a sociologist could chart these ups and downs of social concern and predict where each child (and each adult) would get an increase or a decrease in attention. The decrease in attention is not necessarily debilitating; it is a healthy process for an infant to outgrow the dense surroundings of parental affection, so long as the child develops his or her own new sources of social attention as networks broaden to include other people and there are other activities that build emotional energy. The struggle for attention becomes severe only when there is a decrease in parents' affection that is not compensated by some new source on the child's part.

Let us narrow in for a moment on the microsituational scale, to examine the way in which the struggle for affection operates upon the emotions of parents and children. Consider a typical scene: late in the day, one parent is at home in good-humored conversation with the children. The other spouse comes in; let us say it is the mother coming home from work. She is greeted by a burst of happy cries, reciprocated by hugs and kisses. A few minutes later, however, the children are no longer so good-humored; they are whining and demanding things of her, while she is trying to relax and unwind from her day. Soon she has a burst of anger and the good mood is gone. Interactionally, the situation changed from one in which the children had the undivided attention of one parent to a situation in which two parents are present. There is now a competition for attention; and the children fall from a favorable to an unfavorable position, when the adults want to pay attention to each other, for instance, in debriefing the professional events of the day. There is nothing so very fatal about this micro up-and-down of emotions; whether these small conflicts result in an overall negative situation in the family depends on the total amount of interest conflict going on.

If the balance tends to the negative side, small conflicts escalate into large ones; sometimes this results in situations that the parents interpret as the children getting out of hand, thus calling for punishment. Consider the phenomenon of crying. If one examines in microsociological detail situations of major family violence involving smaller children — ones where an adult severely beats a child — it is likely in many or most cases that the child has been crying, perhaps noisily and at length. Like all emotions overtly expressed, crying evokes answering emotions in persons nearby, usually at first sympathy and concern; but if distress is not alleviated and the crying does not stop, it builds a situation of emotional intensity on all sides, which can explode into anger. For the adult, the crying can be experienced as a move in a conflict; physical punishment is a counterattack and an attempt to put to an end the aggravation. A typical scene of violent child abuse involves the mother, her boyfriend, and her small child. The boyfriend has little or no emotional bond to the child; moreover, they are rivals for the affection of the mother. There is likely to be a three-way conflict, between mother and boyfriend over how to handle the baby and between mother and child too, since the baby is aggressively demanding her attention. Each conflict can exacerbate the others, leading to persistent crying on the part of the baby and built-up anger on the part of the adults. The extreme violence that sometimes takes place may well be precipitated because the child, who is hurt by spanking or slapping, continues to cry; the level of violence escalates until the child is too badly hurt to make any more noise.[7]

Such cases are extreme; a milder version of this dynamic, however, is fairly common. Crying is a resource held by the child; following conflict theory, we can expect the resource to be used in the struggle for control. At a fundamental level, crying is a signal wired into the human nervous system: a cry of distress and a call for help. Children quickly learn that this signal can be deliberately controlled and used to get an adult's attention. In microsociological research, if one listens to children's crying in natural situations, one frequently hears small children crying with an up-and-down flow of intensity. Their voices range from whimpering and whining up to loud crying, and down again; this is particularly common in situations where the child is trying to get something, such as an object from another small child, or attention from a babysitter or parent. The inference is unmistakable that children can modulate their crying in the moderate ranges, deliberately cranking it up or down for its effects on other persons.

A commonly observed situation is one in which an adult is busy working or socializing with other adults and the child makes a demand for attention that the parent attends to only slightly. The child escalates the pitch, turning up the crying mode. Eventually this brings attention, which is initially soothing; but this does not end the crying, since as soon as the parent feels he or she can turn his or her attention back to the main thing he or she is trying to do, the crying begins again. The parent's emotion changes from sympathy to annoyance. The crying becomes a weapon in a conflict; and whether or not the parent consciously perceives it as such, he or she retaliates with punishment. This need not be a violent action, perhaps only an angry word or threat, or a demand that the child go and do something. Since the adult is busy with something else and does not want to spend time on enforcing the threat, it usually does not work. This scenario typically builds up to an outburst on the part of the parent. If this happens, the child has won a victory by provoking the parent's attention. The surface content of the communication is negative; but on the deeper emotional level, there is a flow of momentary connection. The angry outburst is itself an interaction ritual, an expression of relationship tie.

As the result of such dynamics, some children come to take angry words or physical punishment as a positive social reward. Punishment is sometimes interpreted in psychodynamic accounts as a sign of love; from a sociological viewpoint, it is not so much a symbolic displacement as an immediate grati-fication of the demand for attention. Better negative attention than no atten-tion at all. Doubtless there are relatively few families in which children get attention only in negative form. How much of an attraction negative attention is for children, and thus how much they are willing to pay the price of physical punishment in order to get it, depends on the relative balance of their differ-ence sources of social solidarity. What becomes clinically sadomasochistic derives from a social situation in which the child gets very little intense emo-tional contact except in punishment situations. On the other hand, if a child has many other occasions for positive contact, a punishment situation is more purely noxious and is to be avoided.

Punishment has a ritualistic aspect from the side of the parents as well. Many parents regard physical punishment as not only legitimate but also desirable, especially for boys (Straus, Gelles, and Steinmetz 1980). To capture the full force of the situation, we should see that for these parents, punishment is not just a necessary evil but morally proper. This calls for a brief explanation of the sociological theory of rituals (Durkheim 1912/1954; Goffman 1967; Collins 1988: 188–203). A ritual is an interaction that creates or reinforces feelings of social membership, drawing boundaries between insiders and out-siders and setting moral standards for members to show their loyalty to the group and its symbols. The best-known rituals are formal ones: flag salutes, weddings, graduations, holiday gift exchanges, and the like; there is also a class of rituals in everyday life that represent the degree of intimacy in personal interactions: conversational greeting and departure ceremonies, kisses, shared drinks and meals. Since rituals convey membership, the flaunting of an ex-pected ritual carries an implication that the relationship is being violated; and since the history of past rituals has built up an emotional tie between the persons involved, the failure of a ritual causes the emotion experienced as justified anger. This is the reason why a typical minor family quarrel breaks out when family members do not come to dinner on time; sitting together at dinner is a ritual, and failing to do so is not just a practical issue but conveys a little break in family solidarity.

Rituals are not necessarily recognized as such. They can occur as "natural rituals" (Collins 1988: 197–99) whenever the basic ingredients are present: the group assembled face to face; awareness of a common focus of attention, usually promoted by some shared stereotypical action that excludes outsiders; a shared emotional mood. If these are present, the emotion grows more intense among all participants, resulting in an additional emotion: the feeling of at-tunement, which manifests itself in a feeling of membership. It is through this process that particular actions become symbols of relationships. Physical punishment has these ritual characteristics — indeed, more than other kinds of punishment, such as material deprivation ("You can't drive the car on Saturday night") or social isolation ("Go to your room"); the physical punishment situation necessarily brings the punisher and punishee together face to face (or at least face to rump), creating a strong focus of attention and an emotional buildup. The surface contents of the emotion need not be exactly the same on both sides; but there is always some contagion of nervous excitement, anger, and fear. "This is going to hurt me as much as it will hurt you" is not strictly an accurate statement, but it does convey an emotional truth that something is shared.

The result is that physical punishment tends to create a ritual bond between parent and child. The bond can be full of anger; but it is typical of rituals that there are two levels of emotion simultaneously (at a funeral, grief but also solidarity; at a political rally against an enemy, anger but also solidarity). Moreover, it is typical of rituals that the surface emotion dissipates as the situation changes, while the solidarity feeling continues as long as the relationship is periodically reenacted. This is how punishment rituals come to carry a moral connotation in the feelings of persons in whose families such rituals were among the most intense forms of interaction. Men who were brought up with physical punishment will often speak of how their fathers would beat them ("Boy, would I get a whipping!") with an affectionate and nostalgic tone. Children are often punished for ritualistic pranks; these are deliberate violations of conventional order, as if daring and provoking punishment. Many families and communities in the more traditional sector of society have a reciprocating cycle of pranks and physical punishment, not unlike the conflictual cycles of tribal vendettas, in this case carried on as a series of ritual provocations and retaliations between the generations.

The same kind of process occurs when abused women interpret the physical attacks of their sexual partner as a "sign of love" (Henton et al. 1983). In all these cases, the physical violence is experienced as a ritual, in which the solidarity aspects are uppermost. It is important to see that there is a continuum here: at one end, a purely aggressive assault by the male, a violent rape; but further up the continuum, physical struggles set off a flow of emotion that results in sexual arousal. The existence of this continuum is one reason why the more blatant domestic assaults are often ignored or excused. The process is one of ritualistic social interactions, not a static internalized state of sadomasochism or identification with the aggressor. In the case of children who have been routinely subjected to physical punishment and then go on to use it when they become parents, the process is not necessarily a displacement of pent-up aggression onto a weaker victim. The former punishee is not merely taking it out on someone else. To analyze it thus would be to overlook the feelings that usually go along with ritual punishment, that it is *morally proper*. This is the intergenerational transmission of a tradition, a feeling of carrying on family solidarity from generation to generation.[8]

Why does this process characterize some families more than others? The theory of rituals holds that the amount of ritualism varies on a continuum, depending on the density and differentiation of the social structure. Life is most ritualistic where the local community is turned in on itself and there are few contacts with outsiders. This is the "tribal" pattern, found both in non-modern societies and in the modern world in rural areas and small towns. Even within the urban agglomeration, there may be relatively isolated local pockets: ethnic ghettos, households turned in on themselves as the result of recent migration, language, or lack of social networks. We may expect that the naturally occurring ritualism of such families will be high—that is, there is a strong focus of attention, exclusion of outsiders, and emotional contagion among members, whether or not this manifests itself in formalistic ritualism. Here there are strong sources of ritual solidarity. Of course there are other forms of ritualism besides punishment rituals; such families may be tightly integrated around positive interactions. But in an isolated structure, where there are few resources (such as material ones) coming in from the outside, subordinate family members are strongly under parental control. When conflicts escalate, they easily turn into physical punishment rituals, and these flow into the cycle of ritualistic recurrence.[9]

On the other side of the spectrum, ritualism is least likely where the social network is wide and diffuse, with little recurrent focus of attention. The extreme end of the continuum often does not actually exist; a more moderate version is approximated in the cosmopolitan networks of middle-class urban life. Here there is less ritualism of every kind. That is not to say that physical punishment is never used; but when it is, it is less likely to be the focus of attention within a closed family community; in fact it would be more likely to drive the individual away from family interactions, resulting in avoidance rather than solidarity. In all families, there are conflict situations of the various kinds outlined above, which can escalate to the level of violence. In a tightly focused, inwardly turned network, fights and punishments tend to take the form of repetitive rituals, which reinforce family solidarity even in a conflictual and tension-laden form. In the cosmopolitan structure of loose networks embedding family members in many directions, conflicts are centrifugal; the ritualism of violent punishment tends to be self-inhibiting because it undermines the assembly of the group, which is one of its key conditions.

SOME DIRECTIONS FOR RESEARCH

Areas where further research is called for are implicit throughout the preceding pages. By way of summary, let me list some key points that need further study:

Coercive power in the family.

We need systematic comparisons of the relative physical strengths of mothers, fathers, and their children, and especially of changes over time in these strengths, in relation to propensities for violent conflict in the family. We need to pay attention to ways in which children contribute to the chain of conflict escalation in the family, including patterns of physical fighting between siblings leading to parental intervention. A broader context for study is the local neighborhood or schoolyard "geopolitics" of children of varying strengths, with their patterns of alliances, bullying relations, and victimization, as this interrelates with family conflicts.

Material conflicts in the family.

We need comparative studies of the kinds of material conflicts that take place in families of different social classes. One case is the latent "labor/management" struggle between children and parents (often recent immigrants) who continue the patrimonial household tradition of requiring unpaid labor in a family business. We need tests of the extent to which "well-socialized" children of the upper-middle classes are being successfully controlled by material and cultural capital, and thus become a contrast case of especially low family conflict and punishment. Conversely, we need studies of how families pressing their children strongly for achievement, but lacking the cultural capital or other resources to facilitate that achievement, risk escalating patterns of punishment and rebellion, culminating sometimes in high levels of family violence. For lower-class families, a key area of research is the extent to which children in loose, sharing networks are not dependent on any parent consistently for material support and thus live in a world in which few sources of social influence exist besides violence.

Emotional solidarity ritual in families.

Several kinds of studies are relevant here. The dynamics of small children crying needs to be studied in detail, with special attention to the temporal patterns of crying and the emotional responses that this has upon parents or caretakers. Such research could have important applied outcomes, eventually providing material for training programs about how caretakers of small children can avoid getting caught up in the escalation of conflict over emotional control that can build up to violent abuse. We need systematic research on the conflicting demands on parents' attention at various times of the day, on one side from their children, and on the other side from "adult" demands on their time; the focus here should be on microsociological dynamics of whining and other strategies of attention demanding by children, which lead to getting attention *faute de mieux* in the negative mode of punishment. And we need studies of the types of families in which punishment is a traditional ritual, especially one that is a principal (or perhaps even exclusive) form of male contact between the generations; emphasis should be on studying the ritualized conditions that cause belief in the moral rightness of physical punishment. From a theoretical viewpoint, the key comparison is between "tribal" structures of localized, inwardly turned or sharply bounded communities that promote ritualism, on the one hand, and loose cosmopolitan social networks that reduce punishment ritualism, on the other.

DE-ESCALATING FAMILY VIOLENCE: PRACTICAL IMPLICATIONS OF
CONFLICT THEORY

Family violence is usually not very extreme. Unlike in full-scale warfare, comparatively few people get killed or badly wounded, little material wealth is used up for weapons, and little property is destroyed. From the point of view of conflict theory, this is a reason why family violence can be sustained for so long. The main reason why major social conflicts de-escalate is that the burden of costs becomes too high. Since mild conflicts go on longer than severe ones, most family violence, including physical punishment, can be a relatively stable, chronic pattern, especially if it is integrated into other forms of control.

Some conditions do change the amount of corporal punishment used. We have already noted that periods of transition in the relative balance of resources are the times when overt conflict is most likely to beak out. Once the transition is completed and the new balance of family power is recognized, conflict and hence overt violence should subside. Perhaps most important for the long-term diminution of family violence is the pattern of social change away from the "tribalistic" structures of inwardly turning, socially isolated families and communities. To the extent that individuals move into cosmopolitan networks, and into affluent middle-class material conditions, family violence should decline. The trouble is that social change does not inevitably go in this direction; many aspects of modern urban life promote local group isolation rather than reduce it.

Sociological analysis cannot itself change the structure. What it can contribute is greater capacity for diagnoses, and hence alertness to dangerous situations. The more that parents can be made aware of the ritualistic processes of conflict, and of precipitating conditions in balances of power, material resources, and the struggle for attention, the better the chances of heading off the more violent levels of conflict. It may be effective to aim publicity campaigns at children and at parents, via television or schools: to outline typical conditions and scenarios in which family conflicts escalate, similar to informational campaigns of alertness for situational signs of sexual abuse. Raising the level of sociological awareness of conflict situations may thus contribute to reducing their destructiveness.

Notes

1. In the modern Western household physical confrontations between parents and children are for the most part one on one. Historically this was not always the case. In many traditional societies, the state gave heads of families the right or even the obligation to control their children, with whatever force was deemed necessary. Typically such societies were organized in what Weber called patrimonial households; property-owning families had armed servants (Collins 1986: 267–96). Hence even an aging father could control his grown sons by force, by having servants execute his orders. The opportunity for such conflicts was also likely to be high when property consisted in family lands, herds, or business and the son could not inherit until his father died. In societies where the extended kinship network or clan was also the form of government, murder or open warfare between fathers and sons (and also between grown brothers) was not uncommon; there are many instances of this among the herding tribes in the African Sahel region, in ancient India before the rise of the Maurya dynasty, and in the clan politics of Ireland and Scotland until the seventeenth century (Paige and Paige 1981: 122–66; Thapar 1966, 57; Cambridge Modern History 1907: 589).

2. The point is testable: girls who are larger and stronger than other girls should also be more likely to fight back against parents and to use force against other children. Among small children, where differences in strength between boys and girls have not yet developed, scattered observations suggest that girls do a fair amount of provoking fights. I have frequently seen my daughter between the ages of about three to six kick or trip her slightly older brother; conversations with other parents confirm that the pattern is common.

3. Particularly relevant are the forms of warfare found among small tribal bands, with their ritual confrontations and vendettas, typically claiming only one victim at a time. These resemble the "drive-by" pattern of gang fighting and may also operate among smaller children in yet narrower territories of the neighborhood or home.

4. This was not so, however, in small gathering economies, where children often produced a fair amount of the food; in simple band societies, there was a good deal of wandering of individuals from one temporary camp-site group to another (Lee and Devore 1968). This is one reason why such societies have often had very mild child-rearing practices.

5. In my own generation, the son of a Lithuanian immigrant used to complain to his father about being required to work after school in the family grocery store, since none of the other kids in his peer group had to do so. "The other boys?" was his father's reply. "They don't work because they're gangsters!" This was his perception of the American teen peer group, which typically does not exist in the society of traditional households.

6. Another typical instigator of quarrels is the choice of family entertainment; this is in part a struggle over the allocation of material resources too. It is overlaid with the "status-culture" dimension, since different kinds of movies, music, sports, and so forth are emblems of membership in different kinds of groups; and thus a struggle over where a family should go on a Saturday, and indeed whether they can all agree to go together, is a conflict over the relative value of different membership ties.

7. From court files in a child-abuse case: an adult female babysitter held a small child's hand under scalding water in the bath tub until the hand was burned so badly that fingers had to be amputated. The scenario can be reconstructed: the little girl did not like the bath; the babysitter grew exasperated and tried to control the child by holding her in the water; as the child's screaming grew louder, the babysitter tried to make her stop by turning up the hot water.

8. A premodern analogy is tribal rituals, such as tortures in male rites of passage or genital mutilation of girls carried out by older women. For cases see Paige and Paige 1981.

9. Sports violence has much the same structure of ritualistic integration through conflict. Sports is the main forum of large-scale, intense ritualistic group assembly in modern society; it manifests especially strong attachment in communities where there are relatively few other activities competing for attention, that is, where the social density of interaction is narrowly focused and cosmopolitan networks are lacking. The culture of sports violence and of ritualistic family punishment should thus tend to be correlated.

Punishment of Children from the Perspective of Control Theory

TRAVIS HIRSCHI AND

MICHAEL R. GOTTFREDSON

Control theory (Gottfredson and Hirschi 1993) assumes that individuals are capable of committing delinquent and criminal acts without benefit of example, training, or rewards over and above those inherent in the acts themselves. This assumption, more than any other, distinguishes control theory from other psychological and sociological theories. In control theory, criminal behavior is likely whenever its advantages outweigh immediate and long-term risks, as perceived by the individual. Given the natural ability of individuals to see the immediate advantages of delinquent and criminal acts, the task for society is to persuade them that such acts are not in their long-term interests. Given the natural ability of individuals to see the immediate advantages of crime, society should not be unduly concerned with protecting them from exposure to such information. Put another way: The benefits of speeding, theft, assault, and drug use are obvious. Efforts to control them by denying or distorting their benefits are unlikely to be effective.

Control theory assumes that delinquent and criminal acts provide immediate and obvious benefits, or satisfaction of ordinary human desires, at little expense of time or energy. It assumes that they are, at the same time, costly to others and to the long-term interests of the offender. Contrary to common academic and popular images of crimes, which depict them as highly motivated, complicated, and organized, control theory sees the vast majority of criminal acts as opportunities and simple, requiring little in the way of preparation or skill. These assumptions stress the availability of crimes to everyone, and the idea that no special motivation or training is required for their commission. The question, from a control-theory point of view, is how society can efficiently and effectively monitor the behavior of so many potential offenders and convince them that crime is something to be avoided.

Forms of Control

Since Jeremy Bentham, four methods of crime control or sanction systems have been described:

1. Natural sanctions, which involve the pains of injury, disease, and loss of life imposed as a direct consequence of the act.
2. Moral or social sanctions, which involve the pains of isolation and loss of reputation and affection.
3. Legal sanctions, which involve deprivations of life, liberty, and property imposed by the state.
4. Supernatural sanctions, which involve losses and deprivations in an afterlife.

Let us examine each of these control mechanisms as they apply to child rearing and crime and delinquency.

NATURAL SANCTIONS

Children quickly learn the natural consequences of many forms of behavior. Steps and stoves are dangerous, as are animals, machines, and larger children. These lessons tend to come directly from the environment, are easily learned, and are powerful shapers of behavior. They provide boundaries to natural curiosity and templates for the learning of consequences of behavior more generally. Because natural lessons are so prevalent or so harsh, parents must often intervene to prevent or ameliorate their effects. At the same time, parents may take advantage of these mechanisms to illustrate more generally the connections between acts and their consequences. Because humans are rational and perceptive, they can presumably quickly generalize such lessons to a variety of acts and consequences.

This is not to say that all violations of natural laws are automatically or immediately punished. On the contrary, in many cases the relevant consequences of a certain line of behavior are uncertain and much delayed. Cigarette smoking more often than not produces no immediate illness or disease, and it rarely produces delayed illnesses or diseases for which it can be held wholly responsible. The probability of an accident fatal to a drunken driver on a single trip home from a bar is for all intents and purposes zero. Numerous risky sexual encounters may produce no untoward outcomes for their participants.

Interestingly enough, probabilistic connections between behavior and its consequences, such as these, may be better teachers of reality than deterministic connections, such as those provided by hot stoves and steep stairs. In most cases in real life, penalties are far removed and unlikely. However, the more frequently repeated the behavior, the greater the likelihood of penalty, such that, given a large enough number of occurrences, sanctions become virtually certain. This fact is a major focus of effective education. And indeed, actions with long-term uncertain consequences are more likely to be avoided by educated than by uneducated segments of the public.

SOCIAL SANCTIONS

Social sanctions are penalties provided by others, as when a parent expresses disapproval, a friend withdraws affection, or a stranger expresses outrage. The assumptions of modern social science make these the most serious or severe penalties faced by the individual. The major assumption is that people care about the opinion of others and are therefore punished when others disapprove of their behavior. Unlike natural sanctions, which are automatic, social sanctions presuppose the presence of others, their awareness of the behavior in question, and their concern for it. The complexities of social sanctions obviously make them less reliable than natural sanctions and subject to greater interpretive difficulties in assessing their utility or value.

LEGAL SANCTIONS

Legal sanctions are penalties provided by the state for behavior forbidden by statute. In the contemporary United States, they are largely restricted to fines, probation, and imprisonment, but other systems employ flogging, mutilation, and execution as well. Modern social science is essentially undecided about the efficacy of legal sanctions (Blumstein, Cohen, and Nagin 1978). The general public, however, strongly approves the use of such penalties. More than eight people in ten believe that the courts should deal more harshly with criminals (Maguire and Flanagan 1992: table 2.44).

SUPERNATURAL SANCTIONS

Supernatural sanctions refer to the belief that conduct during one's life is punished and rewarded in the hereafter. Belief in such sanctions is presumably conveyed to children as a means of shaping their behavior. The template established by natural, social, and legal sanctions is sufficiently clear that, in principle, such beliefs could be effective. To the extent they are effective, super-natural sanctions provide one mechanism for the generation of self-control, because the system cannot by definition depend for its success on actual conse-quences of behavior.

RELATIONS AMONG THE SANCTION SYSTEMS

Sanction systems can be ranked in terms of the distance between be-havior and its consequences. Natural sanctions are most immediate and cer-tain. Moral sanctions, which depend on the existence and interest of friends and family, and detection of the act, are less immediate and certain. Legal sanctions, operating at some remove from the act, are notoriously uncertain and much delayed. Supernatural sanctions are of course most removed from the act in terms of immediacy, and their certainty is a matter of belief.

Given this hierarchy, control theorists assume that natural sanctions govern much behavior most of the time; that social sanctions can be highly influential; and that legal and supernatural sanctions are best left to lawyers and priests.

In our view, all of these systems rely ultimately on the threat of some form of physical pain to those who do not conform to their requirements or expecta-tions. The natural and most effective system in fact operates almost exclusively on physical pain. Corporal punishment thus has logical and temporal priority in the sanctions hierarchy. Summarizing Thomas Hobbes, Michael Oakeshott put it this way: "Man is a creature civilized by the fear of death" (Hobbes 1957 [1651]: xxxvi). In recognizing that the ultimate or basic sanction is execution, Hobbes was not advocating its use but pointing out that the task of society is to influence behavior in ways consistent with this premise without having to resort to such drastic methods. The danger that follows from ignoring ulti-mate sanctions is that greater harm to the miscreant follows inappropriate teaching. Ironically, then, in the control-theory view, small punishments, de-signed to teach moral lessons, are at the same time designed to prevent larger penalties.

Given such assumptions, it is hard to overstate the role of natural sanctions. They are the major shapers of behavior and provide the conceptual and factual foundation of all other sanction systems. They teach the value of immediacy, certainty, and severity and thereby define the limits of social, legal, and super-natural systems. Indeed, these secondary systems seek to control behavior that somehow escapes natural sanctions by augmenting or otherwise modify-ing their consequences. Attempts to enhance the natural system tend to take predictable forms. For example, one device is to educate potential offenders about the true risks of unwanted behavior. In this way, governments and societies use natural sanctions as effective weapons to reduce the levels of risky behaviors. It is easy to show that natural sanctions used in these ways are far more effective than legal sanctions. For example, the decline of drug use in the teenage population is undoubtedly a consequence of increased concern about health consequences rather than a reaction to increased legal penalties. By the same token, the large shifts in sexual behavior in modern times are better explained by the appreciated risks of pregnancy and disease than by shifts in moral sanctions. In fact, the extent to which "moral" beliefs in this area have *followed* changes in the actual consequences of sexual behavior is nothing short of phenomenal.

Another device is simply to supplement natural sanctions with secondary sanctions. Thus social and legal systems often add punishments to those naturally connected to risky behavior. For example, burglars run the risk of physical injury or death when they invade a home or business. If they escape such penalties, they may still be ostracized by the community and imprisoned by the state. In this regard, greater use of legal punishments by society is evidence of weakened natural and social sanction systems. Ironically, then, societies, such as the United States, said to be more punitive than others because of their high incarceration rate are, by definition, less punitive than others at the natural- or social-sanction level. Thus, those who advocate lessened social and natural sanctions may be unwittingly responsible for the growth of the criminal-justice system. They may also be unwittingly responsible for the severity of the punishments it imposes. A possible connection between liberty in a society and a heightened level of punitiveness within its justice system has long been noted (see Tocqueville's remarks in Garland 1990: 9). Thus in free societies a larger portion of the population may be incarcerated for a longer period of time. Criminal sanctions tend to be more certain and severe where social sanctions are neither.

The assumption that the primary effect of sanctions, whatever their form or source, is to reduce the prevalence or frequency of sanctioned behavior is largely restricted to control theory. Alternative perspectives emphasize the dangers inherent in sanctioning and prefer some methods of sanctioning to others. Indeed, the standard assumption in the punishment literature is that methods equal in apparent or immediate effectiveness are in all cases to be preferred to physical pain or "verbal aggression." Thus locking a child in a room is better than slapping his or her hands; explaining the reasons for one's disapproval is better than spanking; grounding is better than epithets or bad names; the expression of wounded feelings is better than shaking the child in a vigorous manner; lengthy incarceration is preferable to caning.

In control or rational-choice theory, sanctions are judged by their efficacy, by their effectiveness and cost. Excessive sanctions exact more pain than is required; they are therefore considered cruel or unjust. Alternative perspectives are likely to find something inherently wrong with certain kinds of punishments, whatever their efficacy. Thus physical pain and verbal aggression are not seen as inferior because they are more punishing (they are not more punishing; if they were, they would be more effective) but because they are thought to have *long-term* negative effects, because they "teach the wrong lessons." This, then, is the violence begets (teaches) violence thesis, according to which violence must be observed, felt, or learned before it can become part of one's behavioral repertoire.

This point of view is illustrated in reactions to the American teenager caned in Singapore for allegedly vandalizing automobiles. When he returned to this country, there was considerable interest in his subsequent behavior. Sure enough, it was soon reported that he had assaulted his father (in a manner sufficiently hateful and violent to occasion calling the police). The reaction was, naturally, that this outburst had been triggered by the caning and/or the "83 days in a foreign prison." One headline read: "Wounds from Singapore caning are also to the mind" (*Arizona Daily Star* 1994). A control theorist would guess that these acts of vandalism and assault are connected by the known versatility of offenders and the stability of their tendencies to commit delinquent acts, a connection unaffected by the caning incident.

The standard thesis of the punishment literature is thus contrary to control theory. This thesis is easily recognized as a variant of the notion that crime is (must be) learned. It is also a product of the notion that no worthwhile distinction may be made between aggressive reaction to norm-violating behavior and aggression aimed at advancing selfish personal interests (for a lengthy discussion of the consequences of the failure to make this distinction, see Gottfredson and Hirschi 1993).

We turn now to a discussion of the role of corporal punishment in child rearing as seen from a control perspective.

Control Theory and Child Rearing

The basic model of child rearing from a control-theory perspective is easily described: Proper socialization of children requires that adults monitor their behavior and correct misbehavior when it occurs. Because monitoring and correction are time consuming or expensive, the model presupposes adults who care enough about the child to devote the necessary time and effort to the task. It also of course requires that the adult be able to identify unwanted or deviant behavior.

AFFECTION 1: INTEREST IN THE OUTCOME

A major premise of the model outlined is that the parent, caretaker, or guardian must care enough about the child or the child's behavior to devote the immense amounts of time and energy that monitoring and discipline require. The source of this care or concern does not seem to be especially important, so long as it is reliable. Thus the natural affection of parents for their children (based, in the mother's case, on unavoidable prior connections) may be replaced by the financial or contractual interests of nannies and day-care workers.

Interest in the outcome, whatever its source, tends to assure monitoring and discipline. It also severely limits the range of usable or acceptable sanctions. Thus interested guardians do not allow serious accidents, whatever their teaching potential, and they tend to protect the child from the more severe penalties of the legal system, however much in some sense these penalties might be deserved. Interested guardians will tend to apply the same logic to the sanctions available to them. They will not go beyond the bounds set by their relationship with the child and by their concern for the child's ultimate deportment or behavior. Put another way, cruel or excessive punishment is strictly contrary to the explicit control-theory assumption of interest in the child. Corporal punishment is not excluded by this interest but if used would be expected to be well within the limits set by modern sensibilities.

AFFECTION 2: ATTACHMENT TO THE CAREGIVER

The theory also assumes that attachment to the caregiver is requisite to successful socialization. The caregiver must be interested in the child; the child must have affection or at least respect for the caregiver. This too puts strict limits on the severity and nature of punishments available to the caretaker. Excessive punishments would destroy the relationship and vitiate their effectiveness. Corporal punishment is apparently in this respect risky. It may sometimes exceed the tolerance level of the child and destroy attachment to its source.

A major source of attachment is assumed to be attention, the time and effort devoted to the child by the caregiver. This "attention" is another word for supervision.

SUPERVISION

Monitoring allows groups to determine whether or not individuals "comply with their obligations," and to sanction them accordingly. It is thus a major element in the relation between group control and individual compliance (Hechter 1987: 51). Applied to child rearing, the concept takes on broader meaning, extending beyond misbehavior to concern for the child's happiness, safety, and well-being. When parents give great attention to such matters, they reduce if not obviate the need for explicit punishment. So, the greater the supervision, the less the punishment required. In other words, for control theory, neglect is the principal cause of punishment, especially excessive punishment; it is the primary source of violence by the parent and of misbehavior by the child.

The theoretical centrality of neglect (supervision) is supported by research, where is it routinely found to be a major predictor of delinquency (Glueck and Glueck 1950; McCord 1979). It is also supported by the actions of the juvenile-justice system, where children neglected by their parents or guardians make up a substantial portion of the case load (Widom 1989).

Supervision takes many forms and poses many practical difficulties. In contemporary Western societies, day-care workers and school teachers share the supervision of children with parents or guardians, and adolescents can often arrange large blocks of time relatively free of surveillance by interested adults. All of which means that parents are often forced to rely on indirect measures of conformity (for example, grades, curfew violations), on the reports of other adults, and on the notoriously incomplete self-reports of their own children. For present purposes, a major consequence of the breakdown of direct observation of behavior as the primary mode of supervision is that it has made certain forms of punishment less appropriate or acceptable. Slapping, spanking, and shaking often presuppose instantaneous reaction by an adult fully responsible for the behavior of the child. Any delay between commission of the offensive act and the application of sanctions, and any diminution of adult responsibility for the offender, will thus reduce the likelihood of corporal punishment. This may partially explain why we have less corporal punishment today and why we don't like it as much as we once did.

Discipline

Discussion of a child-rearing model that includes care, monitoring, and punishment of misbehavior quickly reveals that these distinctions are analytic, that in reality the three elements are hard to separate from one another. Thus the research literature occasionally reports that "care" of children is an important predictor of delinquency, where care implies supervision and discipline as much as it implies affection (see Kolvin, Miller, Fleeting, and Kolvin 1988). And the quality of "supervision" is typically gauged as much by the imposition of rules or discipline as by parental awareness of the child's whereabouts or behavior. By the same token, when care and supervision are subtracted from punishment, the techniques that remain may not be particularly important in and of themselves (Rutter 1985: 385). Thus, in context, it may make little difference whether the parent yells, nags, scolds, shakes, slaps, or cries. The important thing is that these particular techniques virtually presuppose the failure of supervision and put at risk the affectional relation between the parent and the child. Consistent with this expectation, use of such techniques is routinely found to be positively correlated with delinquency.

In an attempt to test the effects of parental monitoring and discipline on delinquency, Larzelere and Patterson carefully built multimethod measures of both constructs. A structural equation model forced them to conclude that the correlation between monitoring and discipline was so large (.60) that these two measures could not have "significant direct paths to delinquency simultaneously" (1990: 312). As important for present purposes, none of their individual measures of monitoring or discipline was significantly correlated with delinquency independent of the effects of the parental-management factor produced by combining monitoring and discipline.

The bottom line would appear to be that there is little room in current research for the conclusion that specific disciplinary techniques or forms of punishment have an important effect on subsequent behavior independent of the overall relationship between parent and child (see again Rutter 1985: 357). This suggests that in the causation of delinquency corporal punishment is typically not that important, one way or the other.

The reverse conclusions to be drawn from the analysis above deserve to be made explicit. Severe punishment or abuse is predictable from control theory. It is likely to reflect breakdown or absence of intimate caretaker-child relationships. Caretakers who have no strong interest in the child are much more likely than others to neglect the child and to resort to inappropriate disciplinary techniques. Control theory thus implicates family disintegration in violence, disputing the "normative" interpretation, which sees family violence as a product of training, learning, or modeling. Similarly, control theory explains why family violence seems to run in families. Parents with low self-control have difficulty teaching self-control to their children. As a consequence, children of violent parents tend to be violent themselves.

All of this, it seems to us, should put to rest the idea that control theory advocates corporal punishment, or that it encourages oppressive parental styles and the production of rigid or authoritarian children. It has always been a mistake, in our view, to attempt to judge theories by their basically unexamined or putative policy implications. In this case, dismissal of control theory in favor of alternatives may put at risk the very children the critics wish to save from harm.

16

Punishment, Child Development, and Crime
A Theory of the Social Bond

THOMAS J. SCHEFF

This chapter frames corporal punishment within a general theory of human conduct. The theory of social bonds proposes that personality and basic behaviors and attitudes arise from the nature of relationships with others. The theory suggests that the extent to which children become effective and responsible adults depends upon the quality of their social bonds. Excerpts from videotaped episodes in a family in which spanking frequently occurred are used to illustrate the main thrust of the theory: spanking, along with other frequent behaviors, such as parents lecturing and threatening children, can be viewed as aspects of alienation, of insecure bonds with the family.

I suggest in this chapter that the state of social bonds determines wide reaches of human conduct. General theories of social relationships and their effects on behavior are very rare. The major theories focus on individuals, with little or no attention to relationships. Certainly behaviorism is completely individualistic, as is psychoanalytic theory, at least in its orthodox form. Marx's analysis of social systems allows for the importance of human relationships in theory, in its emphasis on alienation. But in Marx and the writings of his followers, alienation remains abstract and unexplicated, so that in actual applications, social relationships play little role.

The theory proposed here depicts social relationships in terms of alienation and its opposite, solidarity. It suggests that the *structure* of actual social relationships involves mixtures of alienation and solidarity, and that the exact proportion can be determined through the analysis of verbatim discourse. In the scheme to be outlined here, alienation can occur not only from others but also from self. I argue that secure bonds in the family and in later life lead to responsible conduct. Insecure bonds, the concrete carriers of alienation, take two forms: bonds that are either too loose (isolation) or too tight (engulfment). I argue that isolation generates criminal behavior, and that engulfment generates irresponsibility.

The *dynamics* of relationships are explained in terms of the emotion that accompanies solidarity, pride, and the one that accompanies alienation, shame. Pride signals and generates solidarity. Shame signals and generates alienation. I argue that shame is usually a normal part of the process of social control; it becomes disruptive only when it is hidden or denied. I suggest that denial of shame generates self-perpetuating cycles of alienation.

Straus's Theory of Crime and Corporal Punishment

I single out Straus's theory as a springboard, because it is clear, explicit, and testable, and because he has conducted significant studies of corporal punishment. Since most theory is of the armchair variety and most empirical studies eschew theory, his work stands out from the crowd. I have two basic criticisms of Straus's theory of crime. Focusing only on corporal punishment, it is much too narrow, ignoring a wide range of other influences on child development. It also seems to be contradicted by a substantial body of evidence.

Although the format of Straus's work is exemplary, the content is another matter. Basically, Straus's work falls within the behaviorist approach: Straus assumes that human behavior can best be understood solely in terms of rewards and punishments, like the behavior of nonhuman creatures. Behaviorists believe that human actions are largely generated by conditioning (by the regular schedule of rewards and punishments that follow behavior). Within this framework, corporal punishment, which Straus sees as a particularly harsh form of punishment, is envisioned as having large and longtime effects. There is a vast literature supporting the behaviorist position, much of it not quite relevant to the particular issue being considered here, the major and long-term effects of punishment on children. A considerable portion of this literature concerns animals and has only questionable relevance to humans. A further large portion concerns only short-term effects; the typical study involves observation of small spans of time, usually minutes, occasionally hours.

The subjects are often a captive audience, such as undergraduate students in a psychology class; changes in their behavior wrought by conditioning schedules may be short lived, since follow-ups and longitudinal studies are rare in the behavioral tradition. Finally, of the remaining studies, most concern minor behavioral effects outside real-world environments, relative to the issues considered here, criminal versus noncriminal behavior. These effects are seldom checked to see if they transfer to the real world. Within the discipline of child development, however, there is a substantial body of studies that have the characteristics that make them relevant here: they concern human children, often in their own homes; some of them employ longitudinal or follow-up designs, and they trace what are for small children major real-world behaviors, such as degree of obedience to their mother. These behaviors are checked to see if they transfer to the real world.

In an impressive critique of Straus's theory, McCord (1991) has called attention to these and other studies. Since her review is detailed and to the point, I will not repeat it here. Instead, I will summarize her major criticisms and describe as an example one of the studies she cites, Stayton, Hogan, and Ainsworth (1971). Ainsworth has long been a contributor to attachment theory, which is closely related to the theory of social bonds that I develop here. The study by her and her colleagues will be used to represent the body of studies that seem to contradict Straus's theory.

The researchers studied twenty-five infant-mother pairs for a period of *three months* in their homes. They found that the children's obedience was unrelated to the frequency of verbal commands and physical interventions. Instead, it was highly correlated with the mother's degree of acceptance of the child (as against rejection) and the mother's sensitivity and responsiveness to the child. The authors interpret their findings to show that "obedience emerges in a responsive, accommodating social environment without extensive training, discipline, or other massive attempts to shape the infant's course of development" (Stayton, Hogan, and Ainsworth 1971: 1065).

On the basis of this and other studies, McCord argues that Straus's theory is invalid, that it does not offer an accurate account of the causes of adult criminal behavior in its relationship to childhood. As an alternative to Straus's theory, McCord offers what she calls construct theory. She proposes that a child's personality is formed through language. Her theory is much broader than Straus's. She locates the causes of adult behavior in the linguistic world created for a child in the family and other settings.

McCord also argues that even if one restricts oneself to the punishments that occur in the child's world, the scope of causal influences in Straus's theory is much too narrow. In addition to corporal punishment, she argues, children are also punished in many other ways, through abuse of other kinds, neglect, and rejection. Although Ayres and Braithwaite (1991) do not cite child-development studies, their criticisms of rational choice theory, a form of behaviorism, are similar to McCord's. Braithwaite's (1989) image of effective family discipline, reintegrative shaming, also implies mutual understanding and acceptance between parents and children (secure bonds), as I will indicate below.

The theory I offer here, like McCord's, speaks to the formation of personality in terms of the whole world of the family, rather than a single type of reward or punishment. In terms of the scope of the theory, it falls between Straus's, which deals with an extremely narrow causal agent, and McCord's, which in its focus on language is extremely broad. I argue that the key determinant in child development is the *structure of social bonds* in the family. I propose that to the extent the bonds in a family are weak and insecure, to that extent the children from that family will become adults whose behavior is criminal or irresponsible. This hypothesis presents a testable alternative to both Straus's and McCord's theories. I suggest that both McCord's and Ayres and Braithwaite's criticisms of behaviorist theories can be shown to fit within a theory of social bonds, and also that the findings from the studies of child development that McCord cites can be shown specifically to support this theory. The new theory also speaks to gender differences in violence and criminality.

Social Bonds

My model of the social bond is based on the concept of *attunement,* mutual identification and understanding. A secure social bond means that the individuals involved identify with and understand each other, rather than misunderstand or reject each other (Scheff 1990). I assume that in all human contact, if bonds are not being built, maintained, or repaired, they are being damaged. That is to say that in every moment of contact, one's status relative to the other is continually being signaled, usually unintentionally. Goffman (1967: 33) made this point clearly:

> The human tendency to use signs and symbols means that evidence of social worth and of mutual evaluations will be conveyed by very minor things, and these things will be witnessed, as will the fact that they have been witnessed. An unguarded glance, a momentary change in tone of voice, an ecological position taken or not taken, can drench a talk with judgmental significance. Therefore, just as there is no occasion of talk in which improper impressions could not intentionally or unintentionally arise, so there is no occasion of talk so trivial as not to require each participant to show serious concern with the way in which he handles himself and the others present.

Status-relevant verbal and nonverbal signs both signal and determine the state of the bond at any given moment. Although Goffman seemed to be thinking about interaction between adults, his formulation applies equally well to contact between adults and children: each party is supremely sensitive to signals of his or her standing with the other.

Threats to a secure bond can come in two different formats; the bond is either too loose or too tight. I refer to relationships in which the bond is too loose as *isolated:* there is mutual misunderstanding or failure to understand, or mutual rejection. Relationships in which the bond is too tight I call *engulfed:* at least one of the parties in the relationship, say the subordinate, understands and embraces the standpoint of the other at the expense of the subordinate's own beliefs, values, or feelings. The other is accepted by rejecting parts of one's self. In engulfed families, a child can only be "good" by blind obedience and conformity, by relinquishing its curiosity, intuition, or feelings.

In such a relationship the child and parents are alienated. The child is alienated from self, because of having given up important parts of the self out of loyalty to the other or fear of the other. The parties are also alienated from each other, since neither is aware of the parts of the self that the child has rejected. The children in the Smiley family, to be discussed below, seem to be in such a situation: they are still young enough to feel attached and loyal to their parents; the family world is the only one they know. In this world, however, because of the lack of relationship talk, and the frequent punishment and threats of punishment, the children also seem to be intimidated by their parents, and to fear them.

This view of alienation is congruent with, and further develops, Durkheim's theory of social integration, which he derived from his study of the causes of suicide (1905). He argued that suicidal inclinations were generated by bonds that were too loose (egoism) or too tight (altruism). My theory extends Durkheim, by describing the microscopic components of this system and also the structure of a secure bond, which Durkheim ignores, one that is neither too loose nor too tight.

In my scheme, a secure bond involves a balance between the viewpoint of self and other. Although each party understands and accepts the viewpoint of the other, this acceptance doesn't go to the extreme of giving up major parts of one's own viewpoint. The behavior of the responsive mothers in the Stayton et al. study suggests this kind of relationship: the mothers seem to understand and accept the child's point of view. Although Stayton et al. are not explicit on this point, the responsive mothers would also need to stand up for their own points of view in relationship to the child, to avoid engulfment with the child.

A child in an alienated family, such as the one to be described below, is faced with the alternatives of embracing or ignoring the continual flow of instruction, command, and discipline from parents. If the child embraces parental strictures out of loyalty or to avoid punishment, it needs to give up major parts of the self, which is synonymous with engulfment. The self can only develop to the extent that its major features are accepted both by self and significant others. If the child ignores or defies parental strictures, the alternative is isolation, in which the child risks missing the beneficial parts of parental care and knowledge. The small child in such a family can't win. Given this situation, the self may be damaged in such a way as to impede the development of adequate bonds with others as an adult.

The theory of solidarity suggested here overlaps with earlier work by Elias (1977), Buber (1958), and Bowen (1978). The master trope in Elias's approach is *interdependency,* patterns of cooperative relationships between individuals and between groups. A close reading of his work shows that it implies three types of social relationship: dependence, interdependence, and independence. These three types correspond closely to the three levels of integration mentioned above: dependence corresponds to integration that is too tight, independence, too loose, and interdependence, a balance between the individual and the group.

The I-We Balance in Relationships

Elias furthermore suggests a way of connecting these levels of integration to the empirical world: the concept of the *I-we balance:* independence should be marked in discourse by emphasis on the "I," dependence, on the "we," and interdependence, on a balance between *I and we* (Elias 2001). According to Elias, the state of integration between individuals or between groups might be visible in the disposition of pronouns in their discourse. (As was suggested in an earlier publication [Scheff 1994, chapter 1], the mechanical counting of pronouns is too simple for anything but a crude estimate; determining the balance between self and other may require discourse analysis because some adults manipulate pronouns in a way that disguises the state of the bond.)

The idea of the I-we balance can be elaborated by referring to ideas from Buber (1958) and from Bowen (1978). Buber distinguishes between the two types of relationship: I-thou, where each person endows the other with the same humanity as self (which I call mutual identification), and I-it, in which one treats the other as an object. This is an important idea, but it is cast in categorical terms. It can be modified by restating it in terms that will admit *degrees* of connection: I-it represents the self in foreground, the other in the background. I-thou places both self and other in foreground. Other as object represents only the extreme position on a continuum of the relative emphasis on self or other.

An extension of Buber's language is also necessary if one is to consider the third state of the relationship, too much integration. In Buber's framework, this state might be represented as it-thou; one places one's self in the background, the other in the foreground. For example, in a traditional marriage, the wife was expected to subject herself to her husband. It-thou involves subjugation of self, one's own needs, feelings, and point of view, to the other person, or to the group. Blind patriotism provides another example. I-it means that one's own needs, feelings, and points of view are dominant over those of others', but in it-thou, they are swallowed out of a sense of loyalty, or because of fear.

The threefold division discussed here is also related to family-systems theory, especially as formulated by Bowen (1978), one of its principal founders. He referred to dysfunctional relationships as involving either isolation or engulfment. Isolation is marked by "cut-off," dealing with difficulties by withdrawing physically or emotionally. Engulfment, which he also referred to as fusion, by confounding one's own needs, feelings, and viewpoint with those of the other. This latter state is also discussed as a boundary problem; in an engulfed relationship, the parties have difficulty in distinguishing the boundaries of the self.

One aspect of family-systems theory is particularly relevant to the present discussion: the distinction between discourse that is topic oriented, and discourse that is relationship oriented (Watzlawick et al. 1967) Topics involve objects in the outer world, such as eating, chores, money, grades, and so on. Relationships involve the thoughts and feelings that are occurring between the participants. Parents who are oriented toward command and control of children's behavior are unlikely to deal adequately with relationship issues. But secure bonds require relationship talk: the child must understand not only what is expected of it by the parents but also the parents' reasons for the expectation.

Behaviorist theories completely ignore this point. In its most common form, behaviorism proposes that child rearing is merely a matter of shaping outer behavior. This perspective allows no room for relationships or for feelings. It is completely oriented toward topics. From the point of view of this essay, behaviorism both expresses and generates alienation.

Corporal punishment can be used as an example of the importance of the distinction between topic and relationship. Punishment is both a topic and an action in the outer world, but it is also accompanied by attitudes and feelings. Striking a child in anger, without warning or explanation, implies a relationship issue, the status of the child relative to the parent.

Being struck without warning would be experienced as especially intimidating, giving rise to terror on the child's part. Another implication is equally important: that the status of the child is so low that it warrants no respect at all. A child that can be hit in anger, with no warning, or be neglected, verbally abused, or rejected is likely to grow up with little sense of self, lacking the skill and inclination to develop secure bonds with others. Within this framework it is conceivable that if spanking were administered in a way that allowed the child foreknowledge and dignity, it might do less damage to the bond than nonphysical abuse, such as neglect or rejection.

The theory of the social bond provides a framework for organizing the critiques by McCord and by Braithwaite, and the findings in the child-development studies cited by McCord. In particular, the characteristics of the effective mothers (accepting and responsive) found in the study by Stayton, Hogan, and Ainsworth (1971) (and in other studies with similar findings, such as Parpal and Maccoby 1985) are exactly those predicted by the social-bond theory.

The ineffectiveness of training and discipline, as reported in these studies, is also congruent with social-bond theory. Discipline and training are usually oriented to behavior rather than to inner thoughts and feelings, and to topics rather relationships. Overemphasis on behavior and topics, according to the theory, would be expected to damage rather than build or repair bonds. The mothers who were responsive and accepting, on the other hand, would be building and repairing bonds, according to the theory. Similarly, McCord's complaint that Straus ignores other significant punishment, such as neglect and rejection, fits exactly within a theory of the social bond.

The proposed theory also speaks to gender differences in child rearing and in personality. In modern societies, males have been raised to be independent in order to find work roles or careers. By the same token, females, until quite recently, have been raised to be oriented toward families rather than work. Since these influences begin in early childhood and persist throughout the person's lifetime, it would not be surprising to find that personalities and relationships would be strongly gender related. There is a preliminary discussion of this issue in Braithwaite's (1989) masterful theory of crime causation. His discussion is only preliminary, since he does not go into the details of shame dynamics, as I will do in a later section.

A series of studies initiated by Helen Lewis (1971, 1977) concerned the distinction between "field dependence" and "field independence," whether one is primarily oriented toward others' viewpoints or one's own. Lewis's studies and those of others following from hers show that women tend toward field dependence (engulfment), men toward field independence (isolation). Lewis's studies also showed a correlation between field dependence and shame format: she found that women tend toward expressing the overt, undifferentiated type of shame, men toward the bypassed type. That is, women tend to manifest shame and embarrassment more overtly than do men. Men's shame and embarrassment is likely to be disguised and denied. In a later section I will relate this difference to differences in male and female crime rates.

The Smiley Family

As a part of a television broadcast on corporal punishment of children on the program 20/20, the producer recruited four families who volunteered to allow filming of punishment in their homes. Camerapersons spent ten or so hours in each of the homes, focusing on episodes of punishment. In the context of studies of corporal punishment, these films are a valuable adjunct to statistical studies, since they allow us to view naturally occurring behavior in the home. Unlike experiments, surveys, and interviews, the sources of most data in current social science, these videos show moment-by-moment details of interaction in the family.

For this discussion I will use all of the scenes that were filmed showing the Smiley (pseudonym) family, from two different sources, the broadcast itself and the outtakes (extra scenes not used on the 20/20 program.) The broadcast showed spanking episodes, interviews with the parents, and a panel discussion with all of the families and the sociologists Straus and Favarro. The outtakes showed spanking and the breakfast scene that I comment on at length.

For my discussion I have chosen the family in which the parents seemed to punish their children most of the four families, who also were clearly the most resistant to advice that would change their disciplinary practices. In the panel discussion, the other three sets of parents were responsive to the advice offered, but not the Smileys, who were defiant. They represent an extreme case for the problem of changing family behavior in this area.

The rate of punishment in this family seems extremely high, relative to survey results. I counted twenty-four spanking and slapping episodes, fourteen by Mom, ten by Dad. I also noted several instances of threats of punishment that were only verbal. If the filming took place over ten hours, that would be a rate of more than two episodes per hour in the family, which would mean slightly less than one per child (only the three older children were spanked). On the other hand, since most of the episodes are quite brief, considerably under a minute, most of the interaction between parents and children does not involve punishment.

Although I will comment on all of the episodes of punishment observable in the Smiley family, I will emphasize one episode, a five-minute breakfast scene. The cameraperson included it because it contains four spanking incidents, but it is unique among the scenes in that it shows many other kinds of family interaction. It offers a window into the nature of the whole network of relationships among the members of this family, as well as instances of punishment.

The breakfast scene happened to be included by the cameraperson because it included instances of corporal punishment. But it also reveals the poverty of communication within the family. There is dialogue only between husband and wife. Speech directed toward children involves only commands and instructions. There is virtually no interchange between parents and children that is not related to discipline.

A FAMILY BREAKFAST

There are four children in the Smiley family. Ashley and Jordan appear to be identical twins about four years old, Cindy is about three. The infant appears to be less than one year old. The mother is sitting at one end of a round table, Dad at the other. Ashley is next to Mom on her left side, Cindy on Mom's other side. Jordan is next to Ashley, on Dad's right side. The infant is away from the table, to Mom's right in a high chair, off camera most of the time. The parents seem to be in their early thirties. Both are short and stocky, with Mom somewhat overweight.

The scene might have been filmed late in the 1980s. The economic standing of the family seems low. Assuming the filming occurred on a weekday, the presence of both mother and father all day suggests that one or both might work a late shift or, less likely, that one or both are out of work. The house is always in disorder in every scene, even though the parents are present.

The table setting points to their lifestyle: they are using paper plates for breakfast and are drinking Sunny Delight (orange juice flavored punch) instead of orange juice. The only indication of prosperity is the presence in one of the rooms of a new and elaborate climbing toy. The home's exterior has chipped paint and is in need of repair, in what appears to be a low-rent area of a large city. The automobile the family uses is a station wagon from the 1970s.

The transcript of the breakfast episode, which lasts slightly less than five minutes, can be found in appendix I. Appendix II is a transcript of the components of the 20/20 broadcast that involved the Smiley family.

One obvious feature of the breakfast scene is that, with the exception of Mom and the infant, the parents show little interest and affection toward their children. Mom, much more than Dad, seems interested in and proud of the infant, as is clearly indicated in lines 63–68. But neither parent shows any pride, interest, or patience with regard to the other children. Both parents seem embattled. The father is more polite than the mother, who yells and hits. But both are usually exasperated by the children's behavior.

The primary emotion the parents show toward the children is self-righteous, indignant anger, both in the breakfast and in many of the spanking scenes. *"HOW MANY TIMES DO I HAVE TO TELL YOU?" (As is the convention in linguistics, the asterisk * signifies a "hypothetical," a statement not actually made, but one that summarizes many actual statements.) The implication of their attitude is that the children are either stupid or intentionally defiant. The mother seems much more out of control than the father, but both seem near the breaking point. Several of the spankings concern the children not paying attention to the parent. The parents in these instances seem particularly angry and indignant.

The mother states during the broadcast panel that she and her husband always count to ten before spanking. Actually, more than half of the spankings on the tapes involve no hesitation whatsoever. They look impetuous. Moreover, using Retzinger's (1991) scheme for coding overt and covert anger, almost all of the scenes show the parents angry. The mother's anger is often overt; her movements are abrupt, her utterances have a loud, staccato quality, and her facial expression shows the characteristic muscular configuration of anger: eyes narrowed, cheek muscles taut, teeth clenched. The father's anger is usually more covert, except when he spanks the children because they are ignoring him. In these situations, his anger is overt like the mother's.

From the point of view of a theory of the social bond, the key feature of the breakfast scene is the character of the bond between Mom and Dad. Mom is loud and active, Dad soft-spoken and withdrawn to the point that many of his remarks are inaudible. The contrast between the actions of Mom and Dad at breakfast is striking: the father speaks briefly and infrequently; his principle activity is eating. The mother, however, eats nothing at all; she only plays with her food. She does nothing at the table but talk and spank. At several points she seems exasperated not only with the children but also with her husband, culminating in the sarcastic remark about his intelligence (line 41).

The pattern of interaction in this scene is common in dysfunctional marital relationships: one partner is passive and withdrawn, the other angry and aggressive. These patterns are usually *reciprocally related* and self-perpetuating: the more the one partner withdraws, the more angry and aggressive the other, and visa versa. Both sides feel rejected and insulted by the other, but neither expresses these intense feelings openly. In this family, the husband's response to rejection is to withdraw, which causes more anger in the wife. The wife's response to rejection is to become angry and aggressive, which causes more withdrawal in the husband. These parents seem to be equally and jointly entrapped in their emotions and silence.

This pattern is subtly pervasive throughout the breakfast scene. The mother is much more vigilant of the children's behavior than the father. This difference is quite blatant. The mother's resentment of the father's withdrawal from child care is implied in some of her words and gestures, but it is explicit in lines 35–41.

According to earlier studies, the passivity of the husband is somewhat more common, but reverse gender roles also occur, with the husband the active, aggressive one, the wife withdrawn or passive. This dynamic has been documented many times in the family-interaction literature. It has also been described in detail in Retzinger's (1991) study of marital quarrels.

It should be noted that the mother's behavior during the broadcast panel discussion on 20/20 is not consistent with her behavior in the breakfast scene. During the panel discussion, except for one episode, in which she interrupts him, the mother defers to her husband. He is also different in this public situation from the way he is in the private one. He is not passive and withdrawn during the panel; instead, he manifests what comes near to being arrogant self-confidence. Perhaps under what they perceive to be an attack on their child-rearing practices from the interviewer and from the two sociologists, they temporarily band together to resist the common enemy.

I will assume that their customary behavior in their home is more like their behavior in the breakfast scene than during the broadcast panel. The usual way in which psychologists have described this dynamic is in terms of "unmet dependency needs." Which is to say, in my language, that the bond between the parents is insecure. For most people in American society, the marriage bond is by far the most important. Deprived of the emotional support of a secure bond even in their marriage, the parents *misperceive their children's age-specific normal behavior* as signs of rejection. They take personally everything the children do. A child's show of independence, particularly, is perceived as rejection. For this reason, a dysfunctional relationship develops between parent and child similar to that between the parents. One is angry and aggressive, the other passive and withdrawn.

With very young children, as in the case of the Smiley family, it is almost always the parent who takes the active-aggressive role, the child the passive-withdrawn one. As the children grow older, however, the roles may be reversed: the child becomes angry and aggressive, the parent passive and withdrawn. This analysis suggests a model of the way insecure bonds in a child's family of origin may lead to juvenile delinquency and to crime, violence, or irresponsibility as an adult. In this model, corporal punishment plays only a minor role in the causal sequence. It is only one of many indicators of alienation in the family.

One final feature of some of the spanking scenes shows the parents, particularly the mother, insisting that the child who has been punished embrace and kiss the parent. This practice may be fraught with significance for the socialization of the child's emotions. If the parent allowed for a full discussion of the punishment episode, which would permit the child to voice any feelings, including those of unfairness or resentment, such a practice would fit within Braithwaite's model of reintegrative shaming. After punishment is over, the parent takes care to repair the bond.

But in the Smiley family, the practice of having the child show affection toward the parent who has just spanked her smacks of repression, rather than reintegration. The child is not allowed to voice its actual feelings but is required to embrace and kiss the parent. In behavioral perspectives, such a practice might be thought of as "extinguishing" negative feelings. But in a more realistic view of emotion dynamics, the child is surely being taught to repress its feelings, especially anger and resentment.

As already suggested, a detailed theory of the social-bond emotions would also explain the differential crime rates between men and women. Given that the crime and violence rates among men are enormously higher than among women in all industrial societies (Braithwaite 1989), the criticisms of Straus's theory by Kurz (1991) and Loseke (1991) that it ignores gender differences are well taken. In this section I will try to provide a preliminary theoretical explanation for these differences.

Alienation in the family of origin drives men and women in different directions. The socialization of men in such families directs them toward an isolated style of relationships, and toward what Lewis (1971) has called *bypassed* shame. That is, they are taught to swallow their shame, to deny it completely, to the point that it is no longer available to consciousness. This type of shame is correlated with the practice of masking shame with anger, giving rise to a pervasive sense of resentment toward others, including the world outside the family. This emotional pattern could drive the vendetta pattern that governs male violence and criminality, both in first offenses and in repeated ones (Scheff 1994).

On the other hand, alienation in the family of origin would drive women into a different pattern. The normal pattern of socialization of girls moves them, in alienated families, toward the engulfed style of relating to others, which is correlated with what Lewis (1971) has called the *overt, undifferentiated* form of shame. In the bypassed format, shame is so disguised that the bearer is likely to be completely unaware of it. But in the overt form, the sensation of unpleasant affect is exaggerated. For example, the blush is associated with overt shame; blushers become aware of their own blushing, in a feedback loop of increasing arousal.

For these reasons, overt shame is associated with shame-shame sequences: women's socialization in overt shame and engulfment leads them, in the world outside the family, toward passivity and withdrawal rather than hostile aggression. This hypothesis would explain the frequent instances of wives who remain loyal to violent and abusive husbands. In the engulfed style, one gives up important parts of one's self, even the right to fairness and justice.

Although Adler did not use shame terminology, his analysis of the consequences of insecure bonds in childhood (lack of parental love, in his terminology) parallels mine. He argued that children who lack parental love at critical junctures in their development go in two different directions: what he called the "inferiority complex," on the one hand, and the "drive for power," on the other. The inferiority complex corresponds to what I have called the engulfed, overt-shame dynamic, and the drive for power, the isolated, bypassed-shame dynamic. My scheme makes explicit the details of moment-by-moment causal sequences and observable indicators in a way that Adler's does not.

The condition of having no secure bond, not a single one, is so painful that it is usually banished from consciousness: the counterdependent behavior it generates is compulsive. In the emotional dynamics of insecure bonds, the feeling of complete alienation from others or self generates feelings of rejection (shame) so overwhelming that they are bypassed, surfacing only as aggressively active and/or hostile behavior. If this theory is correct, it would explain why the Smiley parents responded so negatively to the good advice about alternatives to corporal punishment that was offered them in the 20/20 broadcast. They were antagonized by the advice offered them, acting as if it were an attack. According to the theory, they have developed a self-righteous rationale for their practices, but their behavior is actually compulsive; they are usually out of control in spanking their children. Their actions are not "rational choices" but involuntary results of denial of their isolation and shame.

To reach parents like the Smileys would require an indirect route, one that would give them time to develop some trust in the instructor, which would probably involve support for their low levels of self-esteem. Given a bond with the instructor, he or she might find a way to allow the parents to acknowledge some of their hidden feelings and their sense of alienation. Such a program might require many sessions rather than a single one, to the extent that the parents are trapped in their patterns of isolation and denial of feeling. To teach parents how to deal with their children without spanking might require changes in the family system as a whole.

Future research directions would be systematically to analyze the Smiley family's interactions, and those of other families, using part/whole analysis of discourse (Scheff 1990, 1994). This method of analysis allows for the systematic interpretation of verbatim discourse, in its biographical and ethnographic context. It can be used to generate a theory of social bonds, as it was here, and, when a sample of families is included, to test it. Such studies might then be used to develop reliable measures of alienation in the family. With such measures, one might perhaps show that spanking of children is associated with later crime, as Straus's findings suggest, but only because it is highly correlated with alienation.

Appendix I: Smiley Breakfast

DAD   1. Your nutu-rous, your nutritious in the morning.
   (Dad being sarcastic towards mother.)
MOM   2. Vit-a-mins, vitamins . . .
   (Mom's response is also sarcastic.)
   (Child one is whining to Mom.)
ASHLEY   3. This is hot!
   (Mom slaps Ashley on the leg and yells.)
MOM   4. This isn't a circus, don't play with your food.
   (Ashley coughs.)
DAD   5. That's what you get.
   (Referring to Ashley, while he removes a glass from Jordan's hand.)
MOM   6. You have a problem?!
   (Raising her voice to Ashley.)
DAD   7. You haven't touched nothing yet.
   (Dad talking to Jordan.)
MOM   8. Eat something Jordan! Eat.
   (Mom raising her voice with a stern expression.)
DAD   9. (Inaudible.)
   (Mom begins to fumble with food in her plate.)
MOM   10. Yeah right, I forgot what happened.
   (Dad continues to eat, while mumbling.)
DAD   11. (Inaudible.)
   (Mom looking down at her plate playing with her food, while talking to Dad.)
MOM   12. Suppose to get cold again though. S'ppose to go down to fifty-eight some
   time this week.
   I'm gonna miss "All My Children" if I have to take her to the doctors.
   (Mom appears frustrated.)
MOM   13. Damn. (Whisper.)
DAD   14. To the doctors?

MOM   15. I should've had an appointment for the morning.

DAD   16. (Inaudible.)

MOM   17. Cause, Sandra told me. Paula has to go too.

(Looking down at the table, with her finger in her mouth. She suddenly screams while getting up to run over to infant in high chair, while Dad continues his breakfast.)

MOM   18. Oh she's got her arm caught under her again.

Your gonna break your arm one of these days.

(Returns to table, being humorous.)

MOM   19. You silly goose.

(Chidren chattering/singing, gesticulating at the table. Mom in high patronizing voice, referring to infant, is talking to Dad.)

MOM   20. There you go. One of these days she's gonna break that arm.

(While resuming her position at the breakfast table Mom smacks Cindy, and then yells.)

MOM   21. Do you want to sit there right and eat?

I just smacked you for that.

CINDY   22. Mama.

DAD   23. (To Cindy) Uhhg. . . . What are you doing?

(Ashley and Jordan chattering and singing.

Mom appears disturbed and disgusted by Cindy, who is picking her nose.)

MOM   24. I can't tell you what she was doing.

(Mom looks at all of the children, appears annoyed and yells.)

MOM   25. Eat! Eat!

MOM   26. (In normal tone.) We don't have to leave right after umm, we take them to school.

(Dad makes eye contact.)

DAD   27. I know . . .

MOM   28. You want lunch first?

29. (Dad nods his head.)

MOM   30. Appointment's not 'til 1:30.

(Cindy chattering.)

CINDY   31. Hey . . .

(Mom mimics Cindy.)

MOM   32. Hey. (To Dad.) We'll be there at one o'clock.

(Ashley points to her chest.)

ASHLEY   33. Mommy right here hurts.

MOM   34. Down there's gonna hurt if you don't eat that. (Mom points to child one's rear, then begins to impatiently tap her fingers on the table. Mom looks around nervously, touching her empty plate.)

MOM   35. It's hot in here . . .

(Dad grunts while eating, not focusing on her.)

DAD   36. Hmmmm?

(Mom seems annoyed.)

MOM   37. It's hot in here.

DAD   38. Something else? . . . Mo, more bacon?

(Mom shakes her head no in silence, looking across at Dad.)

MOM   39. Did you cut the heat back?

DAD   40. (Mumbles, looking down at his plate.) No . . . (inaudible).

MOM   41. Would never nobody never accuse you of being intelligent!

(Mom continues drinking orange juice. Dad is looking down, shuffling his fork
in his plate.

Cindy yells in baby talk.)

DAD   42. Ummm.

(Cindy continues talking and starts to sing.)

CINDY   43. Yum. . . . Yum. . . . Yummy.

(Mom looking in direction of hall door, not focusing on Cindy. Talking in harsh
tone of voice.)

MOM   44. Yummy. . . . Eat.

(Looking at Jordan and Cindy, speaking in an irritated tone to Ashley.)

DAD   45. Ashley don't play with your food . . . if you're not going to eat go put your
plate in the trash. Please. . . . (Mom slaps Ashley on the leg, yelling angrily.)

MOM   46. What do you think your doing?

(Mother grabs Ashley's fork from her hand.)

(Father looks at Ashley.)

DAD   47. Just get down, go put your plate in the trash.

MOM   48. But I've told her that already, about playing with it.

ASHLEY   49. But I can't eat more food.

(Dad looks at Ashley, speaking in a low tone.)

DAD   50. Put it down. . . .

(Mom, sneering, says)

MOM   51. Solves . . . the blanket again.

(Infant in high chair mumbles baby-talk. Ashley and Jordan turn away from
table to look.)

DAD   52. (Speaking to Ashley and Jordan.) Never mind, concentrate on eating.

MOM   53. (Looking at infant, talks to Dad.)

She's got the keys in her mouth, and she's going like this. . . .

(Shaking her head from side to side in a comical manner, then points to infant.)

DAD   54. (Inaudible.)

(Mom screams in a laughing manner for Dad's attention in reference to infant.)

MOM   55. Look at her! She's mugging on them, Oh I bet ya her teeth hurt.

(Mom looks at her finger, picks at it.)

MOM   56. Got some Orajel upstairs.

(Mom looks at Dad. Dad looks at infant and becomes animated.)

DAD   57. Oh, she's struggling . . . all by herself.

MOM   58. (Laughing, referring to infant.) Look at her! Look at her. . . . Look at her. How did I do that, Oh goooh.

(The Mom seems to be speaking for the infant, who's teething. Suddenly she smacks Ashley, who's looking at the infant.)

MOM   59. (Yelling.) Eat! . . . Well I'm tired of telling you. You too, Jordan!

ASHLEY   60. (Crying.) I don't want more pancakes.

MOM   61. We have Sebastian (?) working.

(Mom is fumbling with her wedding ring.)

Appendix II: 20/20 Report

SMILEY FAMILY SPANKINGS AND BROADCAST DISCUSSION

I. Ashley didn't clean her room

REBECCA: Didn't I tell you (pulls her towards her by the arm, rhetorical calm, expressionless)

A: (shrugs away from her and nods her head)

R: (spanks her behind *3)

II. Jordan runs towards the street

S: Get up there (spanks her, Jordan puts her hand behind her to protect her bottom. Rebecca's voice is assertive and angry)

III. Ashley didn't pay attention

R: (turns and faces Ashley) Pay attention to me when I am talking to you (smacks her hand). (Ashley looks up at Rebecca, face has a look of deference, appears nervous calm, says with childlike insecurity, voice is soft, the smack appears to be almost habitual, because she does not seem angry)

IV. Cindy is picking her nose

R: (approaches Cindy) Do not put your fingers in your nose and then put it in your mouth. That's nasty (strikes her hand five to six times. Cindy cringes during the spanking, face tightens up, begins to cry after mom has left, words are punctuated with each smack, appears to be less instruction than a disgust with the action, angry)

V. Ashley plays with her food

R: (smacks her *4) Eat (emphatic frustration, voice is whiney, eyes raised to make pleading-like gesture, helpless anger)

VI. Jordon hits Ashley

R: You like to hit, you like to hit, come here (hits Jordon on the bottom *4. Jordon immediately backs away when she realizes she is about to be hit, puts hands over her eyes, moves out of range of the first attempt, when she is told to "come here" she follows directions and moves towards her mom hesitantly and cowering) (tries striking Jordon twice, when she misses the first time she throws her head back in rage and yells "come here," voice is calm until she is unable to make physical contact and then voice elevates, throws hand down emphatically, tantrum like, spank is forceful but appears not to reflect the intensity of the previous outburst as if the "tantrum" was a result of the humiliation felt when Jordon refused to be punished)

VII. Ashley pulls Jordan's hair

R: (pulls Ashley's hair *4) (Ashley thinks mom is coming at her to smack her, puts hand up instinctively and shies away, mom turns Ashley around, head is thrown back from the force of the pull, Ashley begins to cry and walks away slowly) You like to pull hair (calm, routine-like, after she gets hold of Ashley's hair seems satisfied, appears to act as if she is teaching a lesson, seems pleased with herself)

VIII. Smiley spanks Cindy for wetting pants

S: (touches Cindy's pants and spanks her *4; Cindy lets out a faint moan) You know better than that (again, spanking appears to be habitual, calm, tone doesn't seem angry, picks Cindy up immediately, lovingly)

IX. Child spanked for ignoring Smiley

S: (spanks child several times *5; child looks terrified, standing back afraid to get any closer, bending up and down at the knee in a panic-like state, crying extremely hard) Don't ignore me (calm until gets hold of the child, anger is very apparent seems to "lose it" for a minute, face clenches up, force of spanking intensifies, starts to say something but then becomes so engrossed in spanking he stops and continues his sentence only after spanking is finished, booms out instruction at the end but appears to have regained some control over his anger) s: (child has hand on her bottom) Move your hand, you want more (child moves hand and is spanked several times * 5; child has waited dutifully for her turn to be spanked, face is frozen in a pained expression, appears very fearful when she is called over, crying uncontrollably before, during and after spanking. Most of Dad's anger seems to have dissipated, face seems more relaxed, even during the battle over moving her hand, perfunctory, voice stays calm)

20/20 Broadcast

REPORTER: It seems to me that someone is being spanked all the time
R: Not all the time (tone is indifferent and cool, dismissive as a defense)
s: Well there are certain things they haven't learned yet (defensive)
R: Ya I have thought about that but no better be hit now than electrocuted in the electric chair later (believes in what she is saying, looks detached, indifferent defensive, direct denial with the words "but no," appears fearful about what could happen, almost fanatical, has a warning in her voice, hard direct glaring at end, rhythm irregular)
s: Until they get spanked they won't realize (reserved, mixed smile, appears very confident) ** is interrupted by Rebecca
R: NO means NO (loud, assertive, challenging, eyes averted, rapid condensed speech possibly because she feels uncomfortable with having interrupted Smiley, playing with hands)
s: Most of these kids growing up who don't get spanked are uncontrollable (patiently explains, has air of superiority, mixed smile)
REPORTER: There is a fine line between spanking and abusing your children there's a very fine line and it's easy when you're angry to cross that line
R: We never cross that line we're very careful (seems to have taken on Smiley's calm and confidant mannerism, is direct, monotone, looks to believe that what she is saying is the truth and is the proper way to handle disciplining children, playing the role)
s: Let's try the time out chair and the privileges taken away you know . . . oh please give me a break (laughs) it didn't work . . . it seems to have gone from bad to worse (tone and expression change three times with each segment, first part eyes are darting nervously, tone is monotonous, sarcastic, stops mid-sentence, changes tone, accusatorial, eyes close to emphasize frustration with the situation, third change occurs with the laughed words, authoritative tone, makes eye contact with reporter, looks to be justifying previous "outburst," rhythm irregular, fragmented speech throughout)
REPORTER: Why do the experts say this? (puts hands in the air)
R: It might work for some people but it doesn't work for us (voice gets higher, assertive, heavy stress on word "doesn't" and "work")
REPORTER: Can't she forget she is only two years old?
s: Yes she can forget but there's certain signs with her that I know she knows what

she is doing (mixed smile, condescending tone, words, tone, and facial expression all take on the "I am the parent, I know best, don't try to challenge me" demeanor, seems a bit defensive)

REPORTER: You think she does this just to bother you?

S: No, not particularly to bother me . . . but just to be bad (mixed smile, stammer, rapid speech in conclusion, frustrated, the reporter is challenging his authority, again condescending)

REPORTER: But that's why they are called training pants

S: RRRight, right, but she does know (mixed smile, looks threatened and a bit flustered, stammers, heavy emphasis on words "does know," reporter seems to have been successful putting him on the defensive)

REPORTER: Sometimes in the Smiley house you see fear

S: Fear restrains them from doing bad things . . . you know bad things

REPORTER: The child care experts say that if children behave out of fear that they will never learn how to behave for the right reasons, just because it's right

S: No, I think that is bull too. AAA UMMM (fixed smile, cocky, cool, laughter in speech, indignant, rudeness to the reporter may be sign he's losing his temper)

R: I don't care if they learn it for the right reasons or not as long as they learn it (sarcastic tone, laughter in speech, almost belligerent, again seems to have taken on Smiley's attitude towards the reporter, gaze averted, appears to be overcome with frustration regarding both the reporter and his line of questioning, cynical of the "child care experts," heavy stress on last words)

REPORTER: It is almost as if you're abusive . . . you're you're cruel

R: It might look cruel but it be more cruel not to let them grow and be evil little brats I mean I see kids now that are . . . I mean downright evil and cruel to each other. My kids are not (calm until emphasis on the word "evil," rhythm becomes irregular, rapid speech, eyes light up, voice becomes urgent, face looks frightened, fanatical voice carries with it a warning, speech slows down again, direct gaze at the end)

Conversation with Favarro and Straus

FAVARRO: I have worked with parents who have unintentionally injured their children while spanking and they feel terrible about it

R: Neither of us spank when we're angry. We have time-out first and we talk about it (calm, controlled, direct eye contact, appears to be playing a role, lies)

S: No we don't AAAA (first time he appears nervous, stammers, over-soft tone, hesitation, self-interruption, withdrawn, face is blank, embarrassed that Rebecca has lied and/or appears ashamed about his action on the tape)

R: I'd love something else to work because it makes me feel worse than it makes them feel to do it (tired expression, breathiness, false exasperation, eyes averted, often dart)

FAVARRO: I believe that

R: But nothing else seems to work (voice fades out, almost incoherent, eyes averted, helpless and tired expression, resigned)

STRAUS: (comments on spanking not working)

S: Oh it works most of the time (face lights up when faced with this "challenge," cocks his head to the side, assertive, interrupted by Straus, changes phrasing)

STRAUS: Most of the time it has not worked

R and S: Most of the time it has (unified and defensive, both sound threatened, Rebecca has jumped in to help Smiley)

17

Exchange Theory

RICHARD J. GELLES

Corporal punishment of children is a type of family violence that is more common and more frequent and has more normative approval than the physical abuse of children, violence toward women, and physical violence toward and abuse of the elderly. Various studies of corporal punishment, going back nearly sixty years, find that the vast majority of parents use corporal punishment at some time in their children's lives (Anderson 1936; Goodenough 1931; Sears, Maccoby, and Levin 1957; Straus, Gelles, and Steinmetz 1980; Straus 1994). The rate of corporal punishment varies by age of child, with children under one year of age having the lowest rates. The rate of corporal punishment increases for children two years of age to eight years of age, and then the rates decline with age from the age of nine to seventeen (Straus, Gelles, and Steinmetz 1980; Wauchope and Straus 1990; Straus 1994). Yet almost one in four seventeen-year-olds experiences corporal punishment at least once during the year.

Corporal punishment is not only common but also frequent, and it is sometimes severe. The average parent uses corporal punishment nearly nine times each year, and even this figure is assumed to be an underestimate (Straus 1994). Corporal punishment often is thought to be a swat on the bottom, a spanking, or the use of a light stinging object, such as a switch. Hairbrushes, sticks, and rods are also used by parents. Of the items actually identified by parents as the objects they use when hitting a child, belts were the most common, followed by rulers and then paddles (Schulman, Ronca, and Bucavalas 1995). There are, of course, more severe forms of physical violence used on children. In both National Family-Violence Surveys, one in one thousand parents report that they used a gun or a knife on a child in the previous year (Straus, Gelles, and Steinmetz 1980; Gelles and Straus 1987).

Given how common corporal punishment is, it is not surprising that there is substantial social and cultural approval for its use on children. As Straus (1994) points out, study after study shows that almost all Americans approve of hitting children — at least under some circumstances. Data from the 1968 survey conducted for the National Commission on the Causes and Prevention of Violence found an 86 percent approval rate for corporal punishment (Owens and Straus 1975). Of the adults surveyed in the 1975 National Family-Violence Survey, 77 percent said that spanking a twelve-year-old child was normal and appropriate (Straus, Gelles, and Steinmetz 1980). Of the adults surveyed in the General Social Survey, 86 percent agreed that "it is sometimes necessary to discipline a child with a good hard spanking" (Lehman 1989).

Clearly, corporal punishment of children is both widely practiced and receives widespread normative approval. Thus, unlike physically abusive violence toward children or even physical violence toward women, this form of family violence is not generally thought of as deviant, criminal, abnormal, or aberrant behavior. The extent of practice and approval poses an interesting dilemma for those who attempt to develop and test theoretical explanations for corporal punishment. First, and most obvious, since corporal punishment is neither rare nor socially defined as deviant, traditional theories of deviance are not necessarily directly applicable. Second, a theoretical explanation of corporal punishment ought to be able to explain not only why parents use corporal punishment but also why the minority of parents do not strike their children.

Exchange theory is a theory of social behavior that is quite applicable to the issue of corporal punishment. Exchange theory was first developed as a general theory of human social behavior (see, for example, Blau 1964; Homans 1961; Thibault and Kelley 1959). Although exchange theory was not initially thought to be applicable to intimate family relations, the theory has been used in family studies in general (see, for example, Nye 1979) and family violence in particular (see Gelles 1983).

This chapter presents an exchange-theory perspective for corporal punishment. The first section presents the basic assumptions, concepts, and propositions of exchange theory. The second section applies these assumptions, concepts, and propositions to corporal punishment of children. The final section examines changes in both public attitudes about corporal punishment and trend data on parents' use of corporal punishment and offers an exchange-theory explanation for changes of both attitudes and behaviors.

Exchange Theory

The exchange approach to human behavior has a long history in both sociology and anthropology (Nye 1979). The key assumptions of the exchange perspective are:

1. Social behavior is a series of exchanges.
2. In the course of these exchanges, individuals attempt to maximize their rewards and minimize their costs.
3. Under certain circumstances, a person will accept certain costs in exchange for other rewards.
4. When we receive rewards from others, we are obliged to reciprocate and supply benefits to them in return (from Homans 1961; Blau 1964; Nye 1979).

The key concepts used by exchange theories are:

Rewards.

Rewards are defined as pleasures, satisfactions, and gratifications (Thibault and Kelley 1959). Rewards also include a gain in status, relationships, interaction, experiences other than interaction, and feelings that provide gratification to people (Nye 1979: 2).

Costs.

Costs are defined as any loss in status, loss of a relationship or milieu, or feeling disliked by an individual or group (Nye 1979: 2). There are two types of costs — (1) punishments and (2) losing out on some reward because another alternative was chosen (missing a good movie because you chose to go to a concert).

Reciprocity.

The key to social exchange is reciprocity. In brief, people are expected to help those who help them and not injure those who have helped them (Gouldner 1960).

Applying Exchange Theory to Corporal Punishment

As with the general exchange theory, the key assumption of an exchange theory of corporal punishment is that human interaction is guided by the pursuit of rewards and the avoidance of punishment and costs. This is applicable both to why parents use corporal punishment and to why they believe that corporal punishment is effective.

A second assumption is that a person who supplies reward services to another obliges the other to fulfill the obligation; and thus the second individual must furnish benefits to the first (Blau 1964). Blau (1964) explains that if reciprocal exchange occurs, the interaction continues. If reciprocity is not received, however, the interaction will be broken off. Of course, family relations in general, and parent-child relations in particular, are more complex and have a unique social structure compared to the exchanges that typically exist outside the family. First, given the relationship between parent and child, it is almost impossible to "break off" the interaction, even when there is little or no reciprocity. While one can break off a social interaction with a friend or coworker, quit or be fired from a job, leave one's church or synagogue and join another, and divorce a spouse, breaking off an interaction with a parent or a child is more socially constrained and difficult. Even when one becomes an ex-spouse, it is difficult to become an ex-parent. Parents can disown children or even petition family or juvenile courts to have their parental rights terminated. These, however, are difficult, complex, and rare occurrences. Unless a parent abandons a child, unless the child runs away, or unless there is court-imposed or court-approved termination of the parental responsibilities, parents and children are tied to one another for life, even if there is low or minimal reciprocity.

A second unique aspect of the parent-child relationship is the substantial difference in power — personal, social, and psychological. For most of their interaction with their children, parents are physically larger and more powerful than their children, and have more economic, personal, and social resources. Parents have a legal and constitutional right to raise their children without unwarranted interference by the state. Although child-welfare agencies have the authority to investigate cases of abuse and neglect and to take short-term custody of maltreated children with *ex parte* court orders, state involvement in child rearing is rigorously constrained. Federal and state law requires that state departments of child welfare make reasonable efforts to keep maltreated children with their birth parents, and the process of actually terminating parental rights is typically long and complex. Thus the exchanges between parents and children, especially young children, are inequitable, with the parents holding most of the social power and social resources.

The playing field in parent-child relations, within which costs and rewards are calculated and reciprocity measures, is not an even one. In addition, it is important to understand that the use of corporal punishment is not necessarily a "last resort" that parents use to redress an imbalance of costs and rewards and achieve a certain level of distributive justice or reciprocity. Violence, particularly spanking, may very well be a *first* choice of behavior for many parents. Exchange theory needs to explain not only why corporal punishment is used by parents but also why it may be the first and most desired behavior parents use.

TYPES OF CORPORAL PUNISHMENT

So far, this chapter has proceeded without actually defining the term *corporal punishment*. The term has been defined throughout the book in many, if not all, of the chapters. For the purposes of this chapter, corporal punishment is defined as the use of physical force with the intent of causing a child to experience pain, but not injury, for the purposes of correction or the control of the child's behavior (Straus 1994: 4). Corporal punishment is not child abuse, because child abuse is typically defined as acts of commission (or omission) that are intended to cause injury. Corporal punishment is also not expressive violence where the behavior itself is the goal of the actor.

This definition of corporal punishment is amenable to an exchange-theory explanation because the behavior is rational and occurs as a result of a *choice* made by the parent or caretaker. The choice is to use a behavior (corporal punishment) that is controlled (that will cause pain but not an injury) and has a specifically desired outcome (correction or control of behavior). Corporal punishment, by definition, is not irrational and unconscious and does not arise out of a loss of temper or uncontrolled anger.

THE PROPOSITIONS

A central and oversimplified proposition of an exchange-theory approach to corporal punishment is that *parents use corporal punishment toward their children because they (the parents) can* (Gelles 1983). In applying the principles of exchange theory we expect that parents will use corporal punishment if the costs of using that behavior do not outweigh the rewards.

This initial proposition can be expanded to the following propositions:

1. Parents are more likely to use corporal punishment toward their children when they expect the costs of using this behavior to be lower than the rewards.

2. The likelihood of using corporal punishment is higher in societies, cultures, subcultures, and communities where there is normative approval for using corporal punishment to discipline children.

3. The likelihood of using corporal punishment is higher is societies, cultures, subcultures, and communities where there is the belief that corporal punishment is effective. Effective can mean that corporal punishment can change children's behavior, mold character, and prevent children from engaging in deviant or otherwise socially disapproved behavior.

The use of corporal punishment does vary across situations and settings. Although I have argued that there is widespread social approval for the use of corporal punishment and widespread belief that corporal punishment is effective, there are still social constraints that limit parents' use of corporal punishment. Because there is no widely accepted definition of what constitutes physical abuse of children, parents may be constrained from using corporal punishment if they believe that their behavior could be perceived as child abuse. Thus:

4. Corporal punishment is more likely to be used by parents in private settings, such as the home, than in public settings. In addition, the severity of corporal punishment in public settings will be lower than the severity in private settings.

The above propositions deal with the balance of costs and rewards and suggest that "effectiveness" of punishment and "normative approval" of its use are rewards, while detection and the risk of being labeled or stigmatized a "child abuser" are costs of using corporal punishment. In addition to the balance of costs and rewards, the use of corporal punishment can arise from an imbalance of reciprocity or "distributive justice." Thus:

5. Parents are more likely to use corporal punishment if they perceive a lack of reciprocity in their exchanges with their children. For example, a parent who has spent a great deal of money to take his or her child on an outing or a vacation will be more likely to use corporal punishment to discipline the child when the child misbehaves on the outing or vacation than the parent would given the same behavior or misbehavior in another situation or setting.

6. Children perceived as "difficult," or chronically disobedient, are more likely to receive corporal punishment than children perceived as compliant, or well-behaved.

7. Given the structured power differential in parent-child relations, and the assumption that parents use corporal punishment to redress an imbalance of costs and rewards, we can derive another proposition that parents are more likely to use corporal punishment when they are larger and more powerful than their children and when their children are physically or emotionally unable or unlikely to use violence in response or to inflict other costs for the parent who uses corporal punishment.

EFFECTIVENESS

One of the key "rewards" of using corporal punishment is the perception of its effectiveness. This, as much as normative approval, underlies a calculus that concludes that using corporal punishment brings more rewards than costs. One of the ironies in the field of corporal punishment is the widespread perception that corporal punishment works and that it is withholding corporal punishment that brings about negative outcomes for children. Straus

(1994) notes that the accumulated evidence over nearly fifty years of research negates the belief that corporal punishment is an effective means of changing behavior and developing character. In fact, Straus's summary of the collected body of research finds quite the opposite — that children who experience corporal punishment are more likely to experience a wide range of social and developmental problems as children, as adolescents, and even as adults. Nonetheless, as Straus (1994) also notes, these research findings have not only failed to make their way into the general population of parents, they seem to have been "suppressed" in the social-science community as well.

It seems clear that the normative approval that lowers the costs of using corporal punishment is tied to the long-held cultural belief that corporal punishment is effective and its *absence* is what harms children and society.

It is also clear that the widespread belief in the effectiveness of corporal punishment explains why corporal punishment is often the first response a parent chooses for a child's misbehavior, rather than simply a last resort to be used "when nothing else works."

The widespread belief that corporal punishment is effective is a function of a number of factors. First, from a short-term point of view, corporal punishment *is* effective. Parents who use corporal punishment to get a child to cease an offending behavior find that if the force causes sufficient pain, the child will indeed stop the offending behavior, at least until the pain subsides. Parents are often reinforced in using corporal punishment because children do stop offending behavior. Second, parents often apply their own personal experiences with corporal punishment as testimony that it is effective. When asked why they spank their children, parents often point out that they too were spanked and that is why they turned out as well as they did — or, conversely, some parents will explain that they are sure that if they were not spanked, they would not have turned out well.

POSSIBLE COSTS

There are possible costs of corporal punishment. First, there is the possibility that what a parent perceives as corporal punishment may be perceived by others as physical child abuse. The federal government developed a model definition of child abuse in the mid-1960s (Nelson 1984), and each state has a definition of child abuse embodied in state child-abuse and child-neglect statutes. Nevertheless, there still is no clear national normative standard that clearly and concisely clarifies the boundary between corporal punishment and physical child abuse. Thus there is always the potential that an observer may label a behavior "abuse" that the parent sees as punishment. In the event that the punishment leaves a mark, such as a welt, bruise, black and blue mark, or cut, there is the possibility that someone who observes the mark may label it the result of abusive behavior and report the child to a state department of child welfare. Even though the likelihood of the department of child welfare officially substantiating the case as "child abuse" may be low, simply being reported for child abuse is a cost parents must consider.

In addition, as suggested above, there is always the possibility that an act that begins as an act of corporal punishment may inadvertently produce an injury and thus be considered and substantiated as physical child abuse.

The possible costs of being labeled a child abuser would exist even if there was a sharp definable boundary between corporal punishment and child abuse. The lack of such a clear boundary increases potential costs for parents because they can never be certain which behaviors will be labeled abuse and which will not.

Obviously, one possible cost is that an act of corporal punishment may indeed produce a serious, unintended injury. Children are injured in the course of corporal punishment, sometimes because of accidental factors (poor aim, the child falls against a hard object, the child turns into the direction of the hand or object), and sometimes because the force was great enough to produce the injury without any intervening or situational contributors. Thus parents who use corporal punishment tend to measure the force and object they use against the possibility that their actions will produce an injury.

Given that corporal punishment is designed to cause pain, and if used to bring about a cessation of perceived misbehavior will often cause pain, children who experience corporal punishment will show distress by crying, sobbing, withdrawing, or otherwise showing they have been hurt. For many parents, although corporal punishment may be approved and effective, there still is the cost of hurting one's child. Although our society provides some buffers against this cost, such as the homily "This will hurt me more than it will hurt you," parents still must experience the cost of the crying, sobbing, or angry child who has been struck in the name of discipline.

An additional cost of using corporal punishment is the possibility that the child will hit back and inflict physical costs on the parent. Finally, there is the cost that a child who experiences corporal punishment will be more likely to develop short-term and long-term developmental problems. Straus (1994) has identified a number of short- and long-term consequences of a child's experiencing corporal punishment, including the increased likelihood that the child will engage in juvenile delinquency, be depressed, attempt suicide, be alienated at work, and make less income than children who did not experience corporal punishment. One of the purposes of Straus's program of research on corporal punishment is to illuminate the negative outcomes of corporal punishment.

Perhaps one of Straus's goals in pursuing and publishing this line of research is to change parents' cost-benefit calculation and rethink the assumption that the benefits of using corporal punishment outweigh the costs.

Changes in Behavior and Attitude with Regard to Corporal Punishment

Although we have a great deal of descriptive research on corporal punishment, including data on its extent and frequency, the relationship between a child's age and experiencing corporal punishment, and the correlates and consequences of corporal punishment, there have been few tests of theories of corporal punishment (one exception is Straus's 1971 test of the linkage theory). Thus there has yet to be an empirical test of exchange-theory propositions regarding corporal punishment.

There are data on parents' attitudes toward and use of corporal punishment and their use of corporal punishment toward their children. The National Committee to Prevent Child Abuse conducts annual public-opinion surveys of attitudes and behaviors with respect to child-abuse prevention (Daro and Gelles 1992; Daro 1995). The first survey was conducted in 1986 and the survey has been conducted each year since then. The survey interviews a representative sample of approximately 1,250 adults in the United States. The survey includes a set of questions about attitudes toward parenting behaviors as well as questions that ask parents to report on their use of specific acts of corporal punishment.

In response to the question, "How often do you think physical punishment of a child leads to injury to the child?" anywhere between 32 percent and 40 percent of those sampled said that physical punishment very often or often leads to injury of a child. There has actually been a decrease in recent years of respondents supporting the statement that physical punishment very often or often leads to an injury to the child.

Self-reports of spanking or hitting a child have declined since 1988. In 1988, 64 percent of the parents surveyed reported that they had spanked or hit their child or children in the previous year. This percentage fell to 49 percent in 1995 (Daro 1995).

One reason for the continued decline in the reporting of corporal punishment is that parents who believe that there are harmful consequences to corporal punishment may be less inclined to use corporal punishment. The reduction in self-reports of spanking does not seem to be a function of an increase in parents who believe that there are harmful consequences of corporal punishment—since the surveys find a decrease in the percentage of parents who believe corporal punishment is harmful. The change, as Daro (1995) suggests, may be occurring because parents are finding corporal punishment is ineffective.

The survey results at least suggest that the key component of an exchange theory of corporal punishment may be the actual perceived rewards and costs of corporal punishment. Important as cultural approval of corporal punishment may be in explaining the use of spankings and other forms of corporal punishment, the more important factor in the cost-reward calculus may be whether parents believe that the rewards of actually using corporal punishment exceed the costs.

Summary

Corporal punishment is behavior that has widespread cultural support, is used by individuals who have much more physical, social, and economic power than those on whom the corporal punishment is used, and is believed to be an effective means of changing and molding behavior — at least the behavior of children. It is no surprise, then, that there is widespread use of corporal punishment across social and cultural groups and across the age span of children. On the other hand, there are certain constraints that tend to limit the use of corporal punishment and may explain why there has been a steady decrease in the percentage of parents who report that they use corporal punishment. One constraint is that the same cultural norms that support the use of corporal punishment also negatively sanction parents and caretakers who cross a poorly marked and vaguely defined line that separates corporal punishment from physical child abuse. The fact that the culture also does not provide clear standards for what and who is a "good parent" also creates a possible cost of using corporal punishment. While parents may believe that corporal punishment is appropriate and effective, many are also concerned that too much corporal punishment may be a sign that they are not "good parents." In addition, the fact that corporal punishment causes pain and often produces distress in children who have been hit may also send a message to the parent that he or she is not a "good parent." Similarly, since the measure of a "good parent" is how a child behaves and develops, the possibility that corporal punishment may produce adverse behaviors or poor child outcomes may also constrain parents from using corporal punishment, both in specific situations and in the general course of child rearing.

Exchange theory provides a useful conceptual framework and testable propositions to test the situational and individual use of corporal punishment as well as the broader social and structural patterns of the use of corporal punishment.

18

Corporal Punishment and the Stress Process

HEATHER TURNER

The stress paradigm has been one of the most widely used and enduring conceptual frameworks for understanding the link between the social environment and individual outcomes. Although most stress research has focused on the effect of stressful occurrences or conditions on physical and psychological health, one major appeal of this paradigm is its flexibility and broad range of application. Thus, the stress-process framework provides an approach for examining connections among social structure, a wide array of life circumstances, individual variations in vulnerability, and a range of personal outcomes, including transitory emotions, psychiatric and physical disorder, and behavioral responses, such as aggression.

The purpose of this chapter is to outline the stress-process framework and discuss how it may be used to examine the use of corporal punishment by parents. From the perspective of the parent, I outline how the use of corporal punishment represents a potential outcome of stressful experience. From the perspective of the child, I discuss how corporal punishment itself can represent a stressor with the potential for creating a variety of negative outcomes. Research that has been conducted on outcomes of corporal punishment has focused almost entirely on aggression. Moreover, there has been little research on the antecedents of corporal punishment, and few studies have specifically examined corporal punishment within a stress-process framework.

Consequently, our discussion draws largely on relevant literature from other areas. For example, while we know little of how "normative" corporal punishment affects the behavior and health of children, we know more about the effects of more extreme violence in the home, such as wife beating and physical abuse of children. Similarly, while little research has examined the factors and conditions that may accentuate the use of corporal punishment as a form of discipline, some studies have examined dispositional and situational antecedents to other, less socially sanctioned, forms of domestic violence.

Although we do not contend that corporal punishment is equivalent to physical child abuse or other types of severe domestic violence, we nonetheless treat physical punishment as a form of physical aggression or violence. Despite the fact that the physical punishment of children is normative, sanctioned, and legal, it can be argued that it still falls within a broad definition of violence: "an act of physical force with the intention of causing injury or harm" (Websters 1982). While parents who use corporal punishment usually do not intend to cause injury, they generally *do* intend to cause some degree of pain for the purpose of controlling or correcting a child's behavior.

Overview of the Stress Process

The term *stress* refers to a state of imbalance within an organism that: (1) results from an actual or perceived disparity between environmental demands and the organism's ability to adapt to those demands; and (2) is manifested through a variety of physiological, emotional, or behavioral responses (Stoklos 1986). Thus, stress occurs in response to strained and threatening circumstances in the environment (Pearlin and Schooler 1978). The environmental demands or stimuli that initiate stress are referred to as "stressors." Circumstances within the physical and social environment act as stressors to the extent that they tax an organism's adaptive capacities. Rather than representing a static phenomenon, stress is typically viewed as a dynamic, interactive process involving a number of different components. Specifically, the "stress process" is recognized as consisting of three major dimensions: sources of stress, moderators of stress, and stress outcomes.

SOURCES OF STRESS

Social stressors can take the form of life events or chronic strains (Pearlin et al. 1981; Pearlin 1989). Most stress research conducted by sociologists and psychologists has focused on life events: discrete occurrences or experiences that surface in individuals' lives. Early life-events research was based on the assumption that all types of change-inducing events create stress because they disrupt an individual's equilibrium (Holmes and Rahe 1967). Since this early conceptualization, however, it has become evident that not all change is stressful. Rather, it is events that are perceived as negative, unexpected, and/or uncontrollable that have the most potential to elicit stress-related responses (Thoits 1983). Thus, such events as involuntary job loss, divorce, death of a family member, accidents, sudden illness, and physical assault are usually stress producing.

Some investigators believe that it is the second general category of stressors — chronic life strains — that have the most potential for having negative effects (Pearlin 1989). Unlike eventful stress, chronic strains generally do not have a discrete onset and ending but instead represent the more enduring conditions in people's lives. Usually chronic strains are rooted in the social roles people occupy. They are more persistent role problems that become relatively fixed and perpetual in daily role experiences. Frustrations at work, heavy demands of child care, and ongoing conflict with one's spouse can represent chronic life strains.

MODERATORS OF STRESS

People vary considerably in the extent to which they are affected by potential stressors. Individuals who experience the same type of events and/or the same chronic life conditions do not all experience adverse outcomes. It is widely accepted that at least part of this difference in response to stressors is due to variations in stress moderators. That is, individuals can possess certain social or personal resources that moderate or buffer the negative effects of stress. While there are likely to be numerous stress moderators, the most well known and well researched are social support and coping. Social support, in the most general sense, refers to the extent to which individuals have access to social relationships or resources on which they can rely. These relationships might include those with a spouse, relatives, friends, community groups, and formal social institutions. A popular conceptualization by Cobb (1976) defines social support as information leading the individual to believe he or she is cared for and loved, is esteemed and valued, and belongs to a network of communication and mutual obligation.

While support represents a potential *social* resource, coping represents an important *personal* resource. That is, coping consists of the strategies that the individual himself or herself employs to deal with problems imposed by stressors. One well-known conceptualization of coping focuses on its functions. Pearlin and Schooler (1978) categorize all coping behavior as involving efforts: (1) to change the problem situation itself; (2) to change one's perceptions of the situation to reduce its threatening quality; or (3) to manage or reduce the symptoms of stress once they occur. Similarly, Moos and Billing (1982) view coping as either problem focused (intended to change or modify the sources of stress), appraisal focused (used to define the meaning of the situation), or emotion focused (directed at managing emotions aroused by stressors). These different types of coping response come into play at different points in the process between the initial occurrence or onset of a stressor and the final outcome. All types, however, are aimed at reducing the ultimate impact of stress.

Other potential individual-centered stress moderators include aspects of self-concept — mastery and self-esteem — and personality characteristics, such as Type A behavior and neuroticism. As will be discussed later, factors that may specifically moderate the effects of parental stress on violent behavior, including the use of corporal punishment, may include aspects of childhood experience and socialization, authoritarian attitudes, and other child-rearing practices. Potential moderators of child stress *arising* from corporal punishment may include parental support, consistency of parental demands, and discipline, whether it is applied in a controlled or explosive manner or is accompanied by discussion or explanation.

OUTCOMES OF STRESS

"Outcome" simply refers to a manifestation of stress. The possible outcomes of stress are numerous. Most research has focused on mental-health and physical-health outcomes. For example, research has documented an association between stressful events or strains and depression, anxiety, neuroses, phobias, various somatic symptoms, and physical disorders, such as ulcers and heart disease (Aneshensel 1999; Creed 1993; Dohrenwend and Dohrenwend 1974; Kessler et al. 1985; Levine and Scotch 1970; McGrath 1970; Rabkin and Struening 1976; Syme and Berkman 1976). As will be discussed, there is also reason to believe that stress can manifest itself, either directly or indirectly, in aggressive or violent behavior (Linsky et al. 1995). This may include the use of physical punishment in discipline.

It is important to note that each dimension of the stress process outlined above is significantly influenced by the stratification systems and social institutions of society. Individual experiences are structured by one's location in various stratification systems and by the social roles one occupies. Thus, one's race or ethnicity, age, gender, and social class, in addition to whether one is a spouse, parent, homemaker, employee, or caregiver, provide the contexts that determine the stressors to which one is exposed, the resources available to deal with stressors, and the types of stress outcomes one is likely to experience. As Pearlin (1989) states, "A salient feature of sociological stress research is its concern with the socially patterned distribution of the components of the stress process: stressors, mediators and outcomes. Such patterns provide a cue that individuals' potentially stressful experiences and the ways in which they are affected by their experiences may originate in the social orders of which they are a part" (1989: 242–43). One especially important context that structures and patterns social stress is the family.

Stress and the Family

Issues involving the occurrence and outcomes of corporal punishment are imbedded within the family context. The family represents an important arena for stress experiences as well as for the development and provision of social and personal resources that moderate stress. Thus, while we often think of the family as an important source of nurturance and support, it can also be a very powerful source of stress. Family-related events, such as widowhood, divorce, unwanted pregnancy or childbirth, and accidents or illness among family members, are often highly stress producing. Chronic strains within family roles can be especially impactful. Chronic role strains often arise from excessive demands of childcare and other domestic responsibilities. Indeed, some research suggests that the roles of mother and housewife may be especially stressful, since women occupying these roles often experience the greatest psychological distress (Bird 1997; Gove and Tudor 1973; Gore and Mangione 1983; Horowitz 1982). An especially common type of strain within the family domain involves interpersonal conflict (Croog 1970; Pearlin and Turner 1987). Without a doubt the family is the most conflict-ridden and violent institution in society (Gelles and Straus 1979). Thus, of special relevance to the issue of corporal punishment is the role of the family in teaching, encouraging, and reinforcing aggressive behavior.

In addition to being a potentially powerful source of stress in its own right, the family is greatly affected by stressors affecting family members outside the family domain. In fact, the family often serves as "conduit" for extrafamilial stressors (Pearlin and Turner 1987). For example, several studies have documented the effect of occupational stress on family functioning or the well-being of a spouse or child (Bolger et al. 1990; Weiss 1990; Bromet et al. 1990). The boundaries between work and family are far from impermeable. Stress in the workplace can cross over into the family domain when distress caused by occupational problems are brought home. When a worker is fatigued, anxious, depressed, or irritated at home, family interactions often become strained or conflictive, daily routines may be disrupted, and strategies for managing and disciplining children can change. Strained family relations, in turn, become additional, independent sources of stress.

Despite its potential to generate stress, the family is also the most important life domain for providing individuals with social support and developing their coping strategies. It is often the first place that individuals turn to get advice and instrumental assistance, to obtain affection and nurturance, or to reaffirm their sense of esteem and value. The particular behaviors individuals adopt in their own efforts to deal with problems are learned and reinforced within the family context. Parent's ways of coping with stress and conflict, whether effective or dysfunctional, become incorporated into children's repertoires and are often maintained into adulthood. As will be discussed later, such strategies can include the use of violence in dealing with family conflict and the use of corporal punishment in dealing with children's misbehavior.

In sum, the family represents an important context for the stress process. It provides a context for the occurrence of stress as well as for the development of family and individual strategies to deal with stress. Thus, considering the stress process within the family context is necessary for understanding the phenomenon of corporal punishment.

Corporal Punishment as a Parental-Stress Outcome

STRESS AND VIOLENCE

Aggressive impulses that can lead to violent behavior are frequent reactions to stress. Studies of human responses to a wide range of severe stressors, such as combat, traumatic illness, and community disasters, suggest that aggressively hostile urges, fantasies, and behavior are organismic responses to high levels of acute and chronic stress (cf. Keith 1990). In fact, the concept of stress represents a useful organizing principle for many issues in violence prediction. Even less severe and more common stressors may be associated with violent reactions. Vinokur and Selzer (1975) found that general life-event scores correlate with aggression, most strongly with negative or undesirable events. According to Monahan (1990), employment-related stressors, such as recent firing or layoff, disputes with superiors or coworkers, or dissatisfaction with the nature of work performed or compensation received, represent potential correlates of violent behavior. Peer-group stressors, such as the disruption of friendship patterns or the demand to conform to group standards, also can lead to violence. As already noted, family-related stressors — domestic frustrations, demands, and conflict in husband-wife and parent-child relationships — are especially susceptible to violent resolution.

Family members appear to be the most common target of violent reactions arising from stressful experience. The high frequency of interaction among family members, the norm of privacy concerning the family, the social acceptance of violence as a legitimate means of settling conflict, and the high expectations for families to meet the needs of all family members have been identified as factors that help explain the high incidence of violence within the family (Gelles and Straus 1979). In fact, stressors that arise from both within and outside the family have been associated with family violence. For example, a number of investigators have attributed the association between poverty and domestic violence to excessive exposure to environmental stressors (Gil 1971; Pelton 1981). Thus, poverty-related factors, such as unemployment, dilapidated and overcrowded housing, and inadequate clothing, food, recreation, and opportunity for improvement, can provide the stressful context for abuse. As Gil (1971) suggests, the stress associated with poverty may precipitate child abuse "by weakening the caretaker's psychological mechanisms of self-control and contributing thus to the uninhibited discharge of aggressive and destructive impulses" (1971: 645).

Consistent with this argument, empirical evidence has documented an association between unemployment or other work-related stress and both spousal and child-directed violence (Straus and Kaufman Kantor 1987; Schechter 1982; Barling and Rosenbaum 1986; Justice and Duncan 1976). Stress arising from parenting has also been associated with domestic violence. Child-related life events, frequent interruptions and difficult behavior by children, demands associated with having large numbers of children, and strains associated with caring for physically or mentally impaired children have been found to be correlated with physical child abuse (Gelles and Cornell 1990; Gil 1970; Justice and Duncan 1976; Light 1983; Passman and Mulhern 1977; Friedrich and Boriskin 1976; Straus et al. 1980).

STRESS AND PARENTING BEHAVIOR

It is evident that stressful conditions and experiences can be determinants of violence toward children. As discussed above, exposure to stressors has been linked to both spousal and child abuse. However, in addition to its relationship to more extreme forms of violence, there is reason to believe that stress may be related to less severe, more normative forms of violence, such as corporal punishment. First, there is evidence suggesting an association between the occurrence of domestic violence and the physical punishment of children as a form of discipline (Straus et al. 1980). Moreover, the stressors that precipitate spousal and child abuse appear also to represent causal factors for "ordinary" family violence, including corporal punishment (Straus 1980). Thus, parents that are physically abusive to each other tend also to discipline children physically, and the conditions that precipitate physical abuse of children tend also to contribute to the use of corporal punishment (Straus 1983).

Also relevant to this issue is research examining the effect of environmental factors and conditions on general parenting behavior. There is evidence, for example, that financial strain due to economic loss increases the probability of punitive parenting (Elder and Caspi 1988). In fact, low income in general, often treated as an indicator of chronic stress, is related to authoritarian parenting strategies that include greater use of physical punishment (Gecas 1979; Kohn 1969; Longfellow et al. 1982). One mechanism by which the stress associated with low socioeconomic status (SES) may influence parenting behavior is by reducing perceived self-efficacy or personal control. Specifically, it has been suggested that low SES parents emphasize obedience and external control when disciplining because of a general expectation that they have little personal control over their environment (Kohn 1969). According to Maccoby (1980), parents who experience low personal control may, especially under conditions of high stress, lack the patience and understanding needed to take time to reason with their children. As a result, parents under stress may be more likely to use parenting practices that will achieve immediate compliance (Conger et al. 1984).

Although it may not be effective in the long term, physical punishment is probably more likely to achieve immediate control and compliance of children than other strategies. Indeed, research shows that, in general, stressed parents are less likely to use positive reinforcement and more likely to use punishment in their child-rearing practices (Conger et al. 1984; Maccoby and Martin 1983; Patterson 1983). Forgatch and Weider (cited in Patterson 1982) found that mothers' probability of continuing "aversive" or "irritable" behavior toward children, which includes hitting children to obtain compliance, was significantly related to day-to-day variations in the incidence of life events or "crises." Models outlined by Patterson (1982, 1983, 1988) also show how increases in daily stress are associated with commensurate increases in irritability within social exchanges with children, which in turn are associated with physical "explosive" styles of discipline.

INDIRECT EFFECTS

While the literature mentioned above suggests that environmental stress may directly influence child-rearing practices, it is also possible that stress is related to physical punishment indirectly. For example, a considerable body of evidence indicates a causal association between stress and symptoms of depression (Kessler et al. 1986; Myers et al. 1971; Pearlin et al. 1981; Turner and Lloyd 1999). Depression, in turn, is often associated with hostility, anger, irritability, conflict, and mistrust of family members (Longfellow et al. 1982; Mirowsky and Ross 1983). Thus, depression can directly influence parent-child interactions. In fact, studies indicate that depressed mothers often show anger, hostility, and conflictive behavior toward their children (Rutter and Quinton 1984; Sussman et al. 1985; Weissman 1983). Of particular relevance are suggestions that depression is related to child abuse, which may in part be a function of the greater degree of parental hostility shown to children of depressed parents (cf. Sussman et al. 1985). It seems likely that the effect of parental depression on parenting behavior would extend to forms discipline.

Stress may also influence the use of physical punishment indirectly through its effect on marital conflict and violence. Clearly, the marital relationship, while a potentially important source of support, is often conflict ridden and even violent. Thus, spousal conflict itself represents an especially common source of family stress. Moreover, studies have found an association between stress arising outside the family and subsequent conflict between spouses (Elder and Liker 1982; Pearlin and Turner 1987). As noted earlier, a link between stressful circumstances or experiences and marital violence has been established (Straus 1980; MacEwan and Barling 1988).

Given the interrelatedness of members within the family system, investigators have acknowledged the likelihood of "spillover" of strain between relationship subsystems within the family (Lempers et al. 1989; Pearlin and Turner 1987). As Belsky et al. (1984) point out, "Since the parent-child system is nested within the marital relationship, what happens between husbands and wives—from an ecological point of view—has implications for what happens between parents and their children" (1984: 171). Thus, stressors that influence the marital relationship by initiating conflict or aggression between spouses can, in turn, influence the parent-child relationship. Elder and Caspi (1988) found that strain in the form of financial loss was related to marital discord and suggest that marital discord may, in turn, affect children by undermining effective discipline. Specifically, they contend that marital discord may set the stage for coercive or aggressive parenting behavior. "Under conditions of stress, aggressive behavior in marital disputes is adopted as one means of achieving one's way . . . and its consequences are reflected across family relationships" (1988: 95). As already noted, studies have found an association between the occurrence of violence between spouses and the occurrence of violence toward children, including more moderate violence in the form of punishment (Green 1976; Straus 1980). Indeed, Steinmetz (1977) found that families who use aggressive tactics to resolve marital disputes tend to adopt similar strategies for disciplining their children. While this does not necessarily indicate a causal association, there is some reason to believe the relationship between the two forms of violence is due, in part, to the influence of marital violence on subsequent violence toward children. Even when stress-related marital discord does not result in spouse-directed violence, spousal disputes may still affect the use of corporal punishment in parenting. That is, to the extent that physical punishment of children is considered more socially acceptable than the use of physical force against one's spouse, aggression toward children may result from displaced marital hostility (Belsky et al. 1984).

STRESS MODERATORS AND VIOLENCE

Not all individuals who are exposed to stressors experience adverse outcomes. Moderators — factors that function to increase or decrease susceptibility to a stress outcome — help to explain some of the differences in individuals' reactions to stress. That is, the association between stress and an outcome will become stronger or weaker when a moderating factor is present. As described earlier, social support and coping are two types of resources that often buffer the adverse effects of stress. A number of investigators have suggested the importance of social support in reducing the likelihood of family-related violence under conditions of stress. Abusive parents are often more "insular" than nonabusive parents, having less contact with individuals outside the family (cf. Maccoby and Martin 1983). Straus (1980) found that men who were more socially isolated (who did not participate in social organizations) had higher wife-assault rates than men who were less social isolated.

It is important to note, however, that "social support" does not always lead to positive outcomes. Social networks can also encourage behavior that is detrimental to health (for example, alcohol and drug use) or that is antisocial (for example, violence). In fact, Straus (1980) also found that couples who had many relatives living close to them were more violent toward one another than couples with few relatives close by. Thus, to the extent that one's social network represents a reference group in which the use of violence is normative, social integration can also *increase* violent behavior. Since physical punishment of children is widely accepted and prevalent in our society, it seems plausible that "social support" could sometimes increase its use.

Clearly, even individuals who are adversely affected by stress do not all experience *violence* as an outcome. To a large extent, outcomes of stress vary from person to person, depending on individual characteristics. Differences in individual coping strategies likely represent an important basis for variations in the nature of stress outcomes. Thus, in order for stress to manifest itself in violence, it first needs to be present in the individual's behavioral coping repertoire. An especially important factor predisposing individuals to cope with stress through aggressive behavior is the occurrence of violence in the family or origin. Individuals exposed to violence in their family of origin as children are more likely to respond to stress by showing aggression against family members as adults. For example, Straus (1980), found that childhood exposure to family violence, particularly parent-to-parent violence, moderated the effect of stress on husbands' assaults on wives. Specifically, men whose parents engaged in physical fights were substantially more likely to assault their own wives.

It seems likely that this intergenerational transmission of coping responses to stress would also extend to the use of physical punishment. That is, individuals who were exposed to frequent physical punishment as children will be more likely to incorporate physical punishment into their own strategies for dealing with children. Thus, even though physical punishment is viewed as acceptable by the majority of parents, people are still likely to vary in the degree to which they are socialized to use violence in response to stress and, in particular, to use physical punishment as a desired form of discipline.

Even parents who would prefer not to hit or spank their children may find that they lack alternative parenting skills. Indeed, it has been suggested that parents who physically mistreat their children often had little chance to rehearse the caregiving role, tend to have a poor understanding of child-rearing requirements, and hold unrealistics expectations of children. Even the use of "normative" corporal punishment is negatively related to the use of more positive methods of discipline. Specifically, physical punishment appears to be antithical to the use of reason, discussion, explanation, and compromise as strategies to control children's behavior (Bryan and Freed 1982; Larzelere 1986). Lack of alternative strategies to physical punishment likely contributes to the use of violence for discipline. This may be especially true under stressful conditions that tend to reduce patience and increase hostility.

Parental attitudes concerning the socialization of children and the distribution of power and authority within the family may also moderate the association between stress and the use of physical punishment. Mason and Blankenship (1987) suggest that individuals with a high need for power may be more likely to be physically aggressive toward an intimate when under stress. When the ability to control one's environment is stressed or threatened, an individual with a high need for power will be more likely to respond with violence than an individual without such a disposition. Indeed, research on marital violence and stress found that men's attitudes concerning marital power moderate the effect of stress on wife beating (Straus 1980). Specifically, men who believe that husbands should have ultimate power in family decision making are more likely to assault their wives under conditions of stress than those who are less committed to values of male dominance.

Authoritarianism around parenting is somewhat parallel to the concept of marital power. Authoritarian parents emphasize obedience in children and

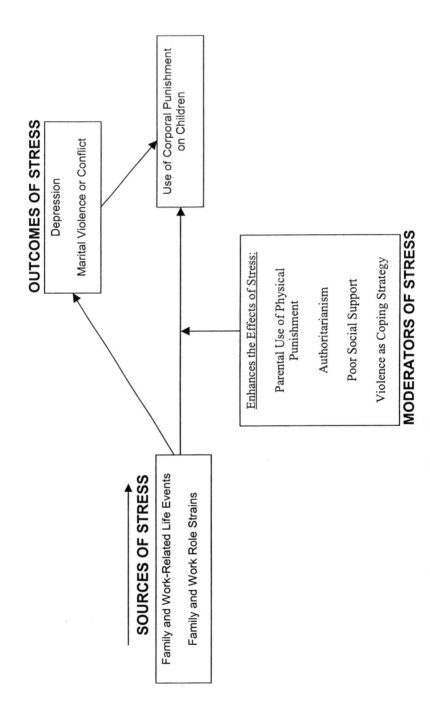

Fig. 18.1. Corporal punishment as an outcome of parental stress.

OUTCOMES OF STRESS

Depression

Marital Violence or Conflict

Use of Corporal Punishment on Children

SOURCES OF STRESS

Family and Work-Related Life Events

Family and Work Role Strains

Enhances the Effects of Stress:

Parental Use of Physical Punishment

Authoritarianism

Poor Social Support

Violence as Coping Strategy

MODERATORS OF STRESS

attach strong values to maintaining their authority. Rather than bargaining or negotiating, they view rules as absolute, and children are not permitted to challenge them. When children deviate from parental requirements, fairly severe punishment, often physical punishment, is likely to be employed (Baumrind 1968; Belsky et al. 1984; Maccoby and Martin 1983). Since authoritarian parents strive to maintain control and power over their children, stressful conditions that reduce perceived power will likely lead to heightened efforts to regain control. Such efforts may include increased use of physical punishment to deal with children, particularly when children are perceived as a source of stress. Thus, an authoritarian style of parenting may moderate the association between stress and corporal punishment, such that authoritarian parents are more susceptible to the use of violence for child discipline when under stress than parents without this parenting style.

To summarize the stress process detailed above, figure 18.1 depicts a theoretical model showing the use of corporal punishment as an outcome of parental stress. Numerous family and work-related stressors experienced by parents can potentially contribute to increased use of corporal punishment in disciplining children. Parental stressors can influence corporal punishment directly, or indirectly through their effects on depression or marital conflict or violence. Several factors or conditions in the lives of parents likely moderate these associations.

GENDER DIFFERENCES

A wide range of research has shown gender differences in aggression and violence across a variety of contexts, with males exhibiting more aggressive behavior than females. However, while men may be more aggressive in general, research suggests that violence by women is more likely to be a response to stress than is violence committed by men. For example, Straus (1980) found that while women are less violent than men under normal circumstances, wives are more likely than husbands to respond with violence under conditions of stress. Similarly, Mason and Blankenship (1987) found that while, in general, men were more likely to use violence to control their partners and solve conflict, women were more likely than men to *respond to stress* with violence. The stronger association between stress and violence among women may have important implications for parenting behavior and the use of physical punishment. Because of their traditional role as caretaker, women typically have substantially more daily contact with children. Moreover, given the often demanding nature of child care, in addition to competing responsibilities of the workplace and other domestic obligations, children are more likely to represent a source of stress for women. In fact, a number of studies suggest that the role of mother, whether alone or in combination with marital or work roles, represents women's primary source of stress (Barnett and Baruch 1985; Gore and Mangione 1983; Kessler and McRae 1981; Pearlin 1975; Ross et al. 1983).

Women may also be more vulnerable to the effects of stress on corporal punishment through indirect paths. As discussed above, stress may influence the use of corporal punishment in part through its effect on depression. Numerous studies drawing on both community and clinical samples have consistently shown women to have higher rates of depression than men (Al-Issa 1982; Dohrenwend and Dohrenwend 1976; Myers et al. 1984; Weissman and Klerman 1992). In fact, the prevalence of major depressive disorder among women is 1.5 to three times greater than it is for men (Kessler and Zhao 1999). Again, investigators have pointed to the demands and conditions of women's social roles as the basis for gender differences in psychological distress. Women, either in caring for children per se or in combining children with employment, experience a greater level of demands than men. Thus, it is argued that this "role overload" experienced by women contributes significantly to their higher rates of depression. To the extent that depression, in turn, elicits hostile parent-child interactions and increases the use of physical punishment, women may be more affected in this regard.

Corporal Punishment as a Childhood Stressor

As discussed earlier, stressors are events or conditions that tax an individual's ability to adjust and adapt to external demands, often leading to negative health or behavioral outcomes. There is reason to believe that acts involving physical punishment can represent stressful events for children. In fact, the high frequency of physical punishment typically experienced and the fact that it continues into adolescence for more than half of American children (Straus and Donnelly 1993) suggest that corporal punishment may often represent a chronic strain.

Justification for considering violence toward children, including corporal punishment, as a source of stress is suggested by evidence of its association with a variety of negative child outcomes. Probably the most well-known outcome of childhood exposure to violence is increased aggression and use of violence by the victimized child. Numerous studies have shown that physically abused children are more likely to be physically aggressive (George and Maine 1979) and to exhibit behavior problems, such as juvenile delinquency (Hirshi 1969; Wisdom 1991). Moreover, the effect of family violence on child aggressiveness is not limited to situations of abuse. Evidence points to the tendency for punitive parenting, especially the use of physical punishment, to be related to elevated levels of aggression and antisocial behavior in children (Larzelere 1986; Lefkowitz et al. 1977; Maurer 1974; Parke and Slaby 1983; Straus 1991; Straus and Mouradian 1998; Straus, Sugarman, and Giles-Sims 1997). For example, Straus (1991) documented an association between "ordinary" physical punishment and violence toward siblings. Specifically, children who experienced only "culturally permissible" physical punishment assaulted a sibling at three times the rate of children who were not physically punished. Similarly, Larzelere (1986) found a positive linear association between frequency of spanking and aggressive acts in three different age groups of children (preschoolers, preadolescents, and teenagers). Based on these findings, Larzelere concludes that moderate physical punishment differs from child abuse only in degree — both lead to childhood aggression. Moreover, the effects of this stressor appear to extend beyond childhood. Exposure to corporal punishment has been related to dating violence in adolescence (Simons, Lin, and Gordon 1998) and other forms of violence in adulthood (cf. Larzelere 1986).

Although much of the research on the effects of violence has focused on child aggression, it is important to acknowledge that a wide range of negative behavioral and health-related outcomes have been observed. Thus, while it could be argued that aggression as an outcome of corporal punishment simply represents the acting out of learned behavior, evidence of multiple outcomes suggests its role in the stress process. Turner and Finkelhor (1996), for example, found positive relationships between frequency of corporal punishment and both psychological distress and clinically relevant depression. Moreover, while children who were frequently exposed to corporal punishment had the highest levels of distress and depression, even moderate or low exposure to corporal punishment had a negative impact on well-being. Several more long-term effects of corporal punishment have also been found, including problems in peer relationships (Bryan and Freed 1982) and elevated levels of depression (Turner and Muller 2004) in young adulthood. Similarly, Straus and Kaufman Kantor (1994) found that corporal punishment experienced in teenage years was positively associated with later drinking problems and thoughts of suicide.

Past research concerning the effects of parenting styles on child development also points to physical punishment as a potential stressor for children. Specifically, authoritarian parenting involving "power-assertive" strategies of discipline that emphasize physical punishment (Maccoby and Martin 1983) has been associated with a number of negative child characteristics. In addition to having a greater tendency toward aggression (Anthony 1970; Feshbach and Feshbach 1972), children of authoritarian parents tend to lack social competence with peers (that is, they are more socially withdrawn), are more likely to have an external rather than internal moral orientation, show less motivation for intellectual achievement, report lower self-esteem, and exhibit lower self-efficacy relative to children of nonauthoritarian parents (Hoffman 1970; Maccoby and Martin 1983).

Patterson (1988) describes how "inept discipline," which includes the use of physical forms of punishment, can set in motion a long chain of negative outcomes. Poor discipline leads to antisocial behavior, which in turn contributes to academic failure and social rejection. These conditions reduce self-esteem and create depressed mood, which in turn increase the likelihood of delinquency in adolescence and ultimately contribute to problems in marriage and careers as adults. Patterson views parental discipline as the malleable determinant in this process. Indeed, his findings show that training parents to use nonphysical forms of punishment reduces the likelihood of negative outcomes.

Importantly, research on parenting practices and child outcomes suggests that not only does corporal punishment itself represent a stressor, it also functions to erode the very resources that have been found to buffer the negative effects of stress. As discussed above, authoritarian parenting, particularly the use of physical punishment, is related to children's social withdrawal and rejection by peers. Thus, children exposed to high levels of corporal punishment may receive less social support from friends than those without such exposure. Personal resources may also be diminished. For example, Bryan and Freed (1982) found that college students who reported receiving high levels of corporal punishment as children or adolescents were more likely than those experiencing less corporal punishment to describe their grades as "below average," even though there was no actual difference in their grades. The investigators attribute this finding to the damaging effect of corporal punishment on self concept. In fact, a number of scholars have suggested that authoritarian discipline contributes to negative self-judgments (self-esteem) as well as lower perceived personal control over life outcomes (mastery) (Belsky et al. 1984; Maccoby and Martin 1983; Patterson 1988). Consistent with this argument, Turner and Muller (2004) found the association between childhood corporal punishment and depression in young adulthood to be partially mediated by reduction in self-esteem and mastery.

MODERATORS OF CORPORAL PUNISHMENT

In addition to peer support and components of self-concept, there may be a number of factors involving the parent or child context that may specifically function to moderate the negative effects of stress arising from corporal punishment. Although experiencing corporal punishment may often be stressful, it does not always (or even usually) lead to psychological or be-havioral problems. While corporal punishment may represent a risk factor for negative outcomes, moderating influences can come into play that reduce or magnify its effects. Straus (1991) points out that the conditions under which corporal punishment is administered, such as whether punishment is con-trolled versus impulsive, whether it is given in the context of a supportive parent-child relationship, or whether parents are consistent in their discipline, likely influence its effects. Thus, physical discipline administered in a sponta-neous or explosive style may be more detrimental than such discipline admin-istered in a more controlled context. For example, Straus and Mouradian (1998) found corporal punishment to be most strongly related to antisocial behavior in children when mothers punished impulsively. Turner and Muller (2004) found that high levels of parental anger during corporal punishment increased its impact on depressive symptoms. Corporal punishment admin-istered in response to parental stress may be particularly likely to have this impulsive and angry quality.

Elder and Caspi (1988) suggest that inconsistent or arbitrary parenting may be especially important in increasing the likelihood of negative child outcomes under conditions of stress: "As long as discipline is consistently applied, chil-dren seem to be resilient under a variety of parenting styles" (1988: 95). Indeed, Agnew (1983) found that the effect of physical punishment on delin-quency interacts with parental consistency. When parents make inconsistent demands on children, physical punishment promotes delinquency. When par-ents make consistent demands, however, physical punishment does not appear to increase delinquent behavior (Agnew 1983). One mechanism by which consistancy of physical punishment may moderate its impact is through its influence on the child's perceptions of the corporal-punishment "event." As noted earlier, research has shown that events perceived as negative, uncontrol-lable, and unexpected are more likely to be experienced as stressful and lead to deleterious outcomes than are events without these qualities. Physical punish-ment that is impulsive, arbitrary, or inconsistant will be more likely to elicit these negative perceptions.

Other aspects of parental context that may moderate negative effects of corporal punishment on children include parental nurturance and praise and the use of discussion and explanation in discipline. Children who receive high levels of nurturance and support from parents may be less adversely affected by corporal punishment. Similarly, physical punishment that is always accom-panied by discussion and explanation may not have harmful side effects. It is important to note, however, that the use of these more "positive" tech-niques (for example, explanation, reason, discussion, compromise) tend to be

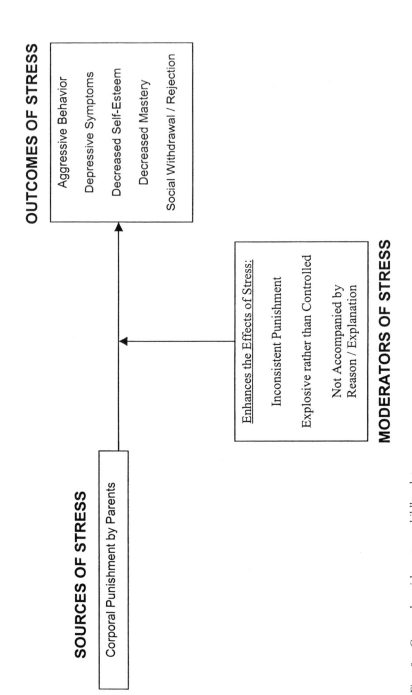

Fig. 18.2. Corporal punishment as a childhood stressor.

inversely related to the use of physical punishment. Thus, parents who spank frequently are less likely to engage in discussion and compromise with their children. Moreover, Larzalere (1986) found that while the use of reasoning reduced the relationship between physical punishment and child aggression, the association remained significant.

Figure 18.2 represents the stress-process model with corporal punishment treated as stressor. As discussed above, children's experience of physical punishment can potentially lead to negative health and behavioral outcomes. Associations between corporal punishment and such outcomes are likely dependent on the relative presence or absence of a number of moderating factors.

A Family-Stress Model: Corporal Punishment as an Intervening Factor

In this chapter, corporal punishment has been considered separately as a potential outcome of parental stress and as a potential source of childhood stress. However, we could also consider both simultaneously within one stress-process model. As depicted in figure 18.3, family-relevant stressors affect child outcomes through their influence on intervening or mediating variables involving changes in parenting practices. Specifically, a stressor like parental unemployment or marital strain can function to increase the use of physical punishment, which in turn leads to negative child health and behavioral outcomes. Thus, corporal punishment as both an outcome and source of stress are represented as the intervening factor in this larger model. Elder and Caspi (1988) and Patterson (1987, 1988) consider similar models in an attempt to understand the effect of family stressors on children's behavior. Elder and Caspi (1988) suggest that economic loss affects "child explosiveness" through its effect on extreme or arbitrary discipline and marital discord, both of which are mutually reinforcing. Similarly, Patterson (1987, 1988) describes how a major crisis, such as unemployment, increases the likelihood of disrupted family-management practices that lead to "inept discipline." Inept discipline, especially physical punishment, in turn, increases the risk of antisocial child behavior. Both these models show how broad economic circumstances can influence specific child outcomes.

Thus, stress-process models that incorporate the broader social context can provide a meaningful framework for understanding how macrosocial and economic conditions are connected to the experiences of individual family members. Specifically, family processes, parent-child interactions in particular, can be viewed as the intermediary link between broad social stress and child development or outcomes. As discussed in this chapter, corporal punishment is

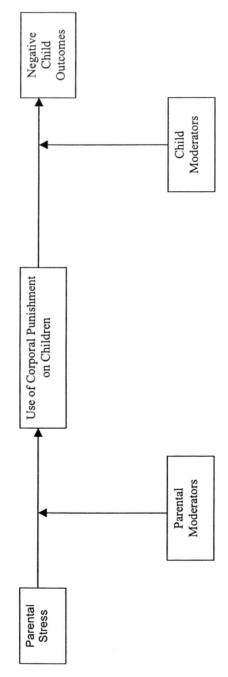

Fig. 18.3. A family-stress model: corporal punishment as an intervening factor.

one potential aspect of this link. Using a stress-process approach also provides a useful framework for examining possible social-structure differences in the prevalence, antecedents, and outcomes of corporal punishment. In seeking to understand variations in the use of physical punishment by social class, parent's age, or gender, one might look for differences in the distribution of stressors and moderators by these social characteristics. For example, an inverse association between social class and the use of corporal punishment may be explained by greater exposure to stressors, such as financial problems, marital instability, and crime among the lower classes. Moreover, lower-class parents may possess fewer social and personal resources that can reduce the negative effects of stress and more characteristics that contribute to the use of violence under stressful conditions.

Summary and Conclusion

This chapter is intended to provide a broad theoretical framework for examining the antecedents and outcomes of corporal punishment. The stress-process model represents a useful organizing tool that links social conditions and circumstances to individual experiences and behavior. The family is an important context for the stress process. It is a place where stress is generated, where coping strategies are learned and carried out, and where the consequences of stress can be transferred across generations. Stress associated with events and ongoing strains, arising both from within the family and from domains outside the family, can influence the use of corporal punishment. The association between parental stress and corporal punishment of children may represent a direct relationship or it may be indirect, through the effect of stress on other factors. Depression and marital conflict represent two such factors that may intervene between parents' stressful experiences and their use of physical punishment. Moderating variables, such as the use of violence as a coping strategy and authoritarian attitudes toward parenting, may increase the likelihood that stress manifests itself in corporal punishment, while non-familial social support and more permissive parenting attitudes may reduce this association.

In addition to viewing corporal punishment as a potential outcome of parental stress, the stress-process model can be extended to consider corporal punishment as a source of childhood stress. Thus, physical pain or discomfort inflicted by parents, even in the context of discipline, can be a stressful experience for children. While research in this area is limited, there is evidence suggesting that corporal punishment is associated with a number of negative child outcomes, including antisocial or delinquent behavior, depressed mood, and reductions in mastery and self-esteem. The extent to which physical punishment translates into negative outcomes will likely depend on the presence or absence of a number of moderating factors. Thus, physical punishment that is administered without reason or explanation in an explosive or angry manner and in the context of inconsistent parental demands will be more likely to have adverse effects on children than physical punishment that is controlled, consistent, and accompanied by explanation.

By considering the above processes, the stress model provides a theoretical framework for understanding how the social environment of adults, reflected in family and work-related experiences and social roles, can importantly influence the development and well-being of children. Parenting practices, including the use of corporal or physical punishment, may represent a crucial causal link between stressful parental experiences and detrimental child outcomes.

19

Corporal Punishment and Black's Theory of Social Control

JAMES TUCKER AND SUSAN ROSS

This chapter extends Donald Black's general theory of social control (Black 1976, 1990, 1993) to the corporal punishment of children. Consistent with a Blackian approach, we seek to explain violent parental social control with the immediate structural context under which it occurs. Specifically, we argue that the likelihood of corporal punishment varies directly with family hierarchy, social distance between parents and children, and isolation of children from potential supporters outside the household.[1]

After briefly reviewing Black's theoretical framework, we describe the central features of corporal punishment as a means of social control. We then introduce several propositions, drawn from the work of Black and others, that address the relationship between family structure and parental violence against children. The chapter concludes with a discussion of how our approach compares to other theories of corporal punishment and a comment on how our propositions might be tested.

The Theory of Social Control

The sociology of social control has as its subject matter all of the ways in which individuals and groups react to behavior they find offensive. Social control includes formal, state-initiated efforts at controlling deviant conduct as well as private strategies of pursuing justice used by people in their daily interactions with family members, friends, neighbors, and others. The theory developed by Black seeks to identify the social structural configurations associated with various formal and informal means of social control. Social control is therefore considered a dependent variable, while the social structure — which includes the social characteristics of all the participants in an act of social control and the social relations among them — is treated as the independent variable.

Unlike most sociological theory, Black's approach explains social life without referring to individuals as such (Black 1995: 858–61, 864–70). The theory is therefore unconcerned with the motivations behind individual conduct. Likewise, it has nothing to say about how people experience themselves as they engage in social action. At the same time, the theory makes none of the assumptions about society that many other theories do. It does not, for example, presume that society is inherently functional or composed of groups with competing interests (Black 1976: 7–8; 1993: 158–59). The theory is solely concerned with showing how social control — or any other type of social behavior — varies with the social structure of relationships (Black 1995).

Black initially applied his structural approach to law, where he demonstrated such factors as the social status of offender and victim and the intimacy of their relationship explain, among other things, what cases attract the police, get settled out of court, and result in long sentences for convicted parties (Black 1976). The theory has been extended in recent years to incorporate third-party supporters (such as lawyers) and settlement agents (such as police officers and judges), both of whom significantly affect the amount and kind of legal action taken in particular cases (Black 1993, chapter 7; Black and Baumgartner 1983; Baumgartner 1992a). In the past two decades, Black and a number of other scholars self-consciously employing his theoretical strategy have turned their attention to extralegal social control. Horwitz (1982, 1984), for example, has written extensively on therapy as a means of handling deviant behavior, while Cooney (1998) has focused on the role of third parties in promoting and preventing violent social control. The Blackian framework has also been applied to research on social control among suburbanites (Baumgartner 1988), factory workers (Tucker 1999), engineers (Tucker 1999), business executives (Morrill 1995), physicians (Mullis 1994), and scientists (Herrmann 1992).

Social control in the family and of children more generally has not been a chief concern of previous research in the Blackian tradition. M. P. Baumgartner's work is a major exception. Her research on conflict in the suburbs, for instance, shows that intrafamily social control is both infrequent and mild, a finding she attributes to the socially atomized and fluid nature of middle-class suburban family life (Baumgartner 1988, chapter 3). In another study, based on cross-cultural research on domestic violence, Baumgartner (1992a) finds that women who lack strong kinship ties are subject to the greatest amount of violent social control by their husbands. A third study relevant to this chapter examines conflict management in a child-care center. Here Baumgartner (1992b) finds that most disputes between children are handled through weak forms of aggression or adult intervention. These types of social control are traced to the subordinate position of children in relation to the adults who supervise them.

In developing his general theory of social control, Black occasionally addresses the social control in the family, including social control initiated by parents against children. He proposes, for example, that the amount of parental discipline aimed at children varies directly with the degree of stratification (inequality of wealth) and centralization of authority in the family (Black 1976: 32, 103). Black also suggests that the severity of punishment increases when parent-child relationships are fragmented (1990: 48) and decreases when families are more intimate (Black 1993: 153). We draw below on Black's theoretical insights and on research by Baumgartner and others as we examine corporal punishment as social control.

Corporal Punishment as Social Control

Parents who hit their children usually do so in response to specific conduct they find offensive. Almost any behavior, including crying, spilling milk, and damaging household objects, can activate a violent response from parents. Children who are disobedient and disrespectful tend to be particularly vulnerable to parental violence (Graziano 1995). In some instances, a single act may lead to corporal punishment, while in other situations violence may be used to sanction a child for a series of perceived misdeeds (see Carson 1986). Whatever the pattern in any particular instance of corporal punishment, most instances can be classified as social control. We can therefore situate corporal punishment within the larger universe of social control and identify its salient characteristics.

Among the most important variable features of social control is its *style,* or the language and logic used to define and respond to deviant behavior (Black 1976: 4–6; 1984: 8–12). Corporal punishment is clearly *penal* in style: It punishes offenders violently for behaving improperly. This style of social control is different from the compensatory style, where wrongdoers are defined as debtors obliged to pay restitution. The penal style also differs from the therapeutic style, where offenders are treated as victims in need of help, and the conciliatory style, where the parties are considered disputants and the chief goal of social control is restoration of harmony.

Violence is certainly not the only kind of penal social control aimed at children. Parents often punish children in other ways as well. They may, for instance, yell at their children, send them to their room, or take away privileges. Parents may also initiate social control characteristic of other styles. Some parents, for example, send their recalcitrant children to therapists.

Social control also varies by the *procedure* in which it is applied, whether authoritarian, negotiatory, or legalistic (Baumgartner 1984: 334–36). Corporal punishment usually follows an *authoritarian* procedure. It is imposed by parents against the wishes of children. Parents may have fixed protocols for using physical punishment (such as when a child arrives late for dinner) and therefore may act legalistically in some circumstances. But most parents hit children without referring to preestablished standards of conduct (Carson 1986).

A third feature of social control is its *form,* or the mechanism by which an aggrieved party expresses a grievance (Black 1984: 7–8). Social control can take on one of three general forms: unilateral, bilateral, or trilateral. Corporal punishment is usually *unilateral,* meaning it flows in one direction, from the parent to the child. It is rarely met with a direct response: Children typically just accept their punishment. Corporal punishment may evolve into bilateral social control if the child fights back, but this is uncommon, especially for younger children who are unable to respond physically. The unilateral character of corporal punishment also distinguishes it from trilateral social control, where a third party helps settle what is defined as a conflict between two adversaries. The only third parties involved with any regularity in corporal punishment are siblings, who sometimes act simply as helpless witnesses.

In summary, corporal punishment is a means of social control distinguished by its penal style, authoritarian procedure, and unilateral form. We now examine the social structural features of family life that are favorable to this kind of violent parental social control.

The Social Structure of Corporal Punishment

While corporal punishment is found in most families in modern America, it is more common in some than others. Moreover, within a particular family, it is used more on some children than others. We identify three features of family life that appear to be associated with parental violence: the degree of hierarchy in the family, the social distance between parents and children, and the isolation of children from supporters outside the household. Below we discuss how each of these is related to the frequency of corporal punishment.

HIERARCHY

The manner in which people in any setting define and respond to deviance is highly contingent on how resources and authority are distributed. In hierarchies, where the distribution of wealth and authority is unequal, the most potent social control tends to be administered by those at the top. The more hierarchy, the more forceful and punitive social control becomes (Black 1990: 47–49; 1993: 149–53; Horwitz 1990: 36–40). When hierarchy is weak, individuals are less able to exert their will on others. Consequently, in egalitarian settings social control tends to be more negotiatory and therapeutic than authoritarian (Tucker 1999).

All families are hierarchical to some degree, and children are almost always subordinate to their parents. In most settings, children possess few resources of their own, and they depend on their parents for various necessities of life, such as food, clothing, and shelter. In fact, parents who do not provide support are usually considered negligent and may be subject to legal social control themselves. Children's lives are therefore largely dictated from above. Even so, families vary in their degree of hierarchy. Some parents, for example, allow children more autonomy than others. Hierarchy varies within families as well. Young children tend to be more subordinate to their parents than their older siblings. As children age they become more independent, and consequently the relationship with their parents becomes more equal.

Following Black's theory, we propose that *corporal punishment varies directly with family hierarchy.* We can find some evidence to support this proposition. In more democratically run households, for example, parents are more likely to talk with children who misbehave rather than strike them (Baumrind 1980). Likewise, young children, who are the most subordinate, are hit at the highest rates. Research consistently shows that more than 90 percent of American children aged one to three are subject to corporal punishment (Straus 1994). Consistent with our proposition, the rate drops to about 50 percent at the age of thirteen and continues to decline to 20 percent by seventeen years of age. At the same time, the frequency of corporal punishment also diminishes as children age. Children three to six years old are hit an average of thirteen times a year, while those fifteen to seventeen years olds are hit 4.5 times a year (Straus 1994).

SOCIAL DISTANCE

Social control also varies by the amount social distance, the strength of people's social ties, and the degree of cultural closeness between the participants. It becomes more aggressive when people who initiate social control are socially distant from the people who subject to social control. The more distant they are, the more the potential for violence increases. In settings where people are intimate and culturally similar, by contrast, social control is more likely to involve negotiation and compromise (Black 1990: 53–56; Horwitz 1990: 67–71).

Families generally have a low degree of social distance among members. Parents and children usually live under the same roof and spend considerable time engaging in common activities. Nonetheless, some children are socially closer to their parents than others. Children living with stepparents, for example, are likely to be more distant than children living with their natural parents. We might also argue that children from larger families are, on average, less intimate with their parents than those from smaller families.

Our proposition is that *corporal punishment varies directly with social distance between parents and children.* Again, we can find some evidence to support this claim. We know, for instance, that stepchildren are subject to a disproportionate amount of corporal punishment. Adopted and foster children, who are arguably somewhat more distant from parents than natural offspring, also experience higher rates of violence at the hands of their parents (Caffey 1972). The family-violence literature also shows, consistent with our proposition, that the probability of parental violence increases with family size (Gil 1971; Goode 1971; Straus, Gelles, and Steinmetz 1980).

We should note that social distance is not necessarily related to physical distance. In fact, it may be that, holding other variables constant, corporal punishment increases when parents and children are constrained to share the same physical space. Spending time together may increase intimacy, but if parties do not have exit or avoidance as a social-control alternative, they may be more apt to resort to violence when they are aggrieved. Thus, in atomized families, where members have their own living space and engage in individual activities rather than family ones, we might predict violent discipline to be infrequent (see Baumgartner 1988, chapter 3). Parents and children in these kinds of families are easily able to avoid one another when tensions arise.

ISOLATION

Social control is also influenced by the presence or absence of third-party supporters. Where support is strong, individuals are able mobilize others to help pursue their grievances and defend themselves from social control initiated by others. Those without support are less able, and therefore less likely, aggressively to confront those who offend them. At the same time, they are more susceptible to social control directed at them, including violence (Black 1993; see also, Cooney 1998). Support or the lack thereof can be especially important in determining the amount of violence in the family (Baumgartner 1992a).

Apart from their internal characteristics, families vary in the degree to which they are isolated from other social institutions: The more isolated a family, the less children are able to mobilize support on their behalf. In some settings, like Japan, families are integrated into the larger community and closely monitored by neighbors (Braithwaite 1989). In other societies, especially modern ones, families are often isolated from others, and children often have little potential support. In the United States, for example, suburban families tend to be socially secluded, and, under these circumstances, neighbors are unlikely to intervene as supporters in intrafamily matters (Baumgartner 1988).

We propose that *corporal punishment varies directly with the isolation of children from supporters outside the household.* While little direct evidence is available to validate this claim, we do know that ties to external parties have an effect on the amount of husband-on-wife violence. For example, rates of domestic violence are lowest in societies where married women live in close proximity to blood relatives (such as brothers) and highest in settings where wives are isolated from their kinship networks (Baumgartner 1992a). Children generally are not able to call on the support of relatives, nor are they likely to have access to others willing to act as advocates on their behalf. Yet, as they get older, attend school, and engage in other outside activities, they come into contact with peers and adults who are potential supporters. We might therefore conclude that the declining frequency of corporal punishment by age is related not only to the declining subordination of children but also to their declining social isolation.

Even more so than other types of support, legal help has historically not been available to children. The law largely ignores them. This is especially true where family matters are involved. Violence within the family is rarely criminalized, and when it is, its enforcement is minimal (Horwitz 1990: 151–52). Corporal punishment, because it is directed downwardly and occurs between intimates, is the least likely type of family violence to attract the law. Even so, in some contemporary societies the legal system has begun to offer children some protection from parental violence. Children in modern America, for example, sometimes rely on the legal system for assistance when they are subject to more severe forms of violence, including what is commonly called "child abuse." Several northern European countries have outlawed all forms of corporal punishment (although offenders receive counseling rather than criminal penalties). Whether similar laws will be passed elsewhere remains to be seen. If they are, perhaps the historical isolation of children, and therefore their vulnerability to parental violence, will decline.

***

Because Blackian theory traces social behavior to the structure of relationships rather than to individuals or societies, it differs significantly from most sociological theories (Black 1995: 852–58), including those that attempt to explain parental violence. Most theories of corporal punishment, for example, focus on the parent, seeking to identify social and psychological factors that compel adults to hit their children (see other chapters in this book). One such theory claims that parents who use violence do so because they were subjected to physical punishment themselves in the past and have learned that it is an appropriate behavior. Other theories focus on such factors as family economic status and parental stress. The theory presented in this chapter does not necessarily contradict explanations that give primacy to forces that motivate parents to hit children. However, by focusing on the social context under which corporal punishment occurs, a Blackian approach recognizes the truly social nature of violent behavior. Violence, after all, depends on more than just a motivated perpetrator.

Our approach also differs from macrolevel theories that view corporal punishment as a consequence of social or historical epochs (see Straus 1994). For example, we do not attribute violence to larger cultural patterns or societal pathologies. We do not rule out the possibility that certain societies may provide a supportive moral framework for corporal punishment. But within any society, the rate of corporal punishment varies across and within families. Black's theory, unlike macrolevel theories, addresses this variation and is therefore able to avoid the theoretical problem of explaining a variable (corporal punishment) with a constant (societal norms supporting violence).

In summary, our approach does not have the limitations of individual-level theories that focus on parents to the exclusion of other parties involved in corporal punishment. At the same time, it is able to obtain a level of precision not possible with societal-level theories.

Testing the Theory

A considerable amount of empirical work has addressed the prevalence, severity, and frequency of corporal punishment. Its social and psychological effects have garnered some attention as well. Research addressing its causes is relatively scarce. When researchers do turn their attention to the explanation of corporal punishment they tend to follow the individual-level approach, seeking to identify factors that motivate parents to discipline their children violently. The typical study of this kind looks for correlations between corporal punishment and such factors as parental experience with violence, social class, employment status, and alcohol and drug use.

As we noted above, some of the previous research provides support for our propositions. But more research is needed, research that addresses the social structure of family life. For example, research would need to examine the relationship between family hierarchy and corporal punishment. Unlike most previous studies of corporal punishment, this would involve going beyond the modern American family, where the range of variation in family hierarchy is relatively limited. In order further to test our theoretical model, we would also need to look at how social distance between parents and children affects the use of parental violence. Such research might involve simply looking at whether the amount of time a parent spends with a child is related to the likelihood of corporal punishment. Another kind of study required to test the theory would explore whether the availability of third-party supporters to children decreases their chances of being hit by their parents. This research should focus on, among other things, when and how friends and others intervene in matters of family discipline. Again, we would need to incorporate historical and cross-cultural materials to adequately test this proposition.

Any test of theory would require using methodologies that allow an in-depth examination of corporal punishment in its social context. Ethnographic methods, including extensive personal interviews, have been useful in research on social control elsewhere (for example, Baumgartner 1988; Morrill 1995; Tucker 1999) and would be particularly appropriate.

The theory is incomplete. Other structural variables that we have not identified may contribute to parental violence as well. So, as well as testing the theoretical model presented here, future research should seek to identify additional features of family life associated with the corporal punishment of children.

Conclusion

This chapter offers a new way to look at corporal punishment. Rather than attribute it to individual or societal characteristics, we have argued that certain structural features of family life foster parental violence. Our approach also has unique implications for those who want to limit the use of corporal punishment in modern society. Democratizing the family, strengthening social ties between parents and their offspring, and increasing external support for children are general strategies for reducing its prevalence consistent with the structural approach outlined in this chapter. More specific efforts might include involving children more in family decision making, encouraging parents to engage in more common activities with their children, and having neighbors become more active in the lives of children in their community. We would expect measures like these to be more effective than moralizing about the evils of corporal punishment or passing laws to criminalize it. Ultimately, however, our approach suggests that it may be impossible to eliminate corporal punishment altogether. Younger children, in particular, seem to be locked in structural situations where corporal punishment is likely. They are subordinates in extremely hierarchical relationships, and their young age, including their inability to communicate, limits the degree of bonding with parents. Moreover, younger children have minimal contact with those outside the household and thus have little third-party support. While we would not claim that the corporal punishment of young children is inevitable, it certainly appears to be strongly embedded in the structure of the family.

Note

1. Donald Black, Mark Cooney, and Arnold Linsky made helpful comments on a previous draft of this chapter.

20

The Structure of Family Rules about Hitting
A Family-Systems Perspective

CARLFRED B. BRODERICK

Family-systems theory is designed to provide a comprehensive approach to understanding interactions among family members and also transactions across family boundaries with the outside world. Many facets of the theory do not seem to have obvious relevance to the question of corporal punishment, for example: those parts dealing with the maintenance of family boundaries, with family transactions with external systems, such as the school, workplace, and neighborhood, with the regulation of family time and space, or with the family mechanisms for achieving change or stability. I treat all of these issues in more complete expositions of the theory elsewhere (Broderick 1990, 1993) and will not discuss them here. Rather, in this chapter, the focus is on another set of constructs central to the theory, the hierarchical arrangement of family rules, more especially the hierarchical arrangement of family rules that lead to the decision in real time to hit or not to hit a particular child in a particular circumstance.

To say that such a spur-of-the-moment decision is rule driven in *not* to suggest that it is necessarily rational or premeditated. Research has repeatedly shown that families are not very perceptive observers of their own rules of interaction. If interviewed on the matter they will almost invariably report what they feel *should* be the family rules, what we might call the *normative rules*. But, alas, too often parents have cause to lament with St. Paul in the

New Testament, "What I would, that do I not; but what I hate, that I do" (Romans 7:15). The rules that govern the actual, observed patterns of behavior (rather than the less often observed code of approved parental conduct) we may call the *system rules*. It is in the nature of such rules to be complexly organized, since they must take into account not only the provocation of the child and the beliefs, temperament, and reactivities of the parent but also the history (immediate and long term) of the relationship and the social and situational circumstances surrounding it.

It is convenient to think of these sets of rules as stacked in a hierarchical pyramid, with the most concrete rules at the bottom of the heap and the most abstract, governing principles at the top. In my own work, I have preferred a four-layer model. At the most concrete level, *direct rules* can be identified that specify the most likely parental responses to particular behaviors of the child. At the next level up are a set of *metarules* (from the Greek, *meta*, meaning beyond, over, transcending) that are contextual indicators, specifying the circumstances in which direct rules apply. One step more general and comprehensive are *midrange policies* that summarize the overall philosophy and cardinal beliefs underlying the parent's actions in this arena (child discipline, in this case). Again, these may incorporate the parent's normative beliefs about child discipline, but they are never restricted wholly to these consciously held values. Also likely to be included are some rather primitive concepts of authority and retribution and some even more primitive emotional responses to particular offenses. Finally, at the very top of the rules pyramid are what Reiss (1981) and others have called the *family paradigm,* which incorporates the family's core philosophy, its most centrally held values and commitments that determine its overall posture toward its members and toward the outside world. Perhaps the chief contribution of family-systems theory to understanding why and when parents hit children might come from an analysis of the issue from the perspective of hierarchically stacked rules.

Direct Rules

In some ways, direct rules are the least interesting and informative, because one can have a great inventory of them but without knowing the metarules and policies have no idea of when or whether any particular rule would be acted upon. In the case of corporal punishment, however, certain features of the inventory have significance in their own right. For example, are there any rules that permit extreme measures against a child under any circumstances or degree of provocation? Is it in the range of conceivable responses to burn, smother, throw, starve, wound, tie up, or beat a child? What are the conceptual limits of what may be done in the name of discipline? If the punishment should fit the crime, what are the full range of punishments that, in this family, can be conceived of as "fitting responses" to the full range of "crimes" that a child might commit? In this regard, it should not be considered a trivial social reform to achieve a shift in the public perception of what is acceptable or nearly so and what is criminal or horrific parent behavior.

Metarules

Metarules specify the contexts within which various direct rules are applied. Within any given range of child offenses, it seems likely that at least half a dozen sets of circumstances govern the probability of particular parental responses occurring.

1. *The parent's mood or condition* (already frustrated, under the influence of a mind-altering substance, tired or ill, otherwise occupied, and so on).
2. *The status of the relationship* (natural versus adopted versus step versus informal, same-sex versus cross-sex, favored versus unfavored, child older versus child younger, and so forth).
3. *Triangular issues* (child as surrogate, scapegoat, ally, and so on).
4. *Audience effects* (public, private, in presence of particular significant others, and so forth).
5. *History of issue at hand* (last straw versus first offence, context of an earlier promise or threat of what would happen if this offence occurred or recurred, previous experience with other children in similar situations, and so on).
6. Child's attitude attending the offensive behavior or the confrontation over it.

Doubtless one can think of other contextual variables that should be added to this list. The point is that without taking them into account, one cannot predict what direct rule will be applied or what the behavioral outcome will be.

Midrange Policies

One step up the hierarchical pyramid are midrange family policies, which, in turn, shape the impact of the various contextual variables. Certain other versions of family systems theory omit this level, positing a simpler, three-layer hierarchy of family rules. To me, it has seemed useful to interpose a level between the overarching family paradigms that occupy the top position in the family-rules pyramid and the contextual metarules level. Unlike family paradigms, midrange policies are specific to particular arenas of family inter-action or transaction. I find it profitable to consider what the family policies on childrearing might be, quite independently of what its policies might be on, for example, boundary maintenance or distance regulation among members. All are surely interrelated in some degree, but each involves enough issues specific to itself to deserve separate consideration.

In the case of the policies concerning child discipline, it seems to me that intrinsic to those policies are certain philosophies of childrearing and familial priorities as well as personal emotional investments that shape the way the metarules we have considered actually operate in the family. By way of il-lustration, let us consider philosophies of childrearing, familial priorities, and personal emotional investments separately.

PHILOSOPHIES OF CHILDREARING

The first issue is whether there is a unified, integrated philosophy at all. In some families there may be a well-developed, well-monitored, family-wide policy; in others the policy permits competing styles of discipline according to the caretaker of the moments's own philosophy; in still others it would be difficult to identify any policy, since each caretaker seems to operate on im-pulse, without much evidence of continuity or philosophy. The content of any given philosophy on childrearing would include views on the appropriate level of surveillance, guidelines for child safety at various ages, the timing of de-velopmental prerogatives, thresholds of response (that is, how far out of line the child is allowed to get before parental response kicks in), and so forth, as well as ideas about appropriate or permissible forms of punishment for vari-ous offenses.

FAMILY PRIORITIES

Among the priorities of various potential caretakers, where does child supervision rank? Given the continual competition for attention among all the duties, diversions, and distractions in the family environment, how well does childrearing compete? In my observation this varies tremendously both within and among families.

PERSONAL EMOTIONAL SENSITIVITIES

The reference here is not to the degree of sensitivity to the child or to the task of childrearing but to certain emotionally laden areas in which children might offend. For example, some caretakers are particularly reactive if the offence involves sex, defacing or destroying property, lying, cheating, stealing, violence, low achievement, or personal defiance. In effect, the playing field of juvenile transgression and punishment is never level ground, and family policy on the matter is shaped by the emotional sensitivities of the caretakers as much as by any more generic standards.

Family Paradigms

At the top of the family-rules pyramid are overarching family paradigms, those more or less shared and integrated philosophies of family governance that shape all family policies and behaviors. From this, the family derives the entire tone and texture of its patterning of interactions and transactions. Reiss (1981) was able to divide the families in his experiments into four groups: those whose overarching posture toward the world he labeled "consensus sensitive," those he labeled "distance sensitive," those he labeled "environment sensitive," and finally those he labeled "achievement sensitive." Similarly, Constantine (1993), elaborating on a typology introduced by Kantor and Lehr (1975), identified four family paradigms, roughly corresponding to Reiss's four, which he labeled "closed," "random," "open," and "synchronous." Rather than elaborate on either of these frequently cited family-system typologies, and at the risk of further cluttering an already overcluttered field, I am going to suggest that for our purposes here, families may more profitably be divided into three basic styles of family governance: "competitive," "policy governed," and "principled."

These levels parallel and are derived from Kolberg's three levels of moral development (Kohlberg 1969; Kolhberg and Turiel 1973; Broderick 1975). The first level of development in his schema Kohlberg labels "premoral hedonism." Like our "competitive" paradigm, it makes the assumption that actors are self-serving in their motivation. The key issue is "what I want." His second level he calls "conventional," which, like our "policy-governed" paradigm, makes the assumption that actors are motivated by a sense of social responsibility and justice. The key issue here is "what is right." His third level he calls postconventional, which, like our "principled" paradigm, makes the assumption that actors are motivated by concern for the general good. The issue is "What would be in the overall best interest of everyone?" or perhaps "What master principle of civilized living governs this question?"

THE COMPETITIVE PARADIGM

Families governed according to this paradigm are organized on the basis of every member competing for the limited resources available to the family as best he or she can. Some families seem to be organized as *zero-sum games* in which every gain for one member is necessarily a loss for some other member.

Others use more sophisticated *mixed-motive games* in which various coalitions may form, within which competition is muted in the interest of improved competitive advantage against other players in the game. Within families operating in the competitive mode, power struggles and contests of will between parents and children (as well as between parents and among children) are the pervasive form of interaction. The policies governing child rearing are likely to be structured along "win-lose" lines, and it is in such families that we should expect to find the greatest incidence of escalating cycles of passive or active defiance on the part of the children and threats and penalties the part of the parents. Because punishment is often embedded in an escalating contest of wills, we should also expect to find parents more often feeling they are "driven" to abusive levels of response. For the same reasons sibling-sibling and husband-wife violence would be expected to be more often found in these families.

It is of interest to note that most studies of the distribution of power in families assume the prevalence of the competitive paradigm, as do most studies based on exchange theory. Perhaps this assumption is fostered, in part, by the fact that most of the families who are seen by family therapists appear to operate in the competitive mode. Although I am aware of no research on the subject, it is my impression that among families who do not seek clinical help, the more common style of family governance is based on Kohlberg's "conventional" level of moral development and constitutes what I have called the "policy-governed" family paradigm.

THE POLICY-GOVERNED PARADIGM

In families operating according to this paradigm the members, children and adults alike, perceive their individual wills as being curbed by a set of overriding policies that all family behavior is judged by. Parents and other caretakers are seen as more or less just administrators of these rules rather than as self-serving players in a zero-sum (or mixed-motive) contest of wills. Corporal punishment may and often does occur in these families, but it is measured, not part of an runaway cycle of response and counterresponse. The difference was vividly illustrated in a study of fathering in the San Diego area (Broderick 1977). Among the traditional Portuguese and Yugoslavian families there were very clear, generations-old policies about what behavior merited what punishment. These policies were understood by the parents and by the children, and when the punishments were administered, no one seemed to take it personally. These are the families in which the children might be required to cut their own birch stick and thank the parent afterwards for the chastisement. These are the families in which a parent might say, with only a modicum of hypocrisy, "I hate to do this, but you know the rules as well as I do." Often quite painful corporal punishment was part of this system, but the children who had broken the rules almost universally admitted that they deserved it. In such cases there was a remarkable absence of bad feelings toward the parents who had administered the punishment. Bitter resentment was reserved for cases where they felt they had been wrongly accused and there had been a miscarriage of justice.

This was in stark contrast to the situation in many of the military families that appeared to operate under a competitive paradigm. In these cases the children seemed to feel that the fathers (or stepfathers), who were at sea for half of every year, had no legitimate authority to come home after such an absence and start ordering them around. The father, used to military discipline, had a very different notion of how things should run. Lacking a shared view of the family policies, these family members resorted to direct power confrontations, which often enough escalated into physical punishment by the father. Mothers frequently got caught in the middle, either trying to protect the children (and sometimes getting physically hurt in the process) or supporting the legitimacy of the father's right to demand obedience ("Robby, do what you father says!"). (Incidently, one of the interesting findings of the study was that mothers were far more likely to intervene on behalf of the child if the male parent were a stepfather and to support the other parent if he was a natural father; as a result the children of natural fathers were more likely to become the victims of serious physical abuse than stepchildren. This is a counterintuitive example of triangulation at work, a major issue in family-systems analysis.) In these families there was tremendous resentment against parents for physical punishment because they were viewed (more or less accurately) as coercive moves in a one-on-one power struggle between the contending parties.

From the viewpoint of an ardent supporter of nonviolence there may be little to choose between these two family types, since in each the child is subject to corporal punishment, but from a sociological point of view they are very different because of the difference in *meaning* attached to the punishment in the two settings, and hence the difference in its personal and familial consequences.

Of course, policy-governed families do not, intrinsically, need to practice corporal punishment, although the evidence is that they are likely to be included in the 95 percent of American families who do include such punishment in their traditional repertoire of legitimate parental responses to children's misconduct. On the face of it, one might hazard the guess that policy-governed families would be resistant to attempts to pressure them into revising their long-standing and highly valued sets of rules and policies. On the other hand, if they do represent the "conventional, law-abiding citizens" that Kohlberg describes them to be, then they should be the segment of the population most responsive to changes in social and legal norms. Moreover, fifty years of research has showed that they tend to adopt "expert opinion" as to the best approaches to child rearing. Once persuaded, through education, the media, informal networks of influence, or whatever other means, they would appear to be better equipped than competitive families to incorporate and implement new child-rearing norms. It should be a lot easier to modify even a long-standing set of policies than to establish an effective dampener or cap for escalating contests of will.

THE PRINCIPLED PARADIGM

Families who operate according to this paradigm might be expected to be among those who have eschewed violence even before the larger society began to reject it. In fact, it seems likely that many of the leaders of the raised national consciousness against family violence might well have been recruited from such families. Since, according to Kohlberg, this style of interaction requires the highest level of moral maturity to attain it, one cannot reasonably expect young children to be fully principled in their behavior no matter what the level of functioning of their parents, and it might be argued that families with young children are not likely to progress beyond the policy-governed mode because so much of their energy is devoted to teaching rules to children. But I have observed that when the parents of young children manage to transcend the challenges and establish a principled mode of family governance, even young children can begin to learn the rules and metarules that are consistent with that paradigm. ("Jamie, I'm sorry, but you just can't hit your sister. We don't ever hit each other in this family." "Let's just stop a minute and try to figure out how Stella might feel about your taking her toys with out asking her." And so forth.) Their comprehension of the underlying humanitarian principles that generate such rules will come as they mature.

Common observation supports Kohlberg's surveys which indicate that at any given time a relatively small percentage of individuals or families operate at this level. Yet it is important to include this paradigm in the general typology of family paradigms because it represents the highest level of moral development and because it may be influential beyond its numbers in defining the conscience of the society.

Punting up and down the Paradigms

Family paradigms are not written in stone, and it is not unheard of for a family to shift its paradigm up or down the ladder. One of the core principles of family systems theory is the *principle of requisite variety*. This principle holds that one of the conditions of normal functioning is that every system must have sufficient variety in its repertory of rules to cover any reasonable range of inputs or challenges. When a system encounters a challenge that it has no preprogrammed response to, it has several options. The most frequently chosen is to develop a new rule or stretch an old one to cover the situation. It is guided in this process by the policies and the paradigm under which it operates. If, for whatever reason, it finds itself unable to generate a rule that satisfactorily covers the new situation, another alternative is to fall back on its all-purpose default response (perhaps to ignore the new situation or to attack the party who introduced it or to head for family therapy). This default response is also sometimes called a "punt," referring to the default play in football where if a team finds itself in a tight corner with no evident means of escape without major damage, it may elect just to get rid of the ball and improve its field position by kicking (or punting) the ball downfield to the other team. I wish to pursue this alternative at some length in terms of its implications for family violence, but first it is necessary to note that there is one other type of response that sometimes occurs if the challenge to the system is completely overwhelming. The most extreme response would be to dissolve the family system altogether, and of course this does occur.

Just for clarity, it might be a good idea to look at a more concrete example of how a family might experience its options when confronted with out-of-range child behavior. Suppose, for example, that an eleven-year-old son attempted suicide. Most families have no prescripted rule for how to respond to such an event. One common response to such a lack of "requisite variety" would be to settle on a definition of the event that permitted them to stretch an old set of rules to cover the case. For example, the family members might say, "This boy is physically hurt and emotionally ill; therefore we must get him to a doctor and a counselor and nurture him back to health." Or they might say, "This boy need to learn that this is intolerable behavior; therefore we must punish him and shame him." Or they might say, "This boy is ungovernable, therefore we need to send him to his aunt in Ohio or to a private boarding school that specializes in incorrigibles." Or they might say, "We have clearly failed this boy as a family; therefore we must change our ways, perhaps seek out pastoral help or family counseling."

In other cases, the family members may search out an altogether new set of rules to deal with the case, perhaps calling a suicide hotline they saw advertized in the newspaper or talking to an acquaintance whose child also attempted suicide a few years earlier, or consulting with their friends, relatives, pastor, doctor, or school counselor about what experience or advice they could offer about what to do in such a situation. Or they could punt. They could fall back on whatever they do when they don't know what to do. Perhaps they just carry on as though nothing significant had happened, as though the son had hurt himself while out riding his bike. Or perhaps their default pattern is that Dad gets drunk and Mom goes to bed and Julie goes over to her girlfriend's. Or perhaps everybody gets upset and yells and screams and accuses everybody else of being at fault and eventually settles back down to normal without doing anything to change the system. Or, and this is not as uncommon as one might think, having run through their whole repertory of rules and policies, they could acknowledge that their whole level of operation is ill suited to deal with this important new problem. That is when they may choose to switch paradigms.

Presumably, it is easier and more common to punt down the ladder of paradigms than to punt up it, although we have evidence that both occur. To punt down, all you have to do is return to a modality that you quite certainly had some experience with at an earlier period in your own moral evolution. If the attempted suicide is interpreted as irrefutable evidence that a principled approach is ineffective with young children, a principled set of parents might return to the more structured approaches of the policy-driven level of parenting with clear rules and consequences rather than lofty principles and empathies. This may well include the reinstitution of corporal punishment into the parental repertoire. Similarly, if the suicide attempt is perceived by policy driven parents as the ultimate defiance of parental control, the ultimate exceeding of the fully understood limits of tolerable behavior, it could easily trigger a return to a very personal contest of wills.

On the other hand, there is a growing clinical literature that indicates that when all else fails, families may be primed for a "second-level change" (that is, a change of paradigms up the ladder, rather than further flailing around in the same, failed modality). To the best of my knowledge, this was first developed as a concept by John Spiegel (1960) in an article on the dynamics of family-conflict resolution. He noted that in his practice nearly all families came into therapy with fully developed repertoires of competitive tactics and countertactics. These tended to exhibit themselves in balanced pairs: one party would criticize and negatively label the other's behavior and character, the response would be denial and counterattack; one party would attempt to provoke, the other would refuse to respond; one would threaten, the other would defy; one would attempt to bribe, the other would reject the offer; one would misrepresent the facts, the other would unmask the deceit. Nothing was ever achieved in these standoffs. Not only did it take a long time to get through one round of the argument, the family also never seemed to run out of rounds, coming back to the same issues again and again. (Since these confrontations occurred in a therapist's office, as might be expected, audience effects kept the exchanges from getting physical, but we must assume that this constraint was not operative at home.)

Eventually, however, Spiegel reports, these families were able to find their way out of these standoffs through adopting noncompetitive tactics. (Spiegel does not discuss his own role in pointing them toward this resolution.) Of the three examples of such tactics he discussed, all seemed to depend on taking perspective. The most frequently used was "role taking," that is, putting yourself in the other's place so that you saw the issue through his or her eyes. The next most common was using nonderisive humor to put things in a lighter perspective. The final category was "mediation," letting an outsider help put things in perspective (presumably the outsider in this case was the therapist, but the principle works with any outsider who is not a fully committed partisan of one side or the other). According to the Broderick typology, these tactics are more typical of "principled" than "policy-governed" approaches. Be that as it may, they clearly represent a paradigm shift, a "second-order change" as contemporary writers are prone to call it (following the terminology of Watzlawick, Weakland, and Fisch 1974).

The point is that families' frustration at their inability to solve a challenge under their current operational and philosophical paradigm may lead them to punt up as well as down the ladder . . . away from psychical confrontations as well as toward them.

Implications

This analysis of the hierarchical structuring of rules that prescribe or permit parental violence as a disciplinary technique suggests that there are a number of points at which those who oppose such rules might have some effect. At the bottom of the paradigmatic pyramid, among families adopting the competitive paradigm, presumably the only effective social mechanism for inducing change is to narrow the limits of legally and morally acceptable parent behavior. The objective is to make violence less prevalent in the ordinary range of most people's concrete rules of parent's response to child's misbehavior. We see some evidence of that occurring even now as we hear traditionally scripted families complain that they can't even raise their kids the way they want to any more without getting turned in by some busybody for child abuse.

At the next level, the level of policy-governed families, the prime effort is educational. Violence needs to be defined as politically and socially incorrect parental behavior so that these conformity-sensitive parents will exclude it from their rules and policies.

At the morally most advanced level, the object would be to recruit more of these parents as educators and leaders in the movement to change the laws and norms. And they may play a role, formal or informal, in helping families at each of the lower levels, who feel stuck, to open themselves to the possibility of punting up.

References

Abraham, K. 1954. "A Short Study of the Development of the Libido in the Light of Mental Disorders." In *Selected Papers of Karl Abraham*. New York: Basic Books.

Agnew, R. 1983. "Physical Punishment and Delinquency: A Research Note." *Youth and Society* 15:225–236.

Ainsworth, M. D. S. 1979. "Infant-Mother Attachment." *American Psychologist* 34:932–937.

Albee, G. 1980. "Politics, Power, Prevention, and Social Change." In *Child Abuse: An Agenda for Action,* edited by G. Gerbner, C. Ross, and E. Zigler. New York: Oxford University Press.

Al-Issa, I. 1982. "Gender and Adult Psychopathology." In *Gender and Psychopathology,* edited by I. Al-Issa. New York: Academic Press.

Almond, G. A., and S. Verba. 1963. *The Civic Culture: Political Attitudes and Democracy in Five Nations.* Boston: Little, Brown.

Altmann, J. 1980. *Baboon Mothers and Infants.* Cambridge, MA.: Harvard University Press.

Altmann, J., and A. Samuels. 1992. "Costs of Maternal Care: Infant-Carrying in Baboons." *Behavioral Ecology and Sociobiology* 29:391–398.

Anderson, J. E. [1936] 1972. *The Young Child in the Home.* Reprint. New York: Arno.

Anderson, M. 1971. *Family Structure in Nineteenth-Century Lancashire.* Cambridge: Cambridge University Press.

Aneshensel, C. S. 1999. "Outcomes of the Stress Process." In *A Handbook for the Study of Mental Health: Social Contexts, Theories and Systems,* edited by A. V. Horwitz and T. L. Scheid. New York: Cambridge University Press.

Aneshensel, C. S., R. R. Fredrichs, and V. A. Clark. 1981. "Family Roles and Sex Differences in Depression." *Journal of Health and Social Behavior* 22:379–393.

Anthony, E. J. 1970. "The Behavior Disorders of Children." In *Carmichael's Manual of Child Psychology,* vol. 2, edited by P. H. Mussen. New York: Wiley.

Argyle, M., and M. Cook. 1976. *Gaze and Mutual Gaze.* Cambridge: Cambridge University Press.

Ariès, Philippe. 1962. *Centuries of Childhood.* Translated by R. Baldick. New York: Random House.

Arnold, R. 1864. *The History of the Cotton Famine.* London: [Publisher unknown].

Aronfreed, J. 1968. *Conduct and Conscience.* New York: Academic Press.

Aronson, E., and J. M. Carlsmith. 1963. "Effect of the Severity of Threat on the Devaluation of Forbidden Behavior." *Journal of Abnormal and Social Psychology* 66:584–588.

Aronson, E., J. M. Carlsmith, and J. M. Darley. 1963. "The Effects of Expectancy on Volunteering for an Unpleasant Experience." *Journal of Abnormal and Social Psychology* 66:220–224.

Axelrod, R. M. 1984. *The Evolution of Cooperation.* New York: Basic Books.

Ayers, Ian, and John Braithwaite. 1992. *Responsive Regulation.* New York: Oxford University Press.

Azrin, N. H., and W. C. Holz. 1966. Punishment. Pp. 380–447 in *Operant Behavior: Areas of Research and Application,* edited by W. K. Honig. New York: Appleton-Century-Crofts.

Azrin, N. H., R. R. Hutchinson, and D. F. Hake. 1967. "Attack, Avoidance, and Escape Reactions to Aversive Shock." *Journal of the Experimental Analysis of Behavior* 10:131–148.

Azrin, N. H., R. R. Hutchinson, and R. McLaughlin. 1965. "The Opportunity for Aggression as an Operant Reinforer during Aversive Stimulation." *Journal of the Experimental Analysis of Behavior* 8:171–180.

Bachman, J. 1967. *Youth in Transition.* Ann Arbor: University of Michigan Institute for Social Research.

Bandura, A. 1965. "Vicarious Processes: A Case of No-trial Learning." Pp 1–55 in *Advances in Experimental Social Psychology,* vol. 2, edited by L. Berkowitz. New York: Academic Press.

———. 1971. *Social Learning Theory.* New York: General Learning.

Bandura, A., and R. H. Walters. 1959. *Adolescent Aggression.* New York: Ronald.

Banfield, E. C. 1958. *The Moral Basis of a Backward Society.* New York: Free Press.

Barkley, R. A. 1987. *Defiant Children: A Clinician's Manual for Parent Training.* New York: Guilford.

———. 1990. *Attention Deficit Hyperactivity Disorder: A Handbook for Diagnosis and Treatment.* New York: Guilford.

Barling, J., and A. Rosenbaum. 1986. "Work Stressors and Wife Abuse." *Journal of Applied Psychology* 71:346–348.

Barnett, R. C., G. K. Baruch. 1985. "Women's Involvement in Multiple Roles and Psychological Distress." *Journal of Personality and Social Psychology* 49:135–145.

Barnett, S. A. 1975. *The Rat: A Study in Behavior,* 2d ed. Chicago, IL: University of Chicago Press.

Baron, L., and M. A. Straus. 1987. "Four Theories of Rape: A Macrosociological Analysis." *Social Problems* 34:468–488.

Baron, L., M. A. Straus, and D. Jaffee. 1988. "Legitimate Violence, Violent Attitudes, and Rape: A Test of the Cultural Spillover Theory." In *Human Sexual Aggression: Current Perspectives*, edited by R. A. Prentky and V. L. Quinsey. Annals of the New York Academy of Sciences, vol. 528.

Baum, W. M. 1973. "The Correlation-Based Law of Effect." *Journal of the Experimental Analysis of Behavior* 20:137–153.

——. 1994. *Understanding Behaviorism: Science, Behavior, and Culture.* New York: Harper Collins.

——. 1995. "Rules, Culture, and Fitness." *The Behavior Analyst* 18:1–21.

Baum, W. M., and H. C. Rachlin. 1969. "Choice as Time Allocation." *Journal of the Experimental Analysis of Behavior* 12:861–874.

Baumgartner, M. P. 1988. *The Moral Order of a Suburb.* New York: Oxford University Press.

——. 1992a. "Violent Networks: The Origins and Management of Domestic Conflict." In *Violence and Aggression: The Social Interactionist Approach*, edited by R. B. Felson and J. Tedeschi. Washington, D.C.: American Psychological Association.

——. 1992b. "War and Peace in Early Childhood." Pp. 1–38 in *Virginia Review of Sociology*, vol. 1, *Law and Conflict Management*, edited by J. Tucker.

Baumrind, D. 1968. "Authoritarian versus Authoritative Parental Control." *Adolescence* 3:255–272.

——. 1971a. "Current Patterns of Parental Authority." *Developmental Psychology Monographs* 4:1–102.

——. 1971b. "Harmonious Parents and Their Preschool Children. *Developmental Psychology* 4:99–102.

——. 1980. "New Directions in Socialization Research." *American Psychologist* 35:639–652.

Bayer, C., and D. Cegala. 1992. "Trait Verbal Aggressiveness and Argumentativeness: Relations with Parenting Style." *Western Journal of Communication* 56:301–310.

Becker, H. S. 1963. *Outsiders.* New York: Free Press.

Bell, R. Q., and L. V. Harper. 1977. *Child Effects on Adults.* Hillsdale, NJ: Erlbaum.

Bell, S. M., and M. D. S. Ainsworth. 1972. "Infant Crying and Maternal Responsiveness." *Child Development* 43:1171–90.

Belsky, J. 1984. "Determinants of Parenting." *Child Development* 55:83–96.

——. 1986. "Infant Day Care: A Cause for Concern?" *Zero to Three* 6.

Belsky, J., R. M. Lerner, and G. B. Spanier. 1984. *The Child in the Family.* Reading, MA: Addison-Wesley.

Berkner, Lutz. 1973. "Recent Research on the History of the Family in Western Europe." *Journal of Marriage and the Family* 35:395–405.

Berkowitz, L. 1962. *Aggression: A Social Psychological Analysis.* New York: McGraw-Hill.

Berman, C. M. 1990. "Intergenerational Transmission of Maternal Rejection Rates among Free-Ranging Rhesus Monkeys." *Animal Behaviour* 39:239–247.

Berman, C. M., K. L. R. Rasmussen, and S. J. Suomi. 1993. "Reproductive Consequences of Maternal Care Patterns during Estrus among Free-Ranging Rhesus Monkeys." *Behavioral Ecology Sociobiology* 32:391–399.

———. 1994. "Responses of Free-ranging Rhesus Monkeys to a Natural Form of Social Separation: I. Parallels with Mother-infant Separation in Captivity. *Child Development* 65:1028–1041.

Bernstein, I. S., and C. L. Ehardt. 1985. "Agonistic Aiding: Kinship, Rank, Age, and Sex Influences." *American Journal of Primatology* 8:37–52.

———. 1986. "The Influence of Kinship and Socialization on Aggressive Behaviour in Rhesus Monkeys (*Macaca mulatta*)." *Animal Behaviour* 34:739–747.

Bird, C. E. 1997. "Gender Differences in the Social and Economic Burdens of Parenting and Psychological Distress." *Journal of Marriage and the Family* 59:809–823.

Black, D. 1976. *The Behavior of Law.* San Diego: Academic Press.

———. 1990. "The Elementary Forms of Conflict Management." Pp. 43–69 in *New Directions in the Study of Justice, Law, and Social Control.* School of Justice Studies, Arizona State University. New York: Plenum Press.

———. 1993. *The Social Structure of Right and Wrong.* San Diego: Academic Press.

———. 1995. "The Epistemology of Pure Sociology." *Law and Social Inquiry* 20:829–870.

Black, D., and M. P. Baumgartner 1983. "Toward a Theory of the Third Party." Pp. 84–114 in *Empirical Theories of the Courts,* edited by K. O. Boyum and L. Mather. New York: Longman.

Blau, P. M. 1964. *Exchange and Power in Social Life.* New York: Wiley.

Block, Ruth. 1975. "American Feminine Ideals in Transition: The Rise of the Moral Mother, 1785–1815." *Feminist Studies* 3:159–172.

Blumstein, A., J. Cohen, and D. Nagin. 1978. *Deterrence and Incapacitation: Estimating the Effects of Sanctions on the Crime Rate.* Washington, D.C.: National Academy Press.

Blurton-Jones, N. C., ed. 1972. *Ethological Studies of Child Behaviour.* Cambridge: Cambridge University Press.

Bolger, N., A. DeLongis, R. C. Kessler, and E. Wethington. 1990. "The Microstructure of Daily Role-Related Stress in Married Couples." In *Stress between Work and Family,* edited by J. Eckenrode and S. Gore. New York: Plenum Press.

Bonacich, Edna. 1972. "A Theory of Ethnic Antagonism: The Split Labor Market." *American Sociological Review* 37:547–559.

Bowen, Murray. 1978. *Family Therapy in Clinical Practice.* New York: Jason Aronson.

Bowers, L., P. Smith, V. and Binney. 1992. "Cohesion and Power in the Families of Children Involved in Bully/Victim Problems at School." *Journal of Family Therapy* 14:371–387.

Bowlby, J. 1969. *Attachment and Loss,* vol. 1: *Attachment.* New York: Basic Books.

Boyle, R. P., and R. M. Coughlin. 1994. "Conceptualizing and Operationalizing Cultural Theory Variables." In *Politics, Culture, and Policy: Applying Grid-Group Analysis,* edited by D. J. Coyle and R. J. Ellis. Boulder, CO: Westview.

Braithwaite, John. 1989. *Crime, Shame, and Reintegration.* Cambridge: Cambridge University Press.

Brassard, M. R., R. B. Germain, and S. N. Hart. 1987. *Psychological Maltreatment of Children and Youth*. New York: Pergamon Press.

Brazelton, T. B., J. S. Robbey, and G. A. Collier, 1969. "Infant Development in the Zinacanteco Indians of Southern Mexico." *Pediatrics* 44:274–290.

British Psychological Society. 1979. *Report of the Society's Working Party on Corporal Punishment in Schools*. Leicester: British Psychological Society.

Broderick, C. B. 1970. "Fathers." *Family Coorinator* 26:269–275.

——. 1975. "Power in the Governance of Families." Pp. 117–130 in *Power in Families*, edited by R. E. Cromwell and D. H. Olson. New York: John Wiley.

——. 1990. "Family Process Theory." Pp. 171–206 in *Fashioning Family Theory: New Approaches*, edited by J. Sprey. Newbury Park, CA: Sage.

——. 1993. *Understanding Family Process: Basics of Family Systems Theory*. Newbury Park, CA: Sage.

Bromet, E. J., M. A. Dew, and D. K. Parkinson. 1990. *Spillover between Work and Family: A Study of Blue-Collar Working Wives*.

Bronfenbrenner, U. 1958. "Socialization and Social Class through Time and Space." In *Readings in Social Psychology*, edited by E. Maccoby, T. Newcomb, and E. Hartley. London: Methuen.

——. 1975. "The Origins of Alienation." In *Influences on Human Development*, edited by U. Bronfenbrenner and M. Mahoney. Hinsdale, IL: Dryden Press.

——. 1979. *The Ecology of Human Development: Experiments by Nature and Design*. Cambridge, MA: Harvard University Press.

——. 1986. "Ecology of the Family as a Context for Human Development: Research Perspectives." *Developmental Psychology* 22:723–742.

Bronson, G. W. 1972. *Infants' Reactions to Unfamiliar Persons and Novel Objects*. Monographs of the Society for Research in Child Development 37.

Bruner, J. S. 1975. "The Ontogenesis of Speech Acts." *Journal of Child Language* 2:1–19.

Bryan, J. W., and F. W. Freed. 1982. "Corporal Punishment: Normative Data and Sociological and Psychological Correlates in a Community College Population." *Journal of Youth and Adolescence* 11:77–87.

Buber, Martin. 1958. *I and Thou*. New York: Scribner's.

Burchard, J. D., and P. T. Harig. 1976. "Behavior Modification and Juvenile Delinquency." Pp. 405–452 in *Handbook of Behavior Modification and Behavior Therapy*, edited by H. Leitenberg. Englewood Cliffs, NJ: Prentice Hall.

Buri, J. 1991. "Parental Authority Questionnaire." *Journal of Personality Assessment* 57:110–119.

Buss, A. H., and A. Durkee. 1957. "An Inventory for Assessing Different Kinds of Hostility." *Journal of Consulting Psychology* 21:343–349.

Caffey, J. 1972. "The Parent-Infant Traumatic Stress Syndrome." *American Journal of Roentgenology, Radium Therapy, and Nuclear Medicine* 114:218–229.

Cambefort, J. P. 1981. "A Comparative Study of Culturally Transmitted Patterns of Feeding Habits in the Chacma Baboon (*Papio ursinus*) and the Vervet Monkey (*Cercopithecus aethiops*)." *Folia Primatologica* 36:243–263.

Campbell, J. C. 1992. "Wife-Battering: Cultural Contexts versus Western Social Sciences." Pp. 229–249 in *Sanctions and Sanctuary: Cultural Perspectives on the Beating of Wives,* edited by D. A. Counts, J. K. Brown, and J. C. Campbell. Boulder, CO: Westview.

Caro, T. M., and M. D. Hauser. 1992. "Is There Teaching in Nonhuman Animals?" *Quarterly Review of Biology* 67:151–174.

Carson, B. A. 1986. "Parents Who Don't Spank: Deviation in the Legitimation of Physical Force." Ph.D. dissertation, University of New Hampshire. *Dissertation Abstracts International* 47:2331-A.

Cheney, D. L., and R. W. Wrangham. 1987. "Predation." Pp. 227–239 in *Primate Societies,* edited by B. B. Smuts, D. L. Cheney, R. M. Seyfarth, R. W. Wrangham, and T. T. Struhsaker. Chicago: University of Chicago Press.

Cheney, D. L., R. M. Seyfarth, S. J. Andelman, and P. C. Lee. 1988. "Reproductive Success in Vervet Monkeys." Pp. 384–402 in *Reproductive Success,* edited by T. H. Clutton-Brock. Chicago: University of Chicago Press.

Cherek, D. R., T. Thompson, and G. T. Heistad. 1973. "Responding Maintained by the Opportunity to Attack during an Interval Food Reinforcement Schedule." *Journal of the Experimental Analysis of Behavior* 19:113–123.

Christophersen, E. R. 1988. *Little People: Guidelines for Commonsense Child Rearing.* 3d ed. Kansas City, MO: Westport.

———. 1992. "Discipline." *Pediatric Clinics of North America* 39:395–411.

Claussen, A. H., and P. M. Crittenden. 1991. "Physical and Psychological Maltreatment: Relations among Types of Maltreatment." *Child Abuse and Neglect* 15:5–18.

Cloninger, R. C. 1987. "A Systematic Method of Clinical Description and Classification of Personality Variants." *Archives General of Psychiatry* 44:573–88.

Clutton-Brock, T. H. 1991. *The Evolution of Parental Care.* Princeton, NJ: Princeton University Press.

Cobb, S. 1976. "Social Support as a Moderator of Life Stress." *Psychosomatic Medicine* 38:300–314.

Cohen, P., and J. S. Brook. 1995. "The Reciprocal Influence of Punishment and Child Behavior Disorder." Pp. 154–164 in *Coercion and Punishment in Long-Term Perspectives,* edited by J. McCord. New York: Cambridge University Press.

Cohen, Y. A. 1966. *A Study of Interpersonal Relations in a Jamaican Community.* Ann Arbor, MI: University Microfilms.

Collinge, N. E. 1991. "Variability in Aspects of the Mother-Infant Relationship in Japanese Macaques during Weaning." Pp. 157–174 in *The Monkeys of Arashiyama,* edited by L. M. Fedigan and P. J. Asquith. Albany, NY: State University of New York Press.

Collins, R. 1975. *Conflict Sociology: Toward an Explanatory Science.* New York: Academic Press.

———. 1986. *Weberian Sociological Theory.* Cambridge: Cambridge University Press.

———. 1988. *Theoretical Sociology.* San Diego: Harcourt, Brace.

———. 1993. "What Does Conflict Theory Predict about America's Future?" *Sociological Perspectives* 36:289–313.

Compass, B., H. Adelman, P. Freundle, and L. Taylor. 1982. "Parent and Children Causal Attributions during Clinical Interviews." *Journal of Abnormal Behaviour* 10:77–84.

Conger, R. D., J. A. McCarty, R. K. Yang, B. B. Lahey, B. B., and J. P. Kropp. 1984. "Perception of Child, Child-Rearing Values, and Emotional Distress as Mediating Links between Environmental Stressors and Observed Maternal Behavior." *Child Development* 55:2234–2247.

Conradt, D. P. 1980. "Changing German Political Culture." Pp. 212–272 in *The Civic Culture Revisited*, edited by G. A. Almond and S. Verba. Boston: Little, Brown.

Constantine, L. L. 1993. "The Structure of Family Paradigms: An Analytic Model of Family Variations." *Journal of Marriage and Family Therapy* 19:39–70.

Cooney, Mark. 1998. *Warriors and Peacemakers*. New York: New York University Press.

Costa, P. T., and R. R. McCrae. 1980. "Still Stable after all These Years: Personality as a Key to Some Issues in Adulthood and Old Age." Pp. 65–102 in *Life-Span development and Behavior*, vol. 3, edited by P. B. Baltes and O. G. Brim. New York: Academic Press.

Cott, Nancy. 1978. "Notes toward an Interpretation of Antebellum Childrearing." *Psychohistory Review* 7:4–20.

Council for Children with Behavioral Disorders. 1990. "Position Paper on Use of Behavior Reduction Strategies with Children with Behavioral Disorders. *Behavioral Disorders* 15:243–260.

Creed, F. 1993. "Stress and Psychosomatic Disorders." Pp. 496–510 in *Handbook of Stress: Theoretical and Clinical Aspects*, 2d ed., edited by L. Goldberger and S. Breznitz. New York: Free Press.

Crittenden, P. M. 1992a. "Quality of Attachment in the Preschool Years." *Development and Psychopathology* 4:209–241.

———. 1992b. "Treatment of Anxious Attachment in Infancy and Early Childhood." *Development and Psychopathology* 4:575–602.

———. 1993. "Peering into the Black Box: A Theoretical Treatise on the Development of Self in Young Children." Pp. 79–148 in *Rochester Symposium on Development and Psychopathology*, vol. 5, *The Self and Its Disorders*, edited by D. Cicchetti and S. L. Toth. Rochester, NY: University of Rochester Press.

———. 2000. "A Dynamic-Maturational Approach to Continuity and Change in Patterns of Attachment." Pp. 343–357 in *The Organization of Attachment Relationships: Maturation, Culture, and Context*, edited by P. M. Crittenden and A. H. Claussen. New York: Cambridge University Press.

———. 2002. "If I Knew Then What I Know Now: Integrity and Fragmentation in the Treatment of Child Abuse and Neglect." Pp. 111–126 in *Prediction and Prevention of Child Abuse: A Handbook*, edited by K. Browne, H. Hanks, P. Stratton, and C. Hamilton. London: Wiley.

———. 1995. "Attachment and Psychopathology." Pp. 367–406 in *John Bowlby's Attachment Theory: Historical, Clinical, and Social Significance*, edited by S. Goldberg, R. Muir, and J. Kerr. New York: Analytic Press.

Crittenden, P. M., A. H. Claussen, and D. B. Sugarman. 1994. "Physical and Psychological Maltreatment in Middle Childhood and Adolescence." *Development and Psychopathology* 6:145–164.

Crittenden, P. M., and Craig, S. E. 1990. "Developmental Trends in the Nature of Child Homicide." *Journal of Interpersonal Violence* 5:202–216.

Crittenden, P. M., and D. DiLalla. 1988. "Compulsive Compliance: The Development of an Inhibitory Coping Strategy in Infancy." *Journal of Abnormal Child Psychology* 16:585–599.

Crittenden, P. M., A. Landini, and A. H. Claussen. 2001. "A Dynamic-Maturational Approach to Treatment of Maltreated Children." Pp. 373–398 in *Handbook of Psychological Services for Children and Adolescents,* edited by J. Hughes, J. C. Conley, and A. La Greca. New York: Oxford University Press.

Crittenden, P. M., M. F. Partridge, and A. H. Claussen. 1991. "Family Patterns of Relationship in Normative and Dysfunctional Families." *Development and Psychopathology* 3:491–512.

Cronkhite, G. 1986. "On the Focus, Scope, and Coherence of the Study of Human Symbolic Activity." *Quarterly Journal of Speech* 72:231–246.

Croog, S. H. 1970. "The Family as a Source of Stress." In *Social Stress,* edited by S. Levine and N. Scotch. Chicago: Aldine.

Dahrendorf, Ralf. 1959. *Class and Class Conflict in Industrial Society.* Stanford, CA: Stanford University Press.

Dake, K., and A. Wildavsky. 1990. "Theories of Risk Perception: Who Fears What and Why?" *Daedalus* 119:41–60.

Dake, K., et al. 1993. "Cultural Characteristics of English Families in the Sixteenth through Nineteenth Centuries." Survey Research Center, University of California, Berkeley. Unpublished manuscript.

Daly, M., and M. Wilson. 1988. "Evolutionary Social Psychology and Family Homicide." *Science* 242:519–524.

———. 1987. "Children as Homicide Victims." In *Child Abuse and Neglect: Biosocial Perspectives,* edited by R. Gelles and J. Lancaster. New York: Aldine.

Dangel, R. F., and R. A. Polster. 1984. "Winning! A Systematic, Empirical Approach to Parent Training." Pp. 162–210 in *Parent Training,* edited by R. F. Dangel and R. A. Polster. New York: Guilford Press.

Daro, D. 1995. "Public Opinion and Behaviors regarding Child Abuse Prevention: The Results of NCPCA's 1995 Public Opinion Poll." Chicago: National Committee to Prevent Child Abuse.

Daro, D., and R. Gelles 1992. "Public Attitudes and Behaviors with respect to Child Abuse Prevention." *Journal of Interpersonal Violence* 7:517–531.

Darwin, C. 1859. *The Origin of Species by Means of Natural Selection.* London: Murray.

Day, D. E., and M. W. Roberts. 1983. "An Analysis of the Physical Punishment Component of a Parent Training Program." *Journal of Abnormal Child Psychology* 11:141–152.

Deese, J., and S. Hulse. 1967. *The Psychology of Learning.* New York: McGraw-Hill.

Degler, Carl. 1982. *At Odds: Women and the Family from the Revolution to the Present.* New York: Oxford University Press.

de Mause, L. 1988. "The Evolution of Childhood." Pp. 1–73 in *The History of Childhood: The Untold Story of Child Abuse,* edited by L. de Mause. New York: Peter Bedrick Books.

Demos, John. 1970. *A Little Commonwealth: Family Life in Plymouth Colony.* New York: Oxford University Press.

deTurk, M. A. 1987. "When Communication Fails: Physical Aggression as a Compliance-Gaining Strategy." *Communication Monographs* 54:106–112.

deTurk, M. A., and G. R. Miller. 1983. "Adolescent Perceptions of Parental Persuasive Message Strategies." *Journal of Marriage and the Family* 45:543–552.

DeVinney, B. J., C. M. Berman, and K. L. R. Rasmussen. 2001. "Changes in Yearling Rhesus Monkeys' Relationships with their Mothers after Sibling Birth." *American Journal of Primatology* 54:193–210.

de Waal, F. 1989. *Peacemaking among the Plimates*. Cambridge, MA: Harvard University Press.

Dillard, J. P., ed. 1990. *Seeking Compliance: The Production of Interpersonal Influence Messages*. Scottsdale, AZ: Gorsuch Scarisbrick.

Dingwall, R., et al. 1984. "Childhood as a Social Problem: A Survey of the History of Legal Regulation." *Journal of Law and Society* 2:297–232.

Dohrenwend, B. P., and B. S. Dohrenwend. 1974. "Social and Cultural Influences on Psychopathology." *Annual Review of Psychology* 25:417–452.

——. 1976. "Sex Differences and Psychiatric Disorders." *American Journal of Sociology* 81:1447–1454.

Douglas, M. 1970. *Natural Symbols: Explorations in Cosmology*. New York: Pantheon.

——. 1978. *Cultural Bias*. London: Royal Anthropological Society.

——. 1982a. *In the Active Voice*. London: Routledge and Kegan Paul.

——, ed. 1982b. *Essays in the Sociology of Perception*. London: Routledge and Kegan Paul.

Douglas, M. 1986. *How Institutions Think*. Syracuse, NY: Syracuse University Press.

Downey, G. L. 1986. "Ideology and the Clamshell Identity: Organizational Dilemmas in the Anti-Nuclear Power Movement." *Social Problems* 33:357–73.

Dunbar, R. I. M., and P. Dunbar. 1988. "Maternal Time Budgets of Gelada Baboons." *Animal Behaviour* 36:970–980.

Dunst, C., and C. Trivett. 1992. "Risk and Opportunity Factors Influencing Parent and Child Functioning." Presented at the Ninth Annual Smoky Mountain Winter Institute, Asheville, NC.

Durkheim, E. [1897] 1951. *Suicide: A Study in Sociology*. Translated by J. Spaulding and G. Simpson. Glencoe, IL: Free Press.

——. [1912] 1995. *The Elementary Forms of the Religious Life*. Translated by Karen Fields. New York: Free Press.

Eaton, G. G. 1972. "Seasonal Sexual Behavior: Intrauterine Contraceptive Devices in a Confined Troop of Japanese Macaques." *Hormones and Behavior* 3:133–142.

Eckstein, H. 1988. "A Culturalist Theory of Political Change. *American Political Science Review* 82:789–804.

Eibl-Eibesfeldt, I. 1979. "Human Ethology: Concepts and Implications for the Sciences of Man." *Behavioral and Brain Sciences* 2:1–57.

Elder, G. H., Jr. 1974. *Children of the Great Depression: Social Change in Life Experience*. Chicago: University of Chicago Press.

Elder, G. H., Jr., and A. Caspi. 1988. "Human Development and Social Change: An Emerging Perspective on the Life Course." In *Persons in Context: Developmental*

Processes, edited by N. Bolger, A. Caspi, G. Downey, and M. Moorehouse. Cambridge: Cambridge University Press.

Elder, G. H., Jr., and J. K. Liker. 1982. "Hard Times in Women's Lives: Historical Influences across Forty Years." *American Journal of Sociology* 88:241–269.

Elias, N. 1978. *What Is Sociology?* New York: Columbia University Press.

Ellis, G. J., and L. R. Peterson. 1992. "Socialization Values and Parental Control Techniques: A Cross-Cultural Analysis of Child Rearing." *Journal of Comparative Family Studies* 23:39–45.

Ellis, R. J. 1993. *American Political Cultures.* New York: Oxford University Press.

Erikson, E. 1950. *Childhood and Society.* New York: Norton.

——. 1959. *Identity and the Life Cycle.* Psychological Issues, Monograph No. 1. New York: International Universities Press.

Erlanger, H. S. 1979. "Childhood Punishment Experience and Adult Violence." *Children and Youth Services Review* 1:75–76.

Eron, L. D. 1982. "Parent-Child Interactions, Television, Violence, and Aggression of Children." *American Psychologist* 37:197–211.

Evans-Prichard, E. E. 1940. *The Nuer: A Description of the Modes of Livelihood and Political Institutions of a Nilotic People.* Oxford: Oxford University Press.

Eyberg, S. M., and S. R. Boggs. 1989. "Parent Training for Oppositional Preschoolers." In *Handbook of Parent Training: Parents as Cotherapists for Children's Behavior Problems,* edited by C. E. Schaefer and J. M. Briesmeister. New York: Wiley.

Eysenck, H. 1993. "Letter to the Editor." *The Psychologist,* September.

Fairbanks, L. A. 1975. "Communication of Food Quality in Captive *Macaca nemestrina* and Free-Ranging *Ateles geoffroyi.*" *Primates* 16:181–190.

——. 1989. "Early Experience and Cross-Generational Continuity of Mother-Infant Contact in Vervet Monkeys." *Developmental Psychobiology* 22:853–859.

——. 1990. "Reciprocal Benefits of Allomothering for Female Vervet Monkeys. *Animal Behaviour* 40:553–562.

——. 1993a. "What Is a Good Mother? Adaptive Variation in Maternal Behavior in Primates." *Current Directions in Psychological Science* 2:179–183.

——. 1993b. "Juvenile Vervet Monkeys: Establishing Relationships and Practicing Skills for the Future." Pp. 211–227 in *Juvenile Primates: Life History, Development, and Behavior,* edited by M. E. Pereira and L. A. Fairbanks. New York: Oxford University Press.

——. 1996. "Individual Differences in Maternal Style of Old World Monkeys." *Advances in the Study of Behavior* 25:579–611.

——. 2003. "Primate Parenting." In *Primate Psychology,* edited by D. Maestripieri. Cambridge, MA: Harvard University Press.

Fairbanks, L. A., and J. Bird. 1978. "Ecological Correlates of Interindividual Distance in the St. Kitts Vervet (*Cercopithecus aethiops sabaeus*)." *Primates* 19:605–614.

Fairbanks, L. A., and M. T. McGuire. 1985. "Relationships of Vervet Mothers with Sons and Daughters from One through Three Years of Age." *Animal Behaviour* 33:40–50.

——. 1987. "Mother-Infant Relationships in Vervet Monkeys: Response to New Adult Males." *International Journal of Primatology* 8:351–366.

——. 1988. "Long-Term Effects of Early Mothering Behavior on Responsiveness to the Environment in Vervet Monkeys." *Developmental Psychobiology* 21:711–724.

——. 1993. "Maternal Protectiveness and Response to the Unfamiliar in Vervet Monkeys." *American Journal of Primatology* 30:119–129.

——. 1995. "Maternal Condition and the Quality of Maternal Care in Vervet Monkeys." *Behaviour* 132:733–754.

——. 1984. "Determinants of Fecundity and Reproductive Success in Captive Vervet Monkeys." *American Journal of Primatology* 7:27–38.

Falk, J. L. 1961. "Production of Polydipsia in Normal Rats by an Intermittent Food Schedule." *Science* 133:195–196.

——. 1971. "The Nature and Determinants of Adjunctive Behavior." *Physiology and Behavior* 6:577–588.

——. 1977. "The Origin and Functions of Adjunctive Behavior." *Animal Learning and Behavior* 5:325–335.

Ferber, R. 1985. *Solve Your Child's Sleep Problems.* New York: Simon and Schuster.

Feshbach, N. D., and S. Feshbach. 1972. "Children's Aggression." In *The Young Child: Review of Research,* vol. 2, edited by W. W. Hartup. Washington, D.C.: National Association for the Education of Young Children.

Feshbach, S. 1970. "Aggression." Pp. 159–259 in *Carmichael's Manual of Child Psychology,* 3d ed., edited by P. H. Mussen. New York: Wiley.

Field, T. M., A. M. Sostek, S. Goldberg, and H. H. Shuman, eds. 1979. *Infants Born at Risk.* New York: SP Medical and Scientific Books.

Fisher, R. A. 1930. *The Genetical Theory of Natural Selection.* Oxford: Clarendon Press.

Fiske, A. P. 1991. *Structures of Social Life: The Four Elementary Forms of Human Relations.* New York: Free Press.

——. 1992. "The Four Elementary Forms of Sociality: Framework for a Unified Theory of Social Relations." *Psychological Review* 90:689–723.

Flugel, J. C. 1945. *Man, Morals, and Society.* New York: International Universities Press.

Flynn, C. P. 1993. "Regional Differences in Attitudes toward Corporal Punishment." Presented at the annual meeting of the American Sociological Association, Miami, FL.

Forehand, R. L. and R. J. McMahon. 1981. *Helping the Noncompliant Child.* New York: Guilford.

Forrester, J. 1969. *Urban Dynamics.* Cambridge, MA: MIT Press.

Franzwa, G., and C. Lockhart. 1994. "Explaining Gender Differences: Communication Styles, Personality Type, and Culture." Texas Christian University, Fort Worth, TX. Unpublished manuscript.

Freeley, A. J. 1966. *Argumentation and Debate: Rational Decision Making,* 2d ed. Belmont, CA: Wadsworth.

Freud, S. 1933. *New Introductory Lectures in Psychoanalysis.* New York: Norton.

——. 1942. *Beyond the Pleasure Principle.* London: Hogarth.

——. 1953. *The Standard Edition of the Complete Psychological Works of Sigmund Freud,* edited by J. Strachey. London: Hogarth Press.

——. 1961. *Civilization and Its Discontents.* New York: Norton.

Friedrich, W. N., and J. A. Boriskin. 1976. "The Role of the Child in Abuse: A Review of the Literature." *American Journal of Orthopsychiatry* 46:580–590.

Furnham, A. 1988. *Lay Theories*. Oxford: Pergamon.

——. 1995. "Attitudes to Spanking." London University. Unpublished manuscript.

Furnham, A., and A. Hume-Wright. 1992. "Lay Theories of Anorexia Nervosa." *Journal of Clinical Psychology* 48:20–36.

Furnham, A., and A. Lewis. 1986. *The Economic Mind*. Brighton: Wheatsheaf.

Furnham, A., and J. Rees. 1988. "Lay Theories of Schizophrenia." *International Journal of Social Psychiatry* 34:212–220.

Furnham, A., and K. Bland. 1983. "The Protestant Work Ethic and Conservatism." *Personality and Individual Differences* 4:205–206.

Furnham, A., and P. Bower. 1992. "A Comparison of Academic and Lay Theories of Schizophrenia." *British Journal of Psychiatry* 161:201–210.

Galef, B. G. 1976. "Social Transmission of Acquired Behavior: A Discussion of Tradition and Social Learning in Vertebrates." Pp. 77–100 in *Advances in the Study of Behavior*, edited by J. S. Rosenblatt, R. A. Hinde, E. Shaw, and C. Beer. New York: Academic Press.

Gallimore, R., R. G. Tharp, and B. Kemp. 1969. "Positive Reinforcing Function of 'Negative Attention.'" *Journal of Experimental Child Psychology* 8:140–146.

Gans, H. 1972. "The Positive Functions of Poverty." *American Journal of Sociology* 78:275–283.

Garbarino, J. 1989. "Troubled Youth, Troubled Families: The Dynamics of Adolescent Maltreatment." Pp. 685–706 in *Child Maltreatment: Theory and Research on the Causes and Consequences of Child Abuse and Neglect*, edited by D. Cicchetti and V. Carlson. Cambridge: Cambridge University Press.

——. 1995 *Raising Children in a Socially Toxic Environment*. San Francisco: Jossey-Bass.

Garbarino, J., and A. C. Garbarino. 1986. *Emotional Maltreatment of Children*. Chicago: National Committee for the Prevention of Child Abuse.

Garbarino, J., and Associates. 1992. *Children and Families in the Social Environment*, 2d ed. Hawthorne, NY: Aldine de Gruyter.

Garbarino, J. and G. Gilliam. 1980. *Understanding Abusive Families*. Lexington, MA: D. C. Heath.

Garbarino, J., and K. Kostelny. 1992. "Child Maltreatment as a Community Problem." *International Journal of Child Abuse and Neglect* 16:455–464.

——. 1995. "The Effects of Political Violence on Palestinian Children's Behavior Problems: A Risk Accumulation Model." *Child Development* 67:33–45.

Garbarino, J., and U. Bronfenbrenner. 1976. "Research on Parent-Child Relations and Social Policy: Who Needs Whom?" Paper presented at the Symposium on Parent-Child Relations: Theoretical, Methodological, and Practical Implications, University of Trier, Trier, West Germany.

Garbarino, J., E. Guttman, and J. Seeley. 1986. *The Psychologically Battered Child: Strategies for Identification, Assessment, and Intervention*. San Francisco: Jossey-Bass.

Garbarino, J., F. Stott, and Faculty of the Erikson Institute. 1989. *What Children Can Tell Us*. San Francisco: Jossey-Bass.

Garland, D. 1990. *Punishment and Modern Society*. Chicago: University of Chicago Press.

Gecas, V. 1979. "The Influence of Social Class on Socialization." In *Contemporary Theories about the Family: Research-Based Theories,* vol. 1, edited by W. R. Burr, R. Hill, F. I. Nye, and I. L. Reiss. New York: Free Press.

Gelles, R., and C. Cornell. 1990. *Intimate Violence in Families.* Beverly Hills, CA.: Sage.

Gelles, R. J. 1977. "Violence in the American Family." In *Violence and the Family,* edited by J. P. Martin. New York: Wiley.

———. "Violence toward Children in the United States." *American Journal of Orthopsychiatry* 48:580–592.

———. 1983. "An Exchange/Social Control Theory." Pp. 151–165 in *The Dark Side of Families: Current Family Violence Research,* edited by D. Finkelhor, R. Gelles, M. Straus, and G. Hotaling. Beverly Hills, CA: Sage.

Gelles, R. J., and E. F. Hargreaves. 1990. "Maternal Employment and Violence toward Children." Pp. 263–277 in *Physical violence in American families,* edited by M. A. Straus and R. J. Gelles. New Brunswick, NJ: Transaction.

Gelles, R. J., and M. A. Straus. 1979. "Determinants of Violence in the Family: Towards a Theoretical Integration." In *Contemporary Theories about the Family,* vol. 1, edited by W. R. Burr, R. Hill, F. I. Nye, and I. L. Reiss. New York: Free Press.

———. 1987. "Is Violence towards Children Increasing?: A Comparison of 1975 and 1985 National Survey Rates." *Journal of Interpersonal Violence* 2:212–222.

George, C., and M. Main. 1979. "Social Interactions of Young Abused Children: Approach, Avoidance, and Aggression." *Child Development* 50:306–318.

Geschwind, N. 1964. "The Development of the Brain and the Evolution of Language." *Monograph Series on Languages and Linguistics* 17:155–169.

Gil, D. G. 1970. *Violence against Children: Physical Child Abuse in the United States.* Cambridge, MA.: Harvard University Press.

———. 1971. "Violence against Children." *Journal of Marriage and the Family* 33:637–648.

Giles-Sims, J., M. A. Straus, and D. B. Sugarman. 1993. "Child, Maternal, and Family Characteristics Associated with Spanking." *Family Relations* 44:170–176.

Glenn, Myra C. 1984. *Campaigns against Corporal Punishment: Prisoners, Sailors, Women, and Children in Antebellum America.* Albany, NY: State University of New York Press.

Glueck, S., and E. Glueck. 1950. *Unraveling Juvenile Delinquency.* Cambridge, MA: Harvard University Press.

Goffman, Erving. 1966. *Behavior in Public Places: Notes on the Social Organization of Public Gatherings.* New York: Free Press.

———. 1967. *Interaction Ritual.* New York: Anchor.

Goldfarb, W. 1958. "Pain Reactions in a Group of Institutionalized Schizophrenic Children." *American Journal of Orthopsychiatry* 28:777–785.

Gomendio, M. 1991. "Parent/Offspring Conflict and Maternal Investment in Rhesus Macaques." *Animal Behaviour* 42:993–1005.

Goode, W. J. 1971. "Force and Violence in the Family." *Journal of Marriage and the Family* 33:624–636.

———. 1982. *The Family.* 2d ed. Englewood Cliffs, NJ: Prentice-Hall.

Goodenough, F. L. [1931] 1975. *Anger in Young Children.* Westport, CT: Greenwood Press.

Goodnow, J. 1981. "Everyday Ideas about Cognitive Development." In *Social Cognition: Perspectives on Everyday Understanding,* edited by J. Forgass. London: Academic Press.

———. 1984. "Parents' Ideas about Parenting and Development." In *Advances in Developmental Psychology,* edited by M. Lamb, A. Brown, and B. Rogoff. Hillsdale, NJ: Erlbaum.

Gorden, W. I., and D. A. Infante. "Employee Rights: Content, Argumentativeness, Verbal Aggressiveness, and Career Satisfaction." Pp. 149–163 in *Communicating Employee Responsibilities and Rights: A Modern Management Mandate,* edited by C. A. B. Osigweh. Westport, CT: Greenwood Press.

———. 1991. "Test of a Communication Model of Organizational Commitment." *Communication Quarterly* 39:144–155.

Gorden, W. I., D. A. Infante, and E. E. Graham. 1988. "Corporate Conditions Conducive to Employee Voice: A Subordinate Perspective." *Employee Responsibilities and Rights Journal* 1:100–111.

Gorden, W. I., D. A. Infante, and J. Izzo. 1988. "Variations in Voice Pertaining to Dissatisfaction/Satisfaction with Subordinates." *Management Communication Quarterly* 2:6–22.

Gordon, Linda. 1988. *Heroes of Their Own Lives: The Politics and History of Family Violence, Boston 1880–1960.* New York: Viking.

Gore, S., and T. Mangione. 1983. "Social Roles, Sex Roles, and Psychological Distress: Additive and Interactive Models of Sex Differences." *Journal of Health and Social Behavior* 24:300–312.

Gottfredson, M. R., and T. Hirschi. 1993. "A Control Theory Interpretation of Psychological Research on Aggression." Pp. 47–68 in *Aggression and Violence,* edited by R. B. Felson and J. T. Tedeschi. Washington, DC: American Psychological Association.

Gouldner, A. 1960. "The Norm of Reciprocity." *American Sociological Review* 25:161–178.

Gove, W. R., and J. F. Tudor. 1973. "Adult Sex Roles and Mental Illness." *American Journal of Sociology* 78:812–835.

Graziano, A., W. A. Plante, and J. Hamblen. 1995. "Use of Sub-abusive Violence in 320 Middle Class Families." Paper presented at the 4th International Family Violence Research Conference, Durham, NH.

Green, A. 1976. "A Psychodynamic Approach to the Study and Treatment of Child Abusing Parents." *Journal of Child Psychiatry* 15:414.

Grendstad, G. 1990. "Europe by Cultures: An Exploration in Grid-Group Analysis." Unpublished master's thesis, University of Bergen, Norway.

Greven, P. 1991. *Spare the Child: The Religious Roots of Physical Punishment and the Psychological Impact of Physical Abuse.* New York: Knopf.

Grusec, J. E., and T. Dix. 1986. "The Socialization of Prosocial Behavior: Theory and Reality." Pp. 218–237 in *Altruism and Aggression: Biological and Social Origins,* edited by C. Zahn-Waxler, E. M. Cummings, and R. Iannotti. Cambridge: Cambridge University Press.

Hall, P. 1986. *Governing the Economy: The Politics of State Intervention in Britain and France.* New York: Oxford University Press.

Hall, R. V., and M. C. Hall. 1980a. *How to Select Reinforcers.* Lawrence, KS: H and H Enterprises.

———. 1980b. *How to Use Planned Ignoring (Extinction).* Lawrence, KS: H and H Enterprises.

Hamilton, V. L., and J. Sanders. 1988. "Punishment and the Individual in the United States and Japan." *Law and Society Review* 22:301–28.

Harbridge, J., and A. Furnham. 1991. "Lay Theories of Rape." *Counselling Psychology Quarterly* 4:3–25.

Harcourt, A. H. 1987. "Dominance and Fertility among Female Primates." *Journal of Zoology* 213:471–487

Hardin, G. 1966. *Biology: Its Principles and Implications.* San Francisco: W. H. Freeman.

Hartmann, H. 1960. *Psychoanalysis and Moral Values.* New York: International Universities Press.

Hauser, M. D. 1993. "Ontogeny of Foraging Behavior in Wild Vervet Monkeys (*Cercopithecus aethiops*): Social Interactions and Survival." *Journal of Comparative Psychology* 107:276–282.

Hauser, M. D., and L. A. Fairbanks. 1988. "Mother-Offspring Conflict in Vervet Monkeys: Variation in Response to Ecological Conditions." *Animal Behaviour* 36:802–813.

Hayes, S. C., ed. 1989. *Rule-Governed Behavior: Cognition, Contingencies, and Instructional Control.* New York: Plenum.

Hechter, M. 1987. *Principles of Group Solidarity.* Berkeley, CA: University of California Press.

Helman, C. 1984. *Culture, Health and Illness.* Bristol: Wright.

Henton, J. R., J. Cate, et al. 1983. "Romance and Violence in Dating Relationships." *Journal of Family Issues* 4:467–82.

Herrmann, J. 1992. "Gossip in Science." Paper presented at the annual meeting of the American Sociological Association, Pittsburgh, PA.

Herrnstein, R. J. 1970. "On the Law of Effect." *Journal of the Experimental Analysis of Behavior* 13:243–266.

Higgins, E. T. 1990. "Personality, Social Psychology, and Person-Situation Relations." Pp. 301–338 in *Handbook of Personality: Theory and Research,* edited by L. A. Pervin. New York: Guilford.

Hinde, R. A. 1983. "Ethology and Child Development." Pp. 27–93 in *Handbook of Child Psychology,* 4th ed., vol. 2, *Infancy and Developmental Psychobiology,* edited by M. M. Haith and J. J. Campos. New York: Wiley.

Hineline, P. N. 1984. "Aversive Control: A Separate Domain?" *Journal of the Experimental Analysis of Behavior* 42:495–509.

Hiner, N. Ray. 1979. "Children's Rights, Corporal Punishment, and Child Abuse: Changing American Attitudes, 1870–1920." *Bulletin of the Menninger Clinic* 43:233–248.

Hirschi, T. 1969. *Causes of Delinquency.* Berkeley, CA: University of California Press.

Hobbes, T. [1651] 1957. *Leviathan.* Oxford: Basil Blackwell.

Hochschild, J. L. 1981. *What's Fair?: American Beliefs about Distributive Justice.* Cambridge, MA: Harvard University Press.

Hoffman, M. L. 1963. "Parent Discipline and the Child's Consideration for Others." *Child Development* 34:573–588.

———. 1970. "Moral Development." In *Carmichael's Manual of Child Psychology,* vol. 2, edited by P. H. Mussen. New York: Wiley.

Hogarth, E. 1971. *Sentencing as a Human Process.* Toronto: University of Toronto Press.

Hold, B. 1976. "Attention and Rank-Order Behaviors in Preschool Children." Pp. 177–201 in *The Structure of Social Attention,* edited by M. R. A. Chance and R. R. Larsen. New York: McGraw-Hill.

Holden, G. W. 1983. "Avoiding Conflict: Mothers as Tacticians in the Supermarket." *Child Development* 54:233–244.

———. 1988. "Adults' Thinking about a Child-Rearing Problem: Effects of Experience, Parental Status, and Gender." *Child Development* 59:1623–1632.

Holden, G. W., and M. J. West. 1989. "Proximate Regulation by Mothers: A Demonstration of How Differing Styles Affect Young Children's Behavior." *Child Development* 60:64–69.

Holden, G. W., and R. J. Zambarano. 1992. "Passing the Rod: Similarities of Parents and Their Children in Orientations toward Physical Punishment." Pp. 143–172 in *Parental Belief Systems: The Psychological Consequences for Children,* 2d ed., edited by I. E. Sigel, A. V. McGillicuddy-DeLisi, and J. J. Goognow. Hillsdale, NJ: Erlbaum.

Holman, S. D., and R. W. Goy. 1988. "Sexually Dimorphic Transitions Revealed in the Relationships of Yearling Rhesus Monkeys Following the Birth of Siblings." *International Journal of Primatology* 9:113–133.

Holmes, T. H., and R. H. Rahe. 1967. "The Social Readjustment Rating Scale." *Journal of Health and Social Behavior* 20:296–300.

Homans, G. 1961. *Social Behavior: Its Elementary Forms.* New York: Harcourt Brace Jovanovich.

Hooley, J. M., and M. J. A. Simpson. 1983. "Influence of Siblings on the Infant's Relationship with the Mother and Others." Pp. 139–142 in *Primate Social Relationships,* edited by R. A. Hinde. Sunderland, MA: Sinauer Associates.

Horowitz, A. 1982. "Sex Role Expectations, Power, and Psychological Distress." *Sex Roles* 8:607–623.

Horrocks, J., and W. Hunte. 1983. "Maternal Rank and Offspring Rank in Vervet Monkeys: An Appraisal of the Mechanisms of Rank Acquisition." *Animal Behaviour* 31:772–782.

Horwitz, A. V. 1982. *The Social Control of Mental Illness.* New York: Academic Press.

———. 1984. "Therapy and Social Solidarity." Pages 211–250 in *Toward a General Theory of Social Control,* vol. 1, *Fundamentals,* edited by D. Black. Orlando: Academic Press.

———. 1990. *The Logic of Social Control.* New York: Plenum Press.

Hough, M., and P. Mayhew. 1985. *Taking Account of Crime.* London: HMSO.

Hrdy, S. B. 1992. "Fitness Tradeoffs in the History and Evolution of Delegated Mothering with Special Reference to Wet-nursing, Abandonment, and Infanticide." *Ethology and Sociobiology* 13:409–442

Hunter, J., and F. Boster. 1987. "A Model of Compliance-Gaining Message Selection." *Communication Monographs* 54:63–84.

Hutchinson, R. R. 1977. "By-products of Aversive Control." Pp. 415–431 in *Handbook of Operant Behavior*, edited by W. K. Honig and J. E. R. Staddon. Englewood Cliffs, NJ: Prentice Hall.

Hyman, I. A. 1990. *Reading, Writing, and the Hickory Stick: The Appalling Story of Physical and Psychological Abuse in American Schools*. Lexington, MA: Heath.

Infante, D. A. 1981. "Trait Argumentativeness as a Predictor of Communicative Behavior in Situations Requiring Argument." *Central States Speech Journal* 32:265–272.

———. 1985. "Inducing Women to be More Argumentative: Source Credibility Effects." *Journal of Applied Communication Research* 13:33–44.

———. 1987. "Aggressiveness." Pp. 157–192 in *Personality and Interpersonal Communication*, edited by J. C. McCroskey and J. A. Daly. Newbury Park, CA: Sage.

———. 1988. *Arguing Constructively*. Prospect Heights, IL: Waveland Press.

———. 1989. "Response to High Argumentatives: Message and Sex Differences." *Southern Communication Journal* 54:159–170.

Infante, D. A., and A. S. Rancer. 1982. "A Conceptualization and Measure of Argumentativeness." *Journal of Personality Assessment* 46:72–80.

Infante, D. A., and C. J. Wigley. 1986. "Verbal Aggressiveness: An Interpersonal Model and Measure." *Communication Monographs* 53:61–69.

Infante, D. A., and W. I. Gorden. 1985. "Superiors' Argumentativeness and Verbal Aggressiveness as Predictors of Subordinates' Satisfaction." *Human Communication Research* 12:117–125.

———. 1987. "Superior and Subordinate Communication Profiles: Implications for Independent-Mindedness and Upward Effectiveness." *Central States Speech Journal* 38:73–80.

———. 1989. "Argumentativeness and Affirming Communicator Style as Predictors of Satisfaction/Dissatisfaction with Subordinates." *Communication Quarterly* 37:81–90.

———. 1991. "How Employees See the Boss: Test of an Argumentative and Affirming Model of Supervisors' Communicative Behavior." *Western Journal of Speech Communication* 55:294–304.

Infante, D. A., A. S. Rancer, and D. F. Womack. 1993. *Building Communication Theory*, 2d ed. Prospect Heights, IL: Waveland Press.

Infante, D. A., B. L. Riddle, C. L. Horvath, and S. A. Tumlin. 1992. "Verbal Aggressiveness: Messages and Reasons." *Communication Quarterly* 40:116–126.

Infante, D. A., C. M. Anderson, M. M. Martin, A. D. Herington, and J. Kim. 1992. "Subordinates' Satisfaction and Perceptions of Superiors' Compliance-Gaining Tactics, Argumentativeness, Verbal Aggressiveness, and Style." *Management Communication Quarterly* 6:307–326.

Infante, D. A., J. D. Trebing, P. E. Shepherd, and D. E. Seeds. 1984. "The Relationship of Argumentativeness to Verbal Aggression." *Southern Speech Communication Journal* 50:67–77.

Infante, D. A., T. A. Chandler, and J. E. Rudd. 1989. "Test of an Argumentative Skill Deficiency Model of Interspousal Violence." *Communication Monographs* 56:163–177.

Infante, D. A., T. C. Sabourin, J. E. Rudd, and E. A. Shannon. 1990. "Verbal Aggression in Violent and Nonviolent Marital Disputes." *Communication Quarterly* 38:361–371.

Inglehart, R. 1990. *Cultural Shift in Advanced Industrial Societies.* Princeton, NJ: Princeton University Press.

Irwin, D. M. 1982. "Moral Development." Pp. 1237–1241 in *Encyclopedia of Educational Research,* 5th ed., vol. 3, edited by H. E. Mitzel. New York: Free Press.

Isbell, L. A. 1990. "Sudden Short-Term Increase in Mortality of Vervet Monkeys (*Cercopithecus aethiops*) due to Leopard Predation in Amboseli National Park, Kenya." *American Journal of Primatology* 21:41–52.

James, Allison, and Alan Prout. 1980. *Constructing and Reconstructing Childhood: Contemporary Issues in the Sociological Study of Childhood.* London: Falmer.

Jay, P. 1963. "Mother-Infant Relations in Langurs." Pp. 282–304 in *Maternal Behavior in Mammals,* edited by H. L. Reingold. New York: Wiley.

Jean-Gilles, M., and P. M. Crittenden. 1990. "Maltreating Families: A Look at Siblings." *Family Relations* 39:323–329.

Jensen, J. V. 1981. *Argumentation: Reasoning in Communication.* New York: Van Nostrand.

Johnson, R. L., C. M. Berman, and I. Malik. 1993. "An Integrative Model of the Lactational and Environmental Control of Mating in Female Rhesus Monkeys." *Animal Behaviour* 46:63–78.

Joreen. 1973. "The Tyranny of Structurelessness." Pp. 285–299 in *Radical Feminism,* edited by A. Koedt, E. Levine, and A. Rapone. New York: Quadrangle.

Justice, B., and D. F. Duncan. 1976. "Life Crisis as a Precursor to Child Abuse." *Published Health Representative* 91:110–115.

Justice, B., and R. Justice. 1976. *The Abusing Family.* New York: Human Sciences Press.

Kadushin, A., and J. A. Martin. 1981. *Child Abuse: An Interactional Event.* New York: Columbia University Press.

Kalmus, D. 1984. "The Intergenerational Transmission of Marital Aggression." *Journal of Marriage and the Family* 46:11–19.

Kandel, E. 1991. "Physical Punishment and the Development of Aggressive and Violent Behavior: A Review." Unpublished manuscript.

Kantor, D., and W. Lehr. 1975. *Inside Families.* San Francisco: Jossey-Bass.

Katona, G. 1971. "Consumer Durable Spending: Explanation and Prediction." *Brookings Papers on Economic Activity* 1:234–239.

Katzenstein, P. 1984. *Corporatism and Change: Austria, Switzerland, and the Politics of Industry.* Ithaca, NY: Cornell University Press.

———. 1985. *Small States in World Markets.* Ithaca, NY: Cornell University Press.

Kazdin, A. E. 1972. "Response Cost: The Removal of Conditioned Reinforcers for a Therapeutic Change." *Behavior Therapy* 3:533–546.

———. 1987. "Treatment of Antisocial Behavior in Children: Current Status and Future Directions." *Psychological Bulletin* 102:187–203.

Keith, C. 1990. "Disturbances of Conduct Following Stress." In *Stressors and the Adjustment Disorders,* edited by J. D. Noshpitz and R. D. Coddington. New York: Wiley.

Keller, H., D. Miranda, and G. Gauda. 1984. "The Naive Theory of the Infant and Some

Maternal Attitudes: A Two-Country Study." *Journal of Cross-Cultural Psychology* 15:165–179.

Kelly, J. F., and D. F. Hake. 1970. "An Extinction-Induced Increase in an Aggressive Response with Humans." *Journal of the Experimental Analysis of Behavior* 14:153–164.

Kelman, H. C. 1961. "Process of Opinion Change." *Public Opinion Quarterly* 25:57–78.

Kessel, Frank S., and A. Siegel, eds. 1983. *The Child and Other Cultural Inventions.* New York: Praeger.

Kessler, R. C., and J. McRae Jr. 1981. "Trends in the Relationship between Sex and Psychological Distress: 1957–1976." *American Sociological Review* 46:443–452.

Kessler, R. C., and S. Zhao. 1999. "The Prevalence of Mental Illness." In *A Handbook for the Study of Mental Health: Social Contexts, Theories, and Systems,* edited by A. V. Horwitz and T. L. Scheid. Cambridge: Cambridge University Press.

Kessler, R. C., R. H. Price, and C. B. Wortman. 1985. "Social Factors in Psychopathology: Stress, Social Support, and Coping Processes." *Annual Review of Psychology* 36:531–572.

Kirshenbaum, M., and C. Foster. 1991. *Parent/Teen Breakthrough: The Relationship Approach.* New York: Penguin.

Klaus, M. H., and J. H. Kennell. 1976. *Maternal-Infant Bonding.* St. Louis, MO: C. V. Mosby.

Knapp, M. L. 1980. *Essentials of Nonverbal Communication.* New York: Holt, Rinehart and Winston.

Kohlberg, L. 1969. "Stage and Sequence: The Cognitive Developmental Approach to Socialization." Pp. 347–480 in *Handbook of Socialization,* edited by D. A. Goslin. Chicago: Rand McNally.

———. 1978. "Revisions in the Theory and Practice of Moral Development." Pp. 83–88 in *Moral Development: New Directions for Child Development,* vol. 2, edited by W. Damon. San Francisco: Jossey-Bass.

———. 1983. *The Psychology of Moral Development.* New York: Harper and Row.

Kohlberg, L., and E. Turiel. 1973. "Overview: Cultural Universals in Morality." In *Recent Research in Moral Development,* edited by L. Kohlberg and E. Turiel. New York: Holt, Rinehart and Winston.

Kohn, M. L. 1977. *Class and Conformity: A Study of Values.* 2d ed. Chicago: University of Chicago Press.

Kolvin, I., F. J. Miller, M. Fleeting, and P. A. Kolvin. 1988. "Social and Parenting Factors Affecting Criminal-Offence Rates: Findings from the Newcastle Thousand Family Study (1947–1980)." *British Journal of Psychiatry* 152:80–90. Reprinted in D. P. Farrington, ed., *Psychological Explanations of Crime.* Aldershot, U.K.: Dartmouth, 1990.

Konner, M. J. 1972. "Aspects of the Developmental Ethology of a Foraging People." Pp. 285–304 in *Ethological Studies of Child Behavior,* edited by N. C. Blurton-Jones. Cambridge: Cambridge University Press.

Kriesberg, L. 1982. *Social Conflicts.* Englewood Cliffs, NJ: Prentice-Hall.

Kurland, J. A. 1977. "Kin Selection in the Japanese Monkey." *Contributions to Primatology,* vol. 12. Basel: S. Karger.

Kurz, D. 1991. "Corporal Punishment and Adult Use of Violence: A Critique of 'Discipline and Deviance.'" *Social Problems* 38:155–161.

Larzelere, R. E. 1986. "Moderate Spanking: Model or Deterrent of Children's Aggression in the Family?" *Journal of Family Violence* 1:27–36.

Larzelere, R. E., and G. R. Patterson. 1990. "Parental Management: Mediator of the Effect of Socioeconomic Status on Early Delinquency." *Criminology* 28:301–323.

Larzelere, R. E., B. R. Kuhn, and B. Johnson. 2004. "The Intervention Selection Bias: An Under-Recognized Confound in Intervention Research." *Psychological Bulletin* 130:289–303.

Larzelere, R. E., P. R. Sather, W. N. Schneider, D. B. Larson, and P. L. Pike. 1998. "Punishment Enhances Reasoning's Effectiveness as a Disciplinary Response to Toddlers." *Journal of Marriage and the Family* 60:388–403.

Laslett, Peter. 1976. "The Wrong Way through the Telescope: A Note on Literary Evidence in Sociology and Historical Sociology." *British Journal of Sociology* 27:319–342.

La Vigna, G. W., and A. M. Donnellan. 1986. *Alternatives to Punishment: Solving Behavior Problems with Nonaversive Strategies.* New York: Irvington.

Lawton, J., S. Schules, N. Fowell, and M. Madser. 1984. "Parents' Perception of Actual and Ideal Child-Rearing Practices." *Journal of Genetic Psychology* 145:77–87.

Leach, P. 1993. "Should Parents Hit Their Children?" *The Psychologist* 5:216–220.

Leathers, D. G. 1986. *Successful Nonverbal Communication: Principles and Applications.* New York: Macmillan.

Lebra, T. S. 1976. *Japanese Patterns of Behavior.* Honolulu: University Press of Hawaii.

Lee, P. C. 1983. "Effects of Parturition on the Mother's Relationship with Older Offspring." Pp. 134–139 in *Primate Social Relationships,* edited by R. A. Hinde. Sunderland, MA: Sinauer Associates.

———. 1984. "Ecological Constraints on the Social Development of Vervet Monkeys." *Behaviour* 91:245–262.

———. 1987. "Nutrition, Fertility, and Maternal Investment in Primates." *Journal of Zoology* 213:409–422.

Lee, P. C., P. Majluf, and I. J. Gordon. 1991. "Growth, Weaning, and Maternal Investment from a Comparative Perspective." *Journal of Zoology* 225:99–114.

Lee, R. B., and I. DeVore. 1968. *Man the Hunter.* Chicago: Aldine.

Lefkowitz, M., L. Eron, L. Walder, and L. Huesmann. 1977. *Growing Up to Be Violent: A Longitudinal Study of the Development of Aggression.* New York: Pergamon.

Lehman, B. 1989. "Spanking Teaches the Wrong Lesson." *Boston Globe,* March 13, p. 27.

Lempers, J. D., D. Clark-Lempers, and R. L. Simons. 1989. "Economic Hardship, Parenting, and Distress in Adolescence." *Child Development* 60:25–39.

Lepper, M. R. 1983. "Social Control Processes and the Internalization of Social Values: An Attribution Perspective." Pp. 294–330 in *Social Cognition and Social Development: A Sociocultural Perspective,* edited by E. T. Higgins, D. N. Ruble, and W. W. Hartup. Cambridge: Cambridge University Press.

Lerner, M. 1980. *The Belief in a Just World.* New York: Plenum Press.

Levine, S., and N. Scotch, eds. 1970. *Social Stress.* Chicago: Aldine.

Levinson, D. 1989. *Family Violence in Cross-Cultural Perspective.* Newberry Park, CA: Sage.

Lewis, H. B. 1977. *Psychic War in Men and Women.* New York: New York University Press.

———. 1971. *Shame and Guilt in Neurosis.* New York: International Universities Press.

Lieske, J. 1993. "Regional Subcultures of the United States." *Journal of Politics* 55:888–913.

Light, R. 1973. "Abused and Neglected Children in America: A Study of Alternative Policies." *Harvard Educational Review* 43:556–598.

Lindblom, C. 1977. *Politics and Markets: The World's Political-Economic Systems.* New York: Basic Books.

Locke, John. [1693] 1947. *Some Thoughts Concerning Education.* In *John Locke: On Politics and Education,* edited by H. Penniman. New York: Van Nostrand.

Lockhart, C., and R. M. Coughlin. 1992. "Building Better Comparative Social Theory through Alternative Conceptions of Rationality." *Western Political Quarterly* 45:793–809.

Loevinger, J., and R. Wessler. 1979. *Measuring Ego Development,* vol. 1. San Francisco: Jossey-Bass.

Longfellow, C., P. Zelkowitz, and E. Saunders. 1982. "The Quality of Mother-Child Relationships." In *Lives in Stress: Women and Depression,* edited by D. Belle. Beverly Hills, CA.: Sage.

Lorenz, K. Z. 1943. "Die angeborenen Formen möglicher Erfahrung." *Zeitschrift für Tierpsychologie* 5:235–409.

Loseke, D. 1991. "Reply to Murray Straus: Readings on 'Discipline and Deviance.'" *Social Problems* 38:162–166.

Lovaas, O. I. 1987. "Behavioral Treatment and Normal Educational and Intellectual Functioning in Young Autistic Children." *Journal of Consulting and Clinical Psychology* 55:3–9.

Lovaas, O. I., and J. E. Favell. 1987. "Protection for Clients Undergoing Aversive/Restrictive Interventions." *Education and Treatment of Children* 10:311–325.

Lovaas, O. I., and C. D. Newsom. 1976. "Behavior Modification with Psychotic Children." Pp. 303–360 in *Handbook of Behavior Modification and Behavior Therapy,* edited by H. Leitenberg. Englewood Cliffs, NJ: Prentice Hall.

Lynch, M. A. and J. Roberts. 1982. *The Consequences of Child Abuse.* New York: Academic Press.

Lytton, H., D. Watts, and B. E. Dunn. 1988. "Continuity and Change in Child Characteristics and Maternal Practices between Ages 2 and 9: An Analysis of Interview Responses." *Child Study Journal* 18:1–15.

Maccoby, E. E. 1980. *Social Development: Psychological Growth and the Parent-Child Relationship.* New York: Harcourt, Brace, Jovanovich.

Maccoby, E. E., and J. Martin. 1983. "Socialization in the Context of the Family: Parent-Child Interaction." Pp. 1–101 in *Handbook of Child Psychology,* vol. 4, *Socialization, Personality, and Social Development,* 4th ed., edited by E. M. Hetherinton. New York: Wiley.

MacEwen, K. E., and J. Barling. 1988. "Multiple Stressors, Violence in the Family of Origin, and Marital Aggression: A Longitudinal Investigation." *Journal of Family Violence* 3:73–87.

Maestripieri, D., and K. A. Carroll. 1998. "Child Abuse and Neglect: Usefulness of the Animal Data." *Psychological Bulletin* 123:211–223.

Maestripieri, D., K. Wallen, and K. A. Carroll. 1997. "Infant Abuse Runs in Families of Group-Living Pigtail Macaques." *Child Abuse and Neglect* 21:465–471.

Maguire, K., and T. Flanagan. 1991. *Sourcebook of Criminal Justice Statistics 1990.* Washington, DC: U.S. Department of Justice.

Mars, G. 1982. *Cheats at Work: An Anthropology of Workplace Crime.* London: Allen and Unwin.

Martin, G., and J. Pear. 1983. *Behavior Modification: What Is It and How to Do It.* 2d ed. Englewood Cliffs, NJ: Prentice-Hall.

Marvin, R. S. 1977. "An Ethological-Cognitive Model for Attenuation of Mother-Child Attachment Behavior." Pp. 25–60 in *Advances in the Study of Communication and Affect,* vol. 3, *The Development of Social Attachments,* edited by T. M. Alloway, L. Kramer, and P. Pliner. New York: Plenum.

Marwell, G. and D. Schmitt. 1967. "Dimensions of Compliance-Gaining Behavior: An Empirical Analysis." *Sociometry* 30:350–364.

Mason, A., and V. Blankenship. 1987. "Power and Affiliation Motivation, Stress, and Abuse in Intimate Relationships." *Journal of Personality and Social Psychology* 52:203–210.

Matson, J. L., and M. E. Taras. 1988. "A 20-Year Review of Punishment and Alternative Methods to Treat Problem Behaviors in Developmentally Delayed Persons." *Research in Developmental Disabilities* 10:85–104.

Maurer, A. 1974. "Corporal Punishment." *American Psychologist* 29:614–626.

———. 1981. *Paddles Away: A Psychological Study of Physical Punishment in the Schools.* Palo Alto, CA: Rand Research Associates.

Maxim, P. 1981. "Dominance: A Useful Dimension of Social Communication." *Behavioral and Brain Sciences* 4:317–335.

McCord, J. 1979. "Some Child-Rearing Antecedents of Criminal Behavior in Adult Men." *Journal of Personality and Social Psychology* 37:1477–1486.

———. 1988. "Parental Behavior in the Cycle of Aggression." *Psychiatry* 51:14–23.

———. 1991. "Questioning the Value of Punishment." *Social Problems* 38:167–179.

McCormick, K. F. 1992. "Attitudes of Primary Care Physicians toward Corporal Punishment." *Journal of the American Medical Association* 267:3161–3165.

McGrath, J. E., ed. 1970. *Social and Psychological Factors in Stress.* New York: Holt.

McGuire, M. T. 1974. "The St. Kitts Vervet." In *Contributions to Primatology.* Basel: S. Karger.

McLoughlin, C. 1985. "Utility and Efficiency of Knowledge of Behavioural Principles as Applied to Children." *Psychological Reports* 56:463–467.

McNeil, C. B., L. Clemens-Mowrer, R. H. Gurwitch, and B. W. Funderburk. 1994. "Assessment of a New Procedure to Prevent Timeout Escape in Preschoolers." *Child and Family Behavior Therapy* 16:27–35.

McNeilly, A. S. 1979. "Effects of Lactation on Fertility." *British Medical Bulletin* 35:151–154.

Mechling, Jay. 1975. "Advice to Historians on Advice to Mothers." *Journal of Social History* 9:44–63.

Meyer, L. H., and I. M. Evans. 1989. *Nonaversive Interventions for Behavior Problems.* Baltimore, MD: Paul H. Brookes.

Miller, G., F. Boster, M. Roloff, and D. Siebold. 1977. "Compliance-Gaining Message Strategies: A Typology and Some Findings Concerning Effects of Situational Differences." *Communication Monographs* 44:37–51.

Milton, K. 1993. "Diet and Social Organization of a Free-Ranging Spider Monkey Population: The Development of Species-Typical Behavior in the Absence of Adults." Pp. 173–181 in *Juvenile Primates: Life History, Development, and Behavior,* edited by M. E. Pereira and L. A. Fairbanks. New York: Oxford University Press.

Mirowsky, J., and C. E. Ross. 1983. "Paranoia and the Structure of Powerlessness." *American Sociological Review* 48:228–239.

Mischel, W. 1968. *Personality and Assessment.* New York: Wiley.

Monahan, J. 1990. "The Social and Economic Context of Violent Behavior." In *Violent Behavior,* vol. 1, *Assessment and Intervention,* edited by L. J. Hertzberg, G. F. Ostrum, and J. R. Field. Costa Mesa, CA: PMA.

Monge, P. R., S. G. Bachman, J. P. Dillard, and E. M. Eisenberg. 1982. "Communication Competence in the Workplace: Model Testing and Scale Development." Pp. 505–527 in *Communication Yearbook 5,* edited by M. Burgoon. New Brunswick, NJ: Transaction.

Moos, R. H., and A. G. Billings. 1982. "Conceptualizing and Measuring Coping Resources and Processes." In *Handbook of Stress: Theoretical and Clinical Aspects,* edited by L. Goldberger and S. Breznetz. New York: Free Press.

Morrill, C. 1995. *The Executive Way: Conflict Management in Organizations.* Chicago: University of Chicago Press.

Mulliss, J. 1994. "Medical Malpractice, Social Structure, and Social Control." *Sociological Forum* 10:135–163.

Murray, L. 1977. "Infants' Capacities for Regulating Interactions with Their Mothers and the Function of Emotions." Unpublished doctoral thesis, University of Edinburgh, U.K.

Myers, J. K., J. J. Lindenthal, and M. P. Pepper. 1971. "Life Events and Psychiatric Impairment." *Journal of Nervous and Mental Disease* 152:149–157.

Myers, J. K., M. M. Weissman, G. L. Tischler, C. C. Holzer III, P. J. Leaf, H. Orvaschel, J. Anthony, J. H. Boyd, J. D. Burke, M. Kramer, and R. Stoltzman. 1984. "Six Months Prevalence of Psychiatric Disorders in Three Communities." *Archives of General Psychiatry* 41:959–967.

Nagel, T. 1973. "Equal Treatment and Compensatory Discrimination." *Philosophy and Public Affairs* 2:348–63.

Nash, L. T. 1978. "The Development of the Mother-Infant Relationship in Wild Baboons (*Papio anubis*)." *Animal Behaviour* 26:746–759.

Nicolson, N. A. 1987. "Infants, Mothers, and Other Females." Pp. 330–342 in *Primate Societies,* edited by B. B. Smuts, D. L. Cheney, R. M. Seyfarth, R. W. Wrangham, and T. T. Struhsaker. Chicago: University of Chicago Press.

Nozick, R. 1974. *Anarchy, State, and Utopia.* New York: Basic Books.

Nye, F. I. 1979. "Choice, Exchange, and the Family." Pp. 1–41 in *Contemporary Theories about the Family,* vol. 2, edited by W. R. Burr, R. Hill, F. I. Nye, and I. L. Reiss. New York: Free Press.

O'Leary, K. D. 1987. "Physical Aggression between Spouses: A Social Learning Theory Perspective." In *Handbook of Family Violence,* edited by V. B. Van Hasselt, R. L. Morrison, A. S. Bellack, and M. Hersen. New York: Plenum Press.

Olson, Dennis. 1984. "The Swedish Ban of Corporal Punishment." *Brigham Young University Law Review* 3:447–456.

O'Neill, O. 1991. "Theories of Justice, Traditions of Virtue." Paper presented at Constructions of Reason: A Conference on the Work of Onora O'Neill and "Explanations of Kant's Practical Philosophy," University of Notre Dame, South Bend, IN.

Onyekwere, E. O., R. B. Rubin, and D. A. Infante. 1991. "Interpersonal Perception and Communication Satisfaction as a Function of Argumentativeness and Ego-Involvement." *Communication Quarterly* 39:35–47.

Ounsted, C., R. Oppenheimer, and J. Lindsay. 1975. "The Psychopathology and Psychotherapy of Families: Aspects of Bonding Failure." Pp. 30–40 in *Concerning Child Abuse,* edited by A. Franklin. Edinburgh: Churchill Livingstone.

Owens, D. J., and M. A. Straus. 1979. "The Social Structure of Violence in Childhood and Approval of Violence as an Adult." *Aggressive Behavior* 1:193–211. Reprinted in Irwin H. Hyman and James H. Wise, eds., *Corporal Punishment in American Education: Readings in History, Practice, and Alternatives,* 107–125. Philadelphia, PA: Temple University Press, 1979.

Paige, K. E., and J. M. Paige. 1981. *The Politics of Reproductive Ritual.* Berkeley, CA: University of California Press.

Parke, R., and R. Slaby. 1983. "The Development of Aggression." In *Handbook of Child Psychology,* vol. 4, edited by P. Mussen. New York: Wiley.

Parke, R. D. 1974. "Rules, Roles, and Resistance to Deviation: Recent Advances in Punishment, Discipline, and Self-Control." Pp. 111–143 in *Minnesota Symposia on Child Psychology,* edited by A. D. Pick. Minneapolis, MN: University of Minnesota Press.

Parpal, M., and E. Maccoby. 1985. "Maternal Responsiveness and Subsequent Child Compliance." *Child Development* 56:1326–1344.

Pasamanick, B. 1987. "Social Biology and Aids." *Division 37 Newsletter* (winter). Washington, DC: American Psychological Association.

Passman, R. H. and R. K. Mulhern. 1977. "Maternal Punitiveness as Affected by Situational Stress: An Experimental Analogue of Child Abuse." *Journal of Abnormal Psychology* 86:563–569.

Patterson, G. R. 1975. *Families.* 2d ed. Champaign, IL: Research Press.

———. 1982. *Coercive Family Process.* Eugene, OR: Castalia Press.

———. 1983. "Stress: A Change Agent for Family Process." In *Stress, Coping, and Development in Children,* edited by N. Garmezy and M. Rutter. New York: McGraw-Hill.

———. 1986. "Performance Models for Antisocial Boys." *American Psychologist* 41:432–444.

———. 1988. "Family Process: Loops, Levels, and Linkages." In *Persons in Context: Developmental Processes,* edited by N. Bolger, A. Caspi, G. Downey, and M. Moorehouse. Cambridge: Cambridge University Press.

Patterson, G. R., and J. B. Reid. 1970. "Reciprocity and Coercion: Two Facets of Social Systems." Pp. 133–177 in *Behavior Modification in Clinical Psychology,* edited by C. Neuringer and J. L. Michael. New York: Appleton-Century-Crofts.

———. 1984. "Social Interaction Processes in the Family: The Study of the Moment-by-Moment Family Transactions in Which Human Social Development is Embedded." *Journal of Applied Developmental Psychology* 5:237–262.

Patterson, G. R., and T. J. Dishion. 1985. "Contribution of Families and Peers to Delinquency." *Criminology* 23:63–79.

Payne, M. J. and T. C. Sabourin. 1990. "Argumentative Skill Deficiency and Its Relationship to Quality of Marriage." *Communication Research Reports* 7:121–124.

Pearlin, L. I. 1975. "Sex roles and Depression." In *Life-Span Developmental Psychology,* edited by N. Datan and L. H. Ginsberg. New York: Academic Press.

———. 1989. "The Sociological Study of Stress." *Journal of Health and Social Behavior* 30:241–256.

Pearlin, L. I., M. A. Lieberman, E. G. Menaghan, and J. T. Mullan. 1981. "The Stress Process." *Journal of Health and Social Behavior* 22:337–356.

Pearlin, L. I., and C. Schooler. 1978. "The Structure of Coping." *Journal of Health and Social Behavior* 19:2–21.

Pearlin, L. I., and H. Turner. 1987. "The Family as a Context of the Stress Process." In *Stress and Health: Issues in Research Methodology,* edited by S. V. Kasl and C. Cooper. New York: Wiley.

Peisner, E. S. 1989. "To Spare or Not to Spare the Rod: A Cultural-Historical View of Child Discipline." Pp. 111–114 in *Child Development in Cultural Context,* edited by J. Valsinger. Lewiston, NY: Hogrefe and Huber.

Pelton, L. H. 1981. *The Social Context of Child Abuse and Neglect.* New York: Human Sciences Press.

Perry, D. G., and L. C. Perry. 1983. "Social Learning, Causal Attribution, and Moral Internalization." Pp. 115–136 in *Learning in Children: Progress in Cognitive Development Research,* edited by J. Bisanz, G. L. Bisanz, and R. Kain. New York: Springer.

Peterson, L. R., G. R. Lee, and G. J. Ellis. 1982. "Social Structure, Socialization Values, and Disciplinary Techniques: A Cross-Cultural Analysis." *Journal of Marriage and the Family* 44:131–42.

Petrovich, S. B., and J. L. Gewirtz. 1991. "Imprinting and Attachment: Proximate and Ultimate Considerations." Pp. 69–93 in *Intersections with Attachment,* edited by J. L. Gewirtz and W. M. Kurtines. Hillsdale, NJ: Erlbaum.

Pfiffner, L. J., and R. A. Barkley. 1990. "Educational Placement and Classroom Management." Pp. 498–539 in *Attention Deficit Hyperactivity Disorder,* edited by R. A. Barkley. New York: Guilford.

Pfohl, Stephen. 1977. "The 'Discovery' of Child Abuse." *Social Problems* 24:310–323.

Phillips, H. P. 1966. *Thai Peasant Personality: The Patterning of Interpersonal Behavior in the Village of Bang Chan.* Berkeley, CA: University of California Press.

Piaget, J. 1952. *The Origins of Intelligence.* New York: International Universities Press.

———. 1965. *The Moral Judgement of the Child.* New York: Free Press.

———. 1970. *Science of Education and the Psychology of the Child.* New York: Orion Press.

Pianka, E. R. 1976. "Natural Selection of Optimal Reproductive Tactics." *American Zoologist* 16:775–784.

Platt, Anthony. 1969. *The Child Savers: The Invention of Delinquency.* Chicago: University of Chicago Press.

Pleck, Elizabeth. 1987. *Domestic Tyranny: The Making of American Social Policy against Family Violence from Colonial Times to the Present.* New York: Oxford University Press.

Plumb, J. H. P. 1975. "The New World of Children in Eighteenth-Century England." *Past and Present* 67:64–93.

Pollock, Linda. 1983. *Forgotten Children: Parent-Child Relations from 1500 to 1900.* Cambridge: Cambridge University Press.

Powers, S. W., and H. C. Rickard. 1992. "Behavior Therapy with Children." Pp. 749–763 in *Handbook of Clinical Child Psychology,* 2d ed., edited by C. E. Walker and M. C. Roberts. New York: Wiley.

Prentice, N. M. 1972. "The Influence of Live and Symbolic Modeling on Promoting Moral Judgement of Adolescent Delinquents." *Journal of Abnormal Psychology* 6:402–408.

Rabkin, J. G., and E. L. Struening. 1976. "Life Events, Stress, and Illness." *Science* 194:1013–1020.

Rachlin, H. 1994. *Behavior and Mind: The Roots of Modern Psychology.* New York: Oxford University Press.

———. 1995. "Self-Control: Beyond Commitment." *Behavioral and Brain Sciences* 18:109–159.

Rancer, A. S., R. A. Baukus, and P. P. Amato. 1986. "Argumentativeness, Verbal Aggressiveness, and Marital Satisfaction." *Communication Research Reports* 3:28–32.

Rancer, A. S., R. L. Kosberg, and R. A. Baukus. 1992. "Beliefs about Arguing as Predictors of Trait Argumentativeness: Implications for Training in Argument and Conflict Management." *Communication Education* 41:375–387.

Ransom, T. W., and T. E. Rowell. 1972. "Early Social Development of Feral Baboons." Pp. 105–144 in *Primate Socialization,* edited by F. E. Poirier. New York: Random House.

Reiss, D. 1981. "The Resolution of Role Conflict within the Family." Pp. 261–281 in *A Modern Introduction to the Family,* edited by N. W. Bell and E. L. Vogel. New York: Free Press.

Reite, M., and N. Caine, eds. 1983. *Child Abuse: The Nonhuman Primate Data.* New York: Alan R. Liss.

Retzinger, S. 1991. *Violent Emotions: Shame and Rage in Marital Quarrels.* Newbury Park, CA: Sage Publications.

Reynolds, G. S. 1975. *A Primer of Operant Conditioning.* 2d ed. Glenview, IL: Scott, Foresman.

Rieke, R. D., and M.O. Sillars. 1984. *Argumentation and the Decision Making Process,* 2d ed. Glenview, IL: Scott, Foresman.

Roberts, M. W. 1982. "Resistance to Timeout: Some Normative Data." *Behavioral Assessment* 4:239–248.

Roberts, M. W., and S. W. Powers. 1988. "The Compliance Test." *Behavioral Assessment* 10:375–398.

——. 1990. "Adjusting Chair Timeout Enforcement Procedures for Oppositional Children." *Behavior Therapy* 21:257–271.

Robertson, P. 1988. "Home as a Nest: Middle-Class Childhood in Nineteenth-Century Europe." Pp. 407–431 in *The History of Childhood: The Untold Story of Child Abuse*, edited by L. de Mause. New York: Peter Bedrick Books.

Rosen, L. A., S. G. O'Leary, S. A. Joyce, G. Conway, and L. J. Pfiffner. 1984. "The Importance of Prudent Negative Consequences for Maintaining the Appropriate Behavior of Hyperactive Students." *Journal of Abnormal Child Psychology* 12:581–604.

Rosenblum, L. A. 1971. "The Ontogeny of Mother-Infant Relations in Macaques." Pp. 315–367 in *The Ontogeny of Vertebrate Behavior,* edited by H. Moltz. New York: Academic Press.

Rosenfield, S. 1989. "The Effects of Women's Employment: Personal Control and Sex Differences in Mental Health." *Journal of Health and Social Behavior* 30:77–91.

Rosenthal, T. L., and J. S. Whitebrook. 1970. "Incentives versus Instructions in Transmitting Grammatical Parameters with Experiments as Models." *Behavior Research and Therapy* 8:189–196.

Ross, C. E., J. Mirowsky, and J. Huber. 1983. "Dividing Work, Sharing Work, and In-between: Marriage Patterns and Depression." *American Sociological Review* 48:809–823.

Rubin, R. B. 1982. "Assessing Speaking and Listening Competence at the College Level: The Communication Competency Assessment Instrument." *Communication Education* 31:19–32.

——. 1985. "The Validity of the Communication Competency Assessment Instrument." *Communication Monographs* 52:173–185.

——. 1990. "Communication Competence." Pp. 94–129 in *Speech Communication: Essays to Commemorate the 75th Anniversary of the Speech Communication Association,* edited by G. M. Phillips and J. T. Wood. Carbondale, IL: Southern Illinois University Press.

Ruppenthal, G. C., G. L. Arling, H. F. Harlow, G. P. Sackett, and S. J. Suomi. 1976. "A Ten Year Perspective of Motherless Mother Monkey Behavior." *Journal of Abnormal Psychology* 85:341–349.

Rutter, M. 1985. "Family and School Influences on Behavioural Development." *Journal of Child Psychology and Psychiatry* 26:349–68. Reprinted in D. P. Farrington, ed., *Psychological Explanations of Crime.* Aldershot, U.K.: Dartmouth, 1990.

Rutter, M., and D. Quinton. 1984. "Parental Psychiatric Disorder: Effects on Children." *Psychological Medicine* 14:853–880.

Ryan, Mary P. 1982. "The Explosion of Family History." *Reviews in American History* 10:181–195.

Rychman, R., M. Burns, and M. Robbins. 1986. "Authoritarianism and Sentence Strategies for Low and High Severity Crimes." *Personality and Social Psychology Bulletin* 12:227–235.

Sackett, G. P. 1966. "Monkeys Reared in Isolation with Pictures as Visual Input: Evidence for an Innate Releasing Mechanism." *Science* 154:1468–1473.

Samalin, N., and D. B. Hogarty. 1994. "The Write Way to Discipline." *Parents* (July).

Sameroff, A., R. Seifer, R. Barocas, M. Zax, and S. Greenspan. 1987. "Intelligent Quotient Scores of 4-Year-Old Children: Social-Environment Risk Factors." *Pediatrics* 79:343–350.

Sampson, R. J., and L. H. Laub. 1993. *Crime in the Making: Pathways and Turning Points through Life*. Cambridge, MA: Harvard University Press.

Sarnoff, C. 1976. *Latency*. New York: Jason Aronson.

Schechter, S. 1982. *Women and Male Violence: The Visions and Struggles of the Battered Women's Movement*. Boston: South End Press.

Scheff, T. 1990. *Microsociology: Discourse, Emotion, and Social Structure*. Chicago: University of Chicago Press.

———. 1994. *Bloody Revenge: Emotion, Nationalism, War*. Boulder, CO.: Westview Press.

Schelling, T. C. 1960. *The Strategy of Conflict*. Cambridge, MA: Harvard University Press.

Schino, G., L. Speranza, and A. Troisi, A. 2001. "Early Maternal Rejection and Later Social Anxiety in Juvenile and Adult Japanese Macaques." *Developmental Psychobiology* 38:186–190.

Schulman, R., and Bucavalas, Inc. 1995. *National Child Abuse Survey*. New York: Schulman, Ronca and Bucavalas, Inc.

Schultz, B. 1982. "Argumentativeness: Its Effect in Group Decision-Making and Its Role in Leadership Perception." *Communication Quarterly* 30:368–375.

Schumacher, E. F. 1973. *Small Is Beautiful: Economics as if People Mattered*. New York: Harper and Row.

Scott, John. 1979. "The History of the Family as an Affective Unit." *Social History* 4:509–16.

Sears, R. R., E. E. Maccoby, and H. Levin. 1957. *Patterns of Child Rearing*. Evanston, IL: Row, Peterson.

Segal, E. F. 1972. "Induction and the Provenance of Operants." Pp. 1–34 in *Reinforcement: Behavioral Analyses,* edited by R. M. Gilbert and J. R. Millenson. New York: Academic Press.

Segrin, C. and M. A. Fitzpatrick. 1992. "Depression and Verbal Aggressiveness in Different Marital Couple Types." *Communication Monographs* 43:79–91.

Seyfarth, R. M. 1981. "Do Monkeys Rank Each Other?" *Behavioral and Brain Sciences* 3:447–448.

Seyfarth, R. M., and D. L. Cheney. 1986. "Vocal Development in Vervet Monkeys." *Animal Behaviour* 34:1640–1658.

Seyfarth, R. M., D. L. Cheney, and P. Marler. 1980. "Monkey Responses to Three Different Alarm Calls: Evidence for Predator Classification and Semantic Communication." *Science* 210:801–803.

Shipley, T. E., Jr. 1987. "Opponent Process Theory." Pp. 346–387 in *Psychological Theories of Drinking and Alcoholism,* edited by H. T. Blane and K. E. Leonard. New York: Guilford Press.

Shorter, Edward. 1975. *The Making of the Modern Family.* New York: Basic Books.

Sicignano-Kupfer, A. 1981. "Examination of the Role of the Response Requirement as a Determinant of Schedule-Induced Behavior. Unpublished master's thesis, University of Florida.

Sidman, M. 1989. *Coercion and Its Fallout.* Boston: Authors Cooperative.

Siegal, M., and J. Cowan. 1984. "Appraisals of Intervention: The Mother's versus the Culprit's Behavior as Determinants of Children's Evaluation of Disciplinary Techniques." *Child Development* 55:1760–1766.

Sigel, I. 1986. "Reflections on the Belief-Behavior Connection: Lessons Learned from a Research Program on Parental Belief Systems and Teaching Strategies." Pp. 35–65 in *Thinking about the Family: Views of Parents and Children,* edited by R. D. Ashmore and D. M. Brodinsky. Hillsdale, NJ: Erlbaum.

Silk, J. B. 1987. "Social Behavior in Evolutionary Perspective." Pp. 330–342 in *Primate Societies,* edited by B. B. Smuts, D. L. Cheney, R. M. Seyfarth, R. W. Wrangham, and T. T. Struhsaker. Chicago: University of Chicago Press.

Simon, H. A. 1957. *Models of Man.* New York: Wiley.

———. 1983. *Reason in Human Affairs.* Stanford, CA: Stanford University Press.

Simons, R., J. Beaman, R. Conger, and W. Chao. 1993. "Childhood Experience Conceptions of Parenting and Attitudes of Spouse as Determinants of Parental Behaviour." *Journal of Marriage and the Family* 55:91–106.

Simons, Ronald L., Kuei-Hsiu Lin, and Leslie C. Gordon. 1998. "Socialization in the Family of Origin and Male Dating Violence: A Prospective Study." *Journal of Marriage and the Family* 60:467–478.

Simpson, M. J. A., and S. Datta. 1991. "Predicting Infant Enterprise from Early Relationships in Rhesus Monkey Infants." *Behaviour* 116:42–63.

Simpson, M. J. A., A. E. Simpson, J. Hooley, and M. Zunz. 1981. "Infant-Related Influences on Birth Intervals in Rhesus Monkeys." *Nature* 290:49–51.

Skinner, B. F. 1938. *The Behavior of Organisms: An Experimental Analysis.* New York: Appleton.

———. 1953. *Science and Human Behavior.* New York: Macmillan.

———. 1957. *Verbal Behavior.* New York: Appleton-Century-Crofts.

———. 1971. *Beyond Freedom and Dignity.* New York: Knopf.

Small, M. F. 1983. "Females without Infants: Mating Strategies in Two Species of Captive Macaques." *Folia Primatologica* 40:125–133.

Snyder, J. J., and G. R. Patterson. 1995. "Individual Differences in Social Aggression: A Test of a Reinforcement Model of Socialization in the Natural Environment." *Behavior Therapy* 26:371–391.

Snyder, J., P. Edwards, K. McGraw, K. Kilgore, and A. Holton. 1994. "Escalation and Reinforcement in Mother-Child Conflict: Social Processes Associated with the Development of Physical Aggression." *Development and Psychopathology* 6:305–321.

Solomon, R. L. 1980. "The Opponent-Process Theory of Acquired Motivation: The Costs of Pleasure and the Benefits of Pain." *American Psychologist* 35:691–712.

Spitzberg, B. H., and W. R. Cupach. 1984. *Interpersonal Communication Competence.* Beverly Hills, CA: Sage.

Stack, C. 1974. *All Our Kin: Strategies for Survival in a Black Family.* New York: Harper and Row.

Staddon, J. E. R. 1977. "Schedule-Induced Behavior." Pp. 125–152 in *Handbook of Operant Behavior,* edited by W. K. Honig and J. E. R. Staddon. Englewood Cliffs, NJ: Prentice-Hall.

Stayton, D., R. Hogan, and M. Ainsworth. 1971. "Infant Obedience and Maternal Behavior: The Origins of Socialization Reconsidered." *Child Development* 42:1057–1069.

Stearns, Carol Z., and Peter Stearns. 1986. *Anger: The Struggle for Emotional Control in America's History.* Chicago: University of Chicago Press.

Stearns, S. C. 1993. *The Evolution of Life Histories.* New York: Oxford University Press.

Steinmetz, S. 1971. "Occupation and Physical Punishment: A Response to Straus." *Journal of Marriage and the Family* 33:664–666.

Steinmetz, S. K. 1977. "The Use of Force for Resolving Family Conflict: The Training Ground for Abuse." *Family Coordinator* 26:19–26.

———. 1979. "Disciplinary Techniques and Their Relationship to Aggressiveness, Dependency, and Conscience." In *Contemporary Theories about the Family,* vol. 1, edited by W. R. Burr, R. Hill, F. I. Nye, and I. L. Reiss. New York: Free Press.

Stevens, J. 1988. "Shared Knowledge about Infants among Fathers and Mothers." *Journal of Genetic Psychology* 149:515–525.

Stoklos, D. 1986. "A Congruence Analysis of Human Stress." In *Stress and Anxiety: A Sourcebook of Theory and Research,* edited by C. D. Spielberger and I. G. Sarason. Washington, DC: Hemisphere.

Stone, Lawrence. 1979. *The Family, Sex and Marriage in England 1500–1800.* London: Weidenfield and Nicolson.

Straus, M. A. 1971. "Some Social Antecedents of Physical Punishment: A Linkage Theory Interpretation." *Journal of Marriage and the Family* 33:658–663.

———. 1980. "Social Stress and Marital Violence in a National Sample of American Families." In *Forensic Psychology and Psychiatry,* edited by F. Wright, C. Bahn, and R. W. Rieber. New York: New York Academy of Sciences.

———. 1983. "Ordinary Violence, Child Abuse, and Wife-Beating: What Do They Have in Common?" Pp. 213–234 in *The Dark Side of Families: Current Family Violence Research,* edited by D. Finkelhor, R. J. Gelles, G. T. Hotaling, and M. A. Straus. Beverly Hills, CA.: Sage.

———. 1985. "Family Training in Crime and Violence." Pp. 164–185 in *Crime and the Family,* edited by A. J. Lincoln and M. A. Straus. Springfield, IL: C. C. Thomas.

———. 1991. "Discipline and Deviance: Physical Punishment of Children and Violence and Other Crime in Adulthood." *Social Problems* 38:133–154.

———. 1994. *Beating the Devil out of Them: Corporal Punishment in American Families.* New York: Lexington Books.

———. 1995. "Corporal Punishment of Children and Depression and Suicide in Adulthood." Pp. 59–77 in *Coercion and Punishment in Long-Term Perspective,* edited by J. McCord. New York: Cambridge University Press.

Straus, M. A., and D. Donnelly. 1993. "Corporal Punishment of Adolescents by American Parents." *Youth and Society* 24:419–422.

Straus, M. A., and G. Kaufman Kantor. 1987. "Stress and Child Abuse." In *The Battered Child,* edited by R. E. Helfer and R. S. Kempe. Chicago: University of Chicago Press.

———. 1994. "Corporal Punishment of Adolescents by Parents: A Risk Factor in the Epidemiology of Depression, Suicide, Alcohol Abuse, Child Abuse, and Wife Beating." *Adolescence* 29:543–561.

Straus, M. A., and R. J. Gelles, eds. 1990. *Physical Violence in American Families.* New Brunswick, NJ: Transaction.

Straus, M. A., R. J. Gelles, and S. K. Steinmetz. 1980. *Behind Closed Doors: Violence in the American Family.* Garden City, NY: Anchor.

Straus, M. A., and H. S. Gimpel. 1992. "Corporal Punishment by Parents and Economic Achievement: A Theoretical Model and Some Preliminary Empirical Data." Paper presented at the annual meeting of the American Sociological Association, Pittsburg, PA.

Straus, M. A., and Vera E. Mouradian. 1998. "Impulsive Corporal Punishment by Mothers and Antisocial Behavior and Impulsiveness of Children." *Behavioral Sciences and the Law* 16:353–374.

Straus, M. A., D. B. Sugarman, and J. Giles-Sims. 1997. "Spanking by Parents and Subsequent Antisocial Behavior of Children." *Archives of Pediatrics and Adolescent Medicine* 151:761–767.

Straus, M. A., S. Sweet, and Y. M. Vissing. 1989. "Verbal Aggression against Spouses and Children in a Nationally Representative Sample of American Families." Paper presented at the meeting of the Speech Communication Association, San Francisco.

Struhsaker, T. T. 1967. "Auditory Communication among Vervet Monkeys (*Cercopithecus aethiops*)." Pp. 281–324 in *Social Communication among Primates,* edited by S. Altmann. Chicago: University of Chicago Press.

———. 1971. "Social Behaviour of Mother and Infant Vervet Monkeys (*Cercopithecus aethiops*)." *Animal Behaviour* 19:233–250.

Stuart, R. B. 1971. "Behavioral Contracting within the Families of Delinquents." *Journal of Behavior Therapy and Experimental Psychiatry* 2:1–11.

Sulzer-Azaroff, B., and E. P. Reese. 1982. *Applying Behavioral Analysis: A Program for Developing Professional Competence.* New York: CBS College Publishing.

Syne, L., and L. Berkman. 1976. "Social Class, Susceptibility, and Illness." *American Journal of Epidemiology* 104:1–8.

Takahashi, K. 1986. "Examining the Strange Situation Procedure with Japanese Mothers and 12-Month-Old Infants." *Developmental Psychology* 22:265–266.

Takahata, Y. 1980. "The Reproductive Biology of a Free-Ranging Troop of Japanese Monkeys." *Primates* 21:303–329.

Takanishi, Ruby. 1978. "Childhood as a Social Issue: Historical Roots of Contemporary Child Advocacy Movements." *Journal of Social Issues* 34:8–28.

Thane, Pat. 1981. "Childhood in History." In *Childhood, Welfare, and Justice,* edited by Michael King. London: Batsford.

Thapar, R. 1966. *A History of India.* Baltimore, MD: Penguin.

Thibaut, J. W., and H. H. Kelley. 1959. *The Social Psychology of Groups.* New York: Wiley.

Thoits, P. A. 1983. "Dimensions of Life Events That Influence Psychological Distress: An

Evaluation and Synthesis of the Literature." In *Psychosocial Stress: Trends in Theory and Research,* edited by H. B. Kaplan. New York: Academic.

Thompson, M. 1982. "The Problem of the Center: An Autonomous Cosmology." Pp. 302–327 in *Essays in the Sociology of Perception,* edited by M. Douglas. London: Routledge and Kegan Paul

Thompson, M., R. Ellis, and A. Wildavsky. 1990. *Cultural Theory.* Boulder, CO: Westview.

Triandis, H. C. 1990. "Cross-Cultural Studies of Individualism and Collectivism." Pp. 41–133 in *Cross-Cultural Perspectives,* edited by J. J. Berman. Lincoln: University of Nebraska Press.

Trivers, R. L. 1972. "Parental Investment and Sexual Selection." Pp. 136–179 in *Sexual Selection and the Descent of Man,* edited by B. Campbell. Chicago: Aldine.

———. 1974. "Parent-Offspring Conflict." *American Zoologist* 14:249–264.

Troisi, A., F. R. D'Amato, R. Fuccillo, and S. Scucchi. 1982. "Infant Abuse by a Wild-Born Group-Living Japanese Macaque Mother." *Journal of Abnormal Psychology* 91:451–456.

Tucker, J. 1999. *The Therapeutic Corporation.* New York: Oxford University Press.

Tucker, M. J. 1988. "The Child in Beginning and End: Fifteenth and Sixteenth Century English Childhood." Pp. 229–257 in *The History of Childhood: The Untold Story of Child Abuse,* edited by L. de Mause. New York: Peter Bedrick Books.

Turiel, E. 1964. "An Experimental Analysis of Developmental Stages in the Child's Moral Judgement." Unpublished Ph. D. dissertation, Yale University, New Haven, CT.

Turner, H. A., and D. Finkelhor. 1996. "Corporal Punishment as a Stressor among Youth." *Journal of Marriage and the Family* 58:155–166.

Turner, H. A., and P. A. Muller. 2004. "Long-Term Effects of Child Corporal Punishment on Depressive Symptoms in Young Adults: Potential Moderators and Mediators." *Journal of Family Issues* 25:761–82.

Turner, James. 1980. *Reckoning with the Beast: Animals, Pain, and Humanity in the Victorian Mind.* Baltimore, MD: Johns Hopkins University Press.

Turner, Jay R., and Donald A. Lloyd. 1999. "The Stress Process and the Social Distribution of Depression." *Journal of Health and Social Behavior* 40:374–404.

Van Houten, R. 1980. *How to Use Reprimands.* Lawrence, KS: H and H Enterprises.

Vincent, C., and A. Furnham. 1994. "The Appeal of Complementary Medicine." Unpublished manuscript.

Vincey, W., P. Waldman, and J. Barchilon. 1982. "Attitudes to Punishment in Relation to Belief in Free Will and Determinism." *Human Relations* 35:939–950.

Vinokur, A., and M. K. Selzer. 1975. "Desirable versus Undesirable Life Events: Their Relationship to Stress and Mental Disorder. *Journal of Personality and Social Psychology* 32:329–337.

Vygotsky, L. 1986. *Thought and Language.* Cambridge, MA: MIT Press.

Wahler, R. G. 1976. "Deviant Child Behavior within the Family: Developmental Speculations and Behavior Change Strategies." Pp. 516–545 in *Handbook of Behavior Modification and Behavior Therapy,* edited by H. Leitenberg. Englewood Cliffs, NJ: Prentice Hall.

Walster, E., E. Aronson, and Z. Brown. 1966. "Choosing to Suffer as a Consequence of

Expecting to Suffer: An Unexpected Finding." *Journal of Experimental Social Psychology* 2:400–406.

Walters, G. C., and J. E. Grusec. 1977. *Punishment*. San Francisco: W. H. Freeman.

Walters, R., J. Cleyne, and R. Banks. 1972. *Punishment*. Harmondsworth, U.K.: Penguin.

Walzer, M. 1983. *Spheres of Justice: A Defense of Pluralism and Equality*. New York: Basic Books.

Watzlawick, P., J. H. Beavin, and D. D. Jackson. 1967. *Pragmatics of Human Communication: A Study of Interactional Patterns, Pathologies, and Paradoxes*. New York: Norton.

Watzlawick, P., J. Weakland, and R. Fisch. 1974 *Change: Principles of Problem Formation and Problem Resolution*. New York: Norton.

Wauchope, B. A., and M. A. Straus. 1990. "Physical Punishment and Physical Abuse of American Children: Incidence Rates by Age, Gender, and Occupational Class." Pp. 133–148 in *Physical Violence in American Families: Risk Factors and Adaptations in 8,145 Families*, edited by M. A. Straus and R. J. Gelles. New Brunswick, NJ: Transaction.

Weimann, J. M. 1977. "Explication and Test of a Model of Communication Competence." *Human Communication Research* 3:195–213.

Weiner, S. G., and S. Levine. 1992. "Behavioral and Physiological Responses of Mother and Infant Squirrel Monkeys to Fearful Stimuli." *Developmental Psychobiology* 25:127–136.

Weiss, B., K. A. Dodge, J. E. Bates, and G. S. Pettit. 1992. "Some Consequences of Early Harsh Discipline: Child Aggression and Maladaptive Social Information Processing Style." *Child Development* 63:1321–1335.

Weiss, R. S. 1990. "Bringing Work Stress Home." In *Stress between Work and Family*, edited by J. Eckenrode and S. Gore. New York: Plenum.

Weissman, M. M., and G. L. Klerman. 1977. "Sex Differences and the Epidemiology of Depression." *Archives of General Psychiatry* 34:98–111.

———. 1992. "Depression: Current Understanding and Changing Trends. Annual Review." *Public Health* 13:319–339.

Welsh, R. 1978. "Delinquency, Corporal Punishment, and the Schools." *Crime and Delinquency* 24:336–354.

Whittaker, J., J. Garbarino, and Associates. 1983. *Social Support Networks on Informal Helping in the Human Services*. Hawthorne, NY: Aldine de Gruyter.

Widom, C. S. 1991. "Childhood Victimization: Risk Factor for Delinquency." In *Adolescent Stress: Causes and Consequences*, edited by M. E. Colten and S. Gore. New York: Aldine de Gruyter.

Wildavsky, A. 1994. "Why Self-interest means less outside of a Social Context: Cultural Contributions to a Theory of Rational Choices." *The Journal of Theoretical Politics* 6:131–59.

Wilson, E. 1978. *On Human Nature*. Cambridge, MA: Harvard University Press.

Wilson, J. Q. 1993. *The Moral Sense*. New York: Free Press.

Wilson, J. Q., and R. J. Herrnstein. 1985. *Crime and Human Nature: The Definitive Study of the Causes of Crime*. New York: Simon and Schuster.

Wishy, Bernard. 1968. *The Child and the Republic: The Dawn of American Child Nurture*. Philadelphia, PA: University of Pennsylvania Press.

Witte, K. L., and E. E. Grossman. 1971. "The Effects of Reward and Punishment upon Children's Attention, Motivation, and Discrimination Learning." *Child Development* 42:537–542.

Wohlford, P., and T. Chicucos. 1975. "Research Evidence on Corporal Punishment in Schools: Need and Roadblocks." Paper presented at the meetings of the American Psychological Association.

Wolf, M., T. Risley, and H. Mees. 1964. "Application of Operant Conditioning Procedures to the Behavior Problems of an Autistic Child." *Behavioral Research and Therapy* 1:305–312.

Wolfgang, M., and F. Ferracuti. 1967. *The Subculture of Violence: Toward an Integrated Theory of Criminology.* London: Tavistock.

Worlein, J. M., G. C. Eaton, D. Johnson, and B. Glick. 1988. "Mating Season Effects on Mother-Infant Conflict in Japanese Macaques, *Macaca fuscata.*" *Animal Behaviour* 36:1472–1481.

Wrangham, R. W. 1980. "An Ecological Model of Female-Bonded Primate Groups." *Behaviour* 75:262–300.

Zelizer, V. A. 1985. *Pricing the Priceless Child: The Changing Social Value of Children.* New York: Basic Books.

Ziegler, E., and D. Smith. 1984. "Discipline: Do Teachers and Psychologists Agree?" *Psychological Reports* 54:835–839.

Zisk, B. 1992. *The Politics of Transformation: Local Activism in the Peace and Environmental Movements.* New York: Praeger.

Contributors

WILLIAM M. BAUM, Professor Emeritus of Psychology, University of California, Davis.

CARLFRED BRODERICK, formerly Professor of Psychology, University of Southern California; d. 1999.

RANDALL COLLINS, Professor of Sociology, University of Pennsylvania.

PATRICIA CRITTENDEN, Ph.D., Family Relations Institute, Miami, Florida.

MICHAEL DONNELLY, Professor of Sociology, Bard College.

LYNN FAIRBANKS, Professor of Neuropsychiatry, UCLA/Department of Veteran's Affairs.

SCOTT FELD, Professor of Sociology, Purdue University.

ADRIAN FURNHAM, Professor of Psychology, University College, London.

JAMES GARBARINO, Professor of Human Development, Cornell University.

RICHARD J. GELLES, Dean, School of Social Work, University of Pennsylvania.

JEAN GILES-SIMS, Professor of Sociology, Texas Christian University.

MICHAEL R. GOTTFREDSON, Vice Chancellor, University of California, Irvine.

TRAVIS HIRSCHI, Professor of Sociology, University of Arizona.

DOMINIC INFANTE, Professor Emeritus, School of Communication Studies, Kent State University.

ANNE S. KUPFER, Faculty Research Associate, Department of Psychology, Arizona State University, Tempe.

ROBERT E. LARZELERE, Professor of Psychology, University of Nebraska Medical Center.

CHARLES LOCKHART, Professor of Political Science, Texas Christian University.

JOHN RICH MARTIN, Professor Emeritus, College of Education, University of Texas, Austin.

JOAN McCORD, formerly Professor, Department of Criminal Justice, Temple University; d. 2004.

MICHAEL T. McGUIRE, Professor of Psychiatry and Biobehavioral Sciences, UCLA.

SCOTT POWERS, Associate Professor of Clinical Pediatrics, University of Cincinnati College of Medicine.

SUSAN ROSS, Assistant Professor of Sociology, Lycoming College.

THOMAS J. SCHEFF, Professor Emeritus of Sociology, University of California, Santa Barbara.

MURRAY A. STRAUS, Professor of Sociology and Co-Director, Family Research Laboratory, University of New Hampshire.

JAMES TUCKER, Associate Professor of Sociology, University of New Hampshire.

HEATHER TURNER, Associate Professor of Sociology, University of New Hampshire.

Index